D0506952

THE COMPLETE
MICROWAVE COOKBOOK

THE COMPLETE
MICROWAVE COOKBOOK

Edited by
Linda Doeser

INTERNATIONAL CULINARY SOCIETY
New York

CONTENTS

USEFUL FACTS AND FIGURES

Measures
All measurements given in this book are assumed to be level unless otherwise stated.

Cookware
Only use microwave-safe cookware and utensils in the microwave oven. Your manufacturer's users' manual will give guidelines.

Covering
When using plastic wrap as a covering during microwave cooking, remove it first from the side away from you, as the build-up of steam can burn you.

Timing
Cooking times may vary slightly depending on the output of your oven, the type and shape of the container used and the temperature of the food. Therefore, always follow the guidelines in your manufacturer's users manual.

Temperature
Recipes assume that the starting temperature of usually non-refrigerated ingredients will be room temperature, and usually refrigerated ingredients will be cold. If for some reason this is different, the cooking times will need to be adjusted accordingly.

Comparison of Some Common Different Microwave Oven Settings

Settings	Approx % Power Input	Use

1 Low
  Stay Warm
  Heat and Hold
	25%	To keep cooked dishes hot for comparatively long periods of time.

2–3 Defrost
  Simmer
  Stew
	30–40%	To defrost foods or for lengthy cooking of less tender foods.

4–5 Medium Bake	50%	Reheating foods or cooking delicate foods.
6–8 Medium–High	60–70%	Reheating foods or cooking delicate foods, or simply slowing down the cooking slightly.

9–10 Cook
  – High
  – Roast
  – Maximum
  – Full power
	100%	Cooking food.

Microwave Cooking Times

All the recipes and information on cooking times in this book are for a 700 watt microwave oven.

■ If your microwave has a higher output, then decrease the cooking time, checking two-thirds of the way through the time suggested and continuing to cook as necessary.

■ If your microwave has a lower output, then you will probably have to increase the cooking times slightly. However, there are many factors which influence cooking times, including the actual size of the oven cavity, so always check well-ahead of the maximum time. Remember, you cannot spoil food by removing it halfway through cooking, then putting it back, but once the food is overcooked it is sometimes beyond salvaging.

INTRODUCTION

The microwave oven has introduced a whole new concept to the kitchen; all the traditional methods of cooking rely on the need for an external source of heat to cook the food. Although the older generations may not have understood electricity, they certainly accepted the fact that hot broilers and stovetops would cook the food just as well as an open fire – this was easy, because the effect of the heat on the food was obvious.

By comparison, the microwave does not offer a source of heat in the traditional sense so it is more difficult to appreciate the ins and outs of how this appliance cooks the food and, of more practical relevance, exactly when the food in the oven cavity is cooked, ready to eat. Instead of relying on previous experience, on rule-of-thumb methods and on teachings passed on from mother, with a microwave you have to follow strict guidelines, taking care to be accurate with timings and thinking ahead about cookware as well as preparation techniques.

Before you can realize the full potential of the microwave you will have to get to know it really well. Using your manufacturer's instruction manual as a guide, experiment with basic cooking, to discover just how your appliance performs. Note down useful cooking times for the amounts of food that you are likely to cook frequently – vegetables, for example. Try different cooking dishes that you have which are suitable for use in the microwave – you will soon discover which bowl or pitcher is best for a sauce, or which dish is just the right shape and size to cook scrambled eggs. The more you experiment at the beginning, the more you will use the microwave as time goes on.

To help you, *The Complete Microwave Cookbook* offers plenty of guidelines on the techniques for preparing and cooking a wide range of foods. At the beginning of each chapter you will find background information, notes and hints on how to achieve the best results. Step-by-step drawings and pictures highlight basic methods, and charts offer a guide to the basic cooking times for a wide variety of foods. When you have mastered all the basic principles of microwave cooking, then you will find the recipes easy to follow. When you are confident about cooking plain foods and are happy to follow microwave recipes, you will find that you can adapt many of your own favorite traditional recipes to this revolutionary new way of cooking. Remember, the key to success is to use the microwave as much as possible – you will soon discover all the advantages, and you are sure to decide which foods you prefer to cook by traditional methods, as well as those which you will never dream of boiling or frying again!

MICROWAVE TECHNOLOGY

Before using your microwave, read through this chapter and study the manufacturer's directions. Here you will find all the background information you need to ensure that you make the best and safest use of your microwave oven.

The concept of cooking food by microwaves has been experimented with by many scientists throughout the world since before the Second World War. The first microwave oven was manufactured in the United States in the late 1940s, but it was not until 1955 that a domestic model was produced. In those early days, the ovens had small cooking cavities but very large cabinets, were expensive to purchase and limited in what they could do.

The modern domestic microwave oven is small enough to be positioned on a counter-top, yet it is so well developed technically that it is able to produce a wide variety of cooked foods to suit individual needs.

The benefits of microwave cooking

The microwave oven is a small appliance which can be accommodated almost anywhere it is required. No special installation is needed because it is plugged into an ordinary wall socket. It gives fast results in minutes rather than hours. Running costs are low, because the energy concentrates on the food and not on the surrounding areas. It is a safe appliance to use, and because it always remains relatively cool, there aren't any hot parts on which a user can be burnt, and the kitchen is more comfortable to work in.

Almost any kitchen utensil can be used, including paper! Depending upon the size of the cooking cavity, almost any quantity of food from a hamburger to a turkey can be cooked. Since the cooking method retains more nutrients, especially in vegetables, the use of a microwave oven contributes to healthier eating. Foods can also be cooked without fat, so those on a diet can enjoy food without the addition of unwanted calories.

What are microwaves?

Microwaves are a form of the electro-magnetic waves which are used every day by all of us in one way or another. Examples are when we watch television, listen to the radio, have an X-ray or cook food. It is the frequency at which the energy is produced which determines the benefits. The microwave oven is designed to generate electro-magnetic waves, and these are contained in the cooking cavity.

How microwaves cook food

To cook raw food in the conventional manner, heat is applied to the outer layer of the food and this gradually penetrates to the center of the food. Various methods of heat transfer are used to achieve different results. These are known as conduction, convection and radiation. By using one or more of these methods, it is possible to carry out cooking operations, such as boiling, broiling, stewing, frying, baking and roasting. Usually, the heat which cooks the food cannot be seen, although the heat source itself can be observed in the form of electricity, gas or coal.

Microwave cooking is an extension of the three basic principles of conventional cooking. The microwaves (short waves) are contained in a cooking cavity and cannot be seen. However, they will act in three different ways:

Absorption Microwaves are attracted to moisture, which is present in all food. Although food looks solid, it is made up of moisture molecules. Once food is placed in the cooking cavity and the microwave energy is switched on, each of the molecules is stimulated and twists back and forth over 2 thousand million times each second. Vibration at such high speed causes the food to heat itself. Unlike conventional cooking, which starts the cooking process on the outer layer of the food, microwaves can penetrate immediately $1\frac{1}{2}$–2 inches all around. Because all the energy is concentrated on cooking the food, the food cooks more quickly than with conventional methods. As a result there is invariably a reduction in energy costs.

Transmission As microwaves are only attracted to moisture molecules and are absorbed by them, they ignore anything else in the cooking cavity and pass through many other materials as if they were invisible. It is rather like sitting in a car on a warm day, with the sun streaming through the window. The warmth of the sun can be felt but the car windows remain cool. Microwaves act in the same manner and are not attracted by internal oven material, only by food.

Reflection Although microwaves are absorbed by food and pass through such materials as glass, china, wood, paper and plastic, they are reflected by metal. Since the walls of the cooking cavity are of metal, the microwaves reflect off the walls, creating an invisible energy pattern which contributes to a good energy distribution in the cavity. This also means that if food is placed in a metal container, it is screened from the microwaves and will not cook.

It is rather like bouncing a ball against a solid wall – it will always bounce back. If a hole was made in the wall, the ball would continue to travel through it.

The basic controls

Microwave ovens have a variety of controls, in the form of buttons, dials or touch-sensitive pads. However, all models will have a timer and cook control. In addition, many include a defrost control and possibly a variable power control to allow slower cooking.

The timer Timing is an essential part of cooking by microwaves. Once the timer has been set, and the cooking control switched on, cooking will continue until the timer automatically switches off the microwave energy. When it stops, it will indicate completion by a ping, buzz or light. If you need to get to the food during the cooking, open the door and the timed sequence will halt. Shut the door again and the oven will continue without needing to be reset in most models.

The cook control This is also sometimes known as the on/off switch. It generally works in conjunction with the timer.

The defrost control This control is for defrosting frozen food fast and, once set, will automatically reduce the microwave energy being applied to the food. Depending upon the model selected, it may either reduce the wattage or pulse the energy on and off. It is a particularly useful feature for thawing large items of food because it ensures even defrosting but prevents food from cooking. A further benefit is to use the control for cooking foods slowly; the energy will cycle on and off alternately in accordance with the selected setting, slowing the cooking process down. When using this control the timer is set for longer, as directed in specific recipes. For other foods, unless directions are given in the manufacturer's users' manual, the exact timing will have to be judged by experience. The selection of defrost setting is often included as part of a variable power control.

Variable power control This control is simply a method of enabling the user to select more or less microwave energy to suit his or her particular cooking needs. Just as a dimmer switch on a light gives a choice of lighting levels, microwave energy levels can be adjusted. There is not a standardization of settings between models, but the users' manual supplied with your oven gives both recipes and guidance about which level is best suited for a specific cooking operation. Like with the

defrost control, the oven will automatically adjust to that cooking level.

Siting the microwave oven

The average microwave oven is about the size of a television. It can be placed in almost any position and in any room, except the bathroom. It may be accommodated on a table top, a countertop, built in or even placed on a cart, so that it can be moved at any time to the most convenient working position. Because it is a "cool" appliance, it is particularly beneficial to the disabled or elderly.

Because air is drawn in by a fan to cool the magnetron, the air inlet grills must not be blocked and the oven should not be placed near an appliance where this air is likely to be hot, for example near the stove top. The magnetron is often referred to as the "heart" of the oven because this component generates the microwave energy.

Safety

Microwave ovens are as safe as any other electrical appliance in the home and must comply with the appropriate safety regulations. For safe operation of the appliance, read the manufacturer's directions and follow them closely.

Cookware and equipment

Cookware for the microwave oven includes not only solid shapes like bowls, pitchers and casseroles, but also bags, plastic wrap and paper towels. Practically any material can be used, except a few exceptions related to metal, and a few plastic materials.

Although microwaves will generally not damage cookwares, it is important to remember that the heat of the

food may sometimes do so. For example, syrup heated in a plastic bowl can reach such a high temperature that the plastic will not be able to withstand it.

Metal Unless the oven manufacturer confirms its use, metal in any form should not be used. China decorated with metal, lead crystal, or any material which contains metal, such as metal ties used for securing roasting bags, are not suitable. Neither are small pieces of foil nor shallow foil containers, unless specifically recommended. Metal can cause "arcing" or sparking and may result in the walls inside the oven becoming pitted. When the walls become pitted, it affects the way the microwaves bounce off them.

Some recipes include directions to cover parts of food with small pieces of aluminum foil. This is a technique to prevent part of the food cooking faster than the other parts. Before you do this, consult the users' manual to make certain this technique is acceptable in your model.

When foil is used on food, it must be small, smooth pieces.

China, ceramic and oven-to-tableware Make sure that containers do not have metal trim or pattern as this will cause arcing (check for gold or silver printing on the underside), and that any handles have not been glued on. The use of antique china should be avoided. Porous pottery is not really suitable for microwave cooking. Moisture absorbed in the pottery itself will heat up, making the container hot – unlike most microwave containers which remain relatively cool – and this absorption will slow down the cooking of the foods by an unknown and variable amount.

Glass Glass such as tumblers, sundae dishes and small bowls are suitable, but should not be

used in recipes where the food is likely to reach such a high temperature that they may crack. Food containing a high proportion of sugar or fat should not be cooked in glass for this reason, unless the glass is ovenproof in conventional cooking. Glass measuring cups, however, are very useful, especially those with extra room beyond the measured capacity. Do not use glass with metal decoration or lead crystal.

Plastic and paper There are several proprietary paper or plastic products designed for microwave cooking. Providing the plastic can withstand the food temperature they can be satisfactory. This includes boil-in-bags, plastic wrap and roasting bags. Thick plastic bags can be used for short-term heating, but preferably not for foods with high fat or sugar content. Avoid using melamine cookware, such as cups, plates or kitchen tools, because these can taint food.

Kitchen paper towels and cardboard can be used, as well as waxed paper.

Never line a browning dish or skillet with plastic wrap or paper towels because they could scorch or burn due to the high temperatures reached by the container.

Wood and baskets Wooden bowls or baskets may be placed in the microwave oven but only for a short time. Do not use baskets which have been bonded with glue or have wire or staples used in their construction.

Selecting the best equipment Unlike conventional cooking, many types of equipment can be used, including cups, mugs, tumblers, cardboard boxes lined with microwave-safe plastic wrap or bowls, and casseroles. Choose the right shape container for the cooking operation, remembering that round dishes give better results than square ones. Also, shallow dishes are usually better than deep ones.

Avoid cooking cakes in a square or oblong container because the food in the corners may overcook and become dry. Ring-shaped molds will frequently give a better cooked result with many cake mixtures.

Although not essential, it is best to choose a container in which the food may be spread evenly. This means it will be evenly exposed to the action of the microwaves. A container which is narrower at one end will cook the food more quickly in the narrow area.

When heating liquids, choose a container large enough to avoid boiling over. Glasses should also be strong enough to withstand the temperature of the heated liquid. When defrosting liquid foods, such as soups, place the frozen block in a tight-fitting container, so that the defrosted liquid is retained close to the frozen block.

Cover foods which need to have the moisture within them to cook the food, for example, stews, soups, fish, peeled fruit, vegetables, steamed puddings, frozen foods. Microwave-safe plastic wrap can be used as a cover, as can plates or lids.

Do not cover foods which are intended to be "dry", for example, cakes, pastry, fruit and vegetables in skins and bread products.

Cooking directions

Sometimes directions are given which may seem unnecessary. As with any cooking operation, the cook is in control, but there are reasons behind instructions.

Stirring liquids such as soups and stews. Certain areas of the liquid tend to get more exposure to microwave energy than others. Therefore by stirring, the liquid will heat more evenly. In the case of sauces, stirring will also help to avoid lumps.

Rearranging food Unevenly shaped foods, such as chops or fish, cook more quickly in the thinnest parts. By rearranging, for example, or changing its position, this can be checked.

Turning food over Large foods like roasts and poultry need turning over. As these foods tend to be irregular in shape, the exposure will vary across the food; by turning over, a more even cooking result can be achieved.

Turning containers around This direction is particularly beneficial when cooking cakes, as it contributes to an even rise.

Standing time After cooking, microwaved food is left to stand for a specific number of minutes. This is not done in order to keep food warm but because foods continue to cook by conduction once the microwave energy has been switched off. Therefore, to avoid dehydration, some foods benefit from being left to stand before serving. This is particularly important with large pieces of meat, some cakes and desserts.

Pricking or scoring food Any food with a skin or membrane, for example unpeeled apples, baked potatoes, whole tomatoes, sausages or egg yolks. This precaution prevents the food from bursting during cooking.

Principles of microwave cooking

By following certain principles when cooking conventionally, a better result will be achieved. The same applies to microwave cooking.

Timing Timing plays a much more important role in the final results obtained from a microwave oven than in conventional cooking. It is wise to undercook, check, and then

Cookware for microwave cooking

Cookware designed specifically for use in the microwave is readily available. It isn't, however, necessary to make any special purchases. A wide variety of ordinary kitchen cookware is suitable for use in the microwave oven. Ovenproof glass dishes, bowls, measuring cups and casseroles are ideal for cooking or reheating foods. Plain ovenproof casseroles and classic white gratin dishes that are free of all metal trim are also useful for microwave cooking. Plain mugs, plates and cereal bowls can be used for a number of cooking processes, while bread dishes and glass ring molds provide variety in shape.

return the food to continue cooking. Overcooking will dehydrate the food and render it unpalatably tough or hard.

The quantity of food that can be cooked in one operation relates to the cooking time. For example, one baked potato may take 5 minutes to cook, but two take 8 minutes. This is simply because the level of microwave energy remains the same and has to be distributed between an increased quantity of food.

The positioning of food

Because the lowest activity of microwave energy is next to the walls, in the corners and absolute center of the cooking cavity, it is better to place the food off-center on the floor, unless otherwise directed by the oven's manufacturer.

The more microwave energy exposure the food gets the more evenly and quickly it cooks. This is particularly beneficial for small individual items of food. For example, items such as small cakes or potatoes should be arranged in a circle with a space between each. For food such as chops, they are best arranged with the thinner areas pointing to the middle of the container.

Browning food Microwave energy heats and cooks food, but since there is no external application of heat, browning in the accepted manner does not usually occur.

Because large pieces of meat and poultry need a longer cooking time, the surface area of fat starts to change color: It may result in an acceptable color but it will not be as crisp or as brown as meat cooked conventionally.

There are several methods available which enable the food to benefit from speedy cooking, yet retain visual appeal.
● After microwave cooking, brown the food under a pre-heated conventional broiler or in a skillet.

● Use a microwave browning dish. This is especially designed to absorb microwave energy over its surface. Once preheated, the surface is hot enough to sear food before cooking.
● If color is the requirement rather than a crisp skin, meat can be brushed with a colorful sauce, such as tomato sauce, soy sauce or fruit jelly, to liven up its appearance.

Maintenance

Like all appliances, if the manufacturer's directions are followed, little or no maintenance is required. However, the majority of manufacturers offer a maintenance service, the cost of which can be discussed at the time of purchase. It is important that no one other than a fully trained microwave service engineer dismantle the oven or endeavor to carry out a repair.

The manufacturer's users'

manual should always be referred to, but in general:
● Wipe any spillage immediately after use.
● Do not use an abrasive cleaning agent.
● Any sharp implement, such as a knife, must never be used to remove hardened food, especially in the area around the door seal.
● A cup of water left in the cavity when the oven is not in use will absorb any microwaves if it is accidentally turned on.

Using the recipes

The recipes in this book have been tested in an oven with a maximum output of 700 watts. If you have a microwave oven with a lower output, you may find it necessary, in some instances, to increase the cooking time slightly. Before doing so, check the food at the time given in the recipe. Only then should any additional cooking time be considered.

Specialist equipment

There are many different types of specialist equipment available for use in the microwave, from light containers manufactured in plastic, to good looking dishes that are designed for use in the freezer, microwave or conventional oven. One of the great advantages of specialist equipment is that it offers plenty of variety in shape and size.

Do not use metal equipment, such as spoons, ladels, pancake turners or whisks. All of these are now widely available in plastic for microwave cooking.

Useful pieces of specialist equipment include plastic or glass ring molds, round muffin dishes and colanders.

MICROWAVE TIPS & TRICKS

The microwave will save time and effort for a wide variety of cooking processes and minor tasks, from defrosting butter to browning almonds. Here are just a few extra snippets of information that will help you to put the microwave to full use.

Browning almonds

Slivered almonds can be browned in butter. Place the nuts in a bowl with a good-sized cube of butter or margarine and cook at Full power (High), allowing about 4 minutes per 1 cup, stirring once. Pour the almonds over cooked fish, such as trout, cooked chicken breasts, vegetables or freshly cooked rice.

Crisping bacon

Cook chopped bacon in a bowl until the fat runs and the bacon is very well cooked. Stir it halfway through the cooking time to separate the bits, then transfer them to a plate lined with paper towels to cool. When cool, the slices should be crisp and dry.

Defrosting butter

Butter which is taken from the freezer can be defrosted rapidly

Browning almonds

Browning almonds in butter, in a small bowl. (Or try using a measuring cup.)

in the microwave for immediate use. Remove the wrapping from the butter, place it on a plate and cook on Medium for 2–3 minutes per 1 cup.

Dissolving gelatine

Sprinkle unflavored gelatine over a small amount of cold water and leave for a minute, then heat in the microwave for about 30 seconds or until the water is hot but not boiling. Stir well until the gelatine has dissolved completely, heating it for a few seconds longer if necessary. Be very careful not to let the liquid boil or all the gelatine's setting properties will be lost.

Crisping crackers

Crackers that have been exposed to the air for any length of time absorb moisture and become soft. They can be crisped up by cooking in the microwave on Full power (High) for a few seconds. Allow to cool and store in an airtight container.

Drying bread crumbs

White bread crumbs can be dried in the microwave. Place them in a dish and cook on Full power (High) for 1 minute, or longer if the quantity is large. Stir to rearrange the crumbs and continue to cook, stirring occasionally, until they are fairly dry, Leave to cool completely by which time they should be crisp. Store in an airtight jar. If the crumbs are not dry when cool, then continue to cook them.

Crisp bacon bits

1. Place diced Canadian bacon in a microwave-safe bowl, separating the pieces rather than leaving them in a lump. Cook on Full power (High) until all the fat has run from them and they are very well cooked. Stir halfway through cooking to separate the bits.

2. As soon as the bacon bits are cooked, use a slotted spoon to transfer the bacon bits to a plate lined with paper towels.

Freshening the kitchen

It is easy to make your kitchen smell as if you have been cooking up a storm – and remove any odors from your microwave at the same time, as well! Simply place lemon slices and 1 tablespoon apple pie spice in a measuring cup and cook on Full power until boiling. Open the microwave door and let the aroma fill the kitchen.

Increasing juice yield

Heat whole lemons, oranges or other citrus fruits in the microwave for about 30 seconds each before squeezing their juice. The warmed fruit will yield the maximum amount of juice.

Making croutons

Make croutons by drying cubes of bread on paper towels until very crisp. Allow 2–3 minutes for 1 cup fresh bread cubes. Cool, then toss well in melted butter.

Melting butter

If you need a small amount of melted butter to fold into a cake or to drizzle over vegetables, then place it in a plain mug or small bowl and melt it in the microwave for about 15 seconds.

Melting chocolate

Melt chocolate by breaking the squares into a bowl and heating in the microwave. Allow about $1-1\frac{1}{2}$ minutes for 4 ounces on

Full power (High). Stir halfway through and at the end of the time. If the chocolate is not quite melted, then heat it for a further 30 seconds.

Warming a baby's bottle

Warm a baby's milk in the microwave. Allow just a few seconds, then shake the milk to distribute the heat evenly and test the milk. The time will depend on the starting temperature of the milk. Once you know the exact timing for your bottle, make a note of it for future reference.

Warming baby food

The microwave is ideal for warming small amounts of puréed foods for a baby. Place them in a small bowl or dish and heat for a few seconds, then stir well and test before heating further, if necessary, or before using.

Warming bread

Warm a whole loaf, French bread or dinner rolls in the microwave. Place on a paper towel on the floor or turntable in the cavity and allow just a few seconds or up to 1 minute on Full power (High). The bread should feel just slightly warm on the outside when you remove it from the oven. Timing depends on quantity – one or two rolls or a French bread heats rapidly.

Warming cake ingredients

Warm the margarine and sugar for a creamed cake mixture to speed up the preparation. Allow just a few seconds on Full power (High) and the ingredients will cream together with ease.

Warming cheese

Bring chilled cheese to room temperature before serving by heating it in the microwave for a few seconds on Medium setting (or allow slightly longer on a Defrost setting). Unwrap the cheese and place it on paper towels on a plate.

Warming honey

Warm honey which has crystallized slightly, allowing a few seconds on Full power (High), then stir well and the crystals should dissolve.

Warming mulled wine

Warm a whole bowl full of mulled wine or heat individual mugs for a few seconds in the microwave. Recipes for mulled wine and other warming drinks are given on pages 188–193.

Warming plates

Warm plates by using them as a cover for the dish in which the food is cooking. Make sure that they do not have any metal trimmings before heating plates in the microwave. Alternatively, if the dish does not need covering, stack the plates underneath the dish to warm them.

Warming sugar for jam

When making jam by conventional methods, warm the sugar in the microwave before adding it to the fruit. Place it in a large microwave-safe bowl and cook on Full power (High) for 1–2 minutes, or longer depending on the quantity. The warm sugar dissolves more quickly and lowers the temperature of the preserve less than it would if it is not warmed. Using special preserving sugar produces less scum during cooking.

Making croutons

1. Cut neat cubes of white or whole-wheat bread, removing the crusts beforehand if you like. Spread them out on paper towels and cook on Full power (High) until firm.

2. The cooled cubes are crisp and they can be tossed in melted butter just before they are to be used.

Melting chocolate

1. Chocolate melts well in the microwave. Break the squares into a small bowl.

2. Stir the chocolate halfway through the recommended time; the squares may still retain their shape even when they are soft, so check even if the chocolate looks firm.

Herbs

These are used in microwave cooking in exactly the same way as for conventional methods. The following notes offer general guidelines on combining individual herbs with main ingredients, and, if necessary, there are notes specifically on using the microwave.

DRYING HERBS

The microwave can be utilized to dry herbs. The sprigs of herb should be washed and dried, then laid on a double thickness of paper towels. Place another piece of paper towel loosely over the top. Cook on Full power (High) for about 2 minutes, then leave the herbs to cool for 5 minutes. When the herbs have been cooked for long enough they will become crisp and dry when they cool. Continue cooking in bursts of 1 or 2 minutes until the sprigs are properly dried. Cool completely before crumbling and storing in an airtight jar.

The exact timing depends on the type of herbs. If you want to prepare a pot of mixed dried herbs, such as Italian seasoning, dry them individually before mixing.

BASIL

Basil has a unique flavor, closely related to its fragrance. It is lost on prolonged heating, so basil should be used as garnish or added toward the end of cooking. Basil has a special affinity with eggs, pasta, vegetable soups and sauces, but its greatest partner is tomatoes.

BAY

BAY

Bay leaves have a strong flavor and are part of the classic *bouquet garni*, and are almost always included in stocks, casseroles and pâtés. Make sure they are tucked well between other ingredients, or covered by liquid, when cooking in the microwave. They should be removed before serving. They make a good garnish, set in aspic on top of a pâté or terrine.

CHERVIL

Chervil has a light, subtle flavor and forms part of the classic mixture called *fines herbes*, for use in omelets and sauces. On its own, chervil is good in bland, creamy soups, with baked or scrambled eggs, pounded into butter for serving with broiled fish, or for flavoring a velouté sauce. Wild chervil is also known as sweet cecily.

CHIVES

CHIVES

Chives are the mildest of the onion family. They are added to dishes just before serving. They make the ideal contrast to pale, creamy dishes like vichyssoise soup and scrambled eggs.

CILANTRO

CILANTRO

Cilantro looks much like flat-leaf parsley, but the leaves have a distinct flavor which complements spiced Tex-Mex foods and curries.

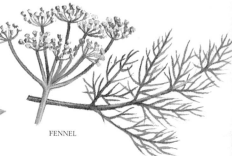
DILL

DILL

Dill resembles fennel, with feathery leaves. It is good with fish and as a garnish.

FENNEL

FENNEL

Fennel leaves, with their aniseed taste, are chopped and added to sauces and fish dishes.

GARLIC

Garlic is a perennial bulb with extensive uses. In the microwave, like onions, garlic should be cooked first to ensure that it does not overpower the finished dish. A peeled clove will flavor a vinaigrette, and it is delicious used to make garlic bread. The flavor becomes milder as it cooks.

BASIL

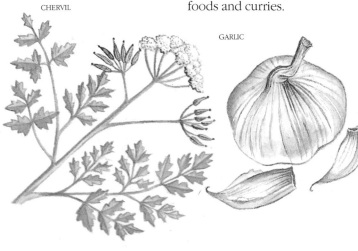
CHERVIL
GARLIC

HORSERADISH

HORSERADISH

The horseradish root is grated and used as a condiment, like mustard, and is a traditional accompaniment to roast beef. When fresh horseradish is not available, it can be bought grated in jars.

LEMON BALM

LEMON BALM

Lemon balm is a perennial, with aromatic leaves which give off a strong lemon fragrance when crushed. The leaves can be chopped and added to stuffings for poultry and game, salads, desserts and fruit cups. They have a flavor somewhat like lemon rind.

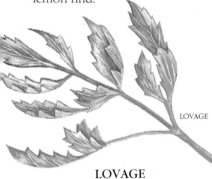

LOVAGE

LOVAGE

Lovage is a hardy perennial growing over 4-feet high, with large, dark green leaves. The chopped leaves are good alone, or combined with other robust herbs, in stuffings, stews and soups, and in fresh tomato sauce for pasta. The flavor is very powerful.

MARJORAM

All majorams dry well and keep their flavors. They give an

MARJORAM

authentic flavor to Provençal, Italian and Greek dishes and go exceptionally well with tomatoes.

MINT

MINT

Mint is a widely available herb and easy to grow. It is used to make mint sauce or jelly to complement roast lamb, and goes well with long summer drinks.

Mint is also widely used in both Mediterranean and Middle Eastern cooking. These cuisines particularly favor the spearmint and applemint varieties.

OREGANO

Oregano is the wild marjoram, similar in taste and aroma, but more powerful. It dries

OREGANO

extremely well and is essential in Italian dishes, especially Spaghetti sauce and pizza. It is also used in commercial chili powders and is an excellent herb for flavoring stuffings and marinades.

PARSLEY

PARSLEY

Parsley is used mainly as a garnish, but with its delicious flavor it can be used much more widely in cooking. Parsley forms part of the *bouquet garni* and *fines herbes* mixtures. Parsley sauce is the traditional accompaniment to boiled ham and poached fish.

ROSEMARY

Rosemary is a bushy shrub with evergreen needles, dark green

ROSEMARY

on top and silvery-gray underneath. It has a robust flavor and the sprigs of the herb are removed before serving.

SAGE

Sage has an extremely powerful flavor and can be used fresh or dried. It dries very well in the microwave.

SAGE

SUMMER SAVORY

SUMMER SAVORY

Savory has a strong, bitter flavor and should be used in moderation. It dries well and is said to have an affinity with bean dishes.

TARRAGON

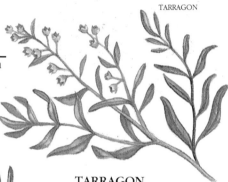

TARRAGON

Tarragon is one of the subtlest of all the herbs, and goes well with foods of delicate flavor, such as eggs, fish and chicken. It is part of the classic *fines herbes* mixture, and is good in marinades and sauces.

THYME

Both common thyme and lemon thyme are very useful since they keep their flavors when dried or after cooking. Common thyme is good with meat and game. Lemon thyme suits chicken and fish.

THYME

SPICES

The art of spicing food has a long and fascinating history, and is one of the most subtle techniques in cooking. When spices are cooked in the microwave, they should be added at an early stage and cooked slightly before the main ingredients are incorporated.

ALLSPICE

Allspice berries are similar to large peppercorns with a spicy flavor, mingling the tastes of cloves, cinnamon and nutmeg. It is used in smoked and pickled

ALLSPICE

foods and traditional savory pork or game pies.

ASAFOETIDA

Asafoetida or "giant fennel" is a huge odiferous member of the parsley family. When used in minute quantities it is a remarkable enhancer of other

ASAFOETIDA

tastes and its frightful smell disappears in cooking. It is used extensively in spicy Middle Eastern dishes.

ANISEED

The small gray-green ribbed seeds of the aromatic anise annual with their spicy/sweet flavor are used in northern and eastern Europe in confectionery, desserts, cookies, cakes and breads. Anise-flavored alcoholic drinks are also often used in cooking. In India, a small plate of aniseed is brought with the check in restaurants, to freshen the mouth.

CARAWAY

CARAWAY SEEDS

Caraway seeds are small, oval and ribbed. Strongly aromatic, they have a warming peppery undertone and should be bought as seeds. Breads such as rye and pumpernickel frequently include caraway.

CARDAMOM

Three types of cardamom pods are available, black, green and

CARDAMOM

white. It is one of the essential spices of Indian cuisine, crucial in biryanis, pilaus, dhals and curries. It is an ingredient of the mixture garam masala and of many Indian dishes.

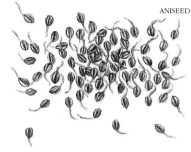
ANISEED

CAYENNE

Cayenne is a very hot pepper which should be used sparingly. It has an affinity with fish and seafood and teams well with cheese and eggs. It is often sprinkled over just before serving.

CHILI

Fiery chili peppers are a very ancient spice, their cultivation stretching back 10,000 years, originating in Latin America.

CHILI

Chilis vary enormously in size, color and strength. They are widely used in Mexican cooking.

CINNAMON

CINNAMON

Cinnamon is a universally popular spice, generally used for sweet dishes in the West and savory ones in the East. In India, it flavors curries and kormas. In Greece, it is used in honeyed pastries.

CAYENNE

CLOVES

Cloves are both sweet and pungent with an unmistakable aroma, but use them with restraint to avoid swamping other tastes. A popular use of cloves is to stud ham for baking

CLOVES

and glazing. They blend well with apples in pies and crumbles and should be included in mulled wine mixes.

CUMIN

Cumin's spicy seeds are small, ridged and greenish-brown in color. They have a strong unmistakable aroma, sweetish and warming. The flavor is

CUMIN

similarly pungent and penetrating. They should be used in moderation, in seed or powdered form. Always buy whole seeds and grind only when needed.

CORIANDER SEEDS

GINGER

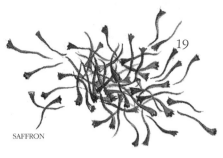

SAFFRON

CORIANDER SEEDS

Coriander seeds look like tiny ridged brown footballs. They are milder than many other spices so can be used in large quantities. The taste, fresh with a hint of bitterness, improves on keeping.

GINGER

Fresh ginger has a distinctive smell and strong taste, the fieriness of which is diminished in the powdered and crystallized form. Ground ginger is an important and traditional baking spice in cakes and cookies.

NUTMEG

Nutmeg is milder than mace but has a similar warm sweetish taste. Grate directly over the

NUTMEG

mixing bowl or cooking dish to flavor a variety of sauces.

SAFFRON

Saffron is the world's most expensive spice. It imparts a distinctive aroma, a bitter honey-like taste and strong yellow color to food. It is traditional in Spain's famous Paella and France's Bouillabaisse.

DILL SEEDS

DILL SEEDS

Dill seeds have a fresh sweet aroma but a slightly bitter taste, similar to caraway seeds. They are good in pickled dishes, including the famous dill pickle, vinegars, marinades and dressings.

JUNIPER BERRIES

JUNIPER BERRIES

Juniper berries with their spicy pine aroma and sweet resinous flavor have an affinity with robust meat dishes and are included in marinades and stuffings.

PAPRIKA

Paprika flavors a profusion of savory foods – from goulashes to vegetables. The mildest kind

PAPRIKA

is the most widely sold and it imparts a wonderful reddish brown to food.

PEPPER

SESAME SEEDS

SESAME SEEDS

Dried sesame seeds have a strong nutty flavor. Dry roast or fry in a little oil before use. They are popular in both Chinese and Japanese cooking and in their ground form make tahini paste.

FENUGREEK

Roast whole fenugreek seeds lightly and grind to a golden powder. It is used most frequently in Indian food, and
FENUGREEK

also in pickles and chutneys and in the Greek sweet, Halva.

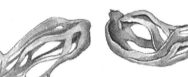
MACE

MACE

Mace is the crimson, lacy cage enclosing the shell of the nutmeg. It is available both as blades and ready ground. Because of its warm pungency it is best suited to savory dishes.

PEPPER

PEPPER

Pepper is the most familiar spice of all. Black is stronger than white, while green peppercorns have a mild, fresh taste. Peppercorns are added to marinades and stocks and are crushed in French recipes.

STAR ANISE

STAR ANISE

Star anise is an attractive oriental spice especially associated with Chinese cooking. Red-cooked Chinese dishes frequently include star anise.

FENNEL SEEDS

FENNEL SEEDS

Fennel is best known as a vegetable but its seeds are also used in cooking, usually with fish. In the West, they are used in marinades, sauces and stuffing. In India, they are used in fish curries.

MUSTARD SEEDS

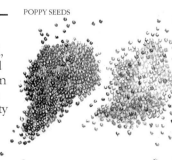

MUSTARD SEEDS

Whole mustard seeds are the basis of all prepared mustards and of the pungent mustard oil, beloved in India. They are used primarily to flavor pickles and in Indian food. Cooked, they lose their heat and have a warm nutty flavor.

POPPY SEEDS

Poppy seeds are mild and sweetish and acquire a bitter sweet, nutty flavor when cooked. They are associated with baking and the seeds decorate many types of bread.

POPPY SEEDS

TURMERIC

Turmeric has a distinctive pungent flavor and is best known for its partnership with fish and rice; notably in Scottish kedgeree, and pickles such as piccalilli.
TURMERIC

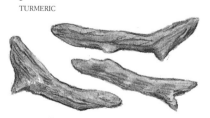

STOCKS AND SOUPS

Home-made soups can be deliciously simple or delicately sophisticated, from main-meal recipes to smooth and light chilled soups, and they can all be cooked with great success in the microwave. Follow the notes for preparing basic stocks, and for adapting your favorite recipes to microwave cooking.

Whether you are preparing a puréed soup or a chunky soup, the microwave can be used to speed up the process considerably, particularly if a few guidelines are followed. When using the microwave for soup-making, the emphasis in the first stage of cooking is on cooking the solid ingredients in the soup and imparting their flavors to a small amount of liquid. Additional liquid is then added to dilute the flavors and to make up the quantity. Soups can be made in advance and reheated in the microwave very successfully.

Cookware

Conventional methods dictate that large saucepans are used to make soup, and when it comes to microwave cooking the same rule applies to the size of the cooking container. You will need a large casserole or bowl in which to cook stocks and soups. This allows plenty of room for rearranging the ingredients and for adding all the liquid. A fairly narrow, deep casserole which has a lid is ideal, but a microwave-safe mixing bowl works just as well with a dinner plate as a cover.

Making stock

1. Add about one third of the water at the first stage of cooking.

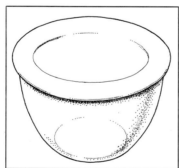

2. The remaining water is added when the ingredients have yielded their flavors and the stock is cooked briefly, then left to stand.

Cookware

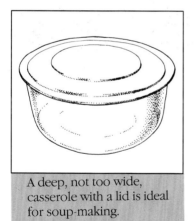

A deep, not too wide, casserole with a lid is ideal for soup-making.

A microwave-safe glass mixing bowl is an ideal alternative to a casserole dish. A plain dinner plate makes a good cover.

Home-made stocks give the best flavor to soups, sauces and casseroles. Use leftover meat bones from a roast or from a ham, the carcass of a cooked or boned chicken, or use ground beef or chicken pieces as the basis for the stock. A vegetable stock should be prepared from a good selection of full-flavored ingredients. Herbs and onions are essential for flavoring all stocks.

Degreasing stock

Leave the strained stock to cool, then chill it and the fat will set on the surface for easy removal.

Freezing

The cooled stock can be frozen in ice cube trays for later use in small quantities to flavor sauces.

Alternatively, to freeze a large amount, pour all the stock into a rigid container, leaving head-space for the liquid to expand slightly as it turns to ice. The stock can also be frozen in bags – plastic or boil-in bags – in which case they should be supported in a bowl or large measuring cup until the stock is solid.

Freezing the stock

The stock can be frozen in a concentrated form, in which case add just enough water to cover the ingredients at the second stage, pressing them down into the liquid. You may have to break the chicken into small pieces to immerse it in liquid.

Continue as above but remember that the frozen concentrated stock will have a stronger flavor and it will need to be diluted when you use it.

Fish Stock

Makes about 1 quart
fish trimmings (heads, tails, fins, bones and skin)
4–6 ounces white fish (the weight depends on the quantity of trimmings used)
1 onion, chopped
1 carrot, thinly sliced
1 bay leaf
2 large parsley sprigs
3¾ cups boiling water
salt and pepper

Preparation time: 10 minutes
Cooking time: 25 minutes, plus 30 minutes standing time
Microwave setting: Full power (High)

1. Cut up the fish trimmings if necessary, then place them in a large bowl or casserole dish.

Cut the fish into chunks and add it to the trimmings.

2. Add the onion, carrot, bay leaf and parsley, then pour in 1¼ cups of the water.

3. Cover the dish and cook for 15 minutes. Pour in the remaining water, then continue to cook the stock for a further 10 minutes.

4. Leave the stock to stand for 30 minutes, before straining it. Press the juices from the flavoring ingredients with the back of a wooden spoon before discarding them.

5. Season the stock to taste, and use as required.

Vegetable Stock

Makes about 5 cups
1 large onion, chopped
1 large carrot, chopped
1 small turnip, chopped
top and root end of 1 bunch of celery, chopped (include all leaves)
2 tablespoons sunflower oil
3 tomatoes, chopped
1 bay leaf
4 large parsley sprigs
thyme sprig
5 cups boiling water
salt and pepper

Preparation time: 15 minutes
Cooking time: 30 minutes, plus 30 minutes standing time
Microwave setting: Full power (High)

1. Mix the onion, carrot, turnip and celery in a bowl or large casserole dish. Add the oil and toss the vegetables in it.

2. Cover the dish and cook the vegetables for 5 minutes. Add the tomatoes, herbs and 1½ cups of the water, then stir.

3. Cover and cook for 15 minutes, stirring once. Add the remaining water and re-cover the dish, then cook for a further 15 minutes.

4. Leave the stock to stand, still covered, for 30 minutes. Strain it, pressing all the juices out.

5. Season to taste and use the stock as required.

Beef Stock

Makes about 1 quart
½ pound lean ground beef
1 large onion, chopped
1 stalk celery, sliced
1 carrot, thinly sliced
1 bay leaf
parsley sprig
thyme sprig
blade of mace
3¾ cups boiling water
salt and pepper

Preparation time: 10 minutes
Cooking time: 30 minutes, plus 30 minutes standing time
Microwave setting: Full power (High)

1. Place the ground beef in a bowl or large casserole dish. Add the vegetables.

2. Tie the bay leaf, parsley, thyme and blade of mace together to make a *bouquet garni* and add to the other ingredients.

3. Pour in 1½ cups of the boiling water, cover the bowl and cook for 15 minutes, stirring once.

4. Pour in the remaining water, stir well, then cover the dish and cook the stock for a further 15 minutes.

5. Leave the stock to stand, covered, for 30 minutes. Remove the herbs, then strain the stock, pressing all the liquid out of the meat mixture. The stock can be seasoned to taste and used as required.

6. The remaining ground beef can be used in another dish if you do not want to waste it. Use it with an equal quantity of fresh ground meat to make a meat sauce, taking care to brown the raw meat first. It should be cooked for the same length of time as the freshly browned meat.

Chicken Stock

Makes about 1 quart
1 chicken carcass or 1 chicken quarter
1 large onion, quartered
1 stalk celery, sliced
1 carrot, thinly sliced
1 bay leaf
parsley sprig
thyme sprig
3¾ cups boiling water
salt and pepper

Preparation time: 10 minutes
Cooking time: 20 minutes, plus 30 minutes standing time
Microwave setting: Full power (High)

1. Break up the carcass and place it in a large bowl. Place the chicken quarter (if used) skin side down in the bowl.

2. Add the vegetables and herbs, putting them around the edges of the chicken and over the top. Pour in 1¼ cups of the boiling water.

3. Cover and cook for 15 minutes. Pour in the remaining water and re-cover the dish. Cook the stock for a further 5 minutes, then leave it to stand for 30 minutes.

4. If the stock is to be cooled, then leave it until cold before straining. Strain, pressing all the juices out of the vegetables. Remove and reserve any chicken meat but discard all the other flavoring ingredients and bones.

5. Season the stock to taste and use as required. It can be used as the base for soups and sauces, in casseroles or to flavor rice during cooking.

SOUPS

As when cooking soup, the important points to remember are to use hot stock or boiling water and to add only a small amount of liquid with the bulk of the ingredients. If all the liquid is added at the first stage, it takes significantly longer to cook the solid ingredients. If the soup is to be frozen, then it can be left in the concentrated form ready to be thinned when it is defrosted and reheated before serving.

Seasoning

Do not add salt at the first stage of cooking – add it when the bulk of the liquid is stirred in, or taste the soup and adjust the seasoning before serving.

Thickening soup

In all other respects the rules for making soup are the same as for those which can be applied to conventional methods.

Vegetables Potatoes and other vegetables thicken a soup which is puréed.

Flour Flour can be used in the form of a roux (a fat and flour mixture) to thicken soup. Chopped onion, or other ingredients, are cooked with butter or oil first, then flour is stirred in before the first quantity of liquid is added. This is a good method of thickening the liquid in a chunky soup.

Cornstarch Used for oriental-style soups, this is mixed with a little cold water and stirred into the full quantity of soup, then cooked for about 3 minutes, until boiling.

Eggs and Cream As with any other cooking method, care should be taken when using eggs or cream as a thickening agent in microwave cooking. Very short heating is required and timings are often measured in seconds rather than minutes. Overheating will result in an unpleasant curdled texture. When hot liquids are taken from the microwave, they should be stirred well and allowed to cool slightly before eggs or cream are added.

Serving ideas

Simple home-made soups or convenience soups are often made more interesting by the addition of a complementary garnish.

Croutons Crunchy cubes of bread can be served in a bowl at the table or sprinkled on to the soup just before it is served.

Browned Almonds Browned slivered almonds can be sprinkled over delicate, creamy soups such as chicken, asparagus or spinach soups.

Shredded Orange Rind Finely shredded orange rind adds a tang to tomato or carrot soups. Cook the rind in a little water in a bowl for 1–2 minutes, until it is tender, then drain and dry it on paper towels. Sprinkle over individual portions of soup that are swirled with cream.

Herbs Chopped fresh parsley, dill, basil or tarragon are all good on soups.

Cream or Yogurt Swirl light cream, sour cream or plain yogurt into bowls of smooth soups before serving.

Bacon Bits Crunchy bacon bits are delicious in smooth or chunky soups.

Sherry Use good-quality consommé to make a quick appetizer. Stir in sherry for extra flavor and whipped cream or sour cream to enrich the soup.

Freezing soups

Many types of soup freeze very well, and they can be defrosted and reheated very quickly in the microwave. However, there are one or two points to remember for success.

Fish and seafood soups do not freeze as well as meat and vegetable soups if they contain pieces of fish because the cooked fish tends to break up on defrosting and reheating.

Soups which are thickened with eggs do not freeze well once the eggs are added as they curdle. Similarly, cream should not be added to soup before it is frozen as it will curdle when defrosted and reheated.

Chunky vegetable soups which are prepared for freezing should be slightly under cooked. Pieces of root vegetable in the soup should be firm and slightly crisp when frozen so that they do not break up when they are defrosted and reheated. Cook the soup for a few minutes once it is hot so that the vegetables are tender and heated through when served.

If the soup has rice or pasta added, then these ingredients should not be frozen with the soup. Once the soup has defrosted and heated, the rice or pasta can be added and cooked before serving.

Packing soup for freezing It is a mistake to pour the soup into large or very tall containers to store in the freezer. Remember that the block of frozen soup will have to fit into a bowl for defrosting. Also, if the block is too tall it may not fit in the microwave.

Convenience foods

Canned soups and consommé can be heated with ease and speed in the microwave. For single portions, simply pour the soup into a suitable serving bowl or mug and heat on Full power (High) for 1–2 minutes. Stir well and continue to heat until the soup is heated through. Stir well before eating. Larger portions can be heated in a bowl, a tureen or large pitcher.

Packaged dried soups can also be prepared in the microwave. Pour the mix into a large bowl and gradually beat in the required amount of water. Heat on Full power (High), beating after 1–2 minutes and at intervals until the soup is boiling and thickened. The time depends on the quantity being cooked. Allow about 4 minutes for $2\frac{1}{2}$ cups.

Packaged cup soups can also be heated in the microwave – slowly stir in the stated quantity of cold water and heat on Full power until boiling. Check the soup after 45 seconds.

Stages in soup-making

1. The vegetables and other solid ingredients are cooked first with the minimum of water, until they are almost tender but not completely cooked.

2. Half the quantity of hot stock is added to the vegetables and cooked until all the ingredients are ready for puréeing.

3. The last of the liquid is added as the soup is puréed or not, depending on the desired thickness. For chunky soups, the stock is added with seasoning, then heated through briefly and served.

Soup which defrosts best in the microwave has been frozen in small containers or blocks. For example, smooth soups can be packed in empty yogurt pots or margarine tubs (put them on a cookie sheet until frozen). Once the soup is hard, it can be removed from the pots and packed in freezer bags for storage. Put the small blocks in a dish to defrost quickly.

Large blocks of soup should be placed in a dish and broken up as they soften to speed up the total defrosting and reheating time.

When the soup is hot, rice or pasta can be added if desired.

Simple Vegetable Soup

Serves 4
1 onion, chopped
1 potato, diced
2 carrots, diced
2 stalks celery, diced
2 tablespoons vegetable oil
3¾ cups hot chicken stock
1 cup frozen peas or cut green beans
3 tablespoons chopped fresh parsley
salt and pepper

Preparation time: 15 minutes
Cooking time: 25 minutes
Microwave setting: Full power (High)

1. Mix all the prepared fresh vegetables in a large bowl or casserole dish. Add the oil and toss the vegetables in it to coat them evenly.

2. Cover the dish and cook the vegetables for 5 minutes. Stir in half the stock, re-cover the dish and cook for a further 10 minutes, stirring once.

3. Add the remaining stock, the frozen peas or beans and the parsley. Sprinkle in a little seasoning, then cover the dish and cook the soup for a further 10 minutes.

4. The vegetables should be tender but still whole. Taste the soup and adjust the seasoning, then stir well before serving with crusty bread.

5. If the soup is to be frozen, then cook it for 2–5 minutes after the second batch of stock is added so that the vegetables are still quite firm. Leave the soup to cool before packing and freezing. After it is defrosted, the soup should be cooked for a few minutes until the vegetables are tender.

Potato and Almond Soup

Serves 4
1 onion, chopped
2 large potatoes, chopped
1 cup blanched almonds
2 tablespoons butter
2½ cups hot chicken stock
1¼ cups light cream or milk
1 tablespoon chopped parsley

Preparation time: 10 minutes
Cooking time: 18–19 minutes
Microwave setting: Full power (High)

1. Mix the onion, potatoes and almonds in a bowl or casserole dish, and add the butter. Cover and cook for 10 minutes, stirring once.

2. Pour in the stock and re-cover the dish, then continue to cook for 7 minutes, or until the potatoes are softened but not fallen.

3. Purée the soup in a blender or food processor, then pour it back into the bowl and stir in the cream or milk. Heat for 1–2 minutes, taking care not to let the soup boil.

4. Stir and taste for seasoning, then sprinkle with parsley before serving.

5. If the soup is to be frozen, then this should be done when it is puréed but before the cream or milk is added. The cream should be added when the purée has been defrosted and reheated.

Potato and Onion Soup

Serves 4

2½ cups peeled and finely
  chopped onions
4 cups peeled and thinly sliced
  potatoes
1 teaspoon Italian seasoning
2½ cups milk
salt
1¼ cups hot beef stock
freshly ground black pepper
2 teaspoons snipped chives, to
  garnish

Preparation time: about 10
minutes
Cooking time: about 17½
minutes
Microwave setting: Full power
(High)

1. Place the onions and
potatoes in a large bowl, cover
and cook for 13 minutes,
stirring halfway through
cooking.

2. Stir in the herbs, milk and salt.
Cover and cook for 4½ minutes,
stirring halfway through
cooking.

3. Stir in the hot beef stock,

pepper and more salt, if
necessary, to taste. Purée in a
blender or food processor.

4. Pour into 4 soup bowls and
garnish.

Potato and onion soup; Lentil and
orange soup.

Lentil and Orange Soup

Serves 4
2 tablespoons butter
heaped ½ cup split red lentils
1 onion, peeled and finely
*   chopped*
1 celery stalk, finely sliced
½ medium carrot, peeled and
*   grated*
¼ teaspoon dried thyme
3¾ cups hot chicken stock
⅔ cup orange juice
grated rind of ½ orange
bay leaf
salt
freshly ground black pepper
orange rind, to garnish

Preparation time: about 10
minutes
Cooking time: about 27
minutes
Microwave setting: Full power
(High)

1. Place the butter and lentils in a large bowl. Cover and cook for 2 minutes, stirring halfway through.

2. Stir in the onion, celery, carrot and thyme. Cover and cook for 7 minutes, stirring halfway through.

3. Stir in 2½ cups of the hot stock with the orange juice, rind, bay leaf, salt and pepper. Cover. Cook for 10 minutes, stirring halfway through cooking.

4. Remove the bay leaf and stir in the remaining hot stock. Cool slightly.

5. Pour the soup into a blender and purée.

6. Return to the bowl and reheat gently for 8 minutes. Adjust the seasoning and garnish with thin strips of orange rind.

Mulligatawny Soup

Serves 4
2 tablespoons vegetable oil
heaped ½ cup red lentils
2 garlic cloves, peeled and
*   crushed*
1 onion, peeled and finely
*   chopped*
1 carrot, peeled and finely
*   chopped*
1 small turnip, peeled and
*   finely chopped*
1 teaspoon curry powder
3¾ cups hot chicken stock
salt
freshly ground black pepper
1–2 tablespoons lemon juice

Preparation time: about 10
minutes
Cooking time: about 27
minutes
Microwave setting: Full power
(High)

1. Mix the oil, lentils, garlic onion, carrot and turnip in a large bowl. Cover and cook for 9 minutes, stirring twice.

2. Stir in the curry powder and pour in 2½ cups of the hot stock, then add seasoning to taste. Stir well, cover and cook for 10 minutes, stirring once.

3. Add the remaining stock, stir well, then purée the soup in a blender or food processor. Pour the soup back into the bowl and heat it for 8 minutes.

4. Taste and adjust the seasoning, then sharpen with lemon juice to taste. Serve crisp Indian popadums or toasted pita bread as an accompaniment.

Corn and Potato Soup

Serves 4–6
1 onion, peeled and finely
*   chopped*
1⅓ cups peeled and thinly sliced
*   potatoes*
1⅓ cup frozen whole-kernel
*   corn*
bay leaf
2½ cups milk
salt
1¼ cups hot chicken stock
freshly ground black pepper
2 scallions trimmed and finely
*   chopped*
4 tablespoons sour cream, to
*   serve*

Preparation time: about 10
minutes
Cooking time: about 19½
minutes
Microwave setting: Full power
(High)

1. Mix the onion, potatoes, corn and bay leaf in a large bowl. Cover and cook for 15 minutes, stirring twice.

2. Pour in the milk and season with a little salt. Cover the bowl and cook for a further 4½ minutes, stirring once.

3. Stir in the hot stock and add some pepper to the soup, then purée it in a blender or food processor until smooth.

4. Taste and adjust the seasoning, add the spring onions to the soup and serve. Swirl a little sour cream into each portion.

Cream of Carrot Soup

Serves 6
6 tablespoons butter
1 onion, peeled and chopped
1 slice Canadian bacon or ham,
*   chopped*
1 teaspoon salt
1 teaspoon sugar
freshly ground black pepper
3 cups peeled and chopped
*   carrots*
1 quart chicken stock
To garnish:
⅔ cup light cream
croutons

Preparation time: about 10
minutes
Cooking time: about 26
minutes
Microwave setting: Full power
(High)

1. Place the butter in a large bowl and cook for 1 minute to melt. Add the onion, bacon, salt, sugar and pepper to taste. Cover and cook for 3 minutes.

2. Stir in the carrots and stock. Cover and cook for 20 minutes.

3. Purée in a blender or food processor until smooth or pass through a fine strainer.

4. Pour the soup into a suitable tureen and cook for 2 minutes to reheat. Serve hot, garnished with a swirl of cream and a few croutons.

Country Vegetable Soup

Serves 4
2 tablespoons butter
1⅓ cups finely shredded cabbage
⅔ cup peeled and diced potatoes
¾ cup peeled and chopped onions
¾ cup peeled and thinly sliced carrots
½ cup cored, seeded and diced red bell pepper
½ cup peeled and diced turnip
1 × 16-ounce can tomatoes with juice
salt
freshly ground black pepper
3¾ cups hot beef stock

Preparation time: about 15 minutes
Cooking time: about 20 minutes
Microwave setting: Full power (High)

1. Place the butter, cabbage, potatoes, onions, carrots, red bell pepper, turnip, tomatoes, salt and pepper in a large bowl. Cover and cook for 10 minutes, stirring halfway through cooking.

2. Stir in the stock. Cover and cook for 10 minutes or until the vegetables are tender, stirring halfway through cooking.

3. Taste and adjust the seasoning before serving.

Tomato Soup with Rice and Basil

Serves 4
2 tablespoons butter
1 large onion, peeled and chopped
⅓ cup all-purpose flour
2 tablespoons tomato paste
6 ripe tomatoes, cut into quarters
¼ teaspoon celery salt
1 teaspoon super-fine sugar
1 teaspoon dried basil
salt
freshly ground black pepper
1¼ cups milk
2 cups hot chicken stock
4 tablespoons cooked rice
2 tablespoons light cream, to serve (optional)

Preparation time: about 5 minutes
Cooking time: about 18 minutes
Microwave setting: Full power (High)

1. Place the butter and onion in a large bowl. Cover and cook for 4 minutes.

2. Stir in the flour, tomato paste, tomatoes, celery salt, sugar, basil, salt and pepper. Add the milk. Cover and cook for 10 minutes, stirring halfway through cooking.

3. Add the hot stock and allow to cool slightly.

4. Pour the soup into a blender or food processor and purée until smooth.

5. Strain the puréed soup to remove the tomato peels and seeds. Stir in the cooked rice.

6. Return the soup to the bowl and reheat uncovered for 3–4 minutes. Adjust the seasoning.

7. Serve the soup with a swirl of cream floating on the top, if liked.

Country vegetable soup; Tomato soup with rice and basil

Fish soup; Pea and mint soup

Fish Soup

Serves 4–6

1 onion, peeled and finely
   chopped
1 small green bell pepper,
   cored, seeded and finely
   diced
1⅓ cups peeled and finely diced
   potatoes
1 tablespoon vegetable oil
1 garlic clove, peeled and
   crushed
½ teaspoon dried rosemary
1 teaspoon chopped fresh
   parsley
salt
2 bay leaves
2½ cups cold water
1½ pounds filleted white fish, cut
   into small pieces
2 cups hot water
freshly ground black pepper

Preparation time: about 20
minutes
Cooking time: about 17½
minutes
Microwave setting: Full power
(High)

1. Place the onion, green bell
pepper, potatoes, oil, garlic,
rosemary, parsley and salt in a
large bowl. Cover and cook for
7½ minutes or until the
vegetables are tender.

2. Stir in the bay leaves, cold
water and fish. Cover and cook
for 10 minutes, stirring halfway
through.

3. Stir the hot water gently into
the fish mixture.

4. Remove the bay leaves. Taste
and adjust the seasoning, then
serve in individual soup bowls.

Pea and Mint Soup

Serves 4–5

2 tablespoons butter
1 onion, peeled and finely
   chopped
1½ 10-ounce packages frozen
   peas
1 tablespoon chopped fresh mint
2½ cups hot chicken stock
salt
freshly ground black pepper
¼ cup all-purpose flour
2 cups milk
4 mint sprigs, to garnish

Preparation time: about 5
minutes
Cooking time: about 19
minutes
Microwave setting: Full power
(High)

1. Place the butter, onion, peas
and mint in a large bowl. Cover
and cook for 8 minutes, stirring
halfway through cooking.

2. Add the hot chicken stock,
salt and pepper. Cover and
cook for 5 minutes.

3. Place the flour in a small bowl
and gradually blend in the milk.
Stir the milk into the soup.

4. Pour the soup into a blender
or food processor and purée
until smooth.

5. Return the soup to the bowl,
cover and cook for 6 minutes,
stirring halfway through
cooking.

6. Taste and adjust the
seasoning, then serve garnished
with sprigs of mint.

Lettuce Soup with Croutons

Serves 4

1 onion, peeled and finely
*   chopped*
$\frac{1}{4}$ cup butter
$\frac{1}{4}$ cup all-purpose flour
2 cups hot chicken stock
$1\frac{1}{4}$ cups milk
4 cups washed and chopped
*   lettuce leaves*
$\frac{1}{4}$ teaspoon grated nutmeg
$\frac{1}{4}$ teaspoon superfine sugar
salt
freshly ground black pepper
1 egg yolk
Croutons:
2 slices fresh white bread, cut
*   into cubes*
4 tablespoons vegetable oil

Preparation time: about 5
minutes
Cooking time: about 19
minutes
Microwave setting: Full power
(High)

1. Place the onion and butter in
a large bowl. Cover and cook
for 4 minutes.

2. Stir in the flour, hot stock,
milk, lettuce, nutmeg, sugar, salt
and pepper. Cover and cook for
9 minutes. Cool slightly.

3. Pour the soup and the egg
yolk into a blender and purée
until smooth.

4. Return soup to the bowl.
Reheat for 2 minutes.

5. Taste and adjust the
seasoning, then serve garnished
with croutons.

6. To make the croutons, toss
the cubes of bread into the oil.
Spread the cubes over a plate.
Cook for 2 minutes. Stir and
cook for a further 2 minutes,
checking and stirring the
croutons frequently until
browned. Drain on paper
towels.

Chicken and Vegetable Soup

Serves 4

1 carrot, peeled and finely
*   sliced*
1 potato, peeled and diced
2 button mushrooms, sliced
1 small red bell pepper, cored,
*   seeded and diced*
1 small turnip, peeled and
*   diced*
$\frac{1}{2}$ leek, finely sliced and washed
1 small onion, peeled and
*   chopped*
$1\frac{1}{4}$ pounds chicken pieces
1 quart hot chicken stock
salt
freshly ground black pepper
parsley, thyme and bay leaf tied
*   together*

Preparation time: about 15
minutes
Cooking time: about 26
minutes
Microwave setting: Full power
(High)

1. Place the carrot, potato,
mushrooms, red bell pepper,
turnip, leek and onion in a large
bowl. Place the chicken pieces
on top of the vegetables. Cover
and cook for 15 minutes,
stirring halfway through.

2. Add the hot chicken stock,
salt, pepper and herbs. Cover
and cook for 8 minutes.

3. Take out the chicken. Remove
and discard the skin, then cut
the flesh from the bones. Chop
the chicken flesh and return it to
the soup.

4. Discard the herbs. Reheat for
3 minutes. Taste and adjust the
seasoning, before serving.

Lettuce soup with croutons; Chicken
and vegetable soup

Vichyssoise

Serves 4–5

2 cups peeled and thinly sliced potatoes
5 cups thinly sliced and washed leeks
1 celery stalk, finely chopped
¼ cup butter
4 tablespons water
3¾ cups hot chicken stock
salt
freshly ground black pepper
⅔–1¼ cups heavy cream
1 tablespoon snipped fresh chives, to garnish

Preparation time: about 10 minutes, plus chilling
Cooking time: about 14 minutes
Microwave setting: Full power (High)

1. Place the potatoes, leeks, celery, butter and water in a large bowl. Cover and cook for 8 minutes, stirring halfway through cooking.

2. Add half the stock, salt and pepper. Cover and cook for 6 minutes. Add the remaining stock.

3. Pour the soup into a blender and purée.

4. Sieve the puréed soup. Taste and adjust the seasoning.

5. Allow to cool completely, then chill for 2 hours.

6. Before serving, stir in the cream and garnish with snipped chives.

Mushroom Soup

Serves 4

2 tablespoons butter
1 onion, peeled and finely chopped
2⅔ cups chopped flat mushrooms
¼ cup all-purpose flour
1¼ cups milk
salt
freshly ground black pepper
2½ cups hot chicken stock
4 tablespoons light cream
2 button mushrooms, thinly sliced, to garnish

Preparation time: about 5–10 minutes
Cooking time: about 13½ minutes
Microwave setting: Full power (High)

1. Place the butter and chopped onion in a large bowl. Cover it and cook for 5 minutes. Stir in the chopped mushrooms, cover again and cook for a further 3 minutes.

2. Stir in the flour, then gradually blend in the milk. Season to taste with salt and pepper. Cover and cook for 2½ minutes.

3. Stir in the hot chicken stock. Purée in a blender or food processor, then pour the soup back into the bowl.

4. Taste and adjust the seasoning, if necessary. Stir in the cream. Reheat gently without boiling, uncovered, for 3 minutes, if required.

5. Pour the hot soup into 4 individual bowls and garnish with the thinly sliced button mushrooms.

Vichyssoise; Mushroom soup

FIRST COURSES

The microwave really does take the trouble out of preparing first courses. Speedy pâtés can be prepared and cooked in advance or mouth-watering hot appetizers can be organized ahead, ready for cooking in minutes just before you sit down at the table.

The key to success when it comes to serving the perfect first course is good planning. Either have the appetizer ready in advance or have it prepared to the stage at which it can be put in the microwave to be quickly cooked or heated just before it is served.

Plan the first course along with the rest of the menu, making sure that there is plenty of contrast in textures and that the flavors are complementary. Before filling main courses serve light appetizers, or if you particularly want to serve a splendid first course, make sure that the main course is simple. If the first course and main courses are both hot, then the dessert can be a cool one, prepared in advance.

The accompaniments which go with the appetizer are also important. Crusty French bread, thinly sliced bread and butter or crisp toast are often served.

Lastly, the garnish is important – this opening dish of the meal should please the eye as well as tempt the palate, so add a few sprigs of fresh seasonal herbs, shredded lettuce, twists of lemon or other simple garnishes that echo the dish's main ingredients.

Fruit appetizers

Fruit appetizers are not always cold and the microwave can be used to prepare quick "baked" grapefruit or light fruit compotes that arouse the appetite. These should be ready prepared, in suitable dishes, to be warmed in the microwave just before you sit down.

Vegetable appetizers

Many classic first courses rely on the simple preparation of perfect vegetables – asparagus with butter, or artichokes with vinaigrette dressing – and the microwave is ideal for this purpose. If you are serving asparagus, have it ready in its cooking container so that it can be cooked just before it is served. To one side have some butter ready to melt as you transfer the cooked asparagus to the plates. Lemon wedges will provide garnish and a refreshing contrast in taste.

Corn-on-the-cob is less expensive and equally easy. The ears can be cooked in one large roasting bag or they look good when individually wrapped in waxed paper or plastic wrap and served in their wrappers. Think ahead and have the ears all ready to go into the microwave well in advance. Remember that you may have to rearrange them halfway through the cooking time to move any from the middle of the dish to the outside.

Pâtés

The microwave is excellent for cooking all types of pâtés. Use the microwave to melt butter for simple fish pâtés which are puréed and chilled, or substitute microwave-poached smoked haddock instead of smoked mackerel for a change. Chicken or turkey liver pâté can be cooked very successfully in the microwave or you can cook heavier, loaf or dish pâtés in the same way. For example, try

serving the Ham Pâté on page 124 as a first course, offering hot toast as an accompaniment. Many of your favorite meat pâtés can be cooked in the microwave but remember that a dense mixture takes time to cook through. It is a good idea to roughly chop and part-cook liver or meat before it is puréed or ground and mixed with the other pâté ingredients. The pâté should be covered to prevent drying out as it cooks. Make sure the mixture is cooked right through by cutting out a tiny sample from the middle before serving up.

Seafood appetizers

Ready-cooked shellfish can be heated rapidly in the microwave and coated in a well-flavored

sauce to make an impressive appetizer. As a change from shrimp cocktails why not sample the Hot Seafood Cocktail on page 35, or cook delicate scallops in a creamy sauce? When cooking delicate fresh shellfish, like scallops or mussels, it is important to remember that they require very little cooking and that they will toughen and lose flavor if they are overcooked. So, the rule of thumb for these ingredients is to check in advance rather than cooking the food for the full length of time suggested.

Cooking corn-on-the-cob

1. Individual ears of corn are generously brushed with melted butter and wrapped in waxed paper or plastic wrap before cooking. (They can be served in the paper wrappings.)

2. Arrange four ears in a shallow dish, placing them as near to the outside of the dish as possible. Rearrange them halfway through cooking, turning the ends from the middle toward the outside.

Hot Game Terrine

Serves 4

*1½ cups finely chopped cold
  cooked game meat, such as
  pheasant or quail*
⅓ cup chopped cooked ham
⅔ cup finely chopped mushrooms
*2 garlic cloves, peeled and
  crushed*
1 teaspoon Italian seasoning
salt
freshly ground black pepper
2 eggs, lightly beaten
watercress sprigs, to garnish
tomato slices, to garnish

Preparation time: 10 minutes
Cooking time: 5–6 minutes
Microwave setting: Full power
(High)

1. Mix the game, ham,
mushrooms, garlic and herbs
together in a bowl. Season to
taste with salt and pepper, then
bind with the eggs.

2. Place a tall straight-sided glass
in the center of a 6½-inch soufflé
dish lined with plastic wrap to

make a ring mold. Spoon in the
game mixture and spread evenly
around the dish.

3. Cover with plastic wrap and
cook 5–6 minutes. Remove the
cover and glass, then unmold
onto a warm serving dish and
remove the plastic wrap.
Garnish with watercress sprigs
and tomato slices. Serve with
hot toast.

Cook's Tip

This terrine is a good way to use
leftover meat. If you don't have
enough cooked game meat, add
cooked chicken, turkey or duck.

Globe Artichokes with Vinaigrette

Serves 4
4 globe artichokes
1¼ cups water
1 tablespoon lemon juice
Vinaigrette:
salt
freshly ground black pepper
1 teaspoon dry mustard
6 tablespoons wine vinegar
¾ cup olive oil

Preparation time: about 10 minutes, plus cooling
Cooking time: about 20 minutes
Microwave setting: Full power (High)

1. Using a pair of scissors, snip off the point from each of the outer leaves of the artichokes. Cut the stems from the bottoms. Rinse the artichokes and turn upside down to drain.

2. Pour the water and lemon juice into a large shallow dish. Cook for 4 minutes.

3. Stand the artichokes in the water and cover the dish with plastic wrap. Cook for 10 minutes.

4. Rearrange the artichokes, so the front ones are at the back, and cook, covered, for a further 10 minutes, or until the bottoms are tender when pricked with a fork.

5. Leave to stand, covered, for 10 minutes. Drain off the water and leave to cool.

6. While the artichokes are cooling, make the dressing. Place the salt, pepper and mustard in a small bowl. Stir in the vinegar. Beat in the oil a little at a time, until smooth.

7. To serve, pour a little vinaigrette over each artichoke. Hand the remaining dressing separately.

Mushrooms in Garlic Butter

Serves 4
5 cups button mushrooms
1 teaspoon Italian seasoning
2 garlic cloves, peeled and crushed
1 tablespoon lemon juice
½ cup butter, cut into pieces
1 tablespoon heavy cream
salt
freshly ground black pepper
chopped fresh parsley, to garnish

Preparation time: about 7 minutes
Cooking time: about 8½ minutes
Microwave setting: Full power (High)

1. Place the mushrooms, herbs, garlic and lemon juice in a large bowl. Cover and cook for 6 minutes. Pour off any excess liquid.

2. Stir in the butter, cream and salt and pepper to taste. Cook, uncovered, for 2½ minutes, stirring every minute. Serve garnished with the parsley. Accompany with crusty French bread if liked.

Globe artichokes with vinaigrette;
Mushrooms in garlic butter

Hot Crab

Serves 4
1 cup fresh white bread crumbs
2 teaspoons vegetable oil
1 tablespoon anchovy extract
1 tablespoon freshly squeezed lemon juice
1 tablespoon Worcestershire sauce
⅔ cup heavy cream
6 ounces crabmeat
salt
freshly ground black pepper
4 pieces fried bread
To garnish:
mild paprika
parsley sprigs

Preparation time: about 10 minutes
Cooking time: about 3 minutes
Microwave setting: Full power (High)

1. Place the bread crumbs, oil, anchovy extract, lemon juice, Worcestershire sauce; cream, crabmeat, salt and pepper in a bowl and mix them all together.

2. Cook for 3 minutes, stirring every minute. Taste and adjust the seasoning.

3. Spoon onto the fried bread and serve garnished with paprika and a sprig of parsley.

Rollmops

Serves 4
4 medium herrings, filleted
1 large onion, peeled and finely sliced
1¼ cups cider vinegar
1 teaspoon superfine sugar
salt
freshly ground black pepper
1 teaspoon apple pie spice
2 teaspoons pickling spice
4 bay leaves

Preparation time: about 5 minutes, plus cooling
Cooking time: about 9 minutes
Microwave setting: Full power (High)

1. Roll up each herring fillet with the skin to the outside and place in a shallow dish. Scatter the onion over the top of the herrings.

2. Mix together the vinegar, sugar, salt, pepper, spice, pickling spice and bay leaves. Pour the mixture over the herrings and onion.

3. Cover and cook for 5 minutes. Turn the plate around and cook for a further 4 minutes.

4. Leave to cool before serving.

From left to right clockwise: Coquilles St Jacques; Hot seafood cocktail; Rollmops; Hot crab

Coquilles St Jacques

Serves 4
2⅔ cups potatoes cut into 1-inch cubes
3 tablespoons water
salt
1⅓ cups sliced button mushrooms
1 garlic clove, peeled and crushed
¼ cup butter
¼ cup all-purpose flour
⅔ cup dry white wine
1 egg yolk
4 large scallops, sliced, with shells
2 tablespoons heavy cream
freshly ground black pepper
1 tablespoon milk
To garnish:
4 parsley sprigs
1 scallop, cooked and sliced

Preparation time: about 17 minutes
Cooking time: about 15 minutes
Microwave setting: Full power (High)

1. Place the roughly cubed potatoes in a medium bowl with the water and a pinch of salt. Cover and cook for 8 minutes, stirring halfway through cooking. Leave to stand, covered.

2. Place the mushrooms, garlic and 2 tablespoons of the butter in a medium bowl. Cover, cook for 3 minutes.

3. Stir in the flour and wine. Cook, uncovered, for 2 minutes.

4. Beat in the egg yolk, then stir in the scallops, cream and salt and pepper to taste. Cook, uncovered, for 2 minutes.

5. Meanwhile, mash the potatoes with the remaining butter, the milk and salt and pepper to taste. Place in a pastry bag filled with a large star tip and pipe around the edges of 4 scallop shells.

6. Spoon the sauce into the center. Reheat if necessary. Serve garnished with parsley and scallop slices.

Hot Seafood Cocktail

Serves 4
¼ cup butter
½ cup all-purpose flour
2½ cups milk
salt
freshly ground black pepper
1 teaspoon tomato paste
3 ounces cooked fresh or frozen mussels
6 ounces shelled and deveined cooked large shrimp
To garnish:
mild paprika
whole cooked shrimp
4 lemon slices

Preparation time: about 5 minutes
Cooking time: about 10 minutes
Microwave setting: Full power (High)

1. Place the butter in a bowl and cook for 1½ minutes.

2. Stir in the flour, then gradually blend in the milk. Stir in the salt and pepper. Cook for 4 minutes, stirring every minute. Taste and adjust the seasoning.

3. Add the tomato paste to color the sauce pink. Stir in the mussels and shrimp. Cook for 4½ minutes, stirring halfway through cooking.

4. Place the mixture in a large dish. Garnish with a sprinkling of paprika, whole shrimp and lemon slices. Serve immediately.

Ratatouille

Serves 4

1 small zucchini, sliced
1 medium eggplant, sliced
6 tomatoes, peeled and chopped
½ green bell pepper, cored,
  seeded and finely sliced
½ red bell pepper, cored, seeded
  and finely sliced
1 onion, peeled and sliced
1 tablespoon tomato paste
2 garlic cloves, peeled and
  crushed
6 tablespoons olive oil
1 teaspoon Italian seasoning
salt
freshly ground black pepper

Preparation time: about 15
minutes, plus cooling
Cooking time: about 15
minutes
Microwave setting: Full power
(High)

1. Place the zucchini, eggplant,
tomatoes, green and red bell
peppers, onion, tomato paste,
garlic, oil, herbs, salt and
pepper in a large bowl. Cover
and cook for 5 minutes.

2. Stir, then cook for 5 minutes.
Stir again and cook for a further
5 minutes.

3. Taste and adjust the
seasoning, then allow to cool
before serving.

Honeyed Grapefruit and Orange

Serves 4

2 large grapefruit, halved, cut
  in sections and drained, with
  shells reserved
1 large orange, pith and rind
  removed, cut in sections and
  drained
1 tablespoon honey
1 tablespoon multi-colored
  sugar crystals or light brown
  sugar

Preparation time: about 15
minutes
Cooking time: about 3½
minutes
Microwave setting: Full power
(High)

1. Place the grapefruit and
orange sections in a bowl. Add
the honey. Cook for 1½ minutes.

2. Divide the mixture between
the grapefruit shells. Sprinkle
the sugar crystals or the brown
sugar over each.

3. Stand the halves on a plate or
in individual sundae dishes or
bowls. Cook for 2 minutes.

*Ratatouille; Honeyed grapefruit and
orange*

Jellied Ham and Chicken

Serves 4
¾ cup finely diced cooked chicken meat
¾ cup finely chopped cooked ham
2 envelopes unflavored gelatine
2 cups well-flavored chicken stock
½ teaspoon meat extract
2 teaspoons chopped fresh parsley
freshly ground black pepper
4 cucumber slices, to garnish

Preparation time: about 8 minutes
Cooking time: about 2½ minutes, plus setting
Microwave setting: Full power (High)

1. Mix together the chicken and ham and divide between 4 ramekins.

Jellied ham and chicken; Corn-on-the-cob with parsley butter

2. Place the gelatine in a small bowl and slowly stir in half the stock. Cook for 2½ minutes or until the gelatine has dissolved, stirring after each minute.

3. Stir in the meat extract, parsley and remaining chicken stock. Season to taste with pepper. Cool, then pour over the chicken and ham. Chill until set.

4. Garnish each ramekin with a slice of cucumber.

Corn-on-the-cob with Parsley Butter

Serves 4
6 tablespoons butter
4 corn-on-the-cob, fresh or frozen
2 tablespoons finely chopped fresh parsley

Preparation time: about 5 minutes
Cooking time: about 14 minutes
Microwave setting: Full power (High)

1. Cut the butter into pieces and place in a small dish. Heat for 1½ minutes or until melted.

2. Brush the corn with melted butter and wrap each ear in plastic wrap.

3. Arrange the corn in a shallow container. Cover and cook for 10 minutes, if using fresh corn, or 12 minutes, if using frozen, until the corn is tender when

pricked with a fork or skewer.

4. Remove the corn from the plastic wrap and put into individual dishes.

5. Stir the parsley into the remaining butter and reheat for 45 seconds. Pour the hot parsley butter over the corn. Alternatively, stir the parsley and unmelted butter together in advance and wrap in plastic wrap and chill until ready to serve. Place thin slices of butter on each ear of corn to serve.

Shrimp with Garlic and Tomatoes

Serves 4

2 tablespoons butter
½ onion, peeled and grated
½ pound shelled and deveined cooked small shrimp
4 tomatoes, peeled and finely chopped
2 garlic cloves, peeled and crushed
1 tablespoon tomato paste
½ teaspoon ground mace
salt
freshly ground black pepper

Preparation time: about 20 minutes
Cooking time: about 7 minutes
Microwave setting: Full power (High)

Shrimp with garlic and tomatoes;
Shrimp in brandy sauce

1. Place the butter and onion in a large bowl, cover and cook for 2 minutes.

2. Stir in the shrimp, tomatoes, garlic, tomato paste, mace, salt and pepper. Cover and cook for 5 minutes, stirring halfway through cooking.

3. Taste and adjust the seasoning.

Shrimp in Brandy Sauce

Serves 4

2 garlic cloves, peeled and crushed
1 medium onion, peeled and finely chopped
2 tablespoons butter
¼ cup cornstarch
1¼ cups milk
2 teaspoons tomato paste
2 tablespoons brandy
1 tablespoon heavy cream
1 pound shelled and deveined jumbo shrimp
salt
freshly ground black pepper
To garnish:
1 tablespoon chopped fresh parsley
lemon wedges.

Preparation time: about 8 minutes
Cooking time: about 12 minutes
Microwave setting: Full power (High)

1. Place the garlic, onion and butter in a large bowl. Cover and cook for 4 minutes.

2. Stir in the cornstarch, then blend in the milk, tomato paste, brandy, cream and shrimp. Season to taste with salt and pepper. Cook, uncovered, for 8 minutes, stirring halfway through cooking.

3. Sprinkle with parsley and serve with lemon.

Shrimp and Lemon Crêpes

Serves 4
1 large egg
1 egg yolk
1¼ cups milk
pinch of salt
1 cup all-purpose flour
vegetable oil for frying
Filling:
3 tablespoons butter
⅓ cup all-purpose flour
1¼ cups milk
salt
freshly ground black pepper
1 teaspoon anchovy extract
grated rind of 1 small lemon
6 ounces shelled and deveined
  cooked shrimp

Preparation time: about 25
minutes, including crêpes
Cooking time: about 6 minutes,
plus 15 minutes to make crêpes
Microwave setting: Full power
(High)

1. Beat together the egg, egg
yolk and milk. Place the salt and
flour into a mixing bowl and
beat in the egg mixture.

2. Make 8 crêpes using the
conventional stovetop. Set aside
and keep warm while making
the filling.

3. Place the butter in a bowl.
Cook for 45 seconds or until
melted.

4. Stir in the flour. Gradually
blend in the milk and add salt
and pepper. Cook for 2½
minutes, stirring every minute.

5. Add the anchovy extract.
Taste and adjust the seasoning.
Stir in the lemon rind and
shrimp.

6. Spread the mixture in a line
down the center of each crêpe.
Fold each edge of the crêpe
over the mixture.

7. Divide the crêpes between 2
plates. Cook each plate of
crêpes for 1½ minutes.

*Shrimp and lemon crêpes; Tomato
pasta bows*

Tomato Pasta Bows

Serves 4
7½ cups boiling water
1 tablespoon vegetable oil
salt
4 cups pasta bows
Sauce:
1 onion, peeled and finely
  chopped
2 garlic cloves, peeled and
  crushed
1 teaspoon cornstarch
1 8-ounce can tomatoes,
  chopped with their juice
1 teaspoon Italian seasoning
2 tablespoons tomato paste
salt
freshly ground black pepper
1 tablespoon butter
2 tablespoons grated Parmesan
  cheese

Preparation time: about 10
minutes, plus standing
Cooking time: about 14
minutes
Microwave setting: Full power
(High)

1. Place the boiling water, oil,
salt and pasta in a large bowl.
Cover and cook for 8 minutes.
Leave to stand, covered, for 10
minutes.

2. Place the onion and garlic in a
small bowl, cover and cook for
3 minutes.

3. Stir in the cornstarch,
undrained tomatoes, herbs,
tomato paste and salt and
pepper to taste. Cook,
uncovered, for 3 minutes,
stirring halfway through.

4. Drain the pasta and stir in the
sauce and butter. Serve
sprinkled with Parmesan
cheese.

Chicken Liver Pâté

Serves 4

2 slices bacon, chopped
½ pound chicken livers
1 garlic clove, peeled and
crushed
⅔ cup butter
1 tablespoon Italian seasoning
freshly ground black pepper
1 tablespoon dry sherry
1 tablespoon cream

Preparation time: about 10
minutes, plus chilling
Cooking time: about 6½
minutes
Microwave setting: Full power
(High)

1. Place the bacon in a medium bowl. Cook for 1 minute.

2. Add the livers, garlic, ½ cup of the butter, herbs and pepper. Cover and cook for 5 minutes, stirring halfway through cooking.

3. Add the sherry and cream. Place the mixture in a blender and purée until smooth. Divide the pâté between 4 ramekin dishes or put in 1 large dish.

4. Place the remaining butter in a bowl. Cook for 30 seconds or until melted. Pour a little butter over each serving of the pâté.

5. Allow to cool completely, then chill for 2 hours.

Smoked Fish Pâté

Serves 4

8 ounces frozen smoked fish
fillets, such as haddock or
trout
1 small onion, peeled and
chopped
¼ cup butter
1 3-ounce package cream
cheese
¼ teaspoon ground mace
1 tablespoon lemon juice
salt
freshly ground black pepper
parsley sprigs, to garnish

Preparation time: about 10
minutes, plus chilling
Cooking time: about 9 minutes
Microwave setting: Full power
(High)

1. Place the fish fillets in a shallow dish. Cover and cook for 2½ minutes.

2. Separate the fillets. Cook for a further 2½ minutes. Set aside.

3. Place the onion and butter in a bowl, cover and cook for 4 minutes.

4. Chop the fish and add to the onion and butter. Stir in the cheese, mace, lemon juice, salt and pepper.

5. Place the mixture in a blender and purée.

6. Divide the pâté between 4 individual ramekin dishes. Allow to cool completely and then chill for 2 hours in a refrigerator. Garnish with parsley sprigs.

Chicken Liver pâté; Smoked fish pâté

Stuffed Tomatoes

Serves 4
*4 large tomatoes, about 1½
    pounds*
*¾ cup fresh whole-wheat bread
    crumbs*
*1 tablespoon finely grated
    Cheddar cheese*
2 tablespoons chopped ham
1 teaspoon Italian seasoning
1 teaspoon mustard
2 tablespoons plain yogurt
salt
freshly ground black pepper
4 parsley sprigs, to garnish

Preparation time: about 10
minutes
Cooking time: about 5½
minutes
Microwave setting: Full power
(High)

1. Slice the top off each of the tomatoes and reserve, then using a grapefruit knife, scoop out the centers. Chop the flesh and seeds, then mix with the bread crumbs, cheese, ham, herbs, mustard, yogurt and salt and pepper to taste.

2. Fill each tomato with the stuffing and replace the "lids" on top of the tomatoes.

3. Place the tomatoes in 4 small dishes and arrange in a circle in the microwave. Cook, uncovered, for 5½ minutes or until soft, rearranging halfway through cooking. Remove any which may be cooked before the total cooking time.

4. Garnish each tomato with a sprig of parsley.

Stuffed Baked Avocado with Shrimp

Serves 4
2 tablespoons butter
*1 cup fresh whole-wheat bread
    crumbs*
1 tablespoon grated lemon rind
*¼ pound shelled and deveined
    cooked small shrimp*
5 tablespoons light cream
salt
freshly ground black pepper
2 large ripe avocados
1 tablespoon lemon juice
To garnish:
lettuce leaves
lemon twists

Preparation time: about 10
minutes
Cooking time: about 5 minutes
Microwave setting: Full power
(High)

1. Place the butter in a bowl. Cook for 30 seconds or until melted.

2. Stir in the bread crumbs. Cook for 1 minute. Stir in lemon rind, shrimp, cream, salt and pepper.

3. Cut the avocados in half. Remove and discard the seeds, then sprinkle the flesh with lemon juice.

4. Pile the shrimp mixture into each of the avocado halves. Arrange on a plate. Cook for 3½ minutes.

5. Serve on lettuce, garnished with lemon.

*Stuffed tomatoes; Stuffed baked avocado
with shrimp*

FISH AND SHELLFISH

Tender, light fish and shellfish cook very successfully in the microwave. Prepared simply, with butter and herbs, or combined with complementary ingredients, the range of dishes which can be created is infinite, from traditional favorites to exotic specialties.

Most fish and shellfish is very light, tender and ideally suited to microwave cooking. Whole fish, fillets, steaks or cubes of fish all cook speedily. Uncooked jumbo shrimp, scallops and mussels are also good candidates for cooking in the microwave. Ready-cooked shellfish can be reheated in sauced dishes in seconds. Since these foods cook so quickly, the rule to follow is to take great care not to overcook them.

Until you are certain of the cooking times for particular foods or recipes in your own microwave, then check the fish ahead of the suggested cooking times given in charts and recipes. If the fish is not quite ready it can be cooked for a while longer but once it is overcooked, then it will be dry and lack flavor. Follow the guidelines given here and you will discover that microwave-cooked fish is succulent, flavorful and particularly easy to prepare.

Cooking containers

Generally, fish and shellfish should be covered when cooked in the microwave. Microwave-safe glassware is ideal – for example, casseroles with lids or bowls which can be covered with plates or plastic wrap. Large shallow dishes are useful for cooking whole fish – quiche dishes can be covered with upturned plates or plastic wrap – and sauced fish dishes can be contained in casseroles or bowls. Fish fillets and steaks are best when cooked in shallow dishes.

Roasting bags or boil-in-bags are also useful to hold steaks or small whole fish. The bag can be placed on a large, plain dinner plate and the fish arranged inside it. This is particularly useful for small neat steaks which do not need rearranging halfway through cooking. Remember to use a special microwave tie to close the bag, leaving room for the steam to escape.

Arranging the ingredients

It is important that the fish or shellfish is arranged to the best advantage in the cooking container to ensure even cooking. Whole fish – for example, mackerel, trout or mullet – should be placed head-to-tail in the cooking container. Halfway through the cooking time the whole fish should be rearranged, moving any from the middle of the dish toward the outside and turning each fish over and around. If two fish are being cooked, then they simply need turning, but if three or four are closely packed into one dish, then those from the middle will need to be moved toward the outside.

Fillets need particular attention to ensure that the thin ends do not dry out before the thicker parts are cooked. When one fillet is cooked in the middle of a shallow dish or on a plate, then simply ensure that the cooking time is not over-long. When ready, the thicker part of the fillet will still be slightly translucent between the flakes but by the time the fish is removed from the oven,

uncovered and transferred to a serving plate it will be cooked.

If a number of fillets are cooked together, then they should be arranged with the thin tails toward the middle of the dish. If the fillets are large ones, tuck the tail of one under the thick part of another to prevent overcooking.

Alternatively, the tail ends of the fillets can be folded under – this is useful when cooking several flounder or whiting fillets. Fish steaks cook very well if they are evenly thick. Tuck the thin flaps of fish neatly into the cavity in the middle of the steaks and secure them with wooden toothpicks.

Large whole fish

A small whole salmon or medium-sized salmon trout will cook well in the microwave. If it is too large for the oven cavity, then curl it into a large quiche dish and use plastic wrap to keep it in place, covering the

dish twice. Remember to pierce the skin of the fish before cooking.

Piercing fish skin

When cooking whole fish, it is important to pierce the skin in one or two places to prevent it from bursting.

Covering during cooking

Most fish and shellfish need covering during cooking, the only exception being when the bulk of the dish is a sauce and the seafood is well coated.

Shielding with foil

Lastly, remember that small pieces of smooth foil can be used to protect areas which are likely to overcook. This is a useful way of protecting the heads and tails of whole fish. If the fish are quite large, by the time the main part of each is cooked, the heads and tails may

Cooking a whole salmon

1. Curve a small whole salmon into a quiche dish.

2. Use microwave-safe plastic wrap to keep the fish in place.

be very shriveled, so use small pieces of foil to shield them.

Seasoning

Do not sprinkle salt on fish before cooking because this results in dried patches. Sauces can be lightly seasoned in advance but check the cooked seafood and add salt to taste before serving.

Shellfish

Delicate items like scallops and shrimp cook very quickly. Scallops should be sliced or cut to prevent them from "bursting" during cooking. They should be cooked with a little liquid if they are not in a sauce. Remember that they will continue to cook slightly after they are removed from the microwave.

Large jumbo shrimp should be arranged around the edge of a shallow dish, a little water added and the dish covered.

Mussels cook particularly well in a large casserole or mixing bowl with a little cooking liquid and covered with a plate or lid. A good shake halfway through the time will ensure even cooking. Any unopened shellfish should be discarded.

Preparing mussels

The mussels should be left in cold water overnight, with a handful of oatmeal sprinkled into the bucket. This process of purging the shellfish rids them of sand. Scrub the shells and scrape off the black hairy beards. Discard any open shellfish which do not close when tapped sharply.

The mussels are cooked in a large container with the minimum of liquid. Any shellfish which are still closed at the end of cooking, when most are open, must be discarded.

Arranging and shielding fish

Arrange whole fish head-to-tail in the dish.

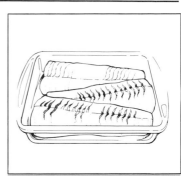

Arrange fillets with the thin tails tucked under.

Use wooden toothpicks to neaten steaks.

Tails and heads can be shielded with smooth foil.

Cooking mussels

1. The mussels are cooked in a large container with the minimum of liquid – here $\frac{2}{3}$ cup warmed dry white wine is added. A mixing bowl is ideal and a plate can be used to cover the bowl. A small chopped onion, a small finely diced carrot, ground pepper, a bay leaf and chopped parsley are added for flavor. A finely chopped clove of garlic can also be added to the mussels. Do not add salt at this stage.

2. Halfway through cooking the bowl is given a good shake. The mussels open when cooked as shown above; any which do not open must be discarded. To cook 2 pounds mussels allow 5–7 minutes on Full power (High). The mussels are ready for seasoning and ladling into individual bowls.

PREPARATION

There are many basic preparation techniques that apply to cooking fish that are useful for microwave cooking. The aim when cooking food in the microwave is to make individual food items as even in shape and size as possible. Boned fish, skinned fillets which can be rolled and even-sized chunks of fish all cook well. A good fish merchant will bone or skin fish but if you have to tackle the task, then follow these guidelines.

Boning round fish

Whole mackerel and trout cook quite successfully in the microwave; there are, however, advantages to cutting the heads off and boning these fish if you are cooking more than two at a time. The boned fish take up less space in the dish and they cook quickly and evenly. The fish should be folded back into shape and a little butter, herbs or other flavoring ingredients can be placed in the body cavity.

Alternatively, the fish can be cut in half lengthwise to yield two fillets which can be rolled and secured with wooden toothpicks before cooking.

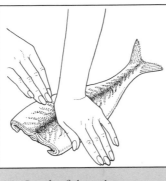

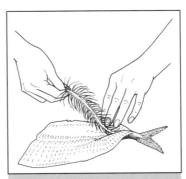

1. Gut the fish and remove the head. Cut off the fins and lay the fish, flesh down on a clean surface. Using the heel of your hand or your thumbs, press along the center back of the fish.

2. Turn the fish over and the bone should be loose. Carefully lift the bone away from the flesh, working from head end to tail. Snip the bone free of the tail end, then lightly run your finger over the flesh and pick out any stray bones.

Skinning fish fillets

Skinned flounder or sole fillets can be rolled and secured with toothpicks, then arranged in a shallow dish or casserole for even cooking in the microwave. The fillets can be sprinkled with lemon rind or chopped herbs before rolling but they must not be seasoned with salt. Larger fish fillets should be skinned if they are cut into pieces for cooking in casseroles or sauces.

Place the fish fillet on a clean surface, skin side down. Rub your fingertips in a little salt and hold the tail firmly. Using a sharp knife and holding it at an acute angle to the skin of the fish, cut between the skin and the flesh. Use a sawing action and avoid breaking the skin of the fish. Roll back the fish flesh as you cut it free of the skin.

Rolling fish fillets

Thin fish fillets cook best if they are rolled. The skinned fillets can be dotted with butter and sprinkled with chopped herbs and grated lemon rind. They should be rolled from head end to tail, then the rolls secured with wooden toothpicks.

Arrange the rolls as far apart as possible for even cooking, ideally around the edge of a round dish. A little liquid is added – water, wine or lemon juice – and the dish is covered before cooking. Pierce the rolls to ensure they are cooked through. Remember that they are ready when still very slightly translucent in the middle. The middle will finish cooking by the time the fish is served.

1. The skinned fish fillets are rolled neatly from head end to tail, with the skinned side inward.

2. The rolls are secured with wooden toothpicks and arranged as far apart as possible in the cooking dish.

Cutting steaks and arranging small portions

Even-sized pieces of fish cook very well in the microwave. Fish which is to be cooked with other ingredients in sauces should be skinned first. The skinned steaks can be cut into even-sized portions or into neat chunks. These can be added to a sauce for cooking, or they can be cooked with vegetables and liquid, casserole-style.

If the chunks are cooked alone, they should be arranged around the outside of a dish, or placed in a large bowl and rearranged halfway through cooking.

Even-sized pieces of shellfish can be cooked in the same way, such as scallops or jumbo shrimp.

Basic preparation methods for fish

These are the essentials which the fish merchant will usually do because these are necessary for all fish, regardless of the cooking method. However, if you buy from a busy market stall or if you have freshly caught fish to prepare, then you may find that you have to gut and scale fish once you have bought it.

Scaling fish

Scaly fish – salmon or mullet, for example – should have the scales removed before cooking. This is a messy job and no matter how well organized you are in your approach, a few scales always manage to escape and make a mess.

The best place to scale fish is in the sink, with the cold water running slowly to wash all the scales away. Using a scaler or cook's knife, hold the fish head upward and at an angle, scrape off the scales working from head to tail. The more vigorously you scrape the fish the farther the scales will fly, so it is best to scrape them off fairly gently to avoid making a mess.

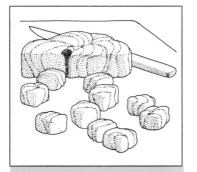

Steaks which are cut into even-sized chunks or pieces will cook evenly.

Once all the scales have been completely removed, rinse the fish thoroughly under cold running water and pat it dry on paper towels. Even if the fish merchant scales the fish for you, it is a good idea to check and remove any scales that may remain before you cook the fish.

Gutting fish

The easiest and most common method of removing the innards from round fish (such as trout or mackerel) is by slitting the fish along the belly, from head to tail. The innards can then be scraped out easily with a knife. The fish should be gutted as soon as possible – do not leave it in the refrigerator overnight before gutting.

It is best to gut the fish near the sink. Have ready two or three layers of newspaper. Holding the fish firmly in one hand, slit it with a sharp kinfe, then scrape out all the innards onto the paper. Rinse the fish under cold water, rubbing away any membranes. Pat the fish dry on paper towels.

Cleaning scallops

Use an oyster knife or stout, short-bladed kitchen knife to

Arrange small portions of fish or shellfish around the edge of a dish for even cooking. Tail ends of jumbo shrimp should be pointed toward the middle of the dish.

open the shells. The shells open more easily if the scallops are warmed for about half a minute under a broiler. As you open the shell, cut the membrane which attaches the scallop to the top part of the shell. The round white flesh is the only part eaten. The membrane, small intestine, pink roe and dark gray, soft area should be discarded. Carefully cut the flesh away from the shell and trim off all membranes, then rinse it briefly under cold water. Do not soak the scallops in water or hold them under the tap for too long as they have a delicate flavor and texture. The rounded shells can be thoroughly scrubbed and washed for serving the cooked scallops.

Shelling shrimp

Shelled cooked shrimp are readily available, both fresh and frozen but you may prefer to buy the whole shrimp and shell them yourself. Uncooked jumbo shrimp are sold with shells on or frozen ready shelled. You can use shrimp shells to flavor stock.

First remove the head of the shrimp. To do this, grip the tail firmly and pull off the head where it joins the back. Next the

Convenience foods

Frozen fish can be first defrosted, then cooked in the microwave in one operation.

Canned fish can be turned into tempting supper dishes in minutes – try adding canned tuna to a cheese or mushroom sauce and serving it with cooked rice or pasta. Canned shrimp, crabmeat or mussels can be added to sauces and briefly reheated. Remember that these foods are already cooked and that they simply require heating through.

Frozen shrimp can be defrosted quickly and used in a variety of ways but again it is important to heat them briefly as they can easily be overcooked and become tough.

shell must be removed from the body of the shrimp. Hold the shrimp with both hands, using your thumbs and index fingers only. Have the under side of the shrimp facing upward, then use your thumbs to push the shell off from the sides. It will slide off easily leaving the middle of the shrimp free of shell. Lastly pull off the tail unless it is to be left in place for serving.

DEFROSTING AND COOKING CHARTS

The following charts provide a guide to the methods and timings for defrosting and cooking a selection of fish and shellfish, and reheating cooked shellfish. Make use of this information to prepare plain cooked fish and shellfish or when you are pre-cooking these foods for use in another recipe, for example to make fish cakes.

GUIDE TO COOKING FISH

Fish		Quantity	Time in minutes on Full power (High)	Method
Bass	whole	1 pound	5–7	Shield the head and tail with smooth foil. Cut the skin in two or three places to prevent it from bursting.
Cod	fillets	1 pound	5–7	Place the fillet tails to the center of the dish or shield with smooth foil. Cut the skin in two or three places to prevent it from bursting.
	steaks	1 pound	4–5	Cover with plastic wrap before cooking.
Haddock	fillets	1 pound	5–7	Place the fillet tails to the center of the dish or shield with smooth foil. Cut the skin in two or three places to prevent it from bursting.
	steaks	1 pound	4–5	Cover with plastic wrap before cooking.
Halibut	steaks	1 pound	4–5	Cover with plastic wrap before cooking.
Mullet and red snapper	whole	1 pound	5–7	Shield the head and tail with smooth foil. Cut the skin in two or three places to prevent it from bursting.
Salmon	steaks	1 pound	4–5	Cover with plastic wrap before cooking.
Salmon trout	whole	1 pound	7–8	Shield the head and tail with smooth foil. Cut the skin in two or three places to prevent it from bursting.
Scallops		1 pound	5–7	Cover with dampened paper towel.
Smoked haddock	whole	1 pound	4–5	Cover before cooking.
Trout	whole	1 pound	8–9	Shield the head and tail with smooth foil, cut the skin in two or three places to prevent it from bursting.

GUIDE TO REHEATING BOILED SHELLFISH

Fish		Quantity	Time in minutes on Full power (High)	Method
Lobster	tails	1 pound	5–6	Turn tails over halfway through the cooking time.
	whole	1 pound	6–8	Turn over halfway through the cooking time. Allow to stand for 5 minutes before serving.
Jumbo shrimp and scampi		1 pound	5–6	Arrange the shelled shrimp in a ring in a shallow dish and cover.
Small shrimp		1 pound	4–5	Arrange the shelled shrimp in a ring in a shallow dish and cover.

GUIDE TO DEFROSTING FISH AND SHELLFISH

Fish	Quantity	Time in minutes on Defrost	Method
Fish fillets	$\frac{1}{2}$ pound 1 pound	5–7 7–9	Place in a shallow dish. Cover. Separate and rearrange when partially defrosted.
Fish steaks	2 × 4 ounces 4 × 4 ounces	5–7 10–12	Arrange thickest parts to outer edge. Cover. Turn or rearrange once, watch timing.
Whole gutted fish (herring, trout, mackerel)	1 pound	4–8	Arrange head-to-tail. Cover. Rearrange and stand halfway through defrosting. Shield tails if necessary.
Shrimp, scallops	$\frac{1}{2}$ pound 1 pound	3–5 6–8	Place in a shallow dish, Stir once or twice. Drain. Use as soon as possible.
Smoked salmon	4 ounces	1–1$\frac{1}{2}$	Unwrap and arrange slices on a plate. Cover.

Serving Suggestions

Fish which is cooked very simply can be turned into a tempting meal by adding a complementary sauce, an interesting topping or an edible garnish. The following suggestions are all fairly simple, they do not take long to prepare or cook and there is no need to follow a complicated recipe. Remember that the fish will cook very quickly in the microwave, so have the sauce made in advance, ready to heat for a minute before serving; the topping should be prepared or any garnishing ingredients should be ready to add to the cooked fish.

Sauced Fish

Parsley sauce A traditional accompaniment, pour the sauce over fish fillets or steaks and serve with creamy mashed or baked potatoes.

Egg sauce Egg sauce is delicious with white or smoked fish. Spoon the sauce over fillets and serve at once. Also good with cooked rice and peas.

Cheese sauce Make a tasty supper dish by coating white fish fillets with cheese sauce,

then browning them under the broiler. Serve with mashed potatoes or pasta. This is very good with cod or haddock.

Tomato sauce Serve cooked white fish on a bed of pasta, breaking the flesh into chunks. Top with hot tomato sauce, plenty of chopped parsley or basil and serve at once. Grated Parmesan cheese can be offered with the fish. Strongly flavored fish fillets, such as mackerel, can be served in this way.

Savory Butters

Butter can be creamed with a variety of different flavoring ingredients. The butter should be formed into a roll and wrapped in plastic wrap or foil, then chilled until it is firm. Cut the roll into neat slices. The slices of butter should be brought to room temperature before they are used then placed on the fish when it is freshly cooked and hot.

Maître d'hôtel butter Cream butter with a little lemon juice, seasoning and chopped fresh parsley. Good with all delicately flavored fish.

Herb butter Chopped fresh tarragon, chives, basil or dill can

be creamed with butter. Alternatively, a mixture of herbs can be used but do not use too much of any one strong herb. Serve with flounder or sole.

Lemon butter Beat grated lemon rind and a little juice into butter. The tangy lemon is particularly good with mackerel or smoked fish and helps counteract oiliness.

Walnut and orange butter An unusual combination but one that complements chunky fish steaks. Beat grated orange rind and finely chopped walnuts into butter. Do not add too many walnuts as they can spoil the texture of the butter.

Anchovy butter A rich butter to accentuate the natural flavor of fish. Beat a can of mashed anchovy fillets into butter, adding the oil if you like. Beat in a dash of lemon juice and some freshly ground black pepper. Good with cod steaks, haddock fillets or rolled whiting fillets which can taste rather bland.

Topping combinations

Buttered crumbs Toss fresh white or whole-wheat bread crumbs in hot melted butter and cook on Full power (High)

about 30–60 seconds until they are piping hot. Mix in some chopped parsley and spoon a little on fish steaks.

Nutty topping Chop some roasted peanuts and mix them with some chopped scallion. Sprinkle a little on fish fillets or steaks and add lemon wedges so that the juice can be squeezed over.

Tomato and chive topping Mix peeled chopped tomatoes with some snipped chives and seasoning. Spoon a little on fillets or steaks before serving.

Steamed Fish

Serves 3–4
*1 pound, fresh white fish, such
    as haddock or cod*
To garnish:
lemon twists
parsley sprigs

Preparation time: about 3
minutes
Cooking time: about 6 minutes,
plus standing
Microwave setting: Full power
(High)

1. Place the fish in a shallow
dish. Cover and cook for 6
minutes.

2. Leave to stand, covered, for
3–4 minutes or until the fish is
opaque and the flesh flakes
easily when tested with a fork.
Serve garnished with lemon
twists and parsley sprigs.

Cook's Tip

The addition of water is
unnecessary in this recipe as the
fish itself is moist and succulent,
and cooked very simply without
extra ingredients.

Cod with Herbs

Serves 4
*1 small onion, peeled and
    chopped*
½ teaspoon dried thyme
½ teaspoon dried parsley
½ teaspoon dried rosemary
½ teaspoon rubbed sage
1 cup fresh white bread crumbs
3 tablespoons water
salt
freshly ground black pepper
*4 cod steaks, total weight 1½
    pounds*
*2 tablespoons butter, cut into
    pieces*

Preparation time: about 10
minutes
Cooking time: about 9½
minutes, plus standing
Microwave setting: Full power
(High)

1. Place the onion in a medium
bowl, cover and cook for 2½
minutes. Stir in the thyme,
parsley, rosemary, sage, bread
crumbs, water, and salt and
pepper to taste. Set aside.

2. Place the cod steaks, thin
ends to the center, in a shallow
casserole. Cover and cook for 4
minutes.

3. Stuff each steak with the herb
mixture. Sprinkle with pepper,
and dot with the butter. Cover
and cook for 3 minutes. Leave to
stand, covered, for 3 minutes
before serving.

4. Serve with green noodles and
Cauliflower in Cheese Sauce
(page 143).

Steamed fish; Cod with herbs

Stuffed Trout

Serves 4

2 tablespoons slivered almonds
4 ounces shelled and deveined cooked shrimp
4 tablespoons fresh white bread crumbs
2 tablespoons lemon juice
salt
freshly ground black pepper
4 trout, total weight 2 pounds, gutted with heads left on
To garnish:
parsley sprigs
lemon slices

Preparation time: about 15 minutes
Cooking time: about 12 minutes, plus standing
Microwave setting: Full power (High)

1. Mix together the almonds, shrimp, bread crumbs, lemon juice, and plenty of salt and pepper to taste.

2. Fill each trout with the stuffing. Cover and cook for 12 minutes, rearranging halfway through cooking. Leave to stand, covered, for 5 minutes before serving.

3. Garnish with parsley and lemon.

Mackerel Roll-ups

Serves 4

1½ cups fresh whole-wheat bread crumbs
½ teaspoon dried marjoram
½ teaspoon dried thyme
½ teaspoon dried parsley
½ teaspoon rubbed sage
grated rind of 1 lemon
2 tablespoons lemon juice
1 teaspoon anchovy extract
6 tablespoons hot water
salt
freshly ground black pepper
4 mackerel, about 12 ounces each, gutted and filleted
To garnish:
lemon slices
flat-leaf parsley

Preparation time: about 15 minutes
Cooking time: about 11 minutes, plus standing
Microwave setting: Full power (High)

1. Mix together the bread crumbs, marjoram, thyme, parsley, sage, lemon rind, lemon juice, anchovy extract, water, and salt and pepper to taste.

2. Spread the stuffing over the fish. Roll up from the head to the tail. Secure with wooden toothpicks. Cover and cook for 11 minutes, rearranging halfway through cooking.

3. Leave to stand, covered, for 5 minutes before serving, garnished with lemon slices and parsley.

Stuffed trout; Mackerel roll-ups

Herrings with Mustard Sauce

Serves 4
*1 small onion, peeled and
    chopped*
½ teaspoon dried thyme
½ teaspoon dried marjoram
grated rind of ½ lemon
*1 cup fresh whole-wheat bread
    crumbs*
salt
freshly ground black pepper
1 small egg
*4 herrings, total weight 12
    ounces, gutted*
Sauce:
3 tablespoons butter
¼ cup all-purpose flour
2 cups milk
1 tablespoon dry mustard
*1 tablespoon white-wine
    vinegar*
1 teaspoon superfine sugar
salt
freshly ground black pepper

Preparation time: about 15 minutes
Cooking time: about 12–14 minutes
Microwave setting: Full power (High)

1. Place the onion in a small bowl, cover and cook for 3 minutes. Stir in the thyme, marjoram, lemon rind, bread crumbs, salt and pepper and bind with egg.

2. Fill the herrings with the stuffing. Close and secure with wooden toothpicks. Place the herrings in a shallow casserole dish, cover and cook for 5 minutes, rearranging halfway through cooking. Set aside, covered, while making the sauce.

3. Place the butter in a large bowl and cook for 1 minute or until melted. Stir in the flour. Gradually blend in the milk, mustard, vinegar, sugar and salt and pepper to taste. Cook for 4–6 minutes, stirring every minute.

4. Remove the toothpicks from the herrings and pour over the sauce. Sprinkle with chopped parsley to garnish and serve with new potatoes.

Cheesy Smoked Haddock

Serves 4
*4 smoked haddock fillets, about
    5 ounces each*
*2 tablespoons butter, cut into
    pieces*
Cheese sauce:
2 tablespoons butter
¼ cup all-purpose flour
1¼ cups milk
1 teaspoon mustard
salt
freshly ground black pepper
½ cup grated Cheddar cheese
flat-leaf parsley, to garnish

Preparation time: about 5 minutes
Cooking time: about 11 minutes
Microwave setting: Full power (High)

1. Place the fillets in a shallow casserole dish. Dot with the butter. Cover and cook for 6 minutes, rearranging halfway through cooking. Set aside, covered, while making the sauce.

2. Place the butter in a large bowl and cook for 1 minute or until melted. Blend in the flour. Stir in the milk, mustard and salt and pepper. Cook, uncovered, for 3 minutes, stirring every minute.

3. Stir in the cheese and cook, uncovered, for 1 minute.

4. Drain the fish and arrange on a serving dish. Pour over the sauce. Garnish with parsley.

Haddock Steaks with Capers

Serves 4
2 tablespoons butter
4 haddock steaks
Sauce:
2 tablespoons butter
¼ cup cornstarch
1¼ cups milk
salt
freshly ground black pepper
*2 tablespoons capers, drained
    and chopped*
1 tablespoon caper juice
dill sprigs, to garnish

Preparation time: about 10 minutes
Cooking time: about 16 minutes
Microwave setting: Full power (High)

1. Place the butter in a small dish. Cook for 1 minute or until melted.

2. Brush the haddock with the butter. Arrange the haddock in a shallow casserole, cover and cook for 4 minutes.

3. Turn the casserole around and cook for a further 4 minutes. Set aside, covered.

4. To make the sauce, place the butter in a 2½-cup measuring cup. Cook for 1 minute or until melted. Stir in the cornstarch, and blend in the milk, salt and pepper. Cook for 4 minutes, stirring every minute.

5. Stir in the capers and their juice and pour the sauce over the fish. Cook for 2 minutes. Garnish with dill and serve.

Fillets of Flounder in White Wine

Serves 4
*⅔ cup finely sliced button
    mushrooms*
*1 onion, peeled and finely
    chopped*
½ cup butter
1¼ cups dry white wine
2 pounds flounder fillets
⅓ cup all-purpose flour
1¼ cups milk
salt
freshly ground black pepper
*⅔ cup peeled, seeded and halved
    green grapes*
To garnish:
4 lemon slices

Preparation time: about 15 minutes
Cooking time: about 21 minutes
Microwave setting: Full power (High)

1. Place the mushrooms, onion, ¼ cup of the butter and wine into a shallow casserole. Cover and cook for 4 minutes or until the onion is translucent.

2. Roll up the flounder fillets and place them in the casserole. Cover and cook for 4 minutes. Turn the casserole around and cook for a further 5 minutes.

3. Drain the fish, reserving the liquid and keep hot.

4. Place the remaining butter in 1-quart measuring cup. Cook for 1 minute or until the butter has melted.

5. Blend in the flour, fish liquid, milk, salt and pepper. Cook for 7½ minutes, stirring every minute.

6. Stir in the grapes. Pour the sauce over the fish, cover and cook for 1 minute. Garnish with lemon.

Clockwise: Herrings with mustard sauce; Haddock steaks with capers; Fillets of flounder in white wine; Cheesy smoked haddock

Cod with Anchovies

Serves 4

4 cod steaks, total weight 1½
    pounds
salt
freshly ground black pepper
2 tablespoons butter, cut into 4
    pieces
1 2-ounce can anchovy fillets,
    drained
16 capers
To garnish:
lemon twists
parsley sprigs

Preparation time: about 5
minutes
Cooking time: about 7 minutes
Microwave setting: Full power
(High)

1. Place the cod steaks in a dish.
Cover and cook for 4 minutes.

2. Season the steaks with salt
and pepper and turn over. Place
a piece of butter on each. Cover
and cook for 1½ minutes.

3. Baste the fish with the melted
butter. Arrange a cross of 2
anchovies on each steak with
capers in between. Cook,
uncovered, for 1½ minutes.
Garnish with lemon twists and
parsley.

Flounder Fillets with Corn

Serves 4

12 skinned flounder fillets, total
    weight 1¼ pounds
6 tablespoons butter, cut into
    pieces
1 8½-ounce can whole kernel
    corn, drained
salt
freshly ground black pepper
parsley sprigs, to garnish

Preparation time: about 10
minutes
Cooking time: about 8½ minutes
Microwave setting: Full power
(High)

1. Roll up the flounder fillets
and arrange them in a shallow
microwave-safe casserole dish.
Cover and cook for 3½ minutes.
Set aside, covered.

2. Place the butter in a
measuring cup and cook,

uncovered, for 1 minute or until
it has melted.

3. Place the butter, corn, and
salt and pepper to taste in a
blender or food processor.
Blend until smooth.

4. Rearrange the fillets. Sprinkle
with salt and pepper to taste,
and spoon the corn mixture
over the top.

5. Cook, uncovered, for 4
minutes.

6. Garnish with sprigs of parsley
and serve immediately.

*Cod with anchovies; Flounder fillets
with corn*

Sole and Shrimp Rolls

Serves 4–6
*7 ounces shelled and deveined
    cooked tiny shrimp, defrosted
    if frozen*
juice of ½ lemon
*12–16 skinned sole fillets, total
    weight 1½ pounds*
*2 tablespoons dried parsley
    flakes*
salt
freshly ground black pepper
¼ cup butter, cut into pieces
*chopped fresh parsley, to
    garnish*

Preparation time: about 16
minutes
Cooking time: about 6 minutes
Microwave setting: Full power
(High)

1. Sprinkle the shrimp with
lemon juice, then spread over
the fillets. Sprinkle over the
parsley flakes, salt and pepper.
Roll up and secure with wooden
toothpicks.

2. Place the fish rolls in a
shallow casserole dish. Cover
and cook for 4 minutes.

3. Rearrange. Dot the fish rolls
with the butter. Cover and cook
for 2 minutes.

4. Remove the toothpicks.
Garnish with chopped parsley,
and serve with duchesse
potatoes and fried zucchini or
green beans.

Spiced Haddock

Serves 4
*1 small onion, peeled and
    chopped*
*1¼ pounds skinned haddock
    fillet, cut into pieces*
*⅔ cup finely sliced button
    mushrooms*
*1 garlic clove, peeled and
    crushed*
*2 tablespoons Worcestershire
    sauce*
1 teaspoon Italian seasoning
½ teaspoon curry powder
1 teaspoon soy sauce
*1 16-ounce can tomatoes,
    chopped with their juice*
salt
freshly ground black pepper

Preparation time: about 10
minutes
Cooking time: about 10
minutes
Microwave setting: Full power
(High)

1. Place the onion in a large
bowl, cover and cook for 2½
minutes.

2. Stir in the haddock,
mushrooms, garlic,
Worcestershire sauce, herbs,
curry powder and soy sauce.
Cover and cook for 3½–4
minutes, stirring halfway
through cooking.

3. Stir in the tomatoes, and salt
and pepper to taste. Cook,
uncovered, for 3½ minutes.

4. Serve surrounded by boiled
rice with peas.

Sole and shrimp rolls; Spiced haddock

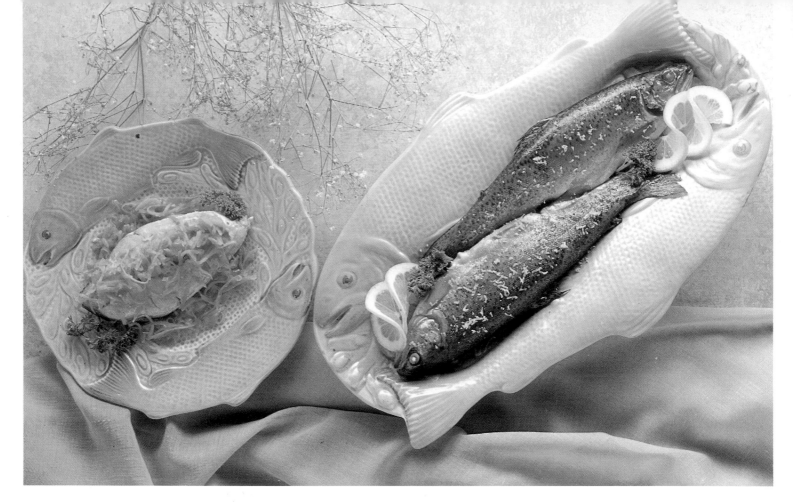

Haddock Steaks with Carrots

Serves 4
1 onion, peeled and finely chopped
1½ cups peeled and finely grated carrots
4 haddock steaks, total weight 1½ pounds
¼ cup butter
salt
freshly ground black pepper
parsley sprigs, to garnish

Preparation time: about 15 minutes
Cooking time: about 17 minutes
Microwave setting: Full power (High)

1. Place the onion in a medium bowl, cover and cook for 2 minutes. Stir in the carrots, cover and cook for 5 minutes. Set aside, covered.

2. Place the haddock steaks, with the thin ends to the center, in a shallow casserole dish, cover and cook for 6 minutes. Set aside.

3. Place the butter in a small cup and cook, uncovered, for 1 minute or until melted. Stir the butter into the vegetables, and season to taste with salt and pepper. Stir in the liquid from the fish.

4. Top the fish steaks with the carrot mixture and pour over any juice. Cook, uncovered, for 3 minutes.

5. Garnish with the parsley sprigs.

Lemon Trout

Serves 4
1 lemon, cut into 8 wedges
4 trout, total weight 2 pounds, gutted, with heads left on
grated rind of 2 lemons
¼ cup butter, cut into 8 pieces
To garnish:
lemon twists
parsley sprigs

Preparation time: about 10 minutes
Cooking time: about 9 minutes, plus standing
Microwave setting: Full power (High)

1. Place 2 wedges of lemon inside each trout. Place in a shallow casserole dish. Cover and cook for 4 minutes.

2. Rearrange the trout. Sprinkle with the lemon rind and dot with the butter. Cover and cook for 5 minutes. Halfway through cooking, baste the trout with the melted butter.

3. Leave to stand, covered, for 3 minutes.

4. Garnish with lemon twists and parsley, and serve with a mixed green salad.

Haddock steaks with carrots; Lemon trout

Cod in Tomato and Onion Sauce

Serves 4
1 onion, peeled and finely
*   sliced*
4 tomatoes, peeled and chopped
1 tablespoon tomato paste
½ teaspoon dried thyme
1 teaspoon chopped fresh
*   parsley*
½ teaspoon dried marjoram
½ teaspoon dried rosemary
1 garlic clove, peeled and
*   crushed*
2 tablespoons butter
salt
freshly ground black pepper
4 cod steaks
fresh dill, to garnish

Preparation time: about 10
minutes
Cooking time: about 14
minutes
Microwave setting: Full power
(High)

1. Place the onion, tomatoes, tomato paste, thyme, parsley, marjoram, rosemary, garlic, butter, salt and pepper in a large bowl. Cover and cook for 6 minutes, stirring halfway through cooking. Set aside, covered, while cooking the fish.

2. Place the fish in a shallow dish. Cover and cook for 3 minutes. Turn the dish around and cook for a further 3 minutes.

3. Pour the sauce over the fish. Cover and cook for 2 minutes, then garnish with dill.

4. Serve with mashed potatoes and green beans.

Cod in tomato and onion sauce;
Mackerel in a bag

Mackerel in a Bag

Serves 4
¼ cup butter
4 mackerel, total weight 3
*   pounds, gutted*
1 tablespoon chopped fresh
*   parsley*
salt
freshly ground black pepper
To garnish:
lemon quarters
parsley sprigs

Preparation time: about 10
minutes
Cooking time: about 12
minutes, plus standing
Microwave setting: Full power
(High)

1. Spread the butter inside each of the fish. Sprinkle the parsley over the butter in the fish. Season with salt and pepper. If the mackerel are too big to fit inside the microwave, remove the heads.

2. Place each mackerel in a roasting bag and secure the end with a non-metallic tie. Prick each bag.

3. Place the mackerel side by side on a large plate, cut sides up. Cook for 4 minutes.

4. Turn the mackerel over and turn the plate around. Cook for a further 4 minutes. Turn the mackerel again and turn the plate around. Cook for 4 minutes.

5. Leave to stand in the bags for 4 minutes. Remove from bags and serve, garnished with lemon quarters and parsley.

Fish Pie

Serves 4
1 pound smoked haddock fillets
3 tablespoons water
salt
4 cups peeled and cubed
    potatoes
about 4 tablespoons milk
1 tablespoon butter
freshly ground black pepper
Sauce:
1¼ cups milk
2 tablespoons butter
¼ cup all-purpose flour
salt
freshly ground black pepper
1 hard-cooked egg, finely
    chopped
parsley sprigs, to garnish

Preparation time: about 10 minutes
Cooking time: about 23½ minutes
Microwave setting: Full power (High)

1. Place the fish in a large bowl. Cover and cook for 6 minutes, rearranging halfway through cooking. Set aside, covered.

2. Place the water, salt and potatoes in a large bowl. Cover and cook for 10 minutes. Set aside, covered.

3. Drain the liquid from the fish and add the milk for the sauce.

4. To make the sauce, place the butter in a large cup and cook for 30 seconds, Stir in the flour, milk/fish liquid, and salt and pepper to taste. Cook for 3 minutes, stirring every minute.

5. Flake the smoked haddock, removing any skin and remaining bones. Fold into the sauce with the chopped egg.

6. Mash the potatoes with the remaining milk and butter, and add pepper to taste.

7. Pour the fish mixture into a 5-cup casserole dish. Pipe the potatoes over the fish. Cook, uncovered, for 4 minutes. Garnish with sprigs of parsley, and serve with peas.

Cook's Tip

If using frozen haddock fillets, cook for a further 3 minutes in step 1 to ensure that the fish has time to defrost, then cook through.

If smoked haddock is not easily available, substitute any other smoked fish.

Fish Risotto

Serves 4
¼ cup butter
1 large onion, peeled and finely
    chopped
½ green bell pepper, cored,
    seeded and finely diced
½ red bell pepper, cored, seeded
    and finely diced
2 tablespoons tomato paste
1 garlic clove, peeled and
    crushed
1 teaspoon Italian seasoning
⅔ cup finely chopped mushrooms
1¾ cups long-grain rice
3 cups hot chicken stock
salt
¼ teaspoon oil
1½ pounds cod fillets, rinsed in
    cold water
freshly ground black peper

Preparation time: about 15 minutes
Cooking time: about 30 minutes, plus standing
Microwave setting: Full power (High)

1. Place the butter, onion, green and red bell peppers, tomato paste, garlic, herbs and mushrooms in a large bowl. Cover and cook for 10 minutes, stirring halfway through the cooking process.

2. Stir in the rice, hot chicken stock, salt and oil. Cover and cook for 13 minutes. Stir halfway through cooking. Set aside, covered.

3. Place the fish fillets in a shallow microwave-safe dish. Cover and cook for 7 minutes, rearranging halfway through cooking. Leave to stand for 4 minutes, covered.

4. Flake the fish, removing any skin. Stir the fish into the rice mixture and season to taste with pepper.

Fish pie; Fish risotto

Tuna Mousse

Serves 4–6
2 tablespoons butter
¼ cup all-purpose flour
1¼ cups cold chicken stock
¼ teaspoon ground mace
2 envelopes unflavored gelatine
4 tablespoons dry sherry
1¼ cups mayonnaise
2 teaspoons anchovy extract
1 14-ounce can tuna fish,
    drained and flaked
salt
freshly ground black pepper
⅔ cup heavy or whipping cream,
    whipped
To garnish:
slices of lemon
parsley sprigs

Preparation time: 10 minutes,
plus setting
Cooking time: 5 minutes
Microwave setting: Full power
(High)

1. Place the butter in a 2½-cup measuring cup and cook for 1 minute or until melted.

2. Blend in the flour, stock and mace. Cook for a further 3½ minutes, stirring every minute, and set aside.

3. Place the gelatine in a small bowl and stir in the sherry. Cook for 30 seconds, or until dissolved. Stir again, the liquid should be clear.

4. Beat the sherry-gelatine liquid into the sauce. Set aside to cool slightly.

5. Stir the mayonnaise, anchovy extract, tuna fish, salt and pepper into the sauce. Fold in the cream.

6. Gently pour the mixture into a 5-cup prepared soufflé dish. Place in the refrigerator and chill for at least 4 hours or until set.

7. Unmold and garnish with lemon and parsley.

Haddock Mousse

Serves 4
1 pound haddock fillets, cut into
    pieces
1 ounce aspic powder
1¼ cups hot water
1 teaspoon dried parsley flakes
salt
freshly ground black pepper
3 tablespoons heavy cream
2 egg whites
To garnish:
cucumber slices
watercress sprigs

Preparation time: about 10
minutes, plus chilling
Cooking time: 6½–7½ minutes
Microwave setting: Full power
(High)

1. Place the fillets in a medium bowl, cover and cook for 6–7 minutes. Rearrange halfway through. Set aside, covered.

2. Stir the aspic into the hot water. Cook, uncovered, for 30 seconds. Stir well to dissolve.

3. Drain, skin and flake the fish. Stir in the aspic, parsley, salt and pepper to taste. Set aside until cold. Stir in the cream.

4. Beat the egg whites until stiff. Gently fold into the fish mixture. Spoon into a 3-cup ring mold. Chill until set. Serve with a garnish of cucumber and watercress.

Tuna mousse; Haddock mousse

MENU PLANNER

The illustration shows a typical menu which can be cooked in advance in the microwave – ideal for entertaining.

Cook the Vichyssoise the day before, then cool and chill. Cook the salmon early on the day, leaving it to cool and allowing time for garnishing. The syrup and some of the fruit for the dessert can be prepared early on the day of serving but prepare fruits that discolor just an hour ahead. The potato salad can be prepared a few hours in advance, allowing time for the flavors to mingle. Alternatively, have new potatoes ready to cook when you serve the first course so that they can be served hot with the salmon.

Poached Salmon

Serves 6–8
1 3-pound salmon, gutted
cucumber slices, to garnish
mayonnaise to serve

Preparation time: about 3 minutes, plus cooling
Cooking time: about 12 minutes, plus standing
Microwave setting: Full power (High)

1. Cover a large plate with plastic wrap and place the salmon on the plate. Cover and cook for 12 minutes, rearranging halfway through cooking. Leave to stand, covered, for 5 minutes. Remove cover and leave to cool.

2. Pipe mayonnaise along length of salmon and garnish with cucumber slices. Serve with mixed green salad and potato salad.

Poached Salmon;
Fruit salad; Vichyssoise;
Mixed green salad and potato salad

POULTRY AND GAME

Tender chicken, turkey and duck cook with great success in the microwave, yielding moist results in minutes. The wide variety of recipes which follow highlight the versatile nature of poultry and its compatibility with microwave cooking. This chapter also contains a selection of delicious game recipes.

Poultry and many types of game are tender, with little tough connective tissue and require fairly quick cooking, making them ideally suited to microwave cooking. Supermarkets offer a wide variety of different poultry products, from quarter of chicken to boneless cuts and breasts, all of which can be cooked in the microwave. The cooking times vary according to the type of portion as well as for different poultry and game.

Regardless of the particular product, there are some general guidelines which can be applied to the microwave method of cooking poultry and game.

Cookware

There is no need to acquire any special utensils or containers for cooking poultry. Sauced dishes can be cooked in microwave-safe casseroles, pieces can be cooked in shallow containers and large plates can be useful for single portions. However, there are special microwave roasting racks which allow the poultry to be raised above the cooking juices and avoid the need for frequent draining off of excess fat. This type of specialist cookware is useful but it certainly is not essential. As an alternative to a rack, whole birds can be positioned on an upturned saucer in a dish, allowing the fat to drain away.

Covering

In most cases poultry and game should be covered during cooking. Casseroles with lids

are ideal, microwave-safe plastic wrap can be used or dinner plates can be useful for covering dishes which do not have lids. Roasting bags with special microwave ties are ideal for cooking whole poultry and game. They retain all the moisture and flavor and can be placed in a quiche dish or other shallow dish in case of any leakage of juices. Roasting racks can be completely enclosed within large bags.

Shielding

Any protruding parts of a whole bird or of pieces can be protected from overcooking by covering with small pieces of smooth foil. The wing tips or the highest point of the breast may benefit from being covered with small pieces of foil.

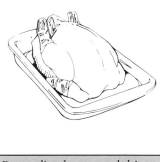

Protruding bones and thin areas can be protected by covering with small pieces of foil.

Seasoning

Poultry and game should not be sprinkled with salt before cooking as this will result in dried patches. Pepper, herbs, spices and other flavoring

ingredients can be added to the poultry, and stuffings can be seasoned with salt. Casseroles and sauces can be seasoned before cooking.

Cooking whole birds

Whole, unboned birds are very irregular in shape, with wing tips that protrude. Whole birds should be covered during cooking to keep them moist, and they should be turned over to ensure that the meat on the underside is cooked through.

The delicate meat on the breast of the bird cooks particularly quickly so it should be placed downward for at least half the cooking time. It is a good idea to start cooking the bird with the breast uppermost, then turn it so that the breast is down and turn it over again for a short period at the end of the cooking time.

Covering the breast with bacon slices helps to protect against overcooking as well as providing flavor and makes the bird more succulent.

Cooking pieces

Poultry pieces can be just as uneven in shape and size as whole birds, and the ins and outs of arranging these cuts for successful cooking are discussed overleaf. In the same way that turning is necessary when cooking a whole bird, the pieces should be covered and turned at least once during cooking. Pieces do not have as thick an area for the microwaves to penetrate, so they take proportionally less cooking time

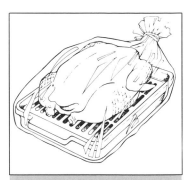

Whole poultry can be cooked on a microwave roasting rack, allowing cooking juices to drain away. Here the bird and rack are completely enclosed in a roasting bag.

than a whole bird, depending on the number which are cooked and on the shape and size of the cooking container.

Trussing and boning

Whole birds should be trussed as neatly as possible, with the wing ends tied as close as possible to the body and the legs tied together tightly.

Boned whole poultry cooks particularly well in the microwave. The preparation of the stuffing is important to ensure even cooking. If bacon, ham, sausage meat or other raw ingredients which require lengthy cooking are included, they should be cooked before being combined with the other stuffing ingredients. This way there is no danger of any dense stuffing being undercooked.

The stuffed bird should be molded into as even a shape as possible for cooking and it should be turned halfway through the time.

A comparison of pieces on the bone and boneless cuts is given on page 62.

Cooking preformed pieces

The evenly shaped, preformed pieces of chicken or turkey can be defrosted and cooked in the microwave but they are very dense and have a greater depth of meat to cook. These do need a short resting time during cooking as well as at the end of the cooking time.

Browning

There are a number of seasonings and browning agents which are sold specifically for use on poultry which is to be cooked in the microwave. Other means of giving whole birds and pieces extra color include brushing with dark sauces, or sprinkling with paprika. However, there is one very successful, and highly preferable, method of browning poultry and game which has been cooked in the microwave, and that is by placing it briefly under a hot conventional broiler.

When the poultry is casseroled with vegetables and

sauce there is not as great a need to brown the outside, because the cooked bird will be coated in sauce. Since the skin does not crisp it is a good idea to remove it before adding pieces to a casserole.

Whole birds can be quickly browned under a hot broiler when they are cooked. Any suggested standing time can be accounted for as the bird browns and the result is an excellent "roast."

For fatty poultry, like duck, this browning is essential for a palatable result – either brown and crisp both sides of the cooked duck under a hot broiler or put the bird in a very hot oven for about 10–15 minutes before it is served. Before the poultry is browned under the broiler it should be basted with cooking juices and sprinkled with a little salt.

Alternatively, pieces or whole birds can be browned before microwaving by cooking them very briefly in hot fat on the conventional stove.

Browning dishes which are manufactured for use in the microwave can also be used to brown poultry and game before cooking. Follow the manufacturer's directions for preheating the browning dish before using.

Broiling to brown

1. The microwave-cooked bird is pale and the skin is not crisp.

2. The skin is basted and seasoned, then the bird is browned for a few minutes under a hot broiler to give the best results.

Testing the cooked bird

Before serving, all poultry should be checked to make sure that it is properly cooked by piercing the meat at the thickest part. This should be done when the bird has been allowed to stand for the recommended standing time. A large bird which is covered by a good

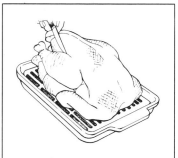

To check that the bird is cooked through, the thick flesh behind the thigh joint is pierced: When the bird is cooked there will not be any trace of blood in the juices.

depth of meat requires longer standing than small birds or pieces. For small portions, the standing time is often accounted for by the time the food is transferred to serving dishes.

Pierce the meat on whole birds at the thickest part, which is just behind the thigh. When cooked, the juices will run clear. If there is any sign of pink meat or blood in the juices, then the bird is not well cooked and, in the case of chicken and turkey, it must be returned to the microwave and cooked for extra time.

Game

When selecting game for microwave cooking, remember that it is only the tender birds that can be cooked successfully by this method.

Young hen pheasants can be cooked in the microwave but older birds, or cocks, which tend to be tougher, are best casseroled or braised by

traditional methods. As a general guide, for microwave cooking use the birds which are suitable for roasting by conventional methods.

Small game birds can be treated in much the same way as chicken quarters and they need to be turned over and around once or twice during cooking for best results.

Boning a chicken

This method can be used for other game and poultry – pheasant, duck or turkey are boned in the same way.

For success, do not try to rush this task – allow plenty of time and you will not have problems. Chicken is easier to bone than pheasant or duck as the bones are larger and the process is less fiddly.

You will need a sharp, pointed knife and a pair of kitchen scissors are useful. Place the bird breast side down on a clean surface with the head end away from you. Cut down the back, from head to tail, then start by working the meat off one side of the carcass.

Cut between the meat and the bones, working as closely as possible to the bones and scraping off all the meat.

Snip the meat and tendons from the wing and leg joints, then scrape the meat off the bones. Chop off the ends of the joints and peel back the meat and skin (in the same way as you would turn the sleeves of a sweater inside out).

When you have boned one side, turn the bird around and work all the meat off the other side. You will be left with the carcass and the meat attached to it along the breastbone. It is important to avoid cutting the skin at all, so turn the bird on its side and carefully cut the meat off the breastbone, taking the slightest sliver of soft bone off with the meat.

COOKING TECHNIQUES FOR POULTRY

One of the key factors which influences the result when cooking poultry and game in the microwave is the shape of the piece of food. Apply the comparison of different portions and the suggestions for arranging them to chicken, duck, turkey, rabbit and pheasant as appropriate. Note the cooking stages for a casserole and use them for all similar recipes. Remember that only tender game microwaves well.

Quarters

Quarter pieces of poultry are usually quite irregular in shape, with protruding leg or wing bones and areas of meat of different thickness.

The rule to apply is that thinner parts should be positioned toward the middle of the cooking container.

The pieces should be turned halfway through cooking, and possibly rearranged in the container, depending on the number which are being cooked. It is a good idea to start cooking the pieces with the skin side down, then turn them over so that the bone side is on top for the second part of the time.

Before cooking you may prefer to brown the pieces or remove the skin.

The pieces should be covered during cooking and the result is more even if the quarters are cooked in a sauce. The ends of the pieces can be shielded with smooth foil, although this should not be necessary as the cooking time is short.

Drumsticks

The thin and thick ends of drumsticks will cook at quite different rates. For small drumsticks off a chicken this does not create a problem, since the main area of meat is at the thick end. Placing the thin bone ends to the middle of the cooking container is usually enough to prevent overcooking.

Turkey drumsticks do have meat at the thinner end and this is likely to overcook if it is not shielded by a small piece of foil.

If the drumsticks are cooked with vegetables or other ingredients, then simply cover the thin end of the meat with food to help prevent overcooking.

Drumsticks are best skinned before cooking and they can be coated in a variety of tasty sauces and herbs to avoid the necessity for browning them separately.

Thighs

Small neat thigh pieces, on the bone, are excellent portions for cooking in the microwave. They have a regular shape and cook evenly. They can be cooked with herbs and butter or they can be prepared in a sauce or casserole.

Fold any meat and skin ends neatly underneath and keep them in shape with wooden toothpicks, if necessary.

Arrange the pieces around the outside of the dish if they are cooked on their own and turn them over halfway through cooking.

Boneless breasts

Both fully boned and part-boned breasts cook well in the microwave. The skin may be removed or browned before cooking and the meat can be cooked on its own or with other ingredients in a sauced dish.

The breasts should be arranged as far apart as possible during cooking and turned halfway through the time. It is best to start cooking with the skin side down.

This meat can be cut into chunks for casseroles, or into strips to make oriental-style recipes. The boneless meat can be flattened, then stuffed and rolled. Boneless breast meat can also be sprinkled with chopped herbs and rolled before cooking.

Casseroles

Poultry and game casseroles cook very well in the microwave. the liquid content of these dishes helps to prevent thin areas of meat from overcooking. Tougher cuts of game are not suitable for microwave cooking and they are best casseroled slowly by conventional methods.

When preparing casseroles there are a few basic guidelines to follow. Because the microwave cooks the poultry or game very quickly, it is essential that any strongly flavored ingredients, or vegetables that will require fairly lengthy cooking, are cooked for a short time before the liquid and main ingredient is added. Onions, garlic and peppers should be cooked first in a little vegetable oil, butter or water. If carrots are added, then they too should be par-cooked before the main ingredients are added, depending on the type of dish. Not only does this method ensure that all the ingredients are evenly cooked but it also avoids any likelihood of the finished dish being dominated by the flavor of raw onion.

The choice of casserole dish also plays a part in determining the result. Ideally, there should be plenty of room in the dish to spread the food out slightly and to allow for easy turning and rearranging of the ingredients halfway through the cooking time. During cooking the dish should be covered.

The liquid which is added should be hot or boiling. The greater the quantity of liquid,

Different-shaped portions

Drumsticks and quarters are uneven in shape and thickness.

Thighs and boned breast halves are neatly shaped and they cook particularly well in the microwave.

then the more important it is to follow this rule. Small quantities, for example a can of tomatoes, will heat quickly in the casserole, but significant amounts of stock, water or wine should be heated before they are added to the casserole. Bouillon cubes should be diluted with boiling water from the kettle, home-made stock can be heated in the microwave first, similarly wine.

Although the pieces of poultry or game should not be individually sprinkled with salt, the sauce in which they are cooked can be seasoned to taste. If the quantity of sauce is very small, then it should be lightly seasoned first, then tasted and the seasoning adjusted at the end of the cooking time.

Duck

Before cooking prick the skin of the duck all over to allow the fat to drain away. During cooking, drain away the fat once or twice. Season the bird after cooking and brown it under a hot broiler or in a very hot oven.

The result is a bird which is tender, moist and well flavored. Unlike duck cooked by conventional methods, microwaved duck is succulent and excellent when browned.

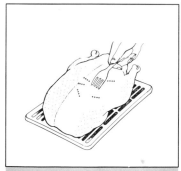

Prick the duck all over before cooking to allow the fat to drain away.

Stages for casseroles

1. Strongly flavored ingredients or those that require fairly lengthy cooking are par-cooked before the poultry and liquid are added. Here chopped onion, diced carrot and crushed garlic are first par-cooked in a little oil.

2. The pieces are arranged in the dish with the thinner parts toward the middle.

3. The remaining ingredients which will cook in the same time required for the poultry or game are added, then hot liquid is poured in. Sliced mushrooms, quartered peeled and seeded tomatoes and a bay leaf are added above. Boiling stock moistens the dish.

Preparing thigh pieces and boneless breast halves for cooking

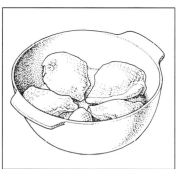

1. Neatly shaped thigh pieces are arranged around the outside of a casserole dish so they will all cook evenly.

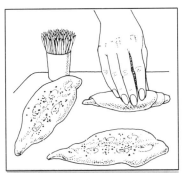

2. Boneless turkey breast halves are rolled into neat shapes so they will cook evenly.

3. The rolls are secured with wooden toothpicks and they are arranged around the outside of the cooking dish, here a quiche dish is used. The dish is covered with an up-turned plate or microwave-safe plastic wrap before cooking.

GUIDE TO COOKING POULTRY AND GAME

Poultry/Game	Cooking time in minutes on Full power (High) per 1 pound	Cooking time in minutes on Medium per 1 pound	Method
Chicken, whole	6–8	9–10	Shield the tips of the wings and legs with smooth foil. Place in a roasting bag in a dish with 2–3 tablespoons stock. Turn the chicken over halfway through cooking.
pieces 1 2 3 4 5 6	2–4 4–6 5–7 6½–10 7½–12 8–14		Place the meatiest part of the chicken piece to the outside of the dish. Cover and turn the pieces over halfway through the cooking time.
Duck, whole	7–8	9–11	Shield the tips of the wings, tail end and legs with smooth foil. Prick the skin thoroughly to release the fat. Place on a roasting rack or upturned saucer and turn over halfway through the cooking time.
Guinea hen, partridge, pheasant, quail and squab	6–8	9–11	Shield the tips of the wings and legs with smooth foil. Smear the breast with a little butter and place in a roasting bag in a dish. Turn over halfway through the cooking time.
Turkey	9–11	11–13	Shield the tips of the wings and legs with smooth foil. Place in a roasting bag in a dish with 2–3 tablespoons stock. Turn over at least twice during the cooking time.

STUFFINGS AND ACCOMPANIMENTS

Stuffings for roast poultry

Sage and onion Finely chop 1 large onion and place in a bowl with a knob of butter. Cook on Full power (High) for 3 minutes. Mix with 4 cups fresh bread crumbs, 1 tablespoon finely chopped fresh sage or rubbed sage, plenty of seasoning and enough milk to bind the ingredients.

Parsley and Thyme Make the stuffing as above, substituting 4 tablespoons chopped fresh parsley and 1 tablespoon chopped fresh or dried thyme for the sage.

Fresh Herb and Walnut Prepare the stuffing as for sage and onion, using 3 cups fresh bread crumbs and 2 tablespoons chopped fresh herbs, such as parsley, basil and tarragon. Add 1 cup finely chopped walnuts before mixing in the milk.

Serving suggestions

Plain cooked chicken, duck or turkey can be served with a variety of simple accompaniments to make deliciously quick meals. If the poultry is skinned before cooking, then the following complementary ingredients can be poured or sprinkled straight over them and served. If the skin is left on, then you may like to brown the skin briefly under a hot broiler before adding the accompaniments.

Herb butter Cream chopped fresh herbs into butter with a little seasoning. Try chopped parsley, dill, tarragon, basil or a mixture of herbs. Shape the butter into a roll on a piece of plastic wrap, wrap it tightly and chill until firm, then cut the roll into slices. Top each poultry piece with a slice of butter just before it is served. Add a lemon wedge for garnish, and so that the juice can be squeezed over to give extra flavor.

Walnut cream Mix finely chopped walnuts into soft cream cheese or sour cream. Add snipped chives and seasoning to taste. Top each piece with a spoonful of the mixture just before serving and garnish with sprigs of parsley.

Spicy peanut sauce Mix a little crunchy peanut butter to a cream with soft cream cheese or sour cream. Season with garlic salt and add a few drops of sesame oil. Serve with chicken or duck, offering thinly sliced onion rings, cucumber slices and shredded lettuce as garnish and decorating with lemon wedges.

Buttered almonds Brown slivered almonds in butter following the instructions on page 14. Pour over the pieces just before serving.

Peach garnish Garnish each portion with thin slices of fresh peeled peach. Sprinkle the fruit with a little lime juice to prevent discoloration.

DEFROSTING POULTRY AND GAME

One of the great advantages of owning a microwave is the facility for rapidly defrosting food. It is important to ensure that poultry is thoroughly defrosted before it is cooked. Check the manufacturer's directions which came with your oven for suggested timings and follow these guidelines to ensure success. When the birds are removed from the microwave, they should still be very slightly icy before standing.

Defrosting whole birds

Leave the bird in its bag and remove any metal clips or ties. Cook for half the recommended time, then unwrap the bird and place it in a dish. If any protruding areas are warm or look as if they are beginning to cook, then cover them with small pieces of smooth foil. Cook for the remaining time and observe the standing time. Place the bird under cold running water to remove any giblets from the inside. When the bird is defrosted it should be soft but still very slightly icy in the cavity. If you are filling the body cavity with a stuffing, then scald it first with plenty of boiling water and cut away any lumps of fat.

Large birds, like turkey, will need frequent turning during defrosting to ensure that each part defrosts evenly.

Defrosting pieces

If the pieces are in a block, then wrap them in a paper towel or place in a covered dish. Arrange individual pieces with meatier parts toward the outside of the dish. Cook for half the recommended defrosting time, uncover and turn the block or individual pieces. Cook for the remaining time, then separate the pieces from the block. Leave to stand as recommended or cook for a further 1–2 minutes if necessary. When defrosted the meat should be soft, moist and very cold. Small game birds should be treated as for chicken quarters.

GUIDE TO DEFROSTING POULTRY AND GAME

Poultry/Game		Cooking time in minutes on Defrost per 1 pound	Method
Chicken	whole	6	Shield the wing tips with smooth foil. Give the dish a quarter turn every $1\frac{1}{2}$ minutes. Remove the giblets at the end of the defrosting time.
	pieces	5	Place the meatiest part of the chicken pieces to the outside of the dish. Turn over halfway through the defrosting time.
Duck		4–6	Shield the wings, tail end and legs with smooth foil. Give the dish a quarter turn every $1\frac{1}{2}$ minutes. Remove the giblets at the end of the defrosting time.
Guinea hen, partridge, pheasant, quail and squab		5–6	Shield the tips of the wings and legs with smooth foil. Turn over halfway through the defrosting time and give the dish a quarter turn every $1\frac{1}{2}$ minutes.
Turkey		10–12	Shield the tips of the wings and legs with smooth foil. Turn over twice during the defrosting time and give the dish a quarter turn every 6 minutes. Shield any warm spots with smooth foil during defrosting. Remove the giblets at the end of the defrosting time.

Note To defrost poultry and game on Full power (High), cook for 1 minute per 1 pound, allow to stand for 10 minutes, then continue cooking in bursts of 1 minute per 1 pound until the poultry or game is defrosted.

Deviled Chicken Drumsticks

Serves 4
8 chicken drumsticks, total
    weight 1½ pounds
1 teaspoon curry powder
1 tablespoon soy sauce
8 tablespoons tomato paste
3 tablespoons soft dark brown
    sugar
2 tablespoons butter, cut into
    pieces
scallion tassels, to garnish

Preparation time: about 5
minutes
Cooking time: about 12½
minutes
Microwave setting: Full power
(High)

1. Place the drumsticks in the
bottom of a shallow oblong
casserole dish. Cook,
uncovered, for 4½ minutes. Set
aside.

2. Place the curry powder, soy
sauce, tomato paste, sugar and
butter in a cup. Cook,
uncovered, for 1½ minutes.

3. Rearrange the drumsticks and
brush with the sauce. Cook,
uncovered, for 4½ minutes.

4. Brush the remaining sauce
over the drumsticks and cook
for 2 minutes. Garnish with the
scallion tassels.

5. Serve with boiled rice and a
green salad or with a bean
sprout salad.

Turkey Breasts Cordon Bleu

Serves 4
4 turkey breast halves, total
    weight 1½ pounds
freshly ground black pepper
¼ cup butter, diced
4 slices cooked ham
4 slices Gruyère cheese
parsley sprigs, to garnish

Preparation time: about 3
minutes
Cooking time: about 7½–9
minutes, plus broiling
Microwave setting: Full power
(High)

1. Place the turkey breast halves
in a shallow casserole dish.
Sprinkle with pepper and dot
with the butter. Cover and cook
for 6 minutes, turning over and
rearranging the meat halfway
through cooking.

2. Transfer to a serving plate.
Place a slice of ham and then a
slice of cheese on top of each
breast. Cook, uncovered, for 3
minutes until the cheese has
melted. Brown under a
preheated conventional broiler,
if preferred.

3. Garnish with the parsley
sprigs. Serve with sauté potatoes
and broccoli.

Deviled chicken drumsticks; Turkey
breasts cordon bleu

Chicken and Peppers

Serves 4
4 chicken pieces, total weight 2½ pounds
1 carrot, peeled and sliced
1 onion, peeled and sliced
1 small red bell pepper, cored, seeded and sliced
1 small green bell pepper, cored, seeded and sliced
1 garlic clove, peeled and crushed
1 teaspoon rubbed sage
1 teaspoon dried parsley flakes
2 tablespoons tomato paste
2 tablespoons butter, cut up
¼ cup all-purpose flour
about 2 cups very hot chicken stock
salt
freshly ground black pepper

Preparation time: about 20 minutes
Cooking time: about 26½ – 29½ minutes
Microwave setting: Full power (High)

1. Place the chicken pieces in a large bowl. Cover and cook for 9–12 minutes, rearranging halfway through cooking. Set aside, covered.

2. Place the carrot, onion, peppers, garlic, sage, parsley and tomato paste in a large bowl. Cover and cook for 10 minutes, stirring halfway through.

3. Stir in the butter until melted, then stir in the flour. Make up the chicken juices to 2 cups with stock, then stir in with salt and pepper. Cook, uncovered, for 3½ minutes, stirring every minute.

4. Stir in the chicken and, cook, uncovered, for 4 minutes.

Chicken Livers and Grapes

Serves 4
1 cup butter
1 garlic clove, peeled and crushed
2 tablespoons tomato paste
1 tablespoon chopped fresh parsley
⅓ cup finely sliced mushrooms
1½ pounds chicken livers, chopped
2 cups halved and seeded red grapes
salt
freshly ground black pepper
¼ cup cornstarch
½ cup red wine
chopped fresh parsley, to garnish

Preparation time: about 20 minutes
Cooking time: about 16½ minutes
Microwave setting: Full power (High)

1. Place the butter, garlic, tomato paste, parsley and mushrooms in a large bowl. Cover and cook for 3 minutes.

2. Stir in the livers. Cover and cook for 6 minutes. Stir in the grapes, salt and pepper. Cover and cook for 5 minutes.

3. Blend together the cornstarch and wine, then stir into the livers. Cook, uncovered, for 2½ minutes, stirring halfway through cooking.

4. Garnish with the chopped parsley and serve with rice and zucchini.

Coq au Vin

Serves 4–6
1 onion, peeled and finely chopped
4 ounces bacon slices, chopped
1⅓ cups button mushrooms
1 3-pound chicken, cut into 8 pieces
⅔ cup chicken stock
2½ cups red wine
2 garlic cloves, peeled and crushed
2 tablespoons butter, cut into pieces
fresh parsley, thyme and bay leaf tied together
salt
freshly ground black pepper

Preparation time: about 20 minutes
Cooking time: about 50 minutes
Microwave setting: Full power (High) and Defrost

1. Place the onion in a large bowl, cover and cook on Full power for 4 minutes. Stir in the bacon and cook, uncovered, for 1 minute. Stir in the mushrooms and cook for 1 minute.

2. Stir in the chicken pieces and cook on Full power, uncovered, for 8 minutes, stirring halfway through.

3. Stir in the stock, wine, garlic, butter, herbs and salt and pepper to taste. Cook, covered, on Full power for 6 minutes.

4. Cook on Defrost, covered, for 30 minutes, stirring halfway through. Before serving, remove the herbs.

Chicken Marengo

Serves 4
1 onion, peeled and finely chopped
4 chicken pieces, total weight 2 pounds
6 tomatoes, peeled and chopped
2 cups button mushrooms
2 tablespoons tomato paste
1 garlic clove, peeled and crushed
½ teaspoon dried rosemary
½ teaspoon rubbed sage
2 tablespoons butter, cut into pieces
¼ cup all-purpose flour
about ⅔ cup hot chicken stock
⅔ cup Marsala wine
salt
freshly ground black pepper
fresh sage, to garnish

Preparation time: about 15 minutes
Cooking time: about 28 minutes
Microwave setting: Full power (High)

1. Place the onion in a bowl, cover and cook for 2 minutes. Add the chicken, cover and cook for 10 minutes, rearranging halfway through cooking. Set aside, covered.

2. Place the tomatoes, mushrooms, paste, garlic, rosemary and sage in a bowl. Cover and cook for 8 minutes, stirring halfway through.

3. Stir in the butter until melted. Stir in the flour. Make up the chicken juices to ⅔ cup with stock, then stir in with the Marsala wine, and salt and pepper. Cover and cook for 4 minutes, stirring halfway through.

4. Stir in the chicken and onions. Cook, uncovered, for 4 minutes. Garnish with sage.

Clockwise: Chicken Marengo; Coq au vin; Chicken livers and grapes; Chicken and peppers

Sherry Chicken

Serves 4
*4 chicken legs, total weight 2
    pounds*
1 zucchini, sliced
1 onion, peeled and sliced
½ teaspoon dried rosemary
*1 teaspoon chopped fresh
    parsley*
½ teaspoon dried tarragon
*1 garlic clove, peeled and
    crushed*
2 tablespoons butter, diced
¼ cup cornstarch
*about 1¼ cups very hot chicken
    stock*
⅔ cup dry sherry
1 tablespoon tomato paste
½ cup slivered almonds
salt
freshly ground black pepper
2 tablespoons heavy cream

Preparation time: about 10
minutes
Cooking time: about 22–25
minutes
Microwave setting: Full power
(High)

1. Place the chicken legs in an
oblong casserole. Cover and
cook for 9–12 minutes,
rearranging halfway through
cooking. Set aside, covered.

2. Place the zucchini, onion,
rosemary, parsley, tarragon and
garlic in a large bowl. Cover and
cook for 5 minutes.

3. Stir in the butter until melted.
Stir in the cornstarch. Make up
the chicken juices to 1¼ cups
with the stock, then stir in with
the sherry, tomato paste,
almonds, salt and pepper. Cook,
uncovered, for 4 minutes,
stirring every minute. Stir in the
cream.

4. Pour over the chicken. Cook
for 4 minutes.

Turkey with Orange and Almonds

Serves 4
*4 turkey breast halves, total
    weight 1½ pounds*
freshly ground black pepper
grated rind of 1 orange
½ cup slivered almonds, toasted
½ cup butter
½ cup orange juice
1 tablespoon Grand Marnier
*2 tablespoons soft dark brown
    sugar*
*1 orange, peeled and sliced, to
    garnish*

Preparation time: about 10
minutes
Cooking time: about 10
minutes
Microwave setting: Full power
(High)

1. Place the turkey breast halves
in a shallow casserole dish and
sprinkle with pepper. Cover and
cook for 6 minutes. Rearrange
and turn over halfway through
cooking. Set aside, covered.

2. Place the orange rind,
almonds, butter, orange juice,
Grand Marnier and sugar in a
cup. Cook, uncovered, for 2
minutes.

3. Drain the juice off the breasts.
Pour the hot sauce over the
turkey. Cook, uncovered, for 2
minutes. Garnish with orange
slices.

Stuffed Chicken

Serves 4–6

1 celery stalk, finely chopped
1 onion, peeled and finely
  chopped
1 eating apple, peeled, cored
  and chopped
¾ cup dried prunes, soaked in ½
  cup port or orange juice
  overnight, and chopped
1 3-pound roasting chicken
2 tablespoons honey
1 teaspoon Worcestershire
  sauce
1 teaspoon soy sauce
parsley sprigs, to garnish

Preparation time: about 20
minutes, plus soaking
Cooking time: about 27½
minutes, plus standing
Microwave setting: Full power
(High)

1. Place the celery, onion and apple in a medium bowl. Cover. Cook for 3½ minutes. Stir in prunes.

2. Spoon stuffing into the chicken, and secure the opening and the legs with trussing thread.

3. Mix the honey, Worcestershire sauce and soy sauce together. Brush the chicken with the sauce.

4. Place the bird in a roasting bag. Secure with a non-metallic tie and prick the bag. Place the bird breast side down in a shallow dish. Cook for 12 minutes. Turn over and cook for a further 12 minutes.

5. Remove the chicken from the bag and wrap tightly in foil. Leave to stand for 15 minutes. Garnish with parsley sprigs.

Turkey Leg Casserole

Serves 4

4 turkey legs, total weight 2½
  pounds
1 celery stalk, chopped
1 small turnip, peeled and
  diced
1 onion, peeled and chopped
1 carrot, peeled and sliced
1 tablespoon tomato paste
½ teaspoon dried marjoram
½ teaspoon dried thyme
1 teaspoon dried parsley flakes
2 tablespoons butter, cut into
  pieces
¼ cup all-purpose flour
about 2 cups very hot chicken
  stock
salt
freshly ground black pepper
chopped fresh parsley, to
  garnish

Preparation time: about 20
minutes
Cooking time: about 29
minutes
Microwave setting: Full power
(High)

1. Place the turkey legs in a large bowl. Cover and cook for 12 minutes, rearranging halfway through cooking. Set aside, covered.

2. Place the celery, turnip, onion, carrot, tomato paste, marjoram, thyme and parsley in a large bowl. Cover and cook for 10 minutes, stirring halfway through cooking.

3. Stir in the butter until melted. Stir in the flour. Make up turkey juices to 2 cups with stock, then stir in with salt and pepper. Cook, uncovered, for 3 minutes, stirring every minute.

4. Pour the vegetable sauce over the turkey. Cook, uncovered, for 4 minutes. Garnish with parsley.

From left to right: Sherry chicken;
Turkey with orange and almonds;
Stuffed chicken; Turkey leg casserole

Chaud-froid Chicken

Serves 4

1 piece of carrot
1 celery stalk, halved
1 small onion, peeled
8 black peppercorns
1 bay leaf
2½ cups milk
2½ cups cold water
1 ounce aspic powder
¼ cup butter
½ cup all-purpose flour
1 teaspoon unflavored gelatine
2 tablespoons heavy cream
salt
freshly ground white pepper
4 chicken legs, total weight 2¼
*   pounds, cooked and skinned*
4 long, thin strips of green bell
*   pepper skin, cut to resemble*
*   flower stems*
16 pieces of red bell pepper skin,
*   cut into petal shapes*
12 pieces of green bell pepper
*   skin, cut into leaf shapes.*

Preparation time: about 50 minutes, plus chilling
Cooking time: about 11 minutes
Microwave setting: Full power (High)

1. Place the carrot, celery, onion, peppercorns, bay leaf and milk in a bowl. Cook, uncovered, for 4 minutes. Set aside for 15 minutes to infuse.

2. Place half of the cold water in a bowl and cook, uncovered, for 3½ minutes. Stir in the aspic until dissolved, then stir in the remaining cold water. Stand the bowl in a larger bowl of hot water.

3. Place the butter in a bowl and cook, uncovered, for 1 minute or until melted. Blend in the flour, then gradually stir in the strained flavored milk. Cook, uncovered, for 2½ minutes, stirring every minute.

4. Stir the gelatine into ⅔ cup of the aspic until dissolved. Beat this mixture into the sauce with the cream and salt and pepper to taste. Continue beating until smooth and glossy.

5. Pour the remaining aspic into a shallow tray and chill until set.

6. Place the chicken legs on a wire tray over a tray. Using a spoon, carefully coat the chicken legs with the sauce. Continue coating the legs until completely covered.

7. Allow the sauce to set slightly before decorating, then garnish the legs with the bell pepper skin pieces to represent flowers.

8. Using a spoon, slowly and gently coat the legs with 2 or 3 layers of the remaining aspic. Chill until set.

9. Using a knife, cut the aspic into small squares. Serve the chicken surrounded by diced aspic.

From left to right: Chicken in sweet-and-sour sauce; Chaudfroid chicken; Chicken à la king

Chicken in Sweet-and-Sour Sauce

Serves 4
4 chicken legs, total weight 2½
  pounds
1 onion, peeled and chopped
½ green bell pepper, cored,
  seeded and diced
½ red bell pepper, cored, seeded
  and diced
1 teaspoon Italian seasoning
1 garlic clove, peeled and
  crushed
2 tablespoons butter, diced
¼ cup all-purpose flour
about 1¼ cups hot chicken stock
2 tablespoons white-wine
  vinegar
1 tablespoon soy sauce
1 tablespoon orange
  marmalade or jelly
⅔ cup pitted and halved dates
¼ cup brown sugar
freshly ground black pepper

Preparation time: about 15
minutes
Cooking time: about 25–27
minutes
Microwave setting: Full power
(High)

1. Place chicken in bowl, cover
and cook for 13 minutes,
rearranging halfway through. Set
aside, covered.

2. Place the onion, peppers,
herbs and garlic in a bowl, cover
and cook for 4–6 minutes,
stirring halfway through. Stir in
butter, cover, cook for 2
minutes.

3. Stir in the flour. Make the
chicken juices up to 1¼ cups
with stock, then stir in with the
remaining ingredients. Cover.
Cook for 3 minutes, stirring
halfway through.

4. Add the chicken, cover and
cook for 3 minutes.

Chicken à la King

Serves 4
⅔ cup diced green bell pepper
1 cup frozen peas
½ cup butter, cut into small
  pieces
1 cup all-purpose flour
3 cups hot chicken stock
3 cups diced skinned cooked
  chicken meat
salt
freshly ground black pepper
To garnish:
4 slices of white bread, cut into
  triangles and fried
chopped fresh parsley

Preparation time: about 15
minutes
Cooking time: about 14½
minutes
Microwave setting: Full power
(High)

1. Place the green bell pepper in
a medium bowl, cover and cook
for 3 minutes. Stir in the peas,
cover and cook for 3 minutes.

2. Stir in the butter until melted.
Stir in the flour and cook for 30
seconds. Slowly blend in the
stock. Stir in the chicken, and
salt and pepper to taste. Cook,
uncovered, for 8 minutes,
stirring every minute.

3. Serve garnished with bread
triangles and parsley.

Turkey Casserole

Serves 4
4 boneless turkey breast halves
1 carrot, peeled and finely
  sliced
1 celery stalk, finely sliced
1 onion, peeled and finely
  chopped
⅔ cup finely sliced button
  mushrooms
3 tablespoons butter
⅓ cup all-purpose flour
⅔ cup sherry
2 cups hot chicken stock
salt
freshly ground black pepper

Preparation time: about 15
minutes
Cooking time: about 18½
minutes
Microwave setting: Full power
(High)

1. Place the turkey breasts in a
large shallow casserole. Cover
and cook for 2 minutes.

2. Turn the casserole around
and cook for a further 2
minutes. Turn the casserole
around again and cook for 1½
minutes. Set aside.

3. Place the carrot, celery,
chopped onion, sliced
mushrooms and butter in a
medium bowl. Cover and cook
for 6 minutes, stirring halfway
through cooking.

4. Stir in the flour, sherry, hot
stock, salt and pepper. Cover
and cook for 2 minutes, stirring
halfway through.

5. Pour over the turkey. Cover.
Cook for 5 minutes.

Glazed Squab Chickens

Serves 4
6 tablespoons butter
1 tablespoon soft dark brown
  sugar
1 tablespoon Worcestershire
  sauce
4 bacon slices
4 squab chickens, total weight
  3 pounds, trussed
watercress sprigs, to garnish

Preparation time: about 10
minutes
Cooking time: about 23
minutes, plus standing
Microwave setting: Full power
(High)

1. Place 1 tablespoon of the
butter, the sugar and
Worcestershire sauce in a small
bowl. Cook, uncovered, for 1
minute. Set aside.

2. Push a slice of bacon into
each chicken. Place the
chickens, breast side down, in a
shallow casserole. Cook,
uncovered, for 12 minutes. Turn
the chickens over and brush
with the sugar glaze. Cook,
uncovered, for 10 minutes.
Wrap the casserole in foil and
leave to stand, covered, for 10
minutes. Garnish with
watercress.

Chicken in Vermouth

Serves 4

*1 onion, peeled and finely
    chopped*
*$\frac{1}{2}$ green bell pepper, cored,
    seeded and finely chopped*
$1\frac{1}{3}$ cups sliced mushrooms
1 teaspoon dried basil
$\frac{1}{4}$ cup butter
salt
freshly ground black pepper
4 chicken quarters
$\frac{1}{2}$ cup cornstarch
$\frac{2}{3}$ cup dry white vermouth
$1\frac{1}{4}$ cups milk
$1\frac{1}{4}$ cups hot chicken stock
*flat-leaf parsley sprigs, to
    garnish*

*From left to right: Turkey casserole;
Chicken in vermouth; Glazed squab
Chickens*

Preparation time: about 15
minutes
Cooking time: about 26
minutes
Microwave setting: Full power
(High)

1. Place the onion and green
bell pepper in a large bowl.
Cover and cook for 4 minutes.
Stir in the mushrooms, basil,
butter, salt and pepper.

2. Arrange the chicken around
the sides of the bowl, cover and
cook for 8 minutes.

3. Stir the chicken and
vegetables together and turn the
bowl around. Cook for a further
7 minutes. Remove the chicken
from the bowl and set aside.

4. Blend the cornstarch and

vermouth together, then
gradually stir in the milk. Add to
the vegetables. Stir in the hot
stock. Cool slightly.

5. Pour into a blender or food
processor and purée until
smooth. Pour the sauce back
into the bowl, cover and cook
for 2 minutes.

6. Return the chicken to the
bowl, cover and cook for 5
minutes. Garnish with sprigs of
parsley.

Cook's Tip

Crisp potato slices are an
excellent accompaniment for
poultry. Speed up the cooking
time by par-cooking the
potatoes in the microwave
before shallow frying them or
browning them under a hot
broiler. Peel and slice the
potatoes, then place them in a
dish with 2 tablespoons water.
Cover and cook on Full power
(High), allowing about 10
minutes for $1\frac{1}{2}$ pounds of
potatoes and rearranging them
halfway through cooking. Lay
the slices on a cookie sheet,
brush with oil and broil to
brown.

Rabbit in White Wine

Serves 4
1 onion, peeled and finely chopped
1 celery stalk, finely sliced
1 carrot, peeled and finely diced
½ green bell pepper, cored, seeded and finely diced
1 garlic clove, peeled and crushed
½ teaspoon dried rosemary
1 teaspoon chopped fresh parsley
¼ cup butter
4 rabbit pieces
½ cup cornstarch
1¼ cups hot chicken stock
⅔ cup milk
⅔ cup white wine
salt
freshly ground black pepper
rosemary sprigs, to garnish

Preparation time: about 20 minutes
Cooking time: about 19 minutes, plus standing
Microwave setting: Full power (High)

1. Place the onion, celery, carrot, green bell pepper, garlic, rosemary, parsley and butter in a large bowl. Cover and cook for 9 minutes, stirring halfway through cooking.

2. Place the rabbit around the sides of the bowl. Cover and cook for 3 minutes.

3. Stir the rabbit and vegetables together and turn the bowl around. Cook for a further 3 minutes.

4. Remove the rabbit. Stir in the cornstarch, then blend in the hot stock, milk, wine, salt and pepper.

5. Return the rabbit to the bowl, cover and cook for 4 minutes. Leave to stand, covered, for 5 minutes before serving, garnished with rosemary.

Duck with Red Wine Sauce

Serves 4
4 duck pieces
3 tomatoes
1 onion, peeled and finely chopped
¼ cup butter
2 tablespoons tomato paste
2 garlic cloves, peeled and crushed
½ teaspoon dried rosemary
½ teaspoon dried basil
salt
freshly ground black pepper
½ cup cornstarch
⅔ cup dry red wine
2 cups hot chicken stock

Preparation time: about 20 minutes
Cooking time: 32 minutes, plus broiling
Microwave setting: Full power (High)

1. Place the pieces of duck in a large bowl. Cover and cook for 8 minutes. Turn the bowl and cook for a further 7 minutes.

2. Meanwhile, peel the tomatoes by pricking them with a fork and placing in a large bowl. Cover with 2½ cups cold water and cook for 6 minutes. Drain immediately to prevent the tomatoes cooking and peel with a knife. Chop the flesh.

3. Place the duck in a broiler pan and brown under a preheated conventional broiler.

4. Place the onion, butter, tomatoes, tomato paste, garlic, rosemary, basil, salt and pepper in a large bowl. Cover and cook for 8 minutes.

5. Blend the cornstarch and wine together. Stir the cornstarch mixture into the vegetables, then stir in the hot stock. Cool slightly.

6. Pour into a blender or food processor and purée until smooth.

7. Pour into a large bowl and cook for 3 minutes or until thickened and hot, stirring once. Spoon over the duck pieces and serve at once.

Roast Pheasant with Bread Sauce

Serves 2
1 onion, peeled
6 cloves
⅔ cup milk
⅔ cup cold chicken stock
2 cups fresh white bread crumbs
6 tablespoons butter
salt
freshly ground black pepper
1 2-pound pheasant, dressed
3 slices bacon
1 tablespoon all-purpose flour
watercress sprigs, to garnish

Preparation time: about 15 minutes
Cooking time: about 23 minutes, plus standing and broiling
Microwave setting: Full power (High)

1. To make the sauce, stud the onion with the cloves and place in a medium bowl. Add the milk, chicken stock, bread crumbs, 4 tablespoons of the butter, salt and pepper. Cook for 5½ minutes, stirring once.

2. Place the remaining butter inside the cavity of the pheasant and secure the opening with trussing thread. Lay the bacon slices over the breast of the pheasant and secure.

3. Place the pheasant in a roasting bag and secure with a non-metallic tie. Prick the bag and place in a shallow casserole. Cook for 7 minutes. Turn the pheasant over and cook for a further 7 minutes.

4. Remove the pheasant from the bag and discard the bacon. Wrap in foil. Stand for 10 minutes.

5. Place the pheasant in a broiler pan. Sprinkle with flour and brown under a preheated conventional broiler.

6. Meanwhile, remove and discard the onion from the sauce. Cook for 3½ minutes, stirring halfway through.

7. Serve the pheasant garnished with watercress and hand the sauce separately.

Braised Squabs

Serves 4

4 bacon slices, rolled
4 squabs, dressed and trussed, total weight 2½ pounds
2 small onions, peeled and sliced
⅔ cup sliced mushrooms
1 tablespoon tomato paste
¼ teaspoon dried thyme
¼ teaspoon dried parsley flakes
¼ teaspoon dried rosemary
¼ teaspoon dried marjoram
1 garlic clove, peeled and crushed

2 tablespoons butter, diced
¼ cup all-purpose flour
1¼ cups hot chicken stock
1¼ cups red wine
salt
freshly ground black pepper
flat-leaf parsley, to garnish

Preparation time: about 10 minutes
Cooking time: about 29 minutes, plus standing
Microwave setting: Full power (High)

1. Place a bacon slice inside each squab. Place the squabs in a 9-inch round, shallow casserole dish, breast sides down. Cover and cook for 8 minutes. Turn the birds over and cook, uncovered, for 5 minutes. Set aside, covered.

2. Place the onions, mushrooms, tomato paste, herbs and garlic in a medium bowl. Cover and cook for 6 minutes, stirring halfway through cooking.

3. Stir in the butter until melted. Stir in the flour, stock, wine, and salt and pepper to taste. Cook, uncovered, for 4 minutes, stirring every minute.

4. Pour the sauce over the squabs. Cover and cook for 6 minutes. Stand, covered, for 5 minutes before serving garnished with parsley.

Clockwise: Rabbit in white wine; Duck with red wine sauce; Roast pheasant with bread sauce; Braised squabs

Roast duck; Spiced duck

Roast Duck

Serves 6–8
1 6-pound duck, washed
1 orange, cut into 8 pieces

Preparation time: about 5 minutes
Cooking time: about 40 minutes, plus standing and broiling
Microwave setting: Full power (High)

1. Stuff the duck with the orange pieces. Truss with string. Place in a roasting bag and tie the opening with string. Pierce the bag.

2. Place the bird, breast side down, on a trivet in a shallow container. Cook for 20 minutes.

3. Drain off the fat and juices. Remove the bag and return to the cooker with the breast side up. Cook uncovered for 20 minutes.

4. Wrap the bird in foil and stand for 15 minutes.

5. Brown under a preheated conventional broiler, cut in to portions if necessary.

Spiced Duck

Serves 4
1 large onion, peeled and chopped
3 tablespoons soft dark brown sugar
1½ teaspoons salt
2 tablespoons paprika
2 tablespoons tomato paste
2 tablespoons Worcestershire sauce
4 tablespoons white-wine vinegar
4 tablespoons lemon juice
½ teaspoon dried rosemary
½ teaspoon dried chives
¼ teaspoon grated nutmeg
3¾ cups cold water
freshly ground black pepper
1 4½-pound duck, quartered
2 tablespoons butter
¼ cup all-purpose flour
scallion tassels, to garnish

Preparation time: about 5 minutes, plus marinating
Cooking time: about 23½ minutes, plus standing and broiling
Microwave setting: Full power (High)

1. Place the onion, sugar, salt, paprika, tomato paste, Worcestershire sauce, vinegar, lemon juice, rosemary, chives, nutmeg, water, and pepper to taste in a large bowl. Add the duck and marinate overnight.

2. Drain the duck, reserving the marinade. Place in a large bowl, cover and cook for 10 minutes. Halfway through cooking, drain off the juice, then rearrange the duck pieces.

3. Leave the duck to stand, covered, for 10 minutes. Drain off the juices and cook, covered, for a further 8 minutes.

4. Place the duck on a broiler pan and broil under a preheated conventional broiler until the skin is crisp; keep warm.

5. Meanwhile, place the butter in a large bowl and cook, uncovered, for 30 seconds or until melted. Stir in the flour. Measure out 2½ cups of the strained reserved marinade. Blend into the butter and flour mixture. Cook, uncovered, for 5 minutes, stirring every minute.

6. Serve the duck with the sauce, garnished with scallion tassels.

MENU PLANNER

Stuffed Roast Turkey

Christmas is the time of year to make the very most of all your cook's gadgets, and your microwave can be put to full use to cut down on time spent working in the kitchen.

Mix the Plum Pudding (page 173) the day before, then cover it and leave overnight.

Make the Cranberry Sauce (page 164) the day before. Prepare the stuffing the day before but do not put it in the bird until just before cooking.

Before the meal, cook the Bread Sauce (page 165) first. Cook the turkey next, then while it stands halfway through cooking, cook the potatoes. Finish cooking the turkey, then make the gravy. Put the potatoes under a slow broiler to brown, heat the appetizer and have the vegetables ready to cook.

Cook the vegetables while the appetizer is being eaten. Heat the sauces and serve the main course. Cook the pudding while the main course is served. Make any sweet sauces just before serving the pudding.

Serves 6–8
2 tablespoons butter
1 large onion, peeled and finely chopped
1 cup fresh white bread crumbs
1 cup fresh whole-wheat bread crumbs
$\frac{2}{3}$ cup hot chicken stock
$\frac{1}{4}$ teaspoon dried thyme
$\frac{1}{4}$ teaspoon dried rosemary
$\frac{1}{4}$ teaspoon dried marjoram
1 teaspoon dried parsley flakes
$\frac{1}{4}$ teaspoon rubbed sage
grated rind of 1 orange
1 orange, peeled and chopped
2 tablespoons golden raisins
salt
freshly ground black pepper
1 7-pound turkey, thawed if frozen, at room temperature
watercress, to garnish
Glaze:
$\frac{1}{4}$ cup butter
2 tablespoons soft dark brown sugar
$\frac{1}{2}$ tablespoon sherry
2 teaspoons soy sauce

Preparation time: about 15 minutes
Cooking time: about 58 minutes, plus standing
Microwave setting: Full power (High)

1. Place the butter and onion in a medium bowl, cover and cook for 4 minutes. Stir in the bread crumbs, stock, thyme, rosemary, marjoram, parsley, sage, orange rind, orange, golden raisins, and salt and pepper to taste. Stuff the turkey.

2. Truss the turkey. Mask the wings and legs with pieces of smooth foil. Place the turkey, breast side down, on an inverted plate or trivet in a shallow dish. Cover with a paper towel. Cook for $26\frac{1}{4}$ minutes. Set aside.

3. Place the butter, sugar, sherry and soy sauce in a small bowl. Cook for $1\frac{1}{2}$ minutes.

4. Remove the foil pieces from the turkey, turn over and brush with the glaze. Cook for $26\frac{1}{4}$ minutes.

5. Wrap in foil and stand for 30 minutes.

6. Garnish with watercress and serve with sauces, gravy and vegetables.

Cook's Tip

If using a different size of turkey, allow $7\frac{1}{2}$ minutes for each 1 pound for turkeys under 10 pounds in weight.

Honeyed grapefruit and orange; Plum pudding; Bread sauce; Peas; Roast Turkey; Potatoes; Cranberry sauce

MEAT

Microwave cooking times for meat are a fraction of those needed for conventional methods but for true success select the tender cuts to prepare by this method. Remember, you can always use the microwave to partially cook large pieces before they are roasted in the conventional oven.

The rule for cooking meat in the microwave is to select the tender cuts which require shorter traditional cooking. Chops, roasts, tender steaks and ground meat recipes all cook well. Microwave cooking is a moist method, however, so the result will be the same as if the meat were steamed. The meat will not be browned at the end of the cooking but this can be remedied by placing pieces under a broiler or by using a browning dish. For sauced dishes the lack of browning is not as important.

To achieve success with traditional roasts, it is a good idea to start the cooking process in the microwave, then to finish the meat in the conventional oven. This way the overall cooking time is greatly reduced and the result is as good as that expected of conventional methods.

The cuts which do not cook as successfully are the tougher ones which require long, moist stewing and braising to tenderize them. These can be cooked on Low power for a longer time and the finished dish will be acceptable but it is not possible to produce meltingly tender casseroles in the microwave. Really it is a question of taste – if you favor slightly chewy casseroles and stews, you will find microwave cooking perfectly acceptable; if you like your meat really tender, then it is best to use traditional methods for stewing and long braising.

Cooking large cuts

Medium power often gives better results for large cuts, allowing time for the meat to cook through evenly. The meat should be covered with plastic wrap or it can be placed in a roasting bag. Plastic ties or elastic bands should be used to close the bag. Do not season meat before cooking – it can be flavored by studding it with herb sprigs or by topping with bay leaves.

Roasts can be cooked in roasting bags which should be loosely closed with elastic bands or special microwave ties that don't contain any metal.

Areas that cook more rapidly than others should be protected with small pieces of smooth foil to prevent them from overcooking.

Using a microwave-safe meat thermometer

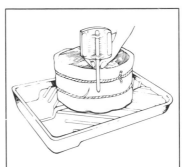

1. Use a special microwave-safe thermometer. Before inserting it into the meat, mark the distance with your middle finger from the outside edge of the meat to the thickest part.

2. Insert the thermometer to the depth marked by your finger, choosing a point at the center of the meat and avoiding contact with bone or fat.

During cooking, the meat should be checked frequently and turned over at least twice, if not more. The larger the cut the more attention it needs.

Observe the suggested standing times as a large piece of meat will continue to cook by means of the residual heat.

Shielding

Shield areas that look as if they are going to overcook by covering them with small pieces of smooth foil.

Using a meat thermometer

Do not use an ordinary meat thermometer. There are special thermometers manufactured for use in the microwave. Insert the thermometer into the thickest part of the meat, pushing it into the center. For an accurate reading, make sure that the thermometer does not touch fat or bone.

Cooking smaller cuts

Small cuts of meat – chops, steaks, burgers or meatballs – can all be cooked in the microwave.

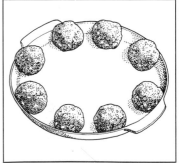

Small portions of meat should be arranged around the edge of a dish for even cooking. Here meatballs are positioned around the edge of a quiche dish.

Turning

Smaller cuts should be turned over and around halfway through the cooking time.

Arranging pieces of meat

As for other foods, small cuts of meat should be arranged around the outside of the dish to promote even cooking. Thin parts should be pointed toward the middle of the dish where they are less likely to overcook. Chops, small steaks, burgers and meatballs should be arranged in this way.

Browning

The meat will not brown in the microwave. A browning dish is useful for chops, burgers or meatballs and the manufacturer's directions should be followed closely. If the pieces are cooked in a sauce, then the fact that they do not brown is less noticeable. If you like crisp, well-browned meat, then you will find traditional cooking methods or combination cooking more acceptable.

Cutting meat

For moist, casserole-style or braised dishes the result is best if the meat is cut across the grain as this method gives the most tender results. Frying

Halfway through cooking the portions of meat should be turned over and around. Here burgers are being cooked in a browning dish.

steak, pork and lamb are all tender and they can be cooked with vegetables and other flavoring ingredients in sauced recipes with great success.

There are two methods of cutting the meat for best results. It can be cut across the grain into small thin slices which can then be cooked in a sauce or they can be flattened and filled with a stuffing. The slices are rolled around the filling and secured with thread or wooden toothpicks. They should be arranged around the edge of a dish for cooking.

Thin strips of meat cook well by this method. The meat should first be cut across the grain into thin slices. The slices are then cut into fine strips. These can be cooked with vegetables, stir-fry style or they can be braised in a sauce.

Defrosting meat

The microwave can be used for defrosting all cuts of meat, whether they are to be cooked by this method or by traditional means. There are a few points which apply to defrosting meat.

When defrosting large pieces it is necessary to turn or rearrange the meat several times during defrosting. About halfway through the defrosting time, check for any areas that are likely to start cooking and shield these with small, smooth pieces of foil. Follow the standing times to ensure that the meat is thoroughly defrosted.

To defrost chunks of meat, place them in a dish and rearrange them once or twice during the recommended time. If the chunks are frozen together in a block, then break them away as soon as they can be loosened and remove any from the microwave if they are likely to start cooking.

Ground meat defrosts particularly speedily. Place a block of ground meat in a dish and defrost for a third of the time, then break up the block

Cutting meat for microwaving

1. The meat is cut across the grain into thin slices to give tender results.

2. The thin slices can be cut into fine strips for cooking with vegetables or moist ingredients.

and continue until completely defrosted. Break up the pieces several times during defrosting.

When defrosting meat still on its styrofoam tray, remove the tray as soon as the meat can be pulled away.

Chops and steaks should be arranged around the edge of a dish for even defrosting. If they are in one block, then defrost them for part of the time until they can be separated and arranged. Turn them once or twice to prevent any areas from cooking and observe the suggested standing times.

Break ground meat down as it defrosts and remove any which is starting to cook.

BEEF

Lean, tender beef steaks cook well in the microwave but the result is not browned as in conventional methods. Frying or braising steak can be cut into thin slices or strips to be cooked successfully. Tender larger cuts cook well and they can be browned under the broiler before serving. Tough stewing cuts do not produce good results, so they are better cooked by conventional methods; ground beef cooks well, with significant savings on time.

Marinating beef

Marinating not only contributes to the flavor of the finished dish but it is also a means of tenderizing the meat before cooking. Thin strips or slices of beef can be marinated for several hours or overnight before cooking. The marinade can be a spicy one, consisting of garlic, grated fresh ginger root, sesame oil and lime or lemon juice. Alternatively, try soaking the meat in a combination of chopped thyme and parsley, a little walnut oil and some dry sherry.

Red-wine marinade

Mix 1 crushed clove of garlic with 2 tablespoons sunflower oil and 1 teaspoon concentrated tomato paste. Add $1\frac{1}{4}$ cups red wine and plenty of freshly ground black pepper. Stir in a bay leaf, 1 teaspoon chopped fresh thyme or $\frac{1}{2}$ teaspoon dried thyme, then add the meat strips or slices. Mix really well, press the meat down into the marinade and cover the dish. Leave for several hours or overnight; ideally, turn the meat several times.

The meat should be drained for the first stages of cooking. The marinade can then be added when the meat is par-cooked to make a delicious sauce.

The marinade can be varied by using different herbs, lightly crushed juniper berries or a blade of mace. The tomato can be omitted and hazelnut or walnut oil can be used instead of the sunflower oil. Both these oils are strongly flavored and they should be used with care.

Cooking ground beef

Ground beef is the most common form of ground meat but the notes given here can also be applied to ground pork, lamb or veal.

Before the meat is cooked, any onions, garlic, peppers or other ingredients which require lengthy cooking, or have strong flavors, should be par-cooked with a little oil, butter or liquid.

The meat is added to the flavoring ingredients and stirred well. The dish should be covered and the meat then cooked for half the recommended time. The meat from the outside of the dish must be stirred into the middle to ensure even cooking. When the meat is partly cooked any other ingredients are added – mushrooms or other quick-cooking vegetables and the liquid.

Unless the quantity is small, the liquid should be heated before mixing into the meat. Bouillon cubes should be dissolved in boiling water. If the dish contains plenty of liquid, then it can be seasoned. If the quantity of liquid is small, only a little of the seasoning should be added at this stage and the balance should be stirred in at the end of the cooking time. Once all the ingredients are added, the dish is covered and the meat sauce is stirred at least once during cooking. It should be left to stand for a few minutes at the end of the cooking time to allow the temperature to equalize, then it should be stirred before serving.

Versatile meat sauce

The basic Bolognese-style meat sauce can be served in many ways or it can form the base for a variety of dishes. In its simplest form it can be ladled over cooked pasta or rice. It can be served in a ring of piped mashed potatoes and sprinkled with a little grated cheese, then browned under the broiler or used to make a lasagne.

Cooking ground beef

1. The onion, bell peppers and garlic are cooked first with a little oil until they are just softened.

2. The meat is added and part cooked, then the meat from the outside of the dish is stirred with that in the middle to ensure even cooking.

3. The remaining ingredients are added; here a Bolognese sauce is prepared. Hot stock is stirred in and, since the mixture is quite moist, the seasoning is added at this stage. The meat sauce is now ready for cooking to completion and it will need stirring once.

GUIDE TO DEFROSTING BEEF

Type of Meat	Defrosting time in minutes on Defrost per 1 pound	
roasts	9	Turn over at least twice during the defrosting time.
steaks (large)	8	
steaks (small)	4	
ground beef	10	Break up during defrosting.

GUIDE TO COOKING BEEF

Type and cut of meat	Cooking time in minutes on Medium power per 1 pound or for quantity given	Cooking time in minutes on Full power (High) per 1 pound or for quantity given	Method
boneless rump roast			Choose a good quality roast with an even covering of fat and a neat shape. Allow to stand for 15–20 minutes, wrapped in foil, before carving.
rare	12	5–6	
medium	14	$6\frac{1}{2}$–$7\frac{1}{2}$	
well done	16	$8\frac{1}{2}$–$9\frac{1}{2}$	
tenderloin			As above.
rare	12	5–6	
medium	14	$6\frac{1}{2}$–$7\frac{1}{2}$	
well done	16	$8\frac{1}{2}$–$9\frac{1}{2}$	
rib roast			Ideally, bone and roll the roast before cooking. Allow to stand for 15–30 minutes, wrapped in foil, before carving.
rare	12–13	$5\frac{1}{2}$–$6\frac{1}{2}$	
medium	14–15	7–8	
well done	16–17	8–10	
ground beef	14–16	10–12	Cover during cooking. Stir once or twice.
sirloin steak			Preheat a browning dish according to the manufacturer's directions. Add the meat and brown. Turn over and cook for the recommended time.
rare		2	
medium	—	3–4	
well done		4	
filet mignon			As above.
rare		2	
medium	—	2–3	
well done		3	
braising steak, such as round steak	16–17	10	Ideally, cook on Medium. If using Full power (High), leave to stand for 10 minutes halfway through cooking time.
hamburgers			Preheat a browning dish. Add the hamburgers and cook for the recommended time, turning the 4-ounce burgers over halfway through the cooking time, and turning the 8-ounce burgers over twice during the cooking time.
1 × 4 ounces		2–3	
2 × 4 ounces		3–4	
4 × 4 ounces		5–6	
1 × $\frac{1}{2}$ pound		$2\frac{1}{2}$–$3\frac{1}{2}$	
2 × $\frac{1}{2}$ pound		6–7	

Beef Tournedos with Pâté

Serves 4

1 onion, peeled and chopped
⅔ cup peeled and sliced button mushrooms
1 garlic clove, peeled and crushed
½ teaspoon dried tarragon
¼ teaspoon dried oregano
1 teaspoon dried rosemary
2 tablespoons butter, cut into pieces
¼ cup all-purpose flour
3 tablespoons tomato paste
1¼ cups hot beef stock
salt
freshly ground black pepper
4 filet mignon steaks, 1 inch thick, 3–4 inches wide, total weight 1¼ pounds
4 slices fried bread, ¼ inch thick
½ pound chicken liver pâté

Preparation time: about 20 minutes
Cooking time: about 12–14 minutes
Microwave setting: Full power (High)

1. Place the onion, mushrooms, garlic, tarragon, oregano and rosemary in a large bowl. Cover and cook for 3 minutes.

2. Stir in the butter until melted. Stir in the flour. Blend in the tomato paste, stock, and salt and pepper to taste. Cook, uncovered, for 3 minutes, stirring every minute. Set aside, covered.

3. Place the steaks in a shallow 2½-quart casserole dish. Cook, uncovered, for 3–5 minutes, depending on how rare you like your steak, and turning over and rearranging halfway through cooking. Pour the steak juices into the sauce.

4. Cut the fried bread to fit the steaks. Spread each piece of bread with pâté. Place steaks on the top. Cook, uncovered, for 3 minutes.

5. Pour the sauce over and serve, with a mixed green salad.

Cook's Tip

This recipe shows how to make the best of microwave-cooked food by adding ingredients or side dishes which offer a contrast in texture. The filet mignon steaks are cooked in the microwave, then heated on circles of crunchy fried bread which are cooked conventionally. Pour the sauce over the steaks just before they are served to keep the bread as crisp as possible.

As well as the button mushrooms in the sauce you may like to add chanterelles or other wild mushrooms. Add ⅔–1 cup to the sauce 1 minute before the end of its cooking time. The sauce and mushrooms may need to be heated for 1 minute before serving.

Beef tournedos with pâté

Garlic Roast Beef

Serves 4
3 pounds boneless rump roast
vegetable oil, to coat
3 garlic cloves, peeled
salt
freshly ground black pepper

Preparation time: about 10 minutes
Cooking time: about 20 minutes, plus standing and broiling
Microwave setting: Full power (High)

1. Rub the beef with the oil, 1 of the garlic cloves, and salt and pepper.

2. Stand the beef on an upturned saucer in a shallow container and cook for 10 minutes.

3. With a sharp knife, cut the remaining garlic cloves into slivers. Make incisions in the meat and insert the slivers of garlic .

4. Cook for 10 minutes.

5. Remove the meat and wrap tightly in foil, with the shiny side inside. Leave the meat to stand for 20 minutes. Brown under a preheated conventional broiler, then carve.

Beef Rolls

Serves 4
⅔ cup mushrooms
1 onion, peeled and quartered
1 tablespoon orange juice
3 tablespoons beef stock
grated rind of 1 lemon
½ teaspoon Italian seasoning
salt
freshly ground black pepper
½ cup fresh white bread crumbs
1 pound boneless rump roast,
*   cut into 4 thin slices and*
*   lightly beaten*
½ green bell pepper, cored,
*   seeded and chopped*
1⅓ cups chopped mushrooms
3 tablespoons butter, diced
2 tablespoons all-purpose flour
⅔ cup white wine
1 teaspoon soy sauce
chopped parsley, to garnish

Preparation time: about 20 minutes
Cooking time: about 13 minutes
Microwave setting: Full power (High)

1. Purée the whole mushrooms, onion, orange juice, stock, lemon rind, herbs and salt and pepper. Stir in the crumbs.

2. Divide the mixture between the slices of beef and roll up. Cook, uncovered, for 6 minutes, turning over halfway through.

3. Place the green bell pepper and chopped mushrooms in a large bowl. Cover and cook for 4 minutes. Stir in the butter until melted. Stir in the flour, wine, soy sauce and meat juices. Season. Pour over the beef. Cook for 3 minutes. Garnish with parsley.

Garlic roast beef; Beef rolls

Tarragon Beef

Serves 4

*3 tablespoons chopped fresh
  tarragon*
*4 filet mignon steaks, total
  weight 1½ pounds, lightly
  beaten*
2 tablespoons butter
about ⅔ cup hot beef stock
1 tablespoon cornstarch
salt
freshly ground black pepper
6 tablespoons heavy cream
fresh tarragon, to garnish

Preparation time: about 6
minutes
Cooking time: about 10
minutes
Microwave setting: Full power
(High)

1. Sprinkle 2 tablespoons of the
tarragon over both sides of the
steaks and rub in well. Place the
steaks in a shallow dish and
cook, uncovered, for 7 minutes,
turning over and rearranging
halfway through cooking. Pour
off and reserve the juices.

2. Place the butter in a large
bowl and cook, uncovered, for
30 seconds or until melted.
Make up the meat juices to ⅔
cup with the stock, then stir in
with the cornstarch, remaining

tarragon, and salt and pepper to
taste. Cook, uncovered, for 2½
minutes, stirring every minute.

3. Stir in the cream and pour
over the steaks and reheat for 1
minute if necessary. Garnish
with tarragon and serve with a
mixed green salad.

Tarragon beef

Beef in Beer

Serves 4
1 onion, peeled and sliced
heaped 1 cup peeled and sliced
*   carrots*
1 celery stalk, chopped
1 pound boneless rump roast,
*   cubed*
2 tablespoons butter, diced
$\frac{1}{4}$ cup all-purpose flour
1 tablespoon tomato paste
1 teaspoon Italian seasoning
$\frac{2}{3}$ cup beer or brown ale
1$\frac{1}{4}$ cups hot beef stock
salt
freshly ground black pepper

Preparation time: about 10
minutes
Cooking time: about 23
minutes, plus standing
Microwave setting: Full power
(High) and Defrost

1. Place the onion, carrots and
celery in a large bowl. Cover and
cook on Full power for 5
minutes, stirring halfway
through cooking.

2. Stir in the beef and butter,
cover and cook on Full power
for 3 minutes. Stir in the flour,
tomato paste, herbs, beer or ale,
stock, and salt and pepper to
taste. Cover and cook for 5
minutes.

3. Cook, uncovered, for a
further 40 minutes on Defrost,
stirring several times during
cooking.

4. Stand, covered, for 10
minutes before serving. Serve
with pasta.

Beef in Cider

Serves 6
$\frac{1}{2}$ green bell pepper, cored,
*   seeded and finely chopped*
2 onions, peeled and sliced
2 pounds top round steak,
*   trimmed and cubed*
3 tablespoons butter, cut up
$\frac{1}{2}$ cup all-purpose flour
1 bay leaf
$\frac{1}{2}$ teaspoon dried oregano
$\frac{1}{2}$ teaspoon dried thyme
1 tablespoon tomato paste
1$\frac{1}{4}$ cups apple cider or applejack
$\frac{2}{3}$ cup hot beef stock
salt
freshly ground black pepper

Preparation time: about 10
minutes
Cooking time: about 52
minutes, plus standing
Microwave setting: Full power
(High) and Defrost

1. Place the green bell pepper
and onions in a large bowl,
cover and cook on Full power
for 5 minutes.

2. Stir in the beef and butter.
Cover and cook on Full power
for 7 minutes, stirring twice.

3. Stir in the flour, bay leaf,
oregano, thyme, tomato paste,
cider, stock and salt and pepper
to taste. Cover and cook on
Defrost for 40 minutes, stirring
twice during cooking. Leave to
stand, covered, for 10 minutes.

4. Discard the bay leaf, then
taste and adjust the seasoning.

Beef in beer; Beef in cider

Beef Goulash

Serves 4
1 large onion, peeled and sliced
2 tablespoons butter
½ cup tomato paste
*1 tablespoon ground
    Hungarian paprika*
2 teaspoons superfine sugar
2 tomatoes, peeled and chopped
*1¼ pounds boneless rump roast,
    cubed*
salt
freshly ground black pepper
2 tablespoons all-purpose flour
1¼ cups hot beef stock
2 tablespoons sour cream
paprika, to garnish

Preparation time: about 15 minutes
Cooking time: about 49 minutes, plus standing
Microwave setting: Full power (High) and Defrost

1. Place the onion in a large bowl, cover and cook on Full power for 4 minutes. Stir in the butter, tomato paste, paprika, sugar, tomatoes, beef and salt and pepper to taste. Cook, covered, on Full power for 5 minutes, stirring halfway through cooking.

2. Stir in the flour and stock. Cover and cook on Defrost for 40 minutes, stirring twice during cooking. Leave to stand, covered, for 10 minutes.

3. Stir in the sour cream and sprinkle with paprika. Serve with ribbon noodles.

Beef Stroganoff

Serves 4–6
¼ cup butter
1 tablespoon tomato paste
*1 large onion, peeled and finely
    diced*
2 cups sliced mushrooms
*1½ pounds beef tenderloin, cut
    into 3- × ½-inch strips*
⅔ cup dry white wine
¼ cup cornstarch
salt
freshly ground black pepper
¼ cup sour cream
*chopped fresh parsley, to
    garnish*

Preparation time: about 15 minutes
Cooking time: about 12 minutes
Microwave setting: Full power (High)

1. Place the butter, tomato paste, onion and mushrooms in a large bowl. Cover and cook for 5 minutes.

2. Stir in the beef, cover and cook for 5 minutes.

3. Blend together the wine and cornstarch, then stir into the beef. Cook, uncovered, for 2 minutes, stirring halfway through cooking.

4. Add salt and pepper to taste, stir in the sour cream and serve on a bed of boiled rice, garnished with parsley.

Beef goulash; Beef stroganoff

Beef, Mushroom and Onion Supper

Serves 4
Pastry:
2 cups self-rising flour
½ teaspoon salt
⅓ cup shredded suet
about ¾ cup water
Filling:
2 tablespoons butter
2 onions, peeled and sliced
2 cups chopped mushrooms
1 garlic clove, peeled and
   crushed
¼ teaspoon dried parsley flakes
¼ teaspoon dried rosemary
¼ teaspoon dried oregano
¼ teaspoon dried marjoram
salt
freshly ground black pepper
¾ pound ground beef
¼ teaspoon meat extract
parsley sprig, to garnish

Preparation time: about 30 minutes
Cooking time: about 18 minutes
Microwave setting: Full power (High)

1. Mix together the flour, salt, suet and enough water to form a smooth dough. Roll out two-thirds of the dough and use to line a greased 5-cup bowl or pudding basin. Roll out the remainder for a lid and set aside.

2. Place the butter, onions, mushrooms, garlic, parsley, rosemary, oregano, marjoram and salt and pepper to taste in a medium bowl. Cover and cook for 5 minutes.

3. Stir in the beef and meat extract. Cover and cook for 4 minutes, stirring halfway through cooking. Drain off the excess liquid.

4. Fill the bowl with the mixture. Place the dough lid in position and seal. Cover loosely with plastic wrap and cook for 9 minutes, turning around halfway through cooking.

5. Serve immediately, garnished with the parsley and accompanied by mashed potatoes and carrots.

Beef, mushroom and onion supper

Chili con Carne

Serves 4
1 large onion, peeled and finely
    chopped
1 garlic clove, peeled and
    crushed
2 teaspoons tomato paste
2 tablespoons butter, cut into
    pieces
$\frac{1}{4}$ cup all-purpose flour
$\frac{1}{2}$ teaspoon dried oregano
$\frac{1}{2}$ teaspoon ground cumin
1 tablespoon chili powder
1 × 16-ounce can chopped
    tomatoes, with their juice
1 pound ground beef
1 × 15$\frac{1}{4}$-ounce can red kidney
    beans, drained
salt
freshly ground black pepper

Preparation time: about 10
minutes
Cooking time: about 17
minutes
Microwave setting: Full power
(High)

1. Place the onion, garlic and
tomato paste in a large bowl.
Cover and cook for 5 minutes.

2. Stir in the butter until melted.
Stir in the flour, oregano, cumin,
chili powder, undrained
tomatoes and beef. Cook,
uncovered, for 8 minutes. Stir
and break up with a fork
halfway through cooking.

3. Stir in the beans and cook,
uncovered, for 4 minutes,
stirring halfway through
cooking.

4. Season to taste with salt and
pepper. Serve with boiled rice
and peas.

Beef Bourguignon

Serves 4–6
2 onions, peeled and chopped
2 bacon slices, chopped
2 cups sliced mushrooms
1$\frac{1}{2}$ pounds top round steak,
    cubed
$\frac{1}{4}$ cup all-purpose flour
1 cup red wine
$\frac{1}{3}$ cup hot beef stock
2 garlic cloves, peeled and
    crushed
1 teaspoon Italian seasoning
salt
freshly ground black pepper

Preparation time: about 15
minutes
Cooking time: about 56
minutes, plus standing
Microwave setting: Full power
(High) and Defrost

1. Place the onions and bacon
in a large bowl, cover and cook
on Full power for 5 minutes.

2. Stir in the mushrooms and
beef, cover and cook on Full
power for 7 minutes, stirring
halfway through.

3. Stir in the flour, red wine,
stock, garlic, herbs and salt and
pepper to taste. Cover and cook
on Full power for 4 minutes,
stirring halfway through
cooking, then reduce to Defrost
and cook for 40 minutes.

4. Leave to stand, covered, for
10 minutes before serving.

Chili con carne; Beef bouguignon

Chinese-style Beef

Serves 4–6

1 tablespoon sesame oil
2 onions, peeled and sliced
1 red bell pepper, cored, seeded
  and thinly sliced
1 garlic clove, peeled and
  crushed
1½ pounds beef tenderloin, cut
  into 3- × ½-inch strips
1⅓ cups sliced button
  mushrooms
1 teaspoon ground ginger
¼ teaspoon ground cumin
¼ teaspoon grated nutmeg
1 teaspoon Italian seasoning
1 tablespoon cornstarch
1 tablespoon lemon juice
¼ cup dry sherry
¾ cup hot beef stock
1 tablespoon Worcestershire
  sauce
1 tablespoon soy sauce
salt
freshly ground black pepper
⅔ 14-ounce can bean-sprouts,
  drained

Preparation time: about 15
minutes
Cooking time: about 12
minutes, plus standing
Microwave setting: Full power
(High)

1. Place the oil, onions, red bell
pepper and garlic in a large
bowl. Cover and cook for 5
minutes, stirring halfway
through cooking.

2. Stir in the beef, mushrooms,
ginger, cumin, nutmeg, and
herbs. Cover and cook for 3
minutes.

3. Stir in the cornstarch, lemon
juice, sherry, stock,
Worcestershire sauce, soy sauce
and salt and pepper to taste.
Fold in the bean-sprouts. Cover
and cook for 4 minutes, stirring
halfway through.

4. Leave to stand, covered, for 4
minutes before serving. Serve
with boiled rice.

Mexican Beef

Serves 4–6

1 onion, peeled and sliced
1 small carrot, peeled and
  sliced
1 green bell pepper, cored,
  seeded and chopped
1 red bell pepper, cored, seeded
  and chopped
1 medium potato, peeled and
  diced
¼ cup butter, cut into pieces
1 teaspoon Italian seasoning
½ teaspoon chili powder
½ teaspoon Worcestershire sauce
1 teaspoon dried parsley flakes
1 garlic clove, peeled and
  crushed
1¼ pounds top round steak, cut
  into strips
salt
freshly ground black pepper
2 tablespoons all-purpose flour
1 × 16-ounce can chopped
  tomatoes, with their juice
⅔ cup hot beef stock

Preparation time: about 20
minutes
Cooking time: about 15½
minutes, plus standing
Microwave setting: Full power
(High)

1. Place the onion, carrot, bell
peppers and potato in a large
bowl. Cover and cook for 6½
minutes.

2. Stir in the butter until melted.
Stir in the herbs, chili powder,
Worcestershire sauce, parsley,
garlic, beef, and salt and pepper
to taste. Cover and cook for 4
minutes, stirring halfway
through.

3. Stir in the flour, undrained
tomatoes and stock. Cover and
cook for 5 minutes, stirring
halfway through cooking.

4. Leave to stand, covered, for 5
minutes before serving.

Chinese-style beef; Mexican beef

Beef with Cheese Sauce

Serves 4

1 onion, peeled and thinly
 sliced
1 medium carrot, peeled and
 sliced
2/3 cup peeled and sliced potato
1 1/3 cups chopped mushrooms
1 tablespoon tomato paste
3/4 pound ground beef
1 teaspoon Italian seasoning
salt
freshly ground black pepper
3 tablespoons butter
1/3 cup all-purpose flour
2 1/2 cups milk
1 cup finely grated Cheddar
 cheese
1 tablespoon chopped fresh
 parsley, to garnish

Preparation time: about 20
minutes
Cooking time: 22 minutes, plus
broiling
Microwave setting: Full power
(High)

1. Place the onion, carrot and
potato in a 1 1/2-quart dish. Cover
and cook for 4 1/2 minutes, stirring
halfway through cooking.

2. Stir in the mushrooms,
tomato paste, beef, herbs, and
salt and pepper to taste. Cover
and cook for 8 minutes. Break
up and stir with a fork halfway
through cooking. Set aside.

3. Place the butter in a large
bowl and cook, uncovered, for
30 seconds or until melted. Stir
in the flour, then gradually
blend in the milk, with salt and
pepper to taste. Cook,
uncovered, for 7 minutes or
until thick, stirring every 2
minutes.

4. Stir in the cheese until melted.
Pour the sauce over the beef
mixture. Cook, uncovered, for 2
minutes. Brown under a
preheated conventional broiler,
if preferred.

5. Sprinkle with parsley to
garnish. Serve with sauté
potatoes and peas.

Beef with cheese sauce

Steak with Water Chestnuts

Serves 4
4 filet mignon steaks, 1 inch thick, total weight 1 pound, lightly beaten
1 small celery stalk, chopped
½ green bell pepper, cored, seeded and chopped
½ red bell pepper, cored, seeded and chopped
1 garlic clove, peeled and crushed
2 tablespoons tomato paste
1 tablespoon cornstarch
3 tablespoons dry sherry
2 tablespoons soy sauce
6 canned water chestnuts, drained and sliced
salt
freshly ground black pepper

Preparation time: about 15 minutes
Cooking time: about 12–14 minutes
Microwave setting: Full power (High)

1. Place the steaks in a casserole dish. Cook, uncovered, for 3–5 minutes, depending on how rare you like your steak, and turning over and rearranging halfway through cooking. Set aside, covered, while making sauce.

2. Place the celery, peppers, garlic and tomato paste in a medium bowl. Cover and cook for 5 minutes, stirring halfway through cooking.

3. Stir in the cornstarch, sherry, soy sauce, water chestnuts, and salt and pepper to taste. Add any juice from the cooked steaks.

4. Pour the mixture over the steaks. Cover and cook for 4 minutes. Serve with baked potatoes.

Steak in Pepper Sauce

Serves 4
1 onion, peeled and finely chopped
¼ cup butter
1 garlic clove, peeled and crushed
⅓ cup cornstarch
1¼ cups hot beef stock
⅔ cup milk
½ teaspoon freshly ground black pepper
16 whole black peppercorns
salt
4 boneless top round steaks
parsley sprig, to garnish

Preparation time: about 10 minutes
Cooking time: about 13½ minutes, plus standing
Microwave setting: Full power (High)

1. Place the onion, butter and garlic in a medium bowl. Cover and cook for 4 minutes.

2. Stir in the cornstarch, hot stock, milk and ground pepper.

Crush 6 of the peppercorns and add them to the sauce with the remaining peppercorns and the salt.

3. Cover and cook for 2 minutes, stirring halfway through cooking. Leave covered and set aside.

4. Place the steaks in a large shallow casserole. Cook for 3 minutes. Turn the steaks over and turn the casserole around. Cook for a further 2½ minutes.

5. Stir any meat juices into the sauce. Pour the sauce over the steaks, cover and cook for 2 minutes.

6. Leave to stand, covered, for 3 minutes before serving garnished with parsley. Serve with a tossed salad.

Steak with water chestnuts; Steak in pepper sauce

Whiskey Steak

Serves 4

*4 rump steaks, total weight 1½
    pounds, lightly beaten*
2 tablespoons whiskey
*1 garlic clove, peeled and
    crushed*
*1 onion, peeled and finely
    chopped*
¼ cup butter
½ teaspoon Worcestershire sauce
freshly ground black pepper
scallion tassels, to garnish

Preparation time: about 7
minutes, plus marinating
Cooking time: about 14
minutes
Microwave setting: Full power
(High)

1. Marinate the steaks in the
whiskey for 2 hours.

2. Place the garlic and onion in a
large bowl. Cook, covered, for 4
minutes. Stir in the butter and
cook, uncovered, for 30
seconds. Set aside while
cooking the steaks.

3. Drain the steaks, reserving the
marinade. Place the steaks in a
shallow casserole dish. Cook,
uncovered, for 7 minutes,
turning over and rearranging
halfway through cooking.

4. Pour the juice from the steaks
into the butter mixture. Stir in
the Worcestershire sauce,
whiskey from the marinade and
pepper to taste.

5. Pour the sauce over the
steaks and cook, uncovered, for
2½ minutes.

6. Garnish with scallions and
serve with boiled rice.

*Whiskey steak; Steak with mushroom
sauce*

Steak with Mushroom Sauce

Serves 4

1 celery stalk, chopped
*1 onion, peeled and studded
    with 6 cloves*
1 carrot, peeled and sliced
2 cups milk
*4 thin boneless top round
    steaks, total weight 1½ pounds*
3 cups sliced mushrooms
¼ cup butter, cut into pieces
*about ⅔ cup hot chicken or
    vegetable stock*
½ cup all-purpose flour
salt
freshly ground black pepper
parsley sprig, to garnish

Preparation time: about 15
minutes, plus infusing
Cooking time: about 20
minutes
Microwave setting: Full power
(High)

1. Place the celery, onion, carrot
and milk in a large bowl. Cook,
uncovered, for 3 minutes. Set
aside to infuse for 15 minutes.
Strain and discard vegetables.

2. Place the steaks in a casserole
dish and cook, uncovered, for 6
minutes, turning over and
rearranging halfway through
cooking. Set aside, covered,
while making the sauce.

3. Place the mushrooms in a
medium bowl, cover and cook
for 3 minutes. Stir in the butter
until melted. Make up the meat
juices to ⅔ cup with the stock,
then stir in with the flour,
strained milk, and salt and
pepper to taste. Cook,
uncovered, for 5 minutes,
stirring every minute.

4. Pour the sauce over the
steaks. Cook, uncovered, for 3
minutes. Garnish with the
parsley.

Meatballs in Mushroom and Tomato Sauce

Serves 4
1 pound ground beef
½ cup fresh whole-wheat bread
   crumbs
1 onion, peeled and grated
1 teaspoon Italian seasoning
1 tablespoon tomato paste
salt
freshly ground black pepper
1 egg
Sauce:
3 tablespoons butter
1⅓ cups finely chopped
   mushrooms
2 large tomatoes, peeled and
   chopped
1 tablespoon tomato paste
⅓ cup all-purpose flour
2 cups hot beef stock
salt
freshly ground black pepper

Preparation time: about 15
minutes
Cooking time: about 20
minutes
Microwave setting: Full power
(High)

1. Mix the beef, bread crumbs, onions, herbs, tomato paste, salt and pepper together. Add the egg and mix well. Form the mixture into 16 balls.

2. Place the meatballs on a plate and cook for 2 minutes. Turn the meatballs over and turn the plate around. Cook for a further 2 minutes.

3. To make the sauce, place the butter, mushrooms, tomatoes and tomato paste in a medium bowl. Cover and cook for 5 minutes. Stir in the flour, then gradually add the hot stock. Cook for 2 minutes. Cool slightly.

4. Pour into a blender and purée until smooth. Stir in salt and pepper to taste.

5. Place the meatballs in a bowl. Pour over the sauce. Cook for 5 minutes. Serve with noodles and grated Parmesan cheese.

Hamburger with Onions

Serves 4
1 onion, peeled and sliced
1 onion, peeled and grated
½ pound ground beef
1 garlic clove, peeled and
   crushed
1 teaspoon Italian seasoning
salt
freshly ground black pepper
¼ cup all-purpose flour
4 hamburger buns, cut in half
lettuce and tomatoes, to garnish

Preparation time: about 10
minutes
Cooking time: about 12¾
minutes
Microwave setting: Full power
(High)

1. Place the sliced onion in a medium bowl. Cover and cook for 4 minutes. Set aside.

2. Place the grated onion in another medium bowl. Cover and cook for 3 minutes.

3. Mix in the ground beef, garlic, herbs, salt, pepper and flour. Shape into 4 hamburgers.

4. Place on a plate and cook for 3 minutes. Turn the hamburgers over and turn the plate around. Cook for a further 2 minutes.

5. Place a few cooked onion slices on 4 of the bun halves. Place a hamburger on top and top with the remaining half buns. Place on a plate and cook for 45 seconds. Garnish with lettuce and tomatoes.

Meatballs in mushroom and tomato sauce; Hamburgers with Onions

Ground Beef with Mixed Vegetables

Serves 4
1 large potato, peeled and diced
1 turnip, peeled and diced
1 carrot, peeled and sliced
1 onion, peeled and sliced
1 celery stalk, chopped
1 pound ground beef
1 teaspoon Italian seasoning
1 tablespoon tomato paste
⅔ cup hot beef stock
salt
freshly ground black pepper

Preparation time: about 20 minutes
Cooking time: about 17 minutes
Microwave setting: Full power (High)

1. Place the potato, turnip, carrot, onion and celery in a large bowl. Cover and cook for 10 minutes.

2. Stir in the beef, herbs, tomato paste, stock, and salt and pepper to taste. Cover and cook for 7 minutes, stirring halfway through cooking.

3. Serve with mashed potatoes.

Ground beef with mixed vegetables;
Potato-topped beef casserole

Potato-topped Beef Casserole

Serves 4
4 cups peeled potatoes cut into 1-inch cubes
3 tablespoons water
1 onion, peeled and chopped
4 tablespoons tomato paste
2 tomatoes, peeled and chopped
3 cups finely chopped cooked beef
1 teaspoon Italian seasoning
3 tablespoons butter
½ teaspoon celery salt
⅔ cup hot beef stock
freshly ground black pepper
2–3 tablespoons milk
salt
parsley sprigs, to garnish (optional)

Preparation time: about 15 minutes
Cooking time: about 23½ minutes
Microwave setting: Full power (High)

1. Place the potatoes in a large bowl with the water. Cover and cook for 12 minutes, stirring halfway through cooking. Leave to stand, covered.

2. Place the onion in a round 5-cup casserole dish, cover and cook for 3½ minutes. Stir in the tomato paste, the chopped tomatoes, the beef, herbs, 1 tablespoon of the butter, the celery salt, stock and pepper to taste. Cover and cook for 4 minutes. Stir.

3. Meanwhile, mash the potatoes with the milk, remaining butter and season with salt and pepper to taste. Using a pastry bag fitted with a large star tip, pipe rosettes of the mashed potatoes to cover the meat. Cook, uncovered, for 4 minutes.

4. Garnish with parsley and serve with mashed rutabaga.

Meat Loaf

Serves 4
1 tablespoon butter
1 onion, peeled and finely chopped
½ pound ground beef
½ pound ground pork
1 garlic clove, peeled and crushed
7 tablespoons fresh white bread crumbs
1 tablespoon tomato paste
¼ teaspoon celery salt
1 teaspoon Italian seasoning
¼ teaspoon dried thyme
salt
freshly ground black pepper
1 egg, beaten

Preparation time: about 10 minutes, plus chilling
Cooking time: about 12–14 minutes
Microwave setting: Full power (High)

1. Place the butter and onion in a 3¾-cup soufflé dish. Cover and cook for 4 minutes.

2. Mix together the beef, pork, garlic, bread crumbs, tomato paste, celery salt, herbs, thyme, salt and pepper to taste. Stir in the onion and beaten egg.

3. Place in the soufflé dish. Cook, uncovered, for 4 minutes. Break up and stir with a fork. Cook, uncovered, for a further 4–6 minutes. Allow to cool.

4. Chill until cold. Turn out, slice and serve with a green salad and sliced tomatoes.

Shepherd's Pie

Serves 6
5⅓ cups peeled potatoes cut into 1-inch cubes
3 tablespoons water
1 onion, peeled and thinly sliced
1¼ pounds ground beef
2 tablespoons tomato paste
½ teaspoon beef extract
¼ teaspoon chopped fresh parsley
¼ teaspoon dried oregano
¼ teaspoon dried marjoram
¼ teaspoon chopped fresh sage
1 teaspoon Worcestershire sauce
salt
freshly ground black pepper
4 tablespoons milk
2 tablespoons butter
parsley sprig, to garnish
gravy (page 99), to serve

Preparation time: 15 minutes
Cooking time: about 26 minutes, plus broiling
Microwave setting: Full power (High)

1. Place the potatoes and water in a large bowl, cover and cook for 12 minutes. Stir once during cooking. Set aside, covered.

2. Place the onion in a large dish. Cover and cook for 4 minutes or until translucent.

3. Stir in the beef, tomato paste, beef extract, parsley, oregano, marjoram, sage, Worcestershire sauce and salt and pepper to taste. Cover and cook for 6 minutes. Stir to break up the ground beef with a fork halfway through cooking. Drain off the excess liquid.

4. Mash the potatoes with the milk, butter and salt and pepper to taste. Spread over the beef mixture and cook for 4 minutes. Brown under a preheated conventional broiler.

5. Garnish with parsley and serve with gravy.

Meat loaf; Shepherd's pie

MENU PLANNER

A traditional meal can be the most difficult to plan, so use your microwave to ease the load. Make a Trifle (page 177) the day before. Prepare the Rollmops (page 35) a few hours in advance; leave them to cool.

Time the meat and vegetables well: Cook the meat before serving the appetizer, then leave it to stand and make the gravy. Cook the potatoes. Cook the vegetables while eating the appetizer.

When ready to serve the main course, heat the gravy and potatoes if necessary.

Alternatively, the vegetables can be three-quarters cooked well in advance, then finish the cooking just before they are served. This works well if you have a divided dish to hold all the vegetables, so that they can be put together for the final cooking.

Roast Beef with Gravy

Serves 6–8
3 pound boneless rolled rump roast
Gravy:
2 tablespoons cold water
2 tablespoons meat sediment
(from the roasting bag)
1 tablespoon all-purpose flour
1¼ cups hot beef stock
¼ teaspoon gravy browning

Preparation time: about 6 minutes
Cooking time: about 23 minutes, plus standing
Microwave setting: Full power (High)

1. Place the beef in a roasting bag. Pierce the bag and tie with a non-metal tie.

2. Place the meat on a trivet or up-turned saucer in a shallow dish. Cook for 21 minutes, turning over halfway through cooking.

3. Remove the bag, wrap the meat tightly in foil, shiny side inward, and stand for 20 minutes.

4. For the gravy, place the water in a measuring cup. Stir in the meat sediment and flour. Add the stock and gravy browning.

5. Cook, uncovered, for 2 minutes, stirring twice.

Roast beef;
Boiled potatoes; Green
beans; Trifle; Rollmops (page 35)

LAMB

Most cuts of lamb which can be broiled or roasted by traditional methods can be cooked to give tender results in the microwave. The majority of cuts are tender, the only exception being the neck of lamb. The guidelines at the beginning of the meat chapter apply to this section, and the following notes relate to specific cuts of lamb and the techniques which should be applied when cooking them in the microwave.

Lamb cooks very well in the microwave but it is important to observe all the basic rules. The size and shape of the meat affects not only the cooking time but also the result.

Boned larger cuts

Boned cuts cook more evenly than meat on the bone. The bone in a large piece of meat becomes very hot during cooking and overcooking can occur where the meat on the bone is thinnest. If meat on the bone is cooked, then it is necessary to shield areas that might overcook with small

Arranging chops

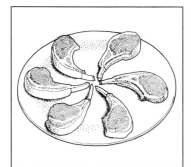

Lamb chops should be trimmed of excess fat before cooking and they should be arranged in a shallow dish with the bones pointing in toward the middle. They can be covered with paper towels. If a little liquid is added, or flavoring ingredients are included, then it is best to cover the dish with a lid, up-turned plate or microwave-safe plastic wrap.

pieces of smooth foil.

Boned lamb not only cooks better but it is easier to carve and serve. Most butchers will oblige by boning out a leg or shoulder of lamb. If you want to bone the meat yourself, the following tips may be of some help in ensuring success.

Use a fairly small, sharp kitchen knife. Work from the widest end at which the bone is exposed. Make small cuts as close as possible to the bone, cutting the meat away from it. Work inward, easing the meat away from the bone with your fingers and cutting carefully around the shape of the bone. A leg is easier to bone than the shoulder because the bone is straight. When you reach any joints in the bone you will find that a pair of kitchen scissors are useful to snip any sinews. Leave all the gristly bits attached to the meat until you have removed the bone, then trim them off. When you are almost through to the far end of the bone you may find it easier to work inward from the thin end. It is important to allow enough time to bone the meat – you will probably find the task far easier if you do not have to rush.

Once the joint is boned, it can be stuffed, flavored with chopped fresh herbs or garlic, then tied into a neat shape. If you have a trussing needle, then the opening in a shoulder joint can be sewn into shape. Mold a boned shoulder of lamb into a neat shape, tucking in any small protruding pieces of meat, and it will cook evenly.

Boneless cuts cook best

1. A boned shoulder of lamb can be tied or sewn into a neat, rounded shape. Before cooking, the thin skin around the roast should be pierced to prevent bursting; here the slits in the skin have been studded with sprigs of rosemary.

Piercing the skin

Cuts of lamb are covered by a thin skin as well as some fat. This should be pierced before cooking to prevent it from bursting. Small slits can be cut into the meat and these studded with sprigs of rosemary or cloves of garlic. The meat should not be seasoned before cooking.

Small cuts

Lamb chops can be microwaved successfully. They should be trimmed of excess fat which will be pale and soft when cooked. A browning dish can be used to brown the fat first. Alternatively, the edges of chops can be browned by rolling the fat on the surface of a very hot skillet on the conventional stove

2. Neat noisettes of lamb are prepared from boned rib or loin chops. They cook particularly successfully either brushed with a little vegetable oil or melted butter, or prepared in a sauce.

before placing them in the dish for microwave cooking.

The chops should be arranged in the dish, as far apart as possible, with thin areas or bone ends toward the middle of the dish.

As with large cuts, boned small cuts cook better than those on the bone, so noisettes of lamb are ideal pieces of meat for successful microwave cooking.

Covering during cooking

Large cuts should be covered during cooking – they can be placed on a microwave roasting rack inside a roasting bag. Alternatively, they can be cooked in a large casserole dish.

Small cuts should be arranged in a shallow dish or on

GUIDE TO COOKING LAMB

Cut of meat		Cooking time in minutes on Medium per 1 pound or for quantity given	Cooking time in minutes on Full power (High) per 1 pound or for quantity given	Method
leg	on bone off bone	11–13 12–13	8–10 9–10	Choose a good quality roast. Roll the meat into a neat shape if it is off the bone. Cover the pointed end with foil to protect it if on the bone. Allow to stand for 25–30 minutes, wrapped in foil, before carving.
breast		14–16	12	Roll and stuff, if liked, before cooking. Allow to stand for 30 minutes, wrapped in foil, before carving.
crown roast		—	5	Cover tips of bones with smooth foil during cooking.
loin roast		11–13	8–10	Choose a good quality roast. Roll into a neat shape if off the bone. Allow to stand for 25–30 minutes, wrapped in foil, before carving.
chops, loin or sirloin	2 4 6	— — —	6–7 7–9 15–17	Preheat the browning dish according to the manufacturer's directions. Add the chops and cook for the recommended time, turning over halfway through the cooking time.
liver		—	5 6	
kidney		—	7–8	

a roasting rack. They can be covered with paper towels, with a lid or, microwave-safe plastic wrap.

Turning and rearranging

Roasts should be turned at least twice during cooking, and it is a good idea to allow a period of standing time when they are turned, particularly if the cut is fairly large and filled with a stuffing.

Small pieces of meat should be turned over halfway through cooking and rearranged in the dish.

Cutting slices and strips

Since lamb is a tender meat it can be braised or cooked with vegetables, stir-fry style. Rather than cutting the meat into chunks, it is better to cut thin slices across the grain or fine strips for tender results when cooked. See pages 80 and 81 for general advice on cutting and preparing meat.

Marinating

Before cooking, lamb benefits from marinating. Large cuts can be rubbed with spices or herbs and marinated in wine, oil or citrus juices to give tender, full-flavored results. The roast should be turned frequently in the marinade and the liquid can be cooked in a sauce to serve with the meat.

Small cuts – chops, noisettes or lamb steaks off the leg – and slices or strips of meat can be thoroughly coated in marinade and left in the refrigerator, covered, for several hours or overnight. For certain spicy lamb recipes, the meat can be marinated for up to 2 days but it must be very fresh.

Ingredients that are particularly complementary to the flavor of lamb include garlic, rosemary, grated fresh ginger root, orange (rind and juice), apricots (puréed), olive oil, ground coriander or crushed coriander seeds, ground cumin and red wine.

GUIDE TO DEFROSTING LAMB

Type of meat	Defrosting time in minutes on Defrost per 1 pound	Method
roasts	10	Turn over at least once during the defrosting time.
chops	5	
kidney	4	Turn over at least once during the defrosting time.
liver	4	Turn over at least once during the defrosting time.

Roast Leg of Lamb

Serves 6–8
1 × 3-pound leg of lamb, lightly beaten

Preparation time: about 5 minutes
Cooking time: about 21 minutes, plus standing and broiling
Microwave setting: Full power (High)

1. Wrap a small, smooth piece of foil around the thin end of the lamb. Place the lamb in a roasting bag. Pierce the bag and tie with a non-metallic tie.

2. Place the lamb on a trivet or up-turned saucer in a shallow dish. Cook for 21 minutes, turning over halfway through cooking.

3. Remove the lamb from the bag and wrap tightly in foil, shiny side inward. Leave to stand for 20 minutes before carving. Brown under a preheated conventional broiler, if preferred.

4. Serve with mint sauce, potatoes and vegetables.

Accompaniments for lamb

Mint sauce The traditional accompaniment to roast lamb. Chop a handful of mint with a sprinkling of sugar. Place in a bowl and pour in just enough boiling water to cover the mint. Add 2 teaspoons sugar and stir until it has dissolved. Stir in enough vinegar to make a small amount of thin sauce. Cider vinegar is excellent because it is not as harsh as others.

Mint cream Stir a little chopped mint into sour cream, then season lightly with garlic salt. Good with noisettes of lamb and zucchini.

Rich red-currant cream Melt 2 tablespoons red currant jelly in a small bowl on Full power – it will take about 30 seconds. Stir in 1 tablespoon port or orange juice, 1 teaspoon grated orange rind and a little garlic salt and pepper. Lightly stir in ⅔ cup yogurt or whipped heavy cream. Good with chops.

Quick tomato relish Peel, seed and finely chop 4 tomatoes and mix them with a finely chopped, seeded fresh green chili. Add 4 finely chopped scallions, plenty of seasoning and 1 teaspoon sugar. Stir in 1 finely chopped clove of garlic and a little chopped fresh mint when in season. Dress with 2 tablespoons sunflower oil and sharpen with 2 teaspoons cider vinegar. Stir well, crushing the tomatoes slightly. It is best left to stand for 1–2 hours before serving.

French-style Lamb

Serves 4
1¼ pounds tenderloin, cubed
3 tablespoons butter
1 tablespoon all-purpose flour
Marinade:
1 cup red wine
2 carrots, peeled and sliced
2 onions, peeled and roughly cut into chunks
1 teaspoon dried thyme
1 bay leaf
small piece of orange rind
salt
freshly ground black pepper

Preparation time: about 15 minutes, plus marinating
Cooking time: 26½ minutes
Microwave settings: Full power (High) and Defrost

1. Place the lamb and marinade ingredients in a bowl. Cover and leave to marinate for 3 hours.

2. Drain the wine from the meat mixture and set aside.

3. Place the butter in a casserole and cook on Full power for ½ minute to melt. Blend in the flour and cook on Full power for 1 minute. Gradually add the reserved wine, blending well. Stir in the meat mixture. Cover tightly and cook on Full power for 15 minutes, stirring twice.

4. Reduce the power setting to Defrost and cook for a further 10 minutes. Remove and discard the bay leaf and orange rind.

Lemon and Herb Marinated Lamb Chops

Serves 4
4 large loin lamb chops
Marinade:
4 tablespoons olive oil
grated rind of 1 lemon
3 tablespoons lemon juice
1 tablespoon chopped fresh parsley
1 tablespoon dried herbes de Provence
1 garlic clove, crushed
4 bay leaves
salt
freshly ground black pepper
Vegetables:
1 bunch celery, trimmed and sliced
1 onion, peeled and chopped
2 tablespoons butter
5 teaspoons water
½ teaspoon salt
1 × 10-ounce package frozen peas
To garnish:
celery leaves.

Preparation time: about 10 minutes, plus marinating
Cooking time: 24–25½ minutes
Microwave settings: Full power (High) and Medium

1. Mix the marinade ingredients together and pour over the chops. Cover and leave to marinate for 4–5 hours.

2. Place the celery, onion, butter, water and salt in a large dish. Cover and cook on Full power for 6 minutes. Add the peas, cover and cook, on Full power for 7–8 minutes, stirring once. Cover and leave to stand while cooking the chops.

3. Preheat a browning dish on Full power for 8 minutes (or according to the manufacturer's directions). Drain the chops and add to the browning dish, turning quickly on all sides to brown evenly. Cook on Full power for 1½ minutes. Turn over and cook on Medium for 1½–2 minutes.

4. To serve, place the cooked vegetables on a preheated serving dish and top with the cooked lamb chops. Garnish with celery leaves.

Roast leg of lamb

Noisettes of Lamb

Serves 4
8 lamb noisettes
1 small carrot, peeled and thinly sliced
1 onion, peeled and chopped
1 celery stalk, chopped
$\frac{1}{3}$ cup sliced button mushrooms
1 teaspoon Italian seasoning
1 teaspoon dried rosemary
2 tablespoons butter, diced
$\frac{1}{4}$ cup all-purpose flour
about 1$\frac{1}{4}$ cups hot chicken stock
2 tablespoons tomato paste
$\frac{2}{3}$ cup red wine
salt
freshly ground black pepper
parsley sprigs, to garnish

Preparation time: about 15 minutes
Cooking time: about 21–22 minutes
Microwave setting: Full power

1. Place the noisettes in a shallow 1$\frac{1}{2}$-quart casserole dish. Cover with a piece of paper towel and cook for 7–8 minutes, turning over and rearranging halfway through cooking. Set aside, covered.

2. Place the carrot, onion, celery, mushrooms and herbs in a medium bowl. Cover and cook for 7 minutes, stirring halfway through cooking.

3. Stir in the butter until melted, then stir in the flour. Make up the meat juices to 1$\frac{1}{4}$ cups with the stock, then stir in with the tomato paste, wine, and salt and pepper to taste. Cook, uncovered, for 4 minutes, stirring every minute.

4. Pour over the meat and cook for 3 minutes.

5. Garnish with the parsley and serve with boiled potatoes and broccoli.

Old-fashioned Casserole

Serves 4
1 onion, peeled and finely sliced
1 carrot, peeled and finely sliced
2 tablespoons butter
8 lambs' kidneys, halved and cores removed
$\frac{2}{3}$ cup sliced mushrooms
$\frac{1}{2}$ cup frozen peas
2 tablespoons chopped fresh parsley
1 garlic clove, peeled and crushed
$\frac{1}{4}$ cup cornstarch
$\frac{2}{3}$ cup dry sherry
1$\frac{1}{4}$ cups hot beef stock
1 tablespoon tomato paste
4 small frankfurters, sliced
salt
freshly ground black pepper

Preparation time: about 25 minutes
Cooking time: about 14$\frac{1}{2}$ minutes, plus standing
Microwave setting: Full power (High)

1. Place the onion, carrot and butter in a large bowl. Cover and cook for 4 minutes.

2. Stir in the kidneys, mushrooms, peas, half the parsley and the garlic. Cover and cook for 5$\frac{1}{2}$ minutes, stirring halfway through cooking.

3. Stir in the cornstarch, sherry, hot stock, tomato paste, frankfurters, salt and pepper. Cover and cook for 5 minutes, stirring halfway through cooking.

4. Leave to stand, covered, for 3 minutes before serving, sprinkled with the remaining parsley.

Noisettes of lamb; Old-fashioned casserole

Liver and Bacon Casserole

Serves 4
4 bacon slices, chopped
2 tablespoons butter
1 carrot, peeled and thinly sliced
½ celery stalk, finely chopped
1 onion, peeled and finely chopped
¼ cup cornstarch
1¼ cups hot beef stock
1½ cups peeled and chopped tomatoes
3 tablespoons tomato paste
1 teaspoon Worcestershire sauce
⅔ cup chopped mushrooms
1 teaspoon Italian seasoning
2 bay leaves
salt
freshly ground black pepper
1 pound lambs' liver, thinly sliced
bay leaves, to garnish

Preparation time: about 20 minutes
Cooking time: about 16½ minutes, plus standing
Microwave setting: Full power (High)

1. Place the bacon, butter, carrot, celery and onion in a large bowl. Cover and cook for 6½ minutes, stirring halfway through cooking.

2. Stir in the cornstarch, then blend in the hot stock.

3. Add the tomatoes, tomato paste, Worcestershire sauce, mushrooms, herbs, bay leaves, salt, pepper and liver. Cover. Cook for 10 minutes, stirring halfway through cooking time.

4. Leave to stand, covered, for 5 minutes. Garnish with bay leaves.

Lamb Chop Casserole

Serves 4
8 lamb loin chops, total weight 2 pounds
1⅓ cups peeled and diced potatoes
1 large onion, peeled and chopped
2 large carrots, peeled and thinly sliced
1 small turnip, peeled and diced
2 zucchini, sliced
3 tablespoons cold water
2 tablespoons butter, cut into pieces
¼ cup all-purpose flour
about 2 cups hot chicken stock
½ teaspoon dried thyme
¼ teaspoon gravy browning
salt
freshly ground black pepper

Preparation time: about 18 minutes
Cooking time: about 28–31 minutes
Microwave setting: Full power (High)

1. Place the chops over the bottom and sides of a large bowl. Cover and cook for 6½–9½ minutes, rearranging halfway through cooking. Set aside, covered.

2. Place the potatoes, onion, carrots, turnip, zucchini and water in another large bowl. Cover and cook for 13 minutes or until tender, stirring halfway through.

3. Stir in the butter until melted. Stir in the flour. Make up the meat juices to 2 cups with the stock, then stir in with the thyme, gravy browning, and salt and pepper. Cover and cook for 4 minutes, stirring halfway through cooking.

4. Stir in the chops. Cook, uncovered, for 4 minutes.

Liver and bacon casserole; Lamb chop casserole

Lamb with Mozzarella Cheese

Serves 4
8 lamb rib chops
4 ounces mozzarella cheese,
thinly sliced
Marinade:
2 tablespoons white-wine
vinegar
⅔ cup dry sherry
2 teaspoons dark brown sugar
1 tablespoon orange juice
¼ teaspoon Worcestershire sauce
salt
freshly ground black pepper
Garnish:
1 tablespoon chopped parsley
1 tomato

Preparation time: about 5
minutes, plus marinating
overnight
Cooking time: about 6–7
minutes
Microwave setting: Full power
(High)

1. Mix together the vinegar,
sherry, sugar, orange juice,
Worcestershire sauce, and salt
and pepper.

2. Arrange the chops in a
shallow dish. Pour over the
marinade and add sufficient
cold water to cover the chops.
Leave to marinate for about 24
hours.

3. Drain the marinade off the
chops. Cover the chops with a
piece of paper towel. Cook for
4–5 minutes, rearranging
halfway through cooking.

4. Pour off the juice and overlap
the chops to look attractive.
Cover the chops with the
cheese. Cook, uncovered, for 2
minutes.

5. Sprinkle with chopped
parsley and garnish with the
tomato.

Sweet-and-Sour Lamb

Serves 4
4 lamb loin chops, total weight
1¼ pounds
1 onion, peeled and finely
chopped
½ green bell pepper, cored,
seeded and finely chopped
½ red bell pepper, cored, seeded
and finely chopped
½ teaspoon dried rosemary
½ teaspoon dried marjoram
½ teaspoon dried parsley flakes
1 garlic clove, peeled and
crushed
2 tablespoons butter, cut into
pieces
¼ cup all-purpose flour
about 1¼ cups hot chicken
stock
2 tablespoons white-wine
vinegar
1 tablespoon light soy sauce
¼ cup brown sugar
salt
freshly ground black pepper

Preparation time: about 18
minutes
Cooking time: about 18
minutes
Microwave setting: Full power
(High)

1. Place the chops in a shallow
1½-quart casserole dish, cover
with a piece of paper towel and
cook for 7 minutes, turning over
and rearranging halfway
through cooking. Set aside,
covered.

2. Place the onion, bell peppers,
rosemary, marjoram, parsley
and garlic in a medium bowl.
Cover and cook for 5 minutes,
stirring halfway through.

3. Stir in the butter until melted.
Stir in the flour. Make up the
meat juices to 1¼ cups with the
stock, then blend into the
vegetables with the vinegar, soy
sauce, sugar, and salt and
pepper to taste. Cook,
uncovered, for 3 minutes,
stirring every minute.

4. Pour the sauce over the
chops and cook, uncovered, for
3 minutes.

5. Serve with buttered noodles.

Lamb with Cherries

Serves 4
4 lamb tenderloins, total weight
1½ pounds, lightly beaten
1 onion, peeled and chopped
2 tablespoons butter, cut into
pieces
1 pound frozen pitted dark
sweet cherries, thawed and
drained (no sugar added)
1 teaspoon dried marjoram
salt
about 1¼ cups hot chicken stock
¼ cup cornstarch

Preparation time: about 10
minutes
Cooking time: about 20½
minutes
Microwave setting: Full power
(High)

1. Place the tenderloins over the
bottom and sides of a large
bowl. Cover and cook for 6½
minutes, rearranging halfway
through cooking. Set aside,
covered.

2. Place the onion in a medium
bowl, cover and cook for 3
minutes. Stir in the butter until
melted. Stir in the cherries,
marjoram and a little salt, cover
and cook for 3 minutes.

3. Make up the meat juices to 1¼
cups with the stock, then stir
into the onion and cherries with
the cornstarch. Cook,
uncovered, for 5 minutes,
stirring occasionally.

4. Arrange the lamb in a shallow
serving dish and pour over the
sauce. Cook, uncovered, for 3
minutes. Serve with piped
mashed potatoes.

Clockwise: Lamb with mozzarella
cheese; Sweet-and-sour lamb; Lamb
with cherries; Lamb chops with spicy
sauce

Lamb Chops with Spicy Sauce

Serves 4
1 onion, peeled and sliced
¼ cup butter
4 sirloin lamb chops
1 tablespoon dark brown sugar
*1 teaspoon Worcestershire
     sauce*
1 teaspoon soy sauce
*1 garlic clove, peeled and
     crushed*
4 tablespoons tomato paste
salt
freshly ground black pepper

Preparation time: about 10 minutes
Cooking time: about 11½ minutes
Microwave setting: Full power (High)

1. Place the sliced onion and butter in a small bowl. Cover and cook for 3½ minutes or until translucent.

2. Place the chops in a shallow casserole. Cover with a piece of paper towel and cook for 5 minutes. Check if cooked to taste. Cook for 1 more minute if necessary.

3. Pour off the fat collected in the casserole.

4. While the chops are cooking, mix the onion and butter with the sugar, Worcestershire sauce, soy sauce, garlic, tomato paste, salt and pepper.

5. Spoon the sauce over the chops in the casserole, cover and cook for a further 3 minutes.

6. Serve with boiled rice and corn.

Crown Roast of Lamb

Serves 4

1 onion, peeled and finely chopped
¼ cup butter, cut into pieces
1 garlic clove, peeled and crushed
meat trimmings (from preparing crown roast), finely chopped
2 cups fresh white bread crumbs
¼ teaspoon dried marjoram
¼ teaspoon dried basil
¼ teaspoon dried parsley flakes
¼ teaspoon celery salt
freshly ground black pepper
1 egg, lightly beaten
1 crown roast of lamb, made from 2 rib roasts with 6 chops each, prepared weight 2¼ pounds
12 candied cherries, to garnish

Preparation time: about 10 minutes
Cooking time: about 29 minutes, plus standing
Microwave setting: Full power (High)

1. Place the onion, butter, garlic and meat trimmings in a medium bowl. Cover and cook for 4 minutes.

2. Stir in the bread crumbs, marjoram, basil, parsley, celery salt, and pepper to taste. Bind with the egg.

3. Stuff the center of the roast and stand on a trivet or up-turned saucer. Cook, uncovered, for 25 minutes, turning around halfway through cooking.

4. Wrap tightly in foil and stand for 20–25 minutes.

5. Place a cherry on top of each bone to garnish. Serve with mashed potatoes and green beans.

Cook's Tip

To prepare the crown roast, bend each rib roast – also called racks – into a semi-circle, fat inward, cutting between, but not dividing chops, if necessary. Sew ends together to form a circle. Most butchers will prepare if ordered in advance.

Lamb in Cream and Cider

Serves 4

8 lamb loin chops, total weight 2 pounds
1 onion, peeled and chopped
½ green bell pepper, cored, seeded and chopped
2⅔ cups sliced mushrooms
1 teaspoon dried rosemary
2 tablespoons butter, cut into pieces
about ⅓ cup hot chicken stock
¼ cup all-purpose flour
1 cup apple cider
salt
freshly ground black pepper
4 tablespoons heavy cream
chopped parsley, to garnish

Preparation time: about 20 minutes
Cooking time: about 17½ minutes
Microwave setting: Full power (High)

1. Place the chops around the bottom and sides of a large bowl, cover and cook for 6½ minutes, rearranging them halfway through. Set them aside, covered.

2. Place the onion and green bell pepper in a large bowl, cover and cook for 4 minutes. Stir in the mushrooms, rosemary and butter. Cover and cook for 3 minutes.

3. Make up the meat juices to ⅓ cup with the stock, then stir in with the flour, cider, and salt and pepper to taste. Add the chops. Cover and cook for 4 minutes, stirring halfway through.

4. Skim if necessary, then stir in the cream and reheat for 1 minute if necessary. Sprinkle with chopped fresh parsley, to garnish.

Crown roast of lamb; Lamb in cream and cider

Lamb Curry

Serves 4

1 onion, peeled and chopped
1 garlic clove, peeled and
    crushed
1 tablespoon ground coriander
1 teaspoon turmeric
½ teaspoon ground cumin
¼ teaspoon chili powder
¼ teaspoon ground ginger
¼ teaspoon grated nutmeg
1 tablespoon all-purpose flour
1 tablespoon tomato paste
1 teaspoon lemon juice
1 tablespoon shredded coconut
¼ teaspoon meat extract
2 tablespoons golden raisins
2 cups chicken stock
2 teaspoons curry paste
5 cups finely chopped cooked
    lamb
salt

Preparation time: about 15 minutes
Cooking time: 14 minutes
Microwave setting: Full power (High)

1. Place the onion, garlic, coriander, turmeric, cumin, chili powder, ginger and nutmeg in a large bowl. Cover and cook for 4 minutes.

2. Stir in the flour, tomato paste, lemon juice, coconut, meat extract, golden raisins, stock, curry paste and lamb. Season. Cover and cook for 10 minutes, stirring twice.

3. Serve with rice, sliced tomatoes and mango chutney.

Moussaka

Serves 4

1 large eggplant, cut into ¼-inch
    slices
salt
2 tablespoons butter
2 onions, peeled and finely
    sliced
2 garlic cloves, peeled and
    crushed
1 pound lean ground lamb
3 tablespoons tomato paste
1 teaspoon Italian seasoning
¼ cup all-purpose flour
⅔ cup hot beef stock
freshly ground black pepper
Sauce:
2 tablespoons butter
¼ cup all-purpose flour
1¼ cups milk
½ cup grated Cheddar cheese
1 teaspoon dry mustard
1 egg, beaten

Preparation·time: about 20 minutes, plus standing
Cooking time: about 29 minutes
Microwave setting: Full power (High)

1. Place the eggplant slices in a colander and sprinkle with salt. Leave for 30 minutes, rinse and drain.

2. Place the eggplant slices in a medium bowl, cover and cook for 3 minutes. Set aside.

3. Place the butter, onions and garlic in a large bowl. Cover and cook for 3 minutes. Stir in the lamb, cover and cook for 4 minutes. Stir in the remaining ingredients. Cover. Cook for 12 minutes. Set aside.

4. To make the sauce, place the butter in a 2½-cup measuring cup. Cook for 45 seconds. Blend in the flour and milk. Cook for 2½ minutes, stirring twice. Stir in the cheese, mustard and egg.

5. Make alternate layers of lamb and eggplant in a large shallow casserole. Pour over the sauce and cook for 5 minutes.

Lamb curry; Moussaka

Stuffed Leg of Lamb

Serves 4–6
1 small onion, peeled and finely
chopped
2 tablespoons butter
1½ cups fresh white bread
crumbs
1 tablespoon dried mint or 2
tablespoons chopped fresh
mint
salt
freshly ground black pepper
1 egg, beaten
2 pounds boned leg of lamb

Preparation time: about 15
minutes
Cooking time: about 18
minutes, plus standing
Microwave setting: Full power
(High)

1. Place the onion and butter in
a large bowl. Cover and cook
for 2 minutes.

2. Stir in the bread crumbs,
mint, salt and pepper. Add the
egg and mix well.

3. Lay the boned leg of lamb out
flat. Spread the stuffing over the
meat, roll up and secure.

4. Wrap in plastic wrap and
place on an up-turned saucer in
a large dish. Cook for 16
minutes.

5. Remove plastic wrap and
wrap the meat in foil, then leave
for 15 minutes before carving.

Stuffed Breast of Lamb

Serves 3–4
1 onion, peeled and chopped
2 tablespoons butter
2 cups fresh white bread crumbs
1 teaspoon Italian seasoning
1 teaspoon dried rosemary
grated rind of 1 orange
1 tablespoon orange juice
salt
freshly ground pepper
1 pound boned breast of lamb

Preparation time: about 20
minutes
Cooking time: about 11
minutes, plus standing and
broiling
Microwave setting: Full power
(High)

1. Place the onion and butter in
a medium bowl, cover and cook
for 3 minutes. Stir in the bread
crumbs, herbs, orange rind and
juice, and salt and pepper to
taste.

2. Spread the stuffing over the
breast, roll up and secure with
string. Stand in a shallow dish
and cook, uncovered, for 8
minutes, turning over halfway
through cooking.

3. Wrap in foil and stand for 10
minutes before serving, with
new potatoes and peas. For a
crispy finish, brown under a
preheated conventional broiler.

Stuffed leg of lamb;
Stuffed breast of lamb

MENU PLANNER

The most successful dinner parties are those that are well planned. Impressive meals do not mean spending time in a hot kitchen while your guests sit waiting expectantly.

The menu suggestion illustrated here is ideal for a formal dinner party. Make a rich, creamy Liver Pâté (page 40) the day before and chill it overnight.

Prepare the lamb in advance – order the guard from your butcher or, if you have to prepare it yourself, then buy two rib roasts – also called racks – with six chops each. Trim the

Vichy Carrots;
Guard of honor; Corn;
Cold strawberry soufflé; Liver pâté

bone ends, then place the racks of ribs together with the fat on the outside and interlock the bones. Sew or tie the guard together. Do this well ahead.

Make a Cold Strawberry Soufflé (page 172) the evening before or early on the day and set it to chill. Prepare the carrots for Vichy Carrots in advance.

Decorate the soufflé a couple of hours before the meal. Cook the lamb just before you serve the appetizer, then leave it to stand.

While the appetizer is served cook the Vichy Carrots. Next cook the corn (see page 141) – this can be done as you take the lamb to the table and serve the carrots.

Guard of Honor

Serves 4
2 tablespoons butter
1 small onion, peeled and
  chopped
$\frac{1}{4}$ teaspoon chopped fresh
  marjoram
$\frac{1}{4}$ teaspoon chopped fresh
  rosemary
$\frac{1}{4}$ teaspoon chopped fresh sage
1 tablespoon chopped fresh
  parsley
$1\frac{1}{2}$ cups fresh white bread
  crumbs
salt
freshly ground black pepper
1 egg, beaten
1 guard of honor, prepared
  weight $1\frac{1}{2}$ pounds, each rack
  comprising 6 chops

Preparation time: about 20 minutes
Cooking time: about 25 minutes, plus standing
Microwave setting: Full power (High)

1. Place the butter, onion and herbs in a small bowl. Cover and cook for 3 minutes. Stir in the bread crumbs, and salt and pepper to taste. Bind with the egg.

2. Stuff the guard and place in a shallow dish. Cook for 22 minutes, turning around halfway through.

3. Wrap tightly in foil and stand for 15–20 minutes.

PORK

Pork, ham and bacon are all tender meats and they cook well in the microwave. Careful preparation is required for some cuts to ensure the best results, and it is essential that these meats are thoroughly cooked before they are served, so standing times should be rigidly observed and the middle of a large cut should be pierced to make sure that the center is cooked – this can be done from the underside.

Tender pork cooks very successfully in the microwave but those cuts with large quantities of fat on them, or portions which are marbled with fat, should be trimmed and prepared with care. Since unbrowned, soft, cooked fat is not attractive or palatable, the outside of chops or roasts benefit from being browned under a pre-heated broiler before serving.

Alternatively, in the case of chops, the fat can be carefully rolled on the surface of a very hot skillet to thoroughly brown it before the chops are arranged in a dish for microwave cooking.

Boneless cuts

As with lamb, those cuts which are boned and neatly tied into shapes cook better than meat on the bone. A special microwave-safe thermometer is useful for making sure that the middle of the meat is cooked. Alternatively, remember that you can combine microwave cooking with a final short period of traditional roasting.

Stuffing

If a large piece of meat is to be stuffed, it is important to weigh it when it is ready for cooking. The cooking time should be calculated with the weight after stuffing.

Seasoning

As with other meats, pork meat should not be seasoned before cooking; however the crackling should be rubbed with salt as this produces a crisp result.

Crackling

Pork crackling is very good when cooked in the microwave and combined with conventional methods for browning – the result is particularly crunchy. The rind should be well scored before cooking and rubbed with salt, avoiding seasoning the meat. At the end of the cooking time the crackling should be well basted with the juices and browned under a conventional broiler.

Small cuts

Follow the directions on pages 80 and 81 for the most tender results.

Pork chops should be trimmed of excess fat before cooking, and they can be cooked with vegetables and liquid to make a delicious casserole. If the chops are cooked on their own, they should be covered with paper towels to prevent spattering the microwave with fat during cooking, and they should be turned and rearranged in the dish halfway through the cooking time.

Fatty cuts

The blade end of pork is a fatty meat from the front of the loin, behind the Boston shoulder and above the belly. Because it is the fattiest, it is very tender meat. The blade roast can be cut into blade chops or country-style ribs.

Another fatty cut is the belly. After the spareribs are removed, the remaining layers of rind, fat and meat are used to make bacon and salt pork.

Spareribs can be cooked with liquid before they are browned under the broiler, or they can be trimmed well before cooking and coated in a rich barbecue sauce to be served unbrowned.

The picnic shoulder, near the front of the belly section, is another fatty cut. The picnic shoulder roast and arm roast both come from this cut. Ground pork is also obtained from the meat in this section of the pig.

Arranging pork chops

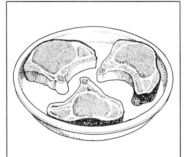

Before cooking, the chops should be trimmed of excess fat. The thin edge of fat which remains is quickly browned on the surface of a hot conventional skillet. The thickest parts of the chops should be placed toward the outside of the dish. Halfway through cooking, turn and rearrange the chops.

Casseroled chops

Pork chops make excellent casseroles. First the chopped onion is cooked with a little oil, then the chops are arranged in the dish and part-cooked. They are turned and, above, the remaining ingredients are added and boiling stock or heated wine is poured in before the dish is covered for the last part of the cooking time.

GUIDE TO COOKING PORK

Type of meat	Cooking time in minutes on Medium per 1 pound or for quantity given	Cooking time in minutes on Full power per 1 pound or for quantity given	Method
Pork boneless loin roast	14–16	10–13	Roll into a neat shape before cooking. Allow to stand for 20 minutes, wrapped in foil, before carving.
tenderloin	—	7	Preheat the browning dish according to the maufacturer's directions. Add the tenderloin and cook for the recommended time, turning over halfway through the cooking time.
chops, rib or loin,	2 14–18 3 19–24 4 26–32 6 33–37	—	Preheat the browning dish according to the manufacturer's directions. Add the chops and cook for the recommended time, turning over halfway through the cooking time.
Ham butt end	11–12	—	Place in a large covered dish with 4–6 tablespoons water. Turn at least twice during cooking. Allow to stand for 10–20 minutes, wrapped in foil, before carving.
shank end	13–15	10	Choose a good quality cut. Cover the pointed end with smooth foil to protect from overcooking. Score fat with a sharp knife and sprinkle liberally with salt to get a crisp crackling. Allow to stand for 20 minutes, wrapped in foil, before carving. Brown under a hot broiler if liked.
steaks (each)	11–12 —	— 14	Cook in a browning dish if liked (observing preheating times) or cover with plastic wrap. Turn halfway through the cooking time.
Bacon	4 slices — 1 pound —	$3\frac{1}{2}$–4 12–14	Place on a plate or roasting rack and cover with paper towels. Turn slices over halfway through cooking.
Sausages	2 — 4 —	$1\frac{1}{2}$–2 3–$3\frac{1}{2}$	Prick thoroughly and arrange on a rack or plate. Cover with paper towels and turn the sausages halfway through the cooking time.

GUIDE TO DEFROSTING PORK

Cut	Defrosting time per 1 pound in minutes on Defrost	Method
roasts	$8\frac{1}{2}$	Turn over at least once during the defrosting time.
chops	5	Turn over and rearrange at least once during the defrosting time.

Cured meat

Salting and smoking are two of the most traditional methods of preserving pork. These types of pork are available in many cuts, from small chops to whole hams, which are the pig's hind leg.

Smoked meat will either be labeled "fully cooked" or "cook before eating." If the meat requires cooking, use a microwave-safe meat thermometer to make certain the internal temperature reaches 160°F.

Most of the country-style hams not only need cooking but also require lengthy soaking (up to 36 hours) before cooking. Country-style hams are usually named after the area they are cured in. One of the most popular and delicious hams is Smithfield ham, from Smithfield, Virginia.

Bacon

Lay bacon slices on a microwave roasting rack or on a large plate lined with paper towels and cover them with a piece of

Bacon slices are laid on a microwave roasting rack or on a double thickness of paper towel. They are covered with a piece of paper towel to prevent spattering during cooking.

paper towel before cooking.

The slices can also be rolled and secured with wooden toothpicks before cooking. Chopped bacon can be cooked until quite dry and used as a crunchy garnish (see page 14).

Cooking sausages

Sausages can be cooked in the microwave but the result is unbrowned and not crisp. A browning dish can be used to brown the skins, giving a more attractive appearance. Skinless sausages can be cooked and cut into chunks for adding to casseroles (for example with chicken or to make a mock cassoulet) or for slicing and adding to heated baked beans for a quick snack. Cold sliced sausages also make good sandwiches with crisp lettuce.

The microwave is good for cooking hot dogs and similar smoked and unsmoked European sausages (prick the skins first).

The microwave is a speedy and convenient way of cooking smoked European sausages, including those like the French *andouilletes*, which need to be boiled before they are cooled and broiled. It is also excellent for preparing combination dishes in which the sausages are poached in stock or wine (again in the French manner) and not intended to be brown or crisp.

Roast Pork

Serves 6
1 tablespoon vegetable oil
3 pounds boneless ham, scored
½ teaspoon salt

Preparation time: about 4 minutes
Cooking time: about 30 minutes, plus standing and broiling
Microwave setting: Full power (High)

1. Rub the oil into the fat on the meat, then rub in the salt. Place the meat in a shallow dish with the fat uppermost. Cover with a paper towel. Cook for 30 minutes. Remove the towel after 15 minutes.

2. Wrap the meat in foil, shiny side inward, and leave for 15–20 minutes before carving. If desired brown under a preheated conventional broiler.

3. Serve with potatoes, peas, carrots, applesauce and gravy.

Accompaniments for pork

Applesauce A traditional accompaniment for roast pork; see the recipe on page 166.
Cumberland sauce Mix the grated rind and juice of 1 orange, 4 tablespoons red-currant jelly and ⅔ cup dry red wine in a bowl. Cook on Full power for about 3 minutes, until the jelly has dissolved. Blend 2 teaspoons cornstarch or arrowroot with a little cold water and add to the sauce, then cook for a further 1–2 minutes, until boiling and thickened. Good with ham slices or pork chops.
Mustard cream Mix 2 tablespoons whole-grain mustard, 1 teaspoon grated orange rind and ½ teaspoon each chopped sage and chopped parsley into ⅔ cup sour cream or fromage frais. Good with smoked ham, chops or stirred into strips of pork cooked with mushrooms.

Pork Chops with Apple

Serves 4

2 teaspoons soy sauce
2 teaspoons Worcestershire sauce
¼ cup butter
2 tablespoons soft dark brown sugar
salt
freshly ground black pepper
4 pork chops, untrimmed
1 large eating apple, peeled, cored and cut into 4 slices

Preparation time: about 10 minutes
Cooking time: about 9 minutes, plus standing
Microwave setting: Full power (High)

1. Place the soy sauce, Worcestershire sauce, butter, sugar, salt and pepper in a small measuring cup. Cook for 1 minute. Stir the sauce.

2. Brush both sides of the chops and apple slices with the sauce.

3. Arrange the pork chops in a shallow casserole. Cover and cook for 4 minutes. Turn the chops over and turn the casserole around.

4. Brush the chops with any remaining sauce and place a slice of apple on each one. Cover and cook for 4 minutes.

5. Leave to stand, covered, for 3 minutes.

Pork Casserole

Serves 4

1 pound pork tenderloin, cut into 1-inch cubes
1 onion, peeled and chopped
2 carrots, peeled and thinly sliced
1 red bell pepper, cored, seeded and chopped
1 garlic clove, peeled and crushed
¼ teaspoon ground mace
¼ teaspoon dried thyme
¼ teaspoon rubbed sage
¼ teaspoon dried parsley flakes
2 tablespoons tomato paste
2 tablespoons butter, cut up
¼ cup all-purpose flour
1¼ cups chicken stock
1 × 7-ounce can whole kernel corn, drained
salt
freshly ground black pepper

Preparation time: about 10 minutes
Cooking time: about 16–18 minutes
Microwave setting: Full power (High)

1. Place the pork in a shallow dish, cover and cook for 4–6 minutes, stirring halfway through cooking. Set aside, covered.

2. Place the onion, carrots, red bell pepper, garlic, mace, thyme sage, parsley and tomato paste in a medium bowl. Cover and cook for 8 minutes, stirring halfway through cooking.

3. Stir in the butter until melted. Stir in the flour. Make up the

Pork Chops with Oregano and Tomato Sauce

meat juices to 1¼ cups with stock, then stir in with the corn, pork and salt and pepper. Cook, uncovered, for 4 minutes, stirring every minute.

4. Serve with mashed potatoes and snow peas.

Serves 4

4 pork loin rib chops, total weight 1½ pounds
1 onion, peeled and finely chopped
1 teaspoon dried oregano
2 tablespoons butter, cut into pieces
¼ cup cornstarch
1 × 16-ounce can chopped tomatoes, with juice
1 tablespoon tomato paste
1 tablespoon chopped fresh parsley
1 cup less 2 tablespoons, hot chicken stock
salt
freshly ground black pepper

Preparation time: about 7 minutes
Cooking time: about 17–19 minutes
Microwave setting: Full power (High)

1. Place the chops around a medium bowl, cover and cook for 7 minutes, rearranging halfway through cooking. Set aside, covered.

2. Place the onion and oregano in a large bowl, cover and cook for 4 minutes, stirring halfway through.

3. Stir in the butter until melted. Stir in the cornstarch, undrained tomatoes, tomato paste, parsley, stock, and salt and pepper to

taste. Cover and cook for 3–5 minutes, stirring halfway through cooking.

4. Add drained chops. Cook, uncovered, for 3 minutes.

From left to right: Pork casserole; Pork chops with apple; Pork chops with oregano and tomato sauce

Glazed Ham

Serves 6–8
3 pounds unsmoked boneless ham
2 tablespoons of marmalade or jelly

Preparation time: about 5 minutes
Cooking time: about $27\frac{1}{2}$ minutes, plus standing and broiling
Microwave setting: Full power (High)

1. Place the ham in a roasting bag and secure with a non-metallic tie. Prick the bag and place the ham in a shallow dish.

Cook for $13\frac{1}{2}$ minutes. Turn the ham over and cook for a further $13\frac{1}{2}$ minutes.

2. Remove the ham from the bag and wrap tightly in foil. Leave to stand for 15 minutes.

3. Place the marmalade or jelly in a small bowl and heat for 30 seconds.

4. Place the ham in a broiler pan and spread the marmalade over the top of the meat. Cook under a preheated conventional broiler until bubbling.

Garlic Bacon Sticks

Makes 8
1 garlic clove
8 bacon slices, stretched
8 thin bread sticks
$\frac{1}{4}$ cup finely grated Cheddar cheese

Preparation time: about 10 minutes
Cooking time: about $5\frac{1}{2}$ minutes
Microwave setting: Full power (High)

1. Rub the garlic over each bacon slice.

2. Twist a slice of bacon around the top half of each bread stick. Place the sticks on a piece of paper towel on a plate. Cook, uncovered, for $5\frac{1}{2}$ minutes or until the bacon is cooked.

3. Twirl the hot bacon in the cheese to coat on all sides.

4. Serve hot or cold with drinks.

Glazed ham; Garlic bacon sticks

Pork with Orange and Cranberries

Serves 4
4 pork tenderloins, total weight
   $1\frac{1}{2}$ pounds
grated rind of 1 orange
$\frac{1}{2}$ cup orange juice
2 tablespoons superfine sugar
$2\frac{1}{4}$ cups fresh cranberries
4 orange slices, to garnish

Preparation time: about 10
minutes
Cooking time: about 17
minutes
Microwave setting: Full power
(High) and Defrost

1. Place the tenderloins in a
shallow dish, cover and cook on
Full power for 6 minutes,
rearranging them halfway
through cooking. Set aside,
covered.

2. Place the orange rind and
juice, sugar and cranberries in a
medium bowl. Cover and cook
on Full power for $2\frac{1}{2}$ minutes.
Stir, re-cover and cook for $5\frac{1}{2}$
minutes on Defrost.

3. Drain the tenderloins and
spoon the cranberry mixture
over them. Cook, uncovered,
for 3 minutes on Full power.

4. Cut into slices and garnish
with orange.

Pork Tenderloins in Wine Sauce

Serves 4
$1\frac{1}{2}$ pounds pork tenderloins, cut
   into 4 pieces
1 onion, peeled and chopped
$1\frac{1}{3}$ cups sliced button
   mushrooms
1 celery stalk, sliced
$\frac{1}{4}$ teaspoon dried parsley flakes
$\frac{1}{4}$ teaspoon rubbed sage
$\frac{1}{4}$ teaspoon dried tarragon
2 tablespoons butter, diced
$\frac{1}{4}$ cup all-purpose flour
about $\frac{2}{3}$ cup hot chicken stock
$\frac{2}{3}$ cup rosé wine
salt
freshly ground black pepper
fried apple rings, to garnish

Preparation time: about 10
minutes
Cooking time: about $16\frac{1}{2}$–$19\frac{1}{2}$
minutes
Microwave setting: Full power
(High)

1. Place the pork tenderloins in
a shallow dish, cover and cook
for 6–9 minutes, turning over
and rearranging halfway
through cooking. Set aside,
covered.

2. Place the onion, mushrooms,
celery, parsley, sage and
tarragon in a medium bowl.
Cover and cook for $5\frac{1}{2}$ minutes.

3. Stir in the butter until melted.
Stir in the flour. Make up the
meat juices to $\frac{2}{3}$ cup with stock,
then stir in with the wine and
salt and pepper. Cook, covered,
for 2 minutes, stirring once.

4. Add the tenderloins and turn
to coat with the sauce. Cook,
covered, for 3 minutes.

5. Garnish with the apple rings.
Serve with new potatoes and
fried zucchini.

Pork with orange and cranberries;
Pork tenderloins in wine sauce

Ham Slices with Pineapple

Serves 4

*4 ham center slices, total weight
    2 pounds
4 slices of canned pineapple,
    drained and cut in half
parsley sprig, to garnish*

Preparation time: about 5
minutes
Cooking time: about 13
minutes, plus standing
Microwave setting: Full power
(High)

1. Arrange the ham slices over
the bottom and sides of a large
bowl. Cover and cook for 10
minutes, rearranging halfway
through cooking.

2. Pour off the juice and arrange
the ham in a serving dish.
Arrange the pineapple halves
over the ham. Cook, uncovered,
for 3 minutes.

3. Cover the dish with foil and
stand for 4 minutes before
serving. Garnish with parsley
sprig and serve with boiled
potatoes.

Bacon and Vegetable Casserole

Serves 3–4

*½ green bell pepper, cored,
    seeded and thinly sliced
2¼ cups peeled and thinly sliced
    onions
1⅔ cups peeled and diced
    potatoes
1 celery stalk, chopped
¾ cup peeled and thinly sliced
    carrots
½ 10-ounce package frozen
    cauliflower florets
12 bacon slices, stretched, rolled
    and secured with wooden
    toothpicks
¼ cup all-purpose flour
2 cups hot chicken stock
1 teaspoon Italian seasoning
salt
freshly ground black pepper*

Preparation time: about 15
minutes
Cooking time: about 20
minutes
Microwave setting: Full power
(High)

1. Place the green bell pepper,
onion, potato, celery, carrot and
cauliflower in a large bowl.
Cover and cook for 10 minutes,
stirring twice during cooking.

2. Place the bacon rolls on top
of the vegetables, cover and
cook for 15 minutes.

3. Remove the bacon and keep
warm. Stir in the flour, stock,
herbs, and salt and pepper to
taste. Cook, uncovered, for 3
minutes.

*Bacon and vegetable casserole;
Ham slices with pineapple*

Ham in Cider

4. Remove the toothpicks from the bacon. Stir the bacon into the vegetables. Cook, uncovered, for 2 minutes. Serve immediately as a complete supper dish.

Cook's Tip

Use red or yellow bell peppers in place of the green bell pepper, and rutabagas or turnips in place of the carrots.

Home-made chicken stock will give the casserole a richer flavor.

Ham in cider

Serves 4

1¼ pounds boneless unsmoked ham, cubed
1 onion, peeled and chopped
1 celery stalk, chopped
1 teaspoon dried marjoram
2 red eating apples, cored and sliced
2 tablespoons butter, cut into pieces
¼ cup cornstarch
⅔ cup hot chicken stock
1¼ cups apple cider
freshly ground black pepper

Preparation time: about 10 minutes
Cooking time: about 15 minutes
Microwave setting: Full power (High)

1. Place the ham in a shallow dish, cover and cook for 4 minutes, stirring halfway through cooking. Remove the ham with its juices and set aside, covered.

2. Add the onion, celery and marjoram to the dish, cover and cook for 3 minutes.

3. Stir in the apples, cover and cook for 2 minutes.

4. Stir in the butter until melted. Stir in the cornstarch, stock, cider and pepper to taste. Cook, uncovered, for 3 minutes, until thickened, stirring every minute.

5. Replace the ham and its juices and heat through for about 3 minutes.

6. Serve with boiled potatoes and broccoli.

Paprika Pork Chops

Serves 4
4 pork country-style sparerib
  chops, total weight 1½ pounds
½ green bell pepper, cored,
  seeded and sliced
½ red bell pepper, cored, seeded
  and sliced
1 celery stalk, chopped
¼ teaspoon Worcestershire sauce
2 tablespoons tomato paste
1 tablespoon paprika
¼ teaspoon dried oregano
¼ teaspoon dried basil
2 tablespoons butter, cut into
  pieces
¼ cup cornstarch
about 2 cups hot chicken stock
salt
freshly ground black pepper
2 tablespoons sour cream

Preparation time: about 10
minutes
Cooking time: about 16–19
minutes
Microwave setting: Full power
(High)

1. Place the chops in a shallow
dish, cover and cook for 6–9
minutes, turning over and
rearranging halfway through
cooking. Set aside, covered.

2. Place the peppers, celery,
Worcestershire sauce, tomato
paste, paprika, oregano and
basil in a medium bowl. Cover
and cook for 5 minutes, stirring
halfway through cooking.

3. Stir in the butter until melted.
Stir in the cornstarch. Make up
the meat juices to 2 cups with
stock, then stir in with salt and
pepper to taste. Cook,
uncovered for 2 minutes,
stirring after 1 minute.

4. Add the chops and cook,
uncovered, for 3 minutes. Stir in
the sour cream.

5. Serve with plain boiled rice
and corn.

Spareribs with Barbecue Sauce

Serves 4
1 tablespoon butter
1 garlic clove, peeled and
  crushed
1 onion, peeled and finely
  chopped
1 × 16-ounce can tomatoes,
  drained
1 tablespoon Italian seasoning
2 tablespoons Worcestershire
  sauce
1 tablespoon honey
1 tablespoon soy sauce
1 tablespoon dark brown sugar
salt
freshly ground black pepper
1½ pounds pork spareribs

Preparation time: about 5
minutes
Cooking time: about 28½
minutes
Microwave setting: Full power
(High)

1. Place the butter, garlic and
onion in a large shallow bowl.
Cover and cook for 3½ minutes.

2. Stir in the tomatoes, herbs,
Worcestershire sauce, honey,
soy sauce, sugar, salt and
pepper. Cover and cook for 5
minutes.

3. Add spareribs. Cover and
cook for 10 minutes.

4. Rearrange the spareribs and
baste with the sauce. Cook for a
further 10 minutes or to taste.
Cut into individual ribs to serve.

Pork Kabobs

Serves 4
Marinade:
3 tablespoons olive oil
⅔ cup water
2 tablespoons Worcestershire
  sauce
1 small onion, peeled and sliced
1 tablespoon wine vinegar
1 teaspoon Italian seasoning
1 tablespoon red currant jelly
salt
freshly ground black pepper
Kabobs:
1 pound pork tenderloin, cut
  into 1½-inch cubes
½ red bell pepper, cored, seeded
  and cut into 8 pieces
½ green bell pepper, cored,
  seeded and cut into 8 pieces
2 tomatoes, halved
Sauce:
2 tablespoons butter
¼ cup all-purpose flour
⅔ cup chicken stock
2 tablespoons tomato paste

Preparation time: about 15
minutes, plus marinating
Cooking time: about 13
minutes
Microwave setting: Full power
(High)

1. Mix the marinade ingredients
together, with salt and pepper
to taste, in a shallow dish. Add
the pork cubes and turn to coat.
Leave for 2 hours.

2. Place the bell peppers in a
medium bowl, cover and cook
for 2 minutes.

3. Drain the pork cubes,
reserving the marinade. Thread
the pork cubes and pepper
pieces alternately onto 4
wooden skewers. Place on a
plate and cover with paper
towels. Cook for 3 minutes.

4. Place half a tomato on each
skewer, cover again and cook
for 4 minutes. Set aside.

5. Place the butter in a bowl and
cook, uncovered, for 1 minute
or until melted. Stir in the flour.

Blend in the strained, reserved
marinade, hot chicken stock
and tomato paste. Cook for 3
minutes, stirring every minute.

6. Serve the sauce separately for
spooning over the kabobs.

Clockwise: Spareribs with barbecue
sauce; Pork kabobs; Cold curried pork;
Paprika pork chops

Cold Curried Pork

Serves 4
1 pound pork tenderloin, cubed
2 eating apples, cored and
diced
2 scallions, trimmed and
chopped
½ red bell pepper, cored, seeded
and chopped
½ small cucumber, peeled and
diced
1 carrot, peeled and grated
2 tablespoons golden raisins
2 tablespoons roasted peanuts

1 celery stalk, chopped
1 tablespoon mild curry powder
1 cup mayonnaise
salt
freshly ground black pepper
scallions, to garnish

Preparation time: about 20
minutes, plus cooling and
chilling
Cooking time: about 5–7
minutes
Microwave setting: Full power
(High)

1. Place the pork in a large
bowl, cover and cook for 5–7
minutes, stirring halfway
through cooking. Leave to
stand, covered, until cold. Drain.

2. Mix together the apples,
scallions, red bell pepper,
cucumber, carrot, golden
raisins, peanuts and celery.

3. Mix together the curry
powder, mayonnaise, and salt

and pepper to taste. Stir in the
pork and the fruit and vegetable
mixture. Chill. Garnish with
scallions.

Cook's Tip

The way in which meat is cut
before cooking affects the result
achieved in the microwave oven.
If cut across the grain into small
slices, rather than chopped into
chunks, the meat will be tender
and will cook more quickly.

Ham Pâté

Serves 4
⅔ *cup mushrooms*
1 onion, peeled and quartered
2½ cups roughly chopped lean
   cooked ham
1 garlic clove, peeled
¼ *teaspoon rubbed sage*
¼ *teaspoon dried parsley flakes*
¼ *teaspoon dried rosemary*
¼ *teaspoon dried marjoram*
freshly ground black pepper
2 eggs, lightly beaten
To garnish:
lettuce
tomato slices

Preparation time: about 6 minutes, plus cooling
Cooking time: about 7½ minutes
Microwave setting: Full power (High)

1. Process or finely grind the mushrooms, onion, ham, garlic, sage, parsley, rosemary, marjoram and pepper to taste. Bind the mixture with the eggs.

2. Line a 6½-inch diameter soufflé dish with plastic wrap and place a microwave-safe glass upside-down in the center. Spread the ham mixture evenly over the bottom.

3. Cover and cook for 7½ minutes, turning around halfway through cooking. Leave to cool before unmolding.

4. Garnish with lettuce and sliced tomatoes and serve with potato salad.

Hot Dogs Wrapped in Bacon

Makes 8
8 slices bacon
8 large hot dogs
parsley sprigs, to garnish

Preparation time: about 5 minutes
Cooking time: about 4 minutes
Microwave setting: Full power (High)

1. Wind the bacon around the hot dogs. Place in a circle on a plate. Cover with a paper towel and cook for 4 minutes.

2. Garnish with parsley and serve with potato salad.

Ham pâté; Hot dogs wrapped in bacon

MENU PLANNER

It is a mistake to leave all the cooking until the last minute when using the microwave to make a meal. The picture below illustrates a well-planned, microwave menu: Jellied Ham and Chicken (page 37) is cooked in advance to serve cold for the first course; this can be done the day before.

Prepare the Croquette Potatoes (page 142) and Applesauce (page 166) early on the day, then set them aside ready to reheat before serving.

Prepare the pork, trimming, stuffing and tying it in a neat roast. Have the broccoli ready to

cook and make the cheese sauce in advance (page 144), covering it with a piece of waxed paper to prevent a skin forming.

Prepare the ingredients for Baked Bananas (page 178) but do not peel the fruit.

Cook the pork and leave it to stand while the first course is served. Cook the broccoli while the appetizer is served. Heat the sauce and pour it over. Heat the potatoes and applesauce just before serving. They will take 3 minutes each or 4–6 minutes together by standing a suitable cup for the sauce in the middle of the dish of croquettes. Remove the sauce as soon as it is hot.

Prepare and cook the bananas just before they are to be served.

Clockwise: Jellied ham and chicken; Baked bananas; Stuffed loin of pork; Croquette potatoes; Applesauce; Broccoli with cheese sauce

Stuffed Pork

Serves 6
1 small onion, peeled and finely chopped
1 garlic clove, peeled and crushed
2 tablespoons butter
½ cup fresh white bread crumbs
grated rind of 1 lemon
¼ teaspoon dried rosemary
¼ teaspoon dried thyme
salt
freshly ground black pepper
2 pound boneless pork center rib roast, skin scored

Preparation time: about 20 minutes
Cooking time: about 14–17 minutes, plus standing and broiling
Microwave setting: Full power (High)

1. Place the onion, garlic and butter in a bowl. Cover and cook for 3 minutes. Stir in the bread crumbs, lemon rind, rosemary, thyme, and salt and pepper to taste.

2. Spread the stuffing over the pork, close up and secure with string. Place in a shallow dish, skin uppermost, and cook, uncovered, for 11–14 minutes, turning around halfway through cooking.

3. Wrap tightly in foil and stand for 10 minutes before carving. If desired, brown the skin under a preheated conventional broiler.

EGGS AND CHEESE

Quick to cook and easy to prepare, both eggs and cheese form the base for a wide variety of tasty supper dishes. Many of your favorite egg and cheese recipes can be cooked with great success in the microwave, as you will discover in this chapter. Do not, however, cook eggs in their shells.

Boths eggs and cheese cook very quickly by conventional methods, and in the microwave they can be prepared with even greater speed. Because they cook so quickly, great care has to be taken to ensure that they cook evenly and that they do not overcook. If you are cooking just one or two eggs, you will have to time them in seconds and check their cooking progress frequently otherwise they may become overcooked and leathery.

In the microwave, the yolk and white of the egg cook at different rates. Conventionally, the white tends to cook before the yolk but in the microwave the yolk cooks faster than the white. So for plain cooked eggs you may prefer to use conventional cooking methods to achieve a perfectly cooked egg with a firmly set white and runny yolk. However, do try scrambled eggs in the microwave as they are very smooth and creamy, and there aren't any pans to scour.

Before cooking, the yolks of eggs should be pierced to prevent them from bursting. Here a toothpick is used.

There are one or two tips that must be remembered for success when microwaving eggs. A thin membrane surrounds the yolk of an egg and this should always be pricked before the egg is cooked in the microwave (unless, of course, it is beaten). Use a wooden toothpick or meat skewer to prick the yolk, otherwise it will burst and spatter yolk everywhere during cooking.

The eggs are ready when they are very slightly undercooked – the residual heat which remains in the food is sufficient to complete the cooking process.

Plain cooked eggs

Whichever way eggs are cooked, they are not the easiest of ingredients to present as perfect. Individual tastes vary enormously, so it is difficult to advize peeople how best to cook eggs in the microwave.

The way in which microwave ovens cook food means that the eggs do not cook in quite the same way as normal. Usually, as the eggs simmer in, or over, the water, or as they bake in the oven, they are cooked from the white inward. So, if you like eggs with firm whites and soft yolks then you are unlikely to achieve this in the microwave. You must become accustomed to a different result.

If you are not too fussy about small areas of soft egg white, then microwaved eggs are fine. They are easy to prepare when you are in a hurry.

A muffin dish especially designed for the microwave

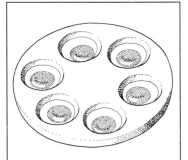

A special microwave muffin dish is ideal for cooking several eggs at once. Microwave-safe plastic wrap can be used as a cover enabling you to see just when the eggs are ready.

oven is the best container to use, otherwise the eggs can be cooked in individual ramekin dishes or saucers. Crack the eggs into the containers and prick the yolk of each one with a toothpick. Top each egg with a small knob of butter and cover with microwave-safe plastic wrap, then cook for the times given below:

2 eggs—1 to $1\frac{1}{4}$ minutes
3 eggs—$1\frac{1}{2}$ to $1\frac{3}{4}$ minutes
4 eggs—$1\frac{3}{4}$ to 2 minutes

Scrambled eggs

Opinion seems to be very divided about whether scrambled eggs cooked in the microwave are successful or not. Cooking scrambled eggs on the top of the stove means standing over the pan every second if you want a creamy result. However, you cannot go away and leave the eggs to cook in the microwave oven either

because they do need regular beating, but you can actually spend time buttering the toast or making coffee during the 2 minute intervals when you are not beating the eggs. So don't let anyone put you off by saying it's more work cooking eggs in the microwave; it's not, but you've got to get used to the frequent beating.

Another plus to microwave scrambled eggs is found when it comes to doing the dishes – washing a bowl in which the eggs were cooked is far easier than cleaning a dirty skillet.

Another advantage is that as the eggs are cooking you can stop the process if necessary. For example, you can leave the eggs at the stage when they just need another half a minute or so, make and butter your toast, and still go back to finish cooking them without having a ruined breakfast or supper. Obviously, this would not be the case if the eggs were virtually cooked, but at the half-set stage they can be left.

Timing scrambled eggs

The timing is fairly crucial and 30 seconds can mean rubbery eggs, so until you know your own particular oven, keep an eye on the eggs to see how they are setting. Once you have cooked your usual two or four eggs you will become used to the time it takes and know how careless you can be with them. Follow the instructions and times, right, keeping a close eye on the eggs until you know *exactly* how long it takes to scramble eggs in your oven.

Preparing scrambled eggs

1. Beat the eggs thoroughly and add a generous knob of butter or margarine. The eggs should be seasoned at this stage.

2. The eggs should be beaten as soon as they have a set rim around the inside of the bowl.

3. As the eggs set around the side of the bowl, they should be beaten again. Here the scrambled eggs are half set.

4. The eggs are ready when they are still very slightly runny. By the time the eggs shown above are beaten and served they will be perfectly creamy. If the eggs are cooked for a longer period, until they are firmly set, by the time they are beaten or stirred and served, they will have started to separate out slightly.

Cooking instructions

2 eggs Beat the eggs thoroughly with 1 tablespoon milk and seasoning to taste. Add about 1 tablespoon (a good knob) of butter or margarine and cook on Full power for 1 minute. Beat thoroughly, then cook for another minute and beat again. Cook for a final 30 seconds and beat before serving.

4 eggs Beat the eggs thoroughly with 2 tablespoons milk, seasoning to taste and 2 tablespoons butter or margarine. Cook on Full power for 2 minutes, then beat the eggs thoroughly. Cook for a further 1 minute and beat again; cook for a final 1 minute, then beat before serving.

6 eggs Beat the eggs thoroughly with 3 tablespoons milk and seasoning to taste. Add 1 large knob of butter or margarine (don't scrimp, because the butter or margarine give the eggs a good flavor) and cook on Full power for 2 minutes. Beat the eggs thoroughly, cook for a further 2 minutes and beat again. Cook for a final 2 to 2½ minutes, then beat the eggs until smooth and serve.

Variations

Creamy eggs Scrambled eggs are delicious made with light or heavy cream instead of milk. Cook them as in the directions, using cream in place of the suggested quantities of milk.

Scrambled eggs with cheese Allow ½ cup finely grated cheese to every 2 eggs. Add the cheese to the eggs when they are half set and stir in a pinch of mustard dry if you like. Continue cooking until the eggs are set, then serve on toast or use to fill a baked potato. The addition of cheese makes the eggs more substantial.

Scrambled eggs with herbs A pinch of thyme, lots of chopped parsley and chives go very well with scrambled eggs. This is particularly tasty if you are serving the eggs with broiled sausages.

Eggs with shrimp For a very special light dish, add 4 ounces shelled and deveined, cooked shrimp to every 2 eggs when they are half set. Serve in small bowls with hot French bread. This also makes a good appetizer.

Smoked salmon special A good one for a very special breakfast treat (try serving this on Christmas morning with a bottle of champagne). Add 1–2 ounces chopped smoked salmon to every 2 eggs (depending on how many you are cooking; if it is only two then use the greater quantity). Stir the smoked salmon into the eggs when they are almost set – the salmon should be warmed through but not cooked. This recipe can also be served as an elegant appetizer, on small circles of buttered toast or with very thin whole-wheat bread and butter.

Bacon eggs Finely chop 2 bacon slices for every 2 eggs and cook them in the bowl for 2 minutes before adding the eggs. Add chopped scallions to the cooked eggs if you like.

Eggs with tomatoes Peel, seed and chop 2 ripe but firm tomatoes for every 2 eggs. Add these to the half-set eggs and continue cooking until the eggs are set. Stir the eggs rather than beating them, but do make sure you thoroughly break up the set bits otherwise they will become leathery.

Ham and eggs Add 2 ounces chopped cooked ham to every 2 eggs when almost set. Then continue cooking.

Cooking cheese

Cheese also cooks very quickly in the microwave, but it too can be overcooked very easily.

Combined with sauces, melted into a fondue or used in stuffings for tomatoes and other vegetables, the cheese will melt quickly and evenly if it is cut into small, even-sized pieces or grated. When cheese is used as a topping for other foods, then care must be taken and the main food should be cooked first so that the cheese can be melted in just a few seconds. If the top of the food to be sprinkled with cheese covers a large area, then it is often better to melt the cheese on a Medium setting instead of Full power. This ensures that the cheese will be evenly melted and not overcooked in some areas before other parts are melted – a problem which can occur when cooking it in a large shallow dish, for example, when making lasagne.

Fried Eggs

Serves 2
1⅓ tablespoons butter
2 eggs
freshly ground black pepper
*   (optional)*

Preparation time: about 2
minutes
Cooking time: about 1¾
minutes, plus standing
Microwave setting: Full power
(High)

1. Divide the butter between
two 5-inch diameter saucers or
dishes. Cook for 30 seconds or
until melted.

2. Break an egg into each saucer
and pierce the yolk with a
toothpick. Sprinkle with pepper,
if desired. Cover tightly with
plastic wrap.

3. Cook for 1¼ minutes, turning
around halfway through
cooking. Leave to stand,
covered, for 1 minute before
serving. If the egg is not cooked,
return to the microwave for 15
seconds.

Baked Eggs

Serves 4
1 tablespoon butter
2 small mushrooms, finely
*   chopped*
½ cup finely chopped lean
*   cooked ham*
4 teaspoons tomato paste
4 large eggs
salt
freshly ground black pepper
4 tablespoons heavy cream

Preparation time: about 5
minutes
Cooking time: about 4½
minutes
Microwave setting: Full power
(High)

1. Divide the butter and the
chopped mushrooms between
4 individual ramekins or dishes.
Cook for 1½ minutes.

2. Place the ham on the
mushrooms and 1 teaspoon of
the tomato paste on the ham in
each dish.

3. Break the eggs onto the ham
and pierce the yolks with a
toothpick. Season with salt and
pepper.

4. Pour 1 tablespoon cream
over each of the eggs. Cook for
1½ minutes.

5. Rearrange the dishes, so the
front ones are at the back, and
cook for a further 1½ minutes.
Serve the eggs at once.

Fried eggs; Baked eggs

Omelet

Serves 2
4 eggs
4 tablespoons milk
salt
freshly ground black pepper
1⅓ tablespoons butter
*1 tablespoon chopped fresh
    parsley, to garnish*

Preparation time: about 3
minutes
Cooking time: 3¾ minutes
Microwave setting: Full power
(High)

1. Beat together the eggs, milk
and salt and pepper to taste.

2. Place the butter in a 9-inch
round shallow casserole. Cook,
uncovered, for 30 seconds.

3. Tilt the casserole to be sure
the bottom is evenly coated with
melted butter, then pour in the
egg mixture. Cover and cook for
2 minutes.

4. Using a fork, draw the edges
of the egg to the center. Cover
and cook for a further 1¼
minutes. If not quite cooked,
stand for 1 minute before
serving.

5. Serve sprinkled with chopped
parsley.

Cook's tip

Chopped cooked ham could be
added at step 4 after the
cooking is completed.

Poached eggs

Serves 2
½ cup water
2 tablespoons distilled vinegar
2 eggs
hot buttered toast, to serve

Preparation time: about 2
minutes
Cooking time: about 3 minutes,
plus standing
Microwave setting: Full power
(High)

1. Divide the water and vinegar
equally between 2 ramekin
dishes. Cook, uncovered, for 2
minutes or until boiling.

2. Break the eggs into the water
and pierce the yolks with a
toothpick. Cook, uncovered, for
1 minute. Leave to stand for 1
minute.

3. Drain off the water and
vinegar, then serve on hot
buttered toast.

Boiled eggs

Eggs must **never** be cooked in
their shells in a microwave oven
because there is a build-up of
pressure within the egg which
causes the shell to "explode"
or burst. As a result, the oven
interior would have to be
cleaned, which is a nuisance.
More important, however, the
impact could cause damage to
the components of the oven.
Even piercing the shell does not
prevent an egg from exploding.

Omelet; Poached eggs

Eggs Benedict

Serves 4
4 slices of cooked ham
4 thick slices of buttered white
*   toast, cut to the size of the*
*   ham*
Poached eggs:
1 cup water
4 tablespoons distilled vinegar
4 eggs
Hollandaise sauce:
2 egg yolks
1 tablespoon lemon juice
½ cup butter, cut into 8 pieces
pinch of cayenne pepper
½ teaspoon dry mustard

Preparation time: about 10 minutes
Cooking time: about 4½ minutes
Microwave setting: Full power (High)

1. Place a piece of ham on each slice of toast. Keep warm.

2. Divide the water and vinegar equally between 4 ramekin dishes. Cook, uncovered, for 2 minutes or until boiling. Break an egg into each dish and pierce its yolk.

3. To make the sauce, prick the egg yolks and place with the lemon juice in a small bowl. Cook, uncovered, for 30 seconds. Beat hard until smooth.

4. Place the eggs for poaching into the microwave and cook for 2 minutes. Stand for 1 minute before draining.

5. Meanwhile, beat one piece of butter at a time into the sauce, until all 8 pieces are incorporated. Beat in the cayenne pepper and mustard.

6. Place the poached eggs on the ham and toast and top with a large spoonful of sauce. Serve at once.

Eggs Florentine

Serves 4
1 × 10-ounce package frozen
*   spinach, thawed and drained*
salt
freshly ground black pepper
¼ teaspoon grated nutmeg
4 eggs

Preparation time: about 4 minutes
Cooking time: about 3¾ minutes, plus standing
Microwave setting: Full power (High)

1. Divide the spinach between 4 ramekin dishes. Cook, uncovered, for 1½ minutes.

2. Sprinkle the spinach with a little salt, pepper and nutmeg. Break the eggs onto the spinach. Prick the yolks and cover dishes with plastic wrap. Arrange in a circle in the microwave.

3. Cook for 2¼ minutes, rearranging the dishes halfway through cooking. If the eggs are not quite cooked, allow to stand, covered, for 1 minute.

4. Serve with hot buttered toast.

Eggs Benedict; Eggs Florentine

Welsh Rabbit

Serves 4

*2 cups finely grated Cheddar
    cheese*
4 tablespoons milk
salt
freshly ground black pepper
1 teaspoon mustard
4 slices toast
parsley sprigs, to garnish

Preparation time: about 5
minutes
Cooking time: about 1½
minutes, plus broiling
Microwave setting: Full power
(High)

1. Place the cheese and milk in a
medium bowl and cook for 1
minute.

2. Stir in the salt, pepper and
mustard and cook for 30
seconds.

3. Spread the cheese mixture
over the toast.

4. If desired, place the Welsh
rabbit under a preheated
conventional broiler, to brown
the top. Garnish with the
parsley.

Cheese and Ham Bake

Serves 4

*4 cups fresh whole-wheat bread
    crumbs*
*½ cup finely chopped cooked
    ham*
pinch of dry mustard
1 teaspoon Italian seasoning
*1½ cups finely grated Cheddar
    cheese*
salt
freshly ground black pepper
3 eggs, lightly beaten
2½ cups milk
*1 tablespoon chopped fresh
    parsley, to garnish*

Preparation time: about 10
minutes
Cooking time: about 10–12
minutes, plus standing
Microwave setting: Full power
(High)

1. Mix together the bread
crumbs, ham, mustard, herbs,
cheese and salt and pepper to
taste. Lightly beat in the eggs
and milk. Pour into a 1¾-quart
soufflé dish. Allow to stand for
10 minutes.

2. Cook, uncovered, for 10–12
minutes, stirring halfway
through cooking.

3. Sprinkle with parsley and
serve with a green vegetable.

Welsh rabbit; Cheese and ham bake

Salami and Cheese Quiche

Serves 4
1 × 8-inch uncooked pastry shell
½ cup milk
3 eggs
3 ounces salami, finely diced
salt
freshly ground black pepper
*½ cup finely grated Cheddar
  cheese*
parsley sprig, to garnish

Preparation time: about 15
minutes
Cooking time: about 9 minutes,
plus broiling
Microwave setting: Full power
(High)

1. Prick the sides and bottom of
pastry shell with a fork. Cook
for 3½ minutes or until the pastry
looks dry. Set aside.

2. Place the milk, eggs, salami,
salt and pepper in a bowl.
Lightly beat together. Cook for 2
minutes, beating with a fork
every 30 seconds.

3. Pour the mixture into the
pastry shell and cook for 3
minutes, stirring gently after 1
and 2 minutes.

4. Sprinkle the cheese over the
egg and brown under a
preheated conventional broiler
for about 5 minutes. Serve
garnished with a sprig of
parsley.

*Salami and cheese quiche; Smoked
haddock with egg sauce*

Smoked Haddock with Egg Sauce

Serves 4
1¼ cups milk
1 bay leaf
1 onion slice
8 smoked haddock fillets
¼ cup butter
¼ cup all-purpose flour
salt
freshly ground black pepper
*2 hard-cooked eggs, finely
  chopped*
*2 tablespoons snipped fresh
  chives*

Preparation time: about 10
minutes, plus infusing
Cooking time: about 11
minutes
Microwave setting: Full power
(High)

1. Place the milk in a bowl with
the bay leaf and onion slice and
cook for 2 minutes. Leave for 15
minutes.

2. Place the haddock fillets in a
shallow dish and dot with 2
tablespoons of the butter. Cover
and cook for 2 minutes. Turn
the dish around and cook for a
further 2 minutes. Keep warm
while making the sauce.

3. Place the remaining butter in
a 2½-cup measuring cup. Cook
for 1 minute or until melted.
Blend in the flour.

4. Strain the hot milk, discarding
the bay leaf and onion, and stir
it into the flour mixture. Add salt
and pepper. Cook for 2
minutes, stirring every minute.

5. Stir in the chopped hard-
cooked eggs and chives.

6. Pour the sauce over the fish
and reheat for 2 minutes before
serving.

Scrambled eggs; Bacon, mushrooms and kidneys

MENU PLANNER

Breakfast time in most homes is not the time to experiment with the newest appliance, so it is worthwhile getting to know how to use your microwave for this meal.

Most of us tend to cook the same breakfast on weekdays so it is a good idea to note the microwave timing for the number of eggs, or slices of bacon which you cook daily.

If the members of the household appear at different times all making different demands, then put the microwave to full use for cooking individual breakfasts. Remember, you can cook a single portion of oatmeal with ease or Baked Eggs (page 128) can be served with hot buttered toast.

If unbuttered toast has long since cooled, then place it on a paper towel to heat for 30 seconds in the microwave. Also, croissants, buns or rolls can be heated in a few seconds to make a delicious breakfast.

Remember, too, that you can make a pot of coffee in the microwave, and use the microwave for heating up individual cups. It is also excellent for heating milk to serve with coffee or with breakfast cereals.

For a change from your daily breakfast, here's an easy to cook country-style breakfast. Iron-rich kidneys were once standard fare as part of farmhouse breakfasts.

Country-style Breakfast

Serves 2
Bacon, mushrooms and
*   kidneys:*
4 bacon slices
4 flat mushrooms
2 lambs' kidneys, membranes
*   and cores removed, halved*
Scrambled eggs:
4 large eggs
1 tablespoon milk
salt
freshly ground black pepper
1 tablespoon butter
parsley sprigs, to garnish
*   (optional)*

Preparation time: about 5 minutes
Cooking time: about $8\frac{1}{2}$ minutes
Microwave setting: Full power (High)

1. Place a piece of paper towel on a plate. Lay the bacon on one side, cover with another piece of paper and cook for 1 minute.

2. Uncover. Place the mushrooms in the center of the plate, cover and cook for $1\frac{1}{2}$ minutes, then put the kidneys around the outside of the plate. Re cover and cook for 2 minutes, turning the kidneys over and rearranging the mushrooms if necessary. Recover and cook for 1 minute.

3. While the kidneys are cooking, beat the eggs, milk, salt and pepper to taste in a bowl and add the butter.

4. Remove the paper towel from the kidneys and bacon, then cover with a warmed plate.

5. Cook the eggs for 3 minutes. Break up the mixture and beat gently once a minute.

6. Serve the scrambled eggs with the bacon, kidneys and mushrooms.

VEGETABLES

Vegetables are among the foods which cook with most success in the microwave. They can be prepared to perfection – no more soggy, overcooked cabbage or broken, watery potatoes. Whether cooking from frozen, serving them plain, or creating a colorful accompaniment, you'll find plenty of vegetable variety in the pages which follow.

Almost all vegetables cook well in the microwave, retaining maximum flavor and nutrients. The color of microwave-cooked vegetables is excellent and their texture is good and firm rather than soft or soggy. Both fresh and frozen vegetables can be cooked, whole or cut into evenly sized pieces as appropriate. Older root vegetables, such as carrots, do not improve with microwave cooking because their own lack of moisture can produce a rather tough, slightly dehydrated result.

Cooking liquid

Very little water or other liquid is necessary when cooking vegetables in the microwave. The moisture which is present in the vegetables produces a certain amount of steam in which the food cooks. Usually a few tablespoons of water are added to increase the moisture content.

If you do cook old, slightly tough, root vegetables in the microwave, then add extra water to help to tenderize them, and remember to increase the cooking time slightly.

Cutting vegetables

As with other ingredients which are to be cooked in the microwave, when preparing vegetables it is best to cut them as evenly as possible both in terms of size and shape.

Cut slices of the same thickness; prepare dice or chunks which are of similar size and sticks that are of roughly the same length and thickness.

Break a cauliflower into florets of similar size unless you plan to cook the vegetable whole. Trim off any very thick pieces of the stem end before cooking. Trim broccoli florets in the same way.

Before cooking, the vegetables which are not left whole should be cut into chunks, slices or sticks which are as even in shape and size as possible.

If vegetables are cooked whole in their skins, then it is important that the skins are pricked to prevent them from bursting during cooking; for example, potatoes, eggplants or tomatoes should be pricked with a fork before they are cooked if they are to be left whole.

Arranging and rearranging

The whole vegetables, such as baked potatoes, may be cooked in a container or straight on the turntable or floor of the microwave. Regardless of whether the individual vegetables are in a dish or not, they should be placed as far apart as possible for the quickest and most even results.

Vegetables which have stems that are tougher than their heads – broccoli, for example – should be arranged with the tougher stems toward the outside of the dish and the heads as close together as possible in the center. Short asparagus spears can be arranged in this way. Alternatively, long asparagus can be cooked in a roasting bag or large shallow dish, placing the tender tips very closely together and overlapping each other at one end, with the tougher stems which require extra cooking separated as far apart as possible at the other end.

Halfway through the cooking time whole vegetables should be turned over or around so that they cook evenly.

If the vegetables are cut in dice or chunks they should be stirred to rearrange them halfway through the cooking time.

Seasoning

Vegetables should not be seasoned with salt before cooking because this results in a dehydrated surface. This is caused by the fact that the liquid content of the vegetables is drawn out during cooking by the salt. Seasoning should be added along with a knob of butter or margarine after the vegetables are drained of any cooking liquid and before they are served.

Covering

It is important to cover the dish in which the vegetables are cooked so that the steam produced by the small amount of cooking liquid is kept within the container. It is this steam which tenderizes the vegetables.

Covered dishes – a casserole, bowl or mixing bowl topped with a plate – are ideal for cooking most vegetables.

Stirring vegetables

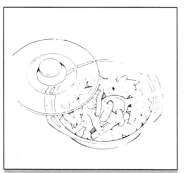

Small vegetables or those which are cut up should be stirred halfway through

cooking to rearrange the pieces and to ensure that they are all evenly cooked.

Roasting bags or boil-in bags are also useful, and frozen vegetables can be stored in these, ready to be transferred straight to the microwave for cooking. Large vegetables, like globe artichokes or a small whole cauliflower, cook very well in bags and they can be easily turned or rearranged during cooking.

Small amounts of small vegetables, such as peas or whole corn kernels, cook very well in a suitable measuring cup which can be covered with microwave-proof plastic wrap or a saucer.

Reheating vegetables

One of the great advantages of microwave cooking is that foods can be successfully reheated without spoiling their texture or making their taste inferior. This is a particularly useful facility when cooking the vegetables for a meal, especially when you are entertaining dinner guests. The vegetables can be prepared and part cooked in advance, then kept tightly covered right up until they are to be served, at which time the cooking can be completed quickly. The liquid should be drained off (it can be saved for use in stocks or sauces) and butter tossed into the vegetables.

If you use the facility often, then it may be worth investing in some practical cookware for the purpose. Divided dishes can be used to contain two or three different types of vegetable which can be reheated together. This is sensible if you often reheat portions to serve two or three but it is not practical for larger quantities.

Alternatively, special microwave plate stackers can also be used for two dishes. These are ideal when family members eat at different times.

Cooking potatoes

1. Before cooking potatoes, the skins should be thoroughly scrubbed and dried, then pricked all over to prevent them bursting.

2. The potatoes are arranged as far apart as possible on the turntable or on a plate. Here they are arranged on a piece of paper towel on the turntable; the paper prevents the turntable from being soiled by juices which escape from the potatoes as they cook. Halfway through cooking, the potatoes are turned over and their positions may be swapped if they are not cooking at quite the same rate.

Cooking broccoli and eggplant

Broccoli spears or cauliflower florets should be arranged with the tender heads toward the center of the dish, pushed closely together, and the stems around the outside. The individual pieces may need turning over halfway through cooking.

Before cooking, the skins should be pricked and the vegetables arranged as far apart as possible on a plate or on paper towels on the floor or turntable in the microwave. The cooked vegetables should be allowed to stand for several minutes before they are ready to be sliced or cut up. To obtain the flesh only (for a purée or to use in a dip), cut the eggplant in half and scoop or cut out the tender middle.

Blanching vegetables for the freezer

The chances are, if you're a keen gardener, pick-you-own fanatic, or simply someone who likes to enjoy fresh vegetables while they are low in price and high in quality, then you probably like to freeze vegetables for year-round eating.

A main advantage of having a microwave is that minutes after the vegetables are picked you can have them blanched and ready to freeze, without spending all day in the kitchen with a bubbling saucepan and a stop watch.

Prepare the vegetables as you would for normal cooking and place them in a covered dish, then add water as given in the chart on page 137. Cook for half the time given in the chart and stir, recover and cook for the remaining time, then stir again. Plunge the vegetables into iced water immediately to prevent further cooking. Drain and spread the vegetables out on paper towels to absorb excess moisture. Pack in freezer containers or boil-in bags, seal and label, then freeze.

Vegetables may be blanched in boil-in bags and then, still in their bags, plunged into iced water up to their necks to cool. This chills the vegetables and expels the air in the bag at the same time, automatically creating a vacuum pack ready for freezing. Seal and label in the usual way.

Cooking frozen vegetables

Most commercially packaged frozen vegetables give microwave cooking directions on the outside of the carton or package. It is best to follow the manufacturer's directions as precisely as possible.

However, if you have frozen your own vegetables you may find the times given on the chart a useful guide when it comes to cooking them.

When you pack vegetables for the freezer it is a good idea to pack them as flat as possible in a bag, with all air excluded, then seal them so that they fall apart easily into individual pieces when you transfer them to the cooking container. Alternatively, they can be frozen on a tray so they do not stick together, then packaged.

If you are cooking a block of frozen vegetables, break them apart as they cook.

Since most frozen vegetables are surrounded by a certain amount of ice, there is no need to add extra liquid. The only exception is whole or cut green beans which may need an extra spoonful or so of water added to the cooking container.

Plain cooked vegetables can be coated with a sauce, served with a gratin topping, lightly tossed in a flavored butter or complemented by the addition of chopped fresh herbs. The following ideas are intended to inspire you to turn some plain cooked vegetables into a tempting first course, or tasty supper dish. Some crusty French bread or mixed grain bread makes an ideal accompaniment to supper dishes, and crisp Melba toast complements a vegetable first course.

Buttered vegetables

Use either butter or margarine for all the following ideas.

Lemon-parsley butter Cream chopped fresh parsley and a little grated lemon rind into

Defrosting frozen spinach

Remove the spinach from its own package if possible and transfer it to a suitable dish. If the frozen spinach cannot be removed from the carton, then cook the whole package on Full power for 1 minute, or until the contents can be released and placed into another dish. Cover and cook on Full power for 2 minutes. Break a whole block of spinach into chunks or rearrange chunks of spinach. Continue cooking until all the spinach is separate and quite watery but still icy. For $\frac{1}{2}$-pound frozen block spinach allow approximately 3–4 minutes, for 1-pound frozen block spinach allow approximately 6–7 minutes. Drain the water from the spinach and use as required – it should still be icy.

softened butter or margarine. Add a dash of lemon juice and seasoning to taste. Serve with freshly cooked asparagus, button mushrooms, or globe artichokes to make a delicious first course. Offer crusty rolls or curly Melba toast as an accompaniment. Toss Jerusalem artichokes, green beans, new potatoes or diced celery root in the butter to make a delicious side dish.

Basil and garlic butter Cream chopped fresh basil, a crushed clove of garlic and seasoning into softened butter. For a delicious supper dish, use the butter to top cooked quartered tomatoes or button mushrooms and serve them on thick slices of hot buttered toast. Toss cooked cubed eggplant, sliced zucchini or cooked endive in the butter to make a full-flavored accompaniment for poultry, lamb or veal.

Almond and orange butter Beat a little grated orange rind and some chopped toasted almonds into softened butter with seasoning to taste. This butter is good with ears of corn for a first course or light lunch dish. Tossed into cooked carrots, pearl onions or cooked shredded spinach it flavors a delicious side dish to serve with pork or ham.

Parmesan-herb butter Beat some grated Parmesan cheese – preferably fresh – and chopped fresh parsley, tarragon or marjoram into softened butter with plenty of freshly ground black pepper. Serve this butter with large open mushrooms or halved tomatoes as a first course, or spoon the mushrooms or tomatoes onto toast as a light lunch. For a more substantial meal, serve the vegetables with plain cooked rice or pasta. Present a tempting side dish by tossing cooked cubed potatoes in the butter – it will enliven simple fish steaks, plain cooked mackerel or trout as well as poultry or meat.

Sauced vegetables

Cheese sauce Prepare a cheese sauce, following the recipe on page 163. Pour it over cooked cauliflower, broccoli, wedges of cabbage, endive or a dish of mixed vegetables.

Egg sauce Prepare an egg sauce following the recipe on page 163. Serve as a topping for asparagus, broccoli, green beans or zucchini and serve the vegetables in small portions as an appetizer or as a side dish.

Mushroom sauce Prepare a mushroom sauce following the directions on page 163. Stir cooked small new potatoes or diced large potatoes into the sauce to make a delicious side dish.

Tomato sauce Prepare a tomato sauce, following the recipe on page 165. Stir cooked zucchini, eggplant or cauliflower florets into the sauce and serve topped with chopped parsley and grated Parmesan cheese.

Simple serving suggestions

Buttered crumbs Toss whole-wheat bread crumbs in melted butter. Add seasoning and some chopped fresh parsley or other herbs. Heat on Full power for about $\frac{1}{2}$–1 minute, or longer depending on the quantity, then sprinkle over cooked cauliflower, carrots, Brussels sprouts, mushrooms or spinach.

Boiled egg Hard-cooked eggs make an excellent topping for vegetables. Cook the eggs conventionally, then immediately cool them in cold water. Separate the whites and yolks, then chop the whites and sieve the yolks. Top cooked asparagus, zucchini, or spinach with first the whites, then the yolks.

Simple serving suggestions

Toss cooked potatoes in Parmesan-herb butter to make a delicious side dish. Used cubed large potatoes, as here, or scrubbed, unpeeled new potatoes.

Top cooked broccoli with an egg sauce. Prepare the sauce before cooking the broccoli, cover and set aside. Heat the sauce on Full power for $\frac{1}{2}$–1 minute, then pour over broccoli and serve. Garnish with hard-cooked egg.

GUIDE TO COOKING FROZEN VEGETABLES

Vegetable	Quantity	Cooking time in minutes on Full power (High)
Asparagus	8 ounces	6–7
	1 pound	11
Beans, green	8 ounces	7
	1 pound	10
Bean, lima	8 ounces	8
	1 pound	10
Broccoli	8 ounces	6–8
	1 pound	8–10
Cabbage	8 ounces	6–7
	1 pound	10–11
Carrots	8 ounces	7
	1 pound	10
Cauliflower florets	8 ounces	5
	1 pound	8
Corn kernels	8 ounces	4
	1 pound	7–8
Corn-on-the-cob	1	4–5
	2	7–8
Diced mixed vegetables	8 ounces	5–6
	1 pound	7–9
Peas, shelled	8 ounces	4
	1 pound	8
Spinach, chopped or leaf	8 ounces	7–8
	1 pound	10–11
Root vegetables, mixed	8 ounces	7
	1 pound	10
Rutabagas	8 ounces	7
	1 pound	11
Turnips	8 ounces	8
	1 pound	12
Zucchini	8 ounces	4
	1 pound	7

GUIDE TO BLANCHING VEGETABLES

Vegetable	Quantity	Water (tablespoons)	Time in minutes on Full power (High)
Asparagus	1 pound	3	3–4
Beans	1 pound	6	5–6
Broccoli	1 pound	6	5–6
Brussels sprouts	1 pound	6	5–6
Cabbage, shredded	5 cups	3	4–4$\frac{1}{2}$
Carrots, sliced	3 cups	3	3–4
whole	1 pound	3	6–7
Cauliflower florets	4 cups	6	4$\frac{1}{2}$–5
Corn-on-the-cob	4	3	5–6
Leeks, sliced	4 cups	3	5–6
Onions, quartered	4 medium	6	4–4$\frac{1}{2}$
Parsnips, cubed	3 cups	3	3–4
Peas, shelled	3 cups	3	4–4$\frac{1}{2}$
	6 cups	3	6–7
Spinach	1 pound	—	3–3$\frac{1}{2}$
Turnips, cubed	4 cups	3	3–4
Zucchini, sliced	4 cups	3	3–3$\frac{1}{2}$

GUIDE TO COOKING FRESH VEGETABLES

Vegetable	Quantity	Water	Preparation	Cooking time in minutes on Full power (High)	Method
Artichokes, globe	1 2 4	½ cup ½ cup 1 cup	Discard the tough, outer leaves. Snip the tips off the remaining leaves and cut off the stems. Cover to cook.	5–6 7–8 14–15	To test for doneness, at the minimum time, pull a leaf from the whole artichoke. If it comes away freely, the artichoke is cooked. Drain upside down before serving.
Asparagus	1 pound	6 tablespoons	Place in a dish, arranging any thicker stems to the outside of the dish and tender tips to the center. Cover to cook.	12–14	Give the dish a half turn after 6 minutes cooking time.
Beans, all except thin French beans	1 pound	½ cup	Cover to cook.	14–16	Stir the beans twice during cooking. Test for doneness after the minimum time.
French beans	1pound	½ cup	Cover to cook.	5–7	
Beets	2 medium 5 medium	½ cup ½ cup	Cover to cook	12–16 22–25	Rearrange halfway through the cooking time. Allow to stand for 10 minutes before peeling.
Broccoli, spears	1 pound	½ cup	Place in a dish arranging the stalks to the outside and heads in the center. Cover to cook.	10–12	Rearrange after 6 minutes.
Brussels sprouts	1 pound	¼ cup	Trim away any damaged or coarse leaves and cut large sprouts in half. Cover to cook.	7–9	Stir the sprouts after 4 minutes cooking time.
Cabbage, finely shredded	1 pound (4 cups)	½ cup	Use a large dish and ensure that the cabbage fits loosely. Cover to cook.	8–9	Stir or rearrange halfway through the cooking time.
Carrots, whole sliced	1 pound 2 pounds 1 pound (3 cups)	½ cup ½ cup ½ cup	Cover to cook. Cut carrots into ½-inch thick slices. Slicing carrots diagonally reduces the cooking time by 2 minutes. Cover to cook.	12–14 18–20 12-14	Stir or rearrange halfway through the cooking time.
Cauliflower, whole	1 medium, about 1½ pounds	½ cup	Cook whole cauliflower on Medium.	13–17	Turn a whole cauliflower or stir the florets halfway through the cooking time. Allow whole cauliflower to stand for 5 minutes after cooking.
florets	1 pound (4 cups)	½ cup	Cover to cook.	10–12	

GUIDE TO COOKING FRESH VEGETABLES

Vegetable	Quantity	Water	Preparation	Cooking time in minutes on Full power (High)	Method
Celery, whole or sliced	1 pound (4 cups)	$\frac{1}{4}$ cup	Cover to cook.	14–16	Turn or stir halfway through the cooking time.
Corn-on-the-cob	1 2 4 6	3 tablespoons 3 tablespoons 5 tablespoons 5 tablespoons	Cover to cook.	4–5 7–8 13–15 17–20	Cook the corn in the husk, if liked, with no extra water. Rearrange halfway through the cooking time if cooking 4–6.
Eggplant	2 medium, halved	2 tablespoons	Cover to cook.	7–9	Scoop out the cooked flesh from the halved eggplants and use as required.
	1 whole, peeled and cubed	2 tablespoons	Cover to cook.	5–6	Stir the cubed eggplants after 3 minutes cooking time.
Mushrooms, whole or sliced	$2\frac{2}{3}$ cups 5 cups	2 tablespoons water or butter	Cover to cook.	2–4 4–6	Stir halfway through the cooking time.
Onions, whole or quartered	4 medium 8 medium	$\frac{1}{4}$ cup $\frac{1}{3}$ cup	Cover to cook.	10–12 14–16	Stir halfway through the cooking time.
Parsnips, cubed	3 cups	$\frac{1}{2}$ cup	Cover to cook.	8–10	Stir halfway through cooking.
Peas, shelled	3 cups 6 cups	$\frac{1}{2}$ cup $\frac{1}{3}$ cup	Cover to cook.	9–11 12–14	Stir halfway through the cooking time. Add 1–2 tablespoons butter after cooking and allow to stand for 5 minutes before serving.
Potatoes, peeled and quartered baked in skins	2 1 2 3 4	$\frac{1}{2}$ cup — — — —	Cover to cook. Prick thoroughly and cook on paper towels.	10–14 4–6 6–8 8–12 12–16	Stir twice during cooking. Potatoes may still feel firm when cooked. Leave to stand for 3–4 minutes to soften.
Spinach	1 pound (8 cups)	—	Wash but do not dry before cooking. Place in a roasting bag and secure loosely with string.	6–8	Drain well before serving.
Tomatoes, halved	2	—	Add a knob of butter and a little pepper to each half before cooking. Cover to cook.	1–1$\frac{1}{2}$	
Turnips, cubed	3 cups (2–3 medium)	$\frac{1}{2}$ cup	Cover to cook.	12–14	Stir twice during cooking.
Zucchini, sliced whole	4 cups 6 small	— —	Cover to cook	5–6 7	Dot lightly with 2 tablespoons butter. Stir or rearrange halfway through the cooking time.

Cabbage with Caraway

Serves 4
3 tablespoons water
salt
4 cups finely shredded cabbage
1 tablespoon caraway seeds
1 tablespoon butter

Preparation time: about 5 minutes

Cooking time: about 8 minutes
Microwave setting: Full power (High)

1. Place the water and salt in a large bowl. Place the cabbage on top. Cover and cook for 8 minutes. Halfway through cooking, stir in the caraway seeds.

2. Stir the butter into the cabbage until melted.

Parsnips with Parsley

Serves 4–6
3 tablespoons water
salt
1 tablespoon chopped fresh parsley
5 cups peeled and quartered parsnips
1 tablespoon butter

Preparation time: about 8 minutes
Cooking time: about 8 minutes, plus standing
Microwave setting: Full power (High)

1. Place the water, salt and parsley in a large bowl. Place the parsnips on top. Cover and cook for 8 minutes, stirring halfway through cooking.

2. Leave to stand, covered, for 5 minutes. Strain, then stir in the butter until melted.

Vichy Carrots

Serves 4
3 tablespoons cold water
1 teaspoon superfine sugar
3 cups peeled and thinly sliced carrots
2 tablespoons butter, cut into pieces
1 tablespoon chopped fresh parsley

Preparation time: about 10 minutes
Cooking time: about 6–9 minutes
Microwave setting: Full power (High)

1. Place the water, sugar and carrots in a medium bowl. Cover and cook for 6–9 minutes or until tender, stirring halfway through cooking.

2. Drain and stir in the butter until melted. Fold in the parsley. Serve hot. If serving with the Guard of Honor (page 111), stand covered until the corn has heated and then drain, and complete the recipe.

Braised Celery

Serves 4
3 tablespoons water
salt
1 bunch celery, about 1 pound, trimmed and stalks halved
1 onion, peeled and thinly sliced
⅔ cup hot chicken stock
2 tablespoons butter, cut into pieces
1 teaspoon chopped fresh parsley
freshly ground pepper

Preparation time: about 5 minutes
Cooking time: about 11 minutes, plus standing
Microwave setting: Full power (High)

1. Place the water and salt in an oblong or oval casserole dish. Place half the celery in the dish and spread over the onion. Cover the onion with the remaining celery. Cover and cook for 8 minutes. After 5 minutes of cooking, stir the vegetables.

2. Mix together the hot stock, butter, parsley, and seasoning. Pour over the celery, cover and cook for 3 minutes. Leave to stand, covered, for 3–4 minutes before serving.

Minted Peas

Serves 4
3 tablespoons water
1 teaspoon chopped fresh mint
salt
4 cups frozen peas
2 tablespoons butter, diced

Preparation time: about 3 minutes
Cooking time: about 7–9 minutes
Microwave setting: Full power (High)

1. Place the water, mint, salt and peas in a medium bowl. Cover and cook for 7–9 minutes, stirring halfway through cooking.

2. Drain the peas and toss in the butter.

Green Beans

Serves 4
1 pound frozen whole green beans
salt

Preparation time: about 2 minutes
Cooking time: about 9 minutes, plus standing
Microwave setting: Full power (High)

1. Place the beans in a medium bowl. Cover and cook for 9 minutes, stirring halfway through cooking. Leave to stand, covered, for 2 minutes. Drain off all excess water.

2. Sprinkle with salt and toss before serving.

Boiled Potatoes

Serves 4
3 tablespoons cold water
pinch of salt
4 potatoes, total weight 1½ pounds, peeled and cut in half
2 tablespoons butter, diced
1 tablespoon chopped fresh parsley

Preparation time: about 10 minutes
Cooking time: about 9 minutes, plus standing
Microwave setting: Full power (High)

1. Place the water and salt in a large bowl. Add the potatoes, cover and cook for 9 minutes, stirring halfway through cooking. Leave to stand, covered, for 8–10 minutes.

Corn

Serves 4–6

2⅓ cups drained canned whole kernel corn

2 tablespoons butter, cut into pieces

Preparation time: about 3 minutes

Cooking time: about 6 minutes

Microwave setting: Full power (High)

1. Place the corn in a casserole dish, cover and cook for 6 minutes, stirring halfway through.

2. Stir in the butter until melted, then serve at once.

Clockwise: Braised celery; Corn; Minted peas; Parsnips with parsley; Green beans; Vichy carrots; Boiled potatoes; Cabbage with caraway

Buttered Jerusalem Artichokes

Serves 4
3 tablespoons water
salt
*1 pound Jerusalem artichokes,
   peeled and sliced*
*3 tablespoons butter, cut into
   pieces*
*1 tablespoon chopped fresh
   parsley, to garnish*

Preparation time: about 10
minutes
Cooking time: about 9 minutes,
plus standing
Microwave setting: Full power
(High)

1. Place the water, salt and
artichokes in a large bowl.
Cover and cook for 9 minutes,
stirring halfway through
cooking.

2. Leave to stand, covered, for 5
minutes.

3. Drain and toss in the butter.
Garnish with parsley.

Croquette Potatoes

Serves 4
3 tablespoons water
salt
*3⅓ cups peeled and chopped
   potatoes*
2 tablespoons butter
½ tablespoon milk
freshly ground pepper
1 egg, lightly beaten
¾ cup toasted bread crumbs

Preparation time: about 10
minutes
Cooking time: about 11½–13
minutes, plus standing
Microwave setting: Full power
(High)

1. Place the water and salt in a
large bowl. Add the potatoes,
cover and cook for 9 minutes.
Leave to stand, covered, for 5
minutes.

2. Beat the butter, milk and salt
and pepper to taste into the
potatoes. Roll the mixture into

Cauliflower in Cheese Sauce

16 cork shapes. Chill for 30 minutes for a firmer texture.

3. Coat the croquettes with egg and roll in bread crumbs. Place on a piece of paper towel in a circle. Prick each with a fork. Cook, uncovered, for 2½–4 minutes, turning over halfway through cooking.

Serves 4

*1 cauliflower, prepared weight
    1½ pounds*
Sauce:
2 tablespoons butter
¼ cup all-purpose flour
1¼ cups milk
salt
freshly ground black pepper
1 teaspoon mustard
½ cup grated Cheddar cheese
*chopped fresh parsley, to
    garnish*

Preparation time: about 10 minutes
Cooking time: about 15 minutes
Microwave setting: Full power (High)

1. Rinse the cauliflower in water and place in a medium bowl. Cover and cook for 10 minutes, turning the cauliflower over halfway through cooking. Keep hot while making the sauce.

2. Place the butter in a 2½-cup measuring cup. Cook for 1

minute or until the butter has melted.

3. Blend in the flour, milk, salt, pepper and mustard. Cook for 3 minutes, stirring, every minute.

4. Stir in the cheese and cook for 1 minute.

5. Pour the sauce over the cauliflower and garnish with the parsley.

From left to right: Buttered Jerusalem artichokes; Croquette potatoes; Cauliflower in cheese sauce

Cabbage Rolls

Serves 4
1 small, tight green cabbage
1 onion, peeled and finely chopped
2 small tomatoes, peeled and chopped
1 tablespoon butter
4 tablespoons all-purpose flour
1¼ cups hot beef stock
½ teaspoon Worcestershire sauce
½ teaspoon Italian seasoning
salt
freshly ground black pepper
4 tablespoons cooked rice

Preparation time: about 15 minutes
Cooking time: about 13 minutes, plus standing
Microwave setting: Full power (High)

1. Cook the whole cabbage conventionally for 4 minutes in rapidly boiling salted water. Drain thoroughly.

2. Gently peel off 8 leaves. Use the remaining cabbage in a vegetable soup.

3. Place the onion, tomatoes and butter in a medium bowl. Cover and cook for 4 minutes.

4. Stir in the flour, stock, Worcestershire sauce, herbs, salt, pepper and rice. Cook uncovered for 2 minutes.

5. Place a little of the mixture on each of the cabbage leaves. Fold them over to enclose the filling and tie with string.

6. Arrange the cabbage rolls in a shallow dish, cover and cook for 7 minutes, turning the dish around halfway through cooking.

7. Leave the cabbage rolls to stand for 5 minutes.

Broccoli with Cheese Sauce

Serves 4
3 tablespoons water
salt
1 pound fresh broccoli, stalks halved lengthwise
chopped fresh parsley, to garnish (optional)
Sauce:
2 tablespoons butter
¼ cup all-purpose flour
1¼ cups milk
1 teaspoon mustard
salt
freshly ground black pepper
½ cup grated Cheddar cheese

Preparation time: about 10 minutes
Cooking time: about 11 minutes, plus standing
Microwave setting: Full power (High)

1. Place the water and salt in a large bowl. Arrange the broccoli in the bowl with stalks standing upward. Cover with plastic wrap and cook for 7 minutes. Set aside, covered.

2. Place the butter in a bowl. Cook for 1 minute or until melted. Blend in the flour, milk, mustard and salt and pepper to taste. Cook for 3 minutes, stirring every minute. Stir in the cheese. Cook for 1 minute.

3. Drain the broccoli. Pour over the sauce and garnish with parsley (if using).

Cook's Tip

Frozen broccoli may be used instead of fresh.

Cabbage rolls; Broccoli with cheese sauce

Stuffed Onions

Serves 4

4 large onions, total weight
  2 pounds, peeled
½ cup fresh white bread crumbs
¼ teaspoon rubbed sage
¼ teaspoon dried tarragon
¼ teaspoon dried parsley flakes
½ egg, lightly beaten
1 teaspoon Worcestershire
  sauce
salt
freshly ground black pepper
1 tablespoon butter

Preparation time: about 25 minutes
Cooking time: about 14–16 minutes, plus standing
Microwave setting: Full power (High)

1. Remove the centers from the onions, using a grapefruit knife, leaving shells about 2–3 layers deep. Set the shells aside, and chop the centers.

2. Mix the chopped onion with the fresh bread crumbs, sage, tarragon, parsley, egg, Worcestershire sauce, and salt and pepper to taste.

3. Stuff each onion with the bread-crumb mixture and top with a small knob of butter.

4 Arrange the onions in a circle on a plate and cook, uncovered, for 14–16 minutes, rearranging halfway through cooking. Leave to stand for 3 minutes before serving.

Stuffed Baked Potatoes

Serves 4

4 medium potatoes, washed
  and dried
¾ cup grated Cheddar cheese
1 tablespoon tomato paste
1 tablespoon Worcestershire
  sauce
1 tablespoon butter
salt
freshly ground black pepper
chopped fresh parsley, to
  garnish

Preparation time: about 10 minutes
Cooking time: about 16 minutes, plus standing
Microwave setting: Full power (High)

1. Place the potatoes on a paper towel, prick them and cook for 6 minutes.

2. Turn the potatoes over and rearrange. Cook for a further 7 minutes.

3. Wrap each potato tightly in foil and leave to stand for 5 minutes.

4. Cut a lengthwise slice off the top of each potato. Scoop out the flesh, leaving each potato shell intact.

5. Mix the potato flesh with the cheese, tomato paste, Worcestershire sauce, butter, salt and pepper.

6. Pile the mixture back into the potatoes and reheat for 3 minutes. Serve garnished with chopped parsley.

Stuffed onions; Stuffed baked potatoes

Zucchini Shells with Bacon

Serves 4

4 zucchini, halved lengthwise
1 bacon slice, chopped
1 small onion, peeled and finely
chopped
1 teaspoon Italian seasoning
½–1 cup fresh white bread
crumbs
1 egg yolk
4 tablespoons stock
salt
freshly ground black pepper

Preparation time: about 10
minutes
Cooking time: about 12
minutes, plus standing
Microwave setting: Full power
(High)

1. Using a teaspoon, scoop the
centers from the zucchini
halves. Set the shells aside, and
chop the scooped-out flesh;
there should be about ¼ cup.

2. Place the zucchini flesh,
bacon, onion and Italian
seasoning in a small bowl.
Cover and cook for 3 minutes.
Stir in the bread crumbs, egg
yolk, stock, and salt and pepper
to taste.

3. Fill one half of each zucchini
shell with the stuffing. Replace
the other half and secure with
wooden toothpicks.

4. Place in a shallow dish, cover
and cook for 9 minutes,
rearranging halfway through
cooking. Leave to stand for 3–4
minutes before serving.

Zucchini shells with bacon; Peppers with
savory rice

Peppers with Savory Rice

Serves 4

1 onion, peeled and finely
chopped
2 tablespoons butter
½ cup finely chopped cooked
ham
1 garlic clove, peeled and
crushed
1 tablespoon tomato paste
1 teaspoon Italian seasoning
salt
freshly ground pepper
½ cup long-grain rice
2 cups hot beef stock
4 green bell peppers, cored,
seeded and blanched

Preparation time: about 10
minutes
Cooking time: about 23
minutes, plus standing
Microwave setting: Full power
(High)

1. Place the onion, butter, ham,
garlic, tomato paste, herbs, salt
and pepper in a large bowl.
Cover and cook for 4 minutes.

2. Stir in the rice and hot stock,
cover and cook for 9 minutes.

3. Leave to stand, covered, for
about 10 minutes.

4. Stand the peppers in a
casserole. Stuff the peppers with
the rice, cover and cook for 5
minutes.

5. Turn the casserole around
and cook for 5 minutes.

6. Leave the peppers to stand,
covered, for 5 minutes before
serving.

Stuffed Zucchini

Serves 4

1 large zucchini, about 1½ pounds, halved and seeds removed
1 onion, peeled and finely chopped
1 small carrot, peeled and grated
2 tomatoes, peeled and chopped
1 teaspoon Italian seasoning
1½ cups fresh whole-wheat bread crumbs
¾ pound ground beef
1 teaspoon Worcestershire sauce
1 tablespoon tomato paste
salt
freshly ground black pepper
Sauce:
2 tablespoons butter
¼ cup all-purpose flour
1¼ cups milk
salt
freshly ground black pepper

Preparation time: 20 minutes
Cooking time: about 30½ minutes, plus broiling
Microwave setting: Full power (High)

1. Place the zucchini halves in a shallow dish. Cover and cook for 14 minutes.

2. Drain the zucchini, cover and set aside.

3. Place the onion, carrot, tomatoes and herbs in a large bowl. Cover and cook for 5 minutes.

4. Stir in the bread crumbs, meat, Worcestershire sauce, tomato paste, salt and pepper. Cover and cook for 4 minutes. Set aside.

5. To make the sauce, place the butter in a 2½-cup measuring cup. Cook for 1 minute or until melted.

6. Blend in the flour, milk, salt and pepper. Cook for 3 minutes, stirring every minute.

7. Fill the zucchini halves with the stuffing. Spoon over the sauce, and cook for 3½ minutes.

8. If preferred, brown under a preheated conventional broiler before serving.

Stuffed zucchini; Stuffed eggplant

Stuffed Eggplant

Serves 4

2 eggplant, about 9 ounces each
salt
vegetable oil for brushing
1 onion, peeled and finely chopped
4 bacon slices, diced
⅔ cup chopped mushrooms
¼ cup butter
2 tablespoons tomato paste
1 tablespoon chopped fresh parsley
2 teaspoons Worcestershire sauce
dash of Angostura bitters (optional)
1 garlic clove, peeled and crushed
freshly ground pepper
1½ cups fresh whole-wheat bread crumbs
½ cup finely grated Cheddar cheese

Preparation time: about 20 minutes, plus salting
Cooking time: about 16¼ minutes
Microwave setting: Full power (High)

1. Cut the eggplant in half lengthwise. Sprinkle the cut edges with salt and set aside. After 30 minutes, rinse them with cold water and pat dry.

2. Scoop out the flesh and dice it. Brush shells with oil.

3. Place the onion in a large bowl. Cover and cook for 2½ minutes. Stir in the bacon and diced eggplant. Cover and cook for 4 minutes.

4. Stir in the mushrooms, butter, tomato paste, chopped parsley, Worcestershire sauce, Angostura bitters (if using), garlic, salt and pepper. Cover and cook for 3 minutes. Leave to stand, covered.

5. Place the eggplant shells on a plate or shallow casserole dish, cover and cook for 2 minutes. Turn each shell around, cover and cook for 2 minutes.

6. Stir the bread crumbs into the stuffing. Spoon the stuffing into the shells. Cook for 2 minutes.

7. Sprinkle the grated cheese on top. Cook for 45 seconds or until the cheese has melted.

Potato Salad

Serves 4
3 tablespoons water
salt
*4 cups peeled potatoes cut into
   1-inch cubes*
1 cup mayonnaise
*1 tablespoon snipped fresh
   chives, to garnish*

Preparation time: about 10
minutes, plus cooling
Cooking time: 9–10 minutes,
plus standing
Microwave setting: Full power
(High)

1. Place the water and salt in a
large bowl. Place the potatoes
on top. Cover and cook for 9–
10 minutes, stirring halfway
through cooking.

2. Leave to stand, covered, for
15 minutes. Remove the cover
and gently stir with a fork to

separate the potato cubes. Leave
to stand until cold.

3. Stir in the mayonnaise and
sprinkle with chives.

*Clockwise: Salami and tomato pizza;
Potato salad; Onion and potato bake;
Vegetarian curry*

Salami and Tomato Pizza

Serves 4
¼ cup milk
1 envelope active dry yeast
pinch of sugar
2 tablespoons butter
1 egg, beaten
1½ cups all-purpose flour, sifted with a pinch of salt
Topping:
1 garlic clove, peeled and crushed
1 onion, peeled and finely chopped
1 tablespoon butter
2 tablespoons tomato paste
2½ cups peeled and chopped tomatoes, or 1½ × 8-ounce cans tomatoes
1 tablespoon dried oregano
salt
freshly ground black pepper
3–4 ounces salami, thinly sliced
¾ cup grated Cheddar cheese
6 anchovy fillets, drained
6 stuffed Spanish olives, halved

Preparation time: about 20 minutes, plus rising
Cooking time: about 11 minutes
Microwave setting: Full power (High)

1. Place the milk in a bowl. Cook for 15 seconds. Sprinkle the yeast and sugar over the milk and leave to stand for 10 minutes or until frothy.

2. Place the butter in a small bowl. Cook for 45 seconds or until melted.

3. Pour the yeast mixture, melted butter and egg into the flour and salt. Knead for 10 minutes or until smooth. Shape into a ball and place in a bowl.

4. Cover and cook for 30 seconds. Leave covered for 10 minutes.

5. Remove the cover and leave dough to rise until it has doubled in size; this will take about 20 minutes.

6. To make the topping, place the garlic, onion and butter in a medium bowl. Cover and cook for 3 minutes. Stir in the tomato paste, tomatoes, oregano, salt and pepper. Cook for 2 minutes. Set aside.

7. Knead the dough and roll it out to make a 9-inch circle. Place on a plate and cook for 2½ minutes.

8. Spread the tomato and onion topping over the pizza crust and cover with the salami slices and grated cheese. Arrange the anchovies on top in a lattice pattern. Garnish with halved olives. Cook for 2 minutes and serve immediately.

Onion and Potato Bake

Serves 4
2⅔ cups peeled and thinly sliced onions
4 cups peeled and thinly sliced potatoes
salt
freshly ground black pepper
2 teaspoons Italian seasoning
about 6 tablespoons milk
parsley sprigs, to garnish

Preparation time: about 12 minutes
Cooking time: about 14 minutes
Microwave setting: Full power (High)

1. Place the onions in a medium bowl, cover and cook for 5 minutes, stirring halfway through cooking.

2. Layer the potatoes and onions in a 5-cup casserole dish. Sprinkle each layer with a little salt, pepper and herbs. Finish with a layer of potatoes. Pour in the milk.

3. Stand the dish on a plate. Cover and cook for 9 minutes, turning around halfway through cooking.

4. Garnish with sprigs of parsley.

Vegetarian Curry

Serves 3–4
1 tablespoon vegetable oil
1 small green bell pepper, cored, seeded and finely chopped
2 carrots, peeled and finely sliced
1 celery stalk, finely chopped
2 large onions, peeled and finely chopped
3 tomatoes, peeled and chopped
1 tablespoon lemon juice
1 large eating apple, peeled, cored and chopped
2 tablespoons dark brown sugar
2 tablespoons curry powder
2 teaspoons turmeric
2 tablespoons shredded coconut
¼ cup all-purpose flour
1¼ cups hot vegetable stock
2 tablespoons golden raisins
2 tablespoons peanuts
salt
freshly ground black pepper

Preparation time: about 20 minutes
Cooking time: about 19 minutes
Microwave setting: Full power (High)

1. Place the oil, green bell pepper, carrots and celery in a bowl. Cover and cook for 5 minutes.

2. Stir in the onions, tomatoes, lemon juice, apple, sugar, curry powder, turmeric and coconut. Cover and cook for 10 minutes, stirring halfway through cooking.

3. Stir in the flour, hot stock, golden raisins, peanuts, salt and pepper. Cover and cook for 4 minutes, stirring halfway through cooking.

4. Serve with brown rice.

RICE, PASTA AND DRIED BEANS

Rice, pasta and dried beans can be turned into such a wide variety of dishes, from authentic Italian first courses to simple side dishes and delicious supper-time specials. As well as all the basic cooking directions you need, this chapter also gives you lots of good ideas and a selection of interesting dishes.

Rice

All types of rice cook very well in the microwave. The great saving is not on the cooking time but on the clean up and on the effort involved. With conventional cooking methods there is always the risk of the rice boiling over or sticking to the bottom of the pan; in the microwave there is no danger of sticking and, if you use a large casserole or bowl, the rice will not boil over. The rice should be lightly salted before cooking and, when all the water has been absorbed, it should be allowed to stand briefly. Before serving, fluff up the grains with a fork.

Types of rice

Most supermarkets offer a wide variety of rice, from plain unprocessed long-grain white rice to exotic, dark-colored, wild rice. The cooking times for the types of rice vary, as does the quantity of liquid needed to tenderize them.

Dark-grained wild rice requires the longest cooking time, and unprocessed brown rice takes longer than the varieties of white rice. Unprocessed white rice cooks quickly and easily, and far more successfully in the microwave than by traditional methods. Easy-cook rice is already partly cooked and when it is ready to serve the grains are all completely separate. Round-grain rice is used for making puddings, and certain types are used for risottos and they are usually sold as "risotto rice."

Different types of rice

Delicious ways with rice

Rice, like pasta, comes in various shapes and sizes from round-grain to long-grain and from wild to easy-cook, so you won't have any trouble in providing plenty of variety in rice-type meals. Sometimes a meal calls for something a little more than plain boiled rice. Why not try one of the following suggestions:

Chicken or beef-flavored rice Cook the rice according to the table but using boiling stock – either beef or chicken.

Herb-flavored rice Cook the rice according to the table but add a large pinch of Italian seasoning before cooking.

Peppered rice Place ½ chopped green bell pepper, ½ chopped red bell pepper and 4 tablespoons chopped scallions in a bowl with 2 tablespoons butter. Cook on Full power for 2 minutes, then add to the rice ingredients before cooking.

Curried rice Place 2 tablespoons butter in a bowl with 2 small peeled and chopped onions, a pinch of grated nutmeg and ½–1 teaspoon curry powder, according to taste. Cook on Full power for 3–4 minutes until, soft and golden. Add to the cooked rice with ½ cup light cream and reheat on Full power for 1 minute.

Risotto alla Milanese Place 2 tablespoons butter in a bowl with 1 peeled and finely chopped onion and a little powdered saffron. Cook on Full power for 2 minutes. Add to the rice, substituting an equal quantity of dry white wine for a quarter of the water.

Herbed orange rice Place $\frac{1}{4}$ cup butter in a bowl with 2 chopped stalks celery and 2 tablespoons grated onion. Cook on Full power for 2 minutes. Add to the rice with 1 tablespoon grated orange rind and substitute an equal quantity of unsweetened orange juice for half of the water. Cook the rice according to the chart.

Vegetable rice Cook the rice according to the chart, then add 1 cup cooked chopped green beans and 1 cup cooked peas.

Cooking Rice

1. The rice is placed in a large casserole or bowl with the water and seasoning. It is covered during cooking.

2. At the end of the cooking time the water has been absorbed but the rice is still very moist.

3. At the end of the standing time the grains have absorbed all the water and they are fluffed up with a fork before being served.

Pasta

Pasta comes in all shapes and sizes, as well as a variety of colors. The shape and size of the pasta is one of the key factors in determining its suitability for microwave cooking, simply because it has to be cooked in a large container with plenty of boiling water. The smaller the shapes, the easier it is to fit them into a suitable cooking dish.

To ensure even cooking, do not mix pasta of different sizes. Remember to use boiling water from the kettle and a large mixing bowl or very large casserole dish. The dish should be covered during cooking, and a lid or large plate, or microwave-safe plastic wrap can be used for this purpose.

The success with which pasta cooks in the microwave depends to a certain extent on its shape. Lasagne is probably the most difficult pasta to accommodate, and second comes spaghetti. These pasta shapes will need plenty of room in the cooking dish – a large oblong dish (if you can fit it on the turntable in the microwave) is ideal for lasagne, and a mixing bowl will usually accommodate the spaghetti.

Smaller pasta shapes – shells, bows, spirals and stars – and

Different types of pasta

noodles cook very successfully in a large bowl of boiling water. They should be stirred halfway through cooking to ensure that the pieces do not stick together and the standing times should always be observed since they are important for tenderizing the pasta.

Remember to take advantage of the partly cooked lasagne which is best to use if you are layering the pasta with a moist meat sauce and coating the dish with a cheese sauce.

Lastly, as with any conventional cooking method, it is best to be sensible and recognize the limitations of the microwave oven. If you are cooking a vast quantity of pasta, you are better off using the traditional method of boiling it in a large saucepan on the stove. However, the microwave reheats cooked pasta perfectly.

The pasta can be cooked in advance and drained, then rinsed in cold water to prevent it sticking. When it is thoroughly drained, place it in a dish suitable for microwave cooking and cover. Before serving, add butter or vegetable oil, and heat the pasta in the microwave on Full power for a few minutes. Toss well and it is ready to serve – as good as it was freshly cooked.

Delicious ways with pasta

There is nothing more delicious than pasta tossed with a knob of butter to give a golden buttery glaze, seasoned to taste and topped with freshly grated Parmesan cheese. But here are more ideas to try – simply return the pasta to the oven with one of the following flavorings and cook for 1 minute on Full power.

Creamy pasta with garlic Add a little chopped garlic and 1–2 tablespoons heavy cream and toss well.

Herbed pasta Add a few snipped chives or chopped parsley and toss well.

Caraway pasta For a crunchy effect, add a few poppy seeds and caraway seeds and toss well.

Almond pasta Place 2 tablespoons almonds in a shallow dish with 1 tablespoon butter. Cook on Full power for 2–4 minutes, until golden brown. Add to the pasta and toss well.

Peppered pasta Place ½ small chopped green bell pepper and 1 small peeled and chopped onion in a bowl with 2 tablespoons butter and cook on Full power for 2 minutes. Add to the pasta and toss well.

Creamed pasta Mix 1 egg yolk with ¼ cup heavy cream and stir into the hot cooked pasta. Do not reheat.

Mushroom and ham pasta Place 1 cup sliced mushrooms in a bowl with 1 tablespoon butter. Cover and cook on Full power for 2 minutes. Add to the pasta with ½ cup shredded cooked ham and toss well. Dress with sour cream for a delicious result.

Pasta with garbanzo beans Cook 1 chopped onion, 3 tablespoons olive oil and 1 chopped red or green chili on Full power for 3 minutes. Toss in a 15-ounce can garbanzo beans, well drained. Add the cooked pasta; heat for 2 minutes and serve.

Three-onion pasta Cook 1 small chopped onion in ¼ cup butter for 3 minutes. Toss into the pasta with 4 finely chopped scallions and 2 tablespoons snipped chives. Top with sour cream.

Fresh pasta

Fresh pasta cooks very well in the microwave. You will need a large bowl of boiling salted water, with a little oil added. The cooking time depends more on the type of pasta than on the quantity which is cooked. Noodles or shapes (usually twists, spirals, bows or shells) cook in about 5 minutes, with a standing time of 5 minutes, before the pasta can be drained and tossed with butter.

Stuffed fresh pasta (such as tortellini) requires longer cooking if the filling is made of raw meat or poultry. Cheese and spinach fillings do not require extra cooking.

GUIDE TO COOKING RICE AND PASTA

Rice	Quantity	Preparation	Cooking time in minutes on Full power (High)	Standing time
Brown rice	1⅓ cups	Place in a deep, covered container with 2½ cups boiling salted water.	20–25	5–10
Easy-cook rice	1½ cups	Place in a deep, covered container with 2½ cups boiling salted water.	10–12	5–10
Long-grain rice	1 cup	Place in a deep, covered container with 2½ cups boiling salted water and 1 tablespoon oil.	8–10	5–10

Rice	Quantity	Preparation	Cooking time in minutes on Full power (High)	Standing time
Egg noodles and tagliatelle	⅔ 12-ounce package	Place in a deep, covered container with 2½ cups boiling salted water and 1 tablespoon vegetable oil.	6	3
Macaroni	½ 16-ounce package	Place in a deep, covered container with 2½ cups boiling salted water and 1 tablespoon vegetable oil.	10	3
Pasta shells and shapes	½ 16-ounce package	Place in a deep, covered container with 2½ cups salted water and 1 tablespoon vegetable oil.	12–14	5–10
Spaghetti	1 8-ounce package	Hold in a deep, covered container with 1 quart boiling salted water to soften, then submerge or break in half and add 1 tablespoon vegetable oil.	9–10	5–10

Dried Beans

Dried beans can be cooked in the microwave without having to pre-soak them. The cooking time is as long as for conventional methods but the advantage is in avoiding the necessity for soaking in advance, and in the fact that the beans will not boil over if they are in a large cooking container.

Boiling is essential

It is essential when cooking red kidney beans to ensure that they come to a full boil and that the boiling is maintained for 5 minutes to make certain the toxins which are naturally present in the beans are destroyed. You will have to watch the beans closely as they come to the boil and make absolutely sure that all the liquid boils, and that the boiling point is maintained.

Lentils

Lentils cook very well in the microwave and there are two options. They can be cooked in a very large bowl on Full power. Alternatively they can be cooked in an average-sized casserole or bowl on a lower power. If you decide to cook them on Full power, make sure that there is plenty of room in the bowl for the water to froth up as the lentils cook. If you do not have a very large casserole, then cook the lentils according to the basic recipe, on Defrost and leave them to stand. This is ideal for making either lentil stuffings or burgers.

Canned beans

Canned beans are ready cooked and they require heating through – rather than cooking – before serving. They are ideally suited to microwave cooking and they can be added to other ingredients halfway through the cooking time or at the end of the time, depending on the dish.

Alternatively, they can be quickly heated in their canned juice, drained and tossed with butter and chopped parsley or scallions to be served very simply instead of rice, pasta or potatoes.

Ways with dried beans

Plain cooked beans and dried peas and lentils can be seasoned or flavored in a variety of ways. They can be served as a side dish for meat, fish or poultry, or as the main dish for a vegetarian meal.

Beans with tomatoes Cook 1 chopped onion with 1 crushed garlic clove in 4 tablespoons olive oil on Full power for 3 minutes. Add cooked lima beans, season and stir in 4 peeled and chopped tomatoes. Heat on Full power for 2 minutes, then serve.

Spiced garbanzo beans Cook 1 tablespoon cumin seeds in 2 tablespoons butter, then pour over cooked **garbanzo beans**. Sprinkle with chopped fresh flat-leaf parsley.

Green lentils with nuts Toss a knob of butter, some chopped walnuts and chopped parsley into cooked green lentils.

GUIDE TO COOKING DRIED BEANS

Beans	Quantity	Preparation and cooking time
Kidney, great-northern, navy and fava beans	2 cups	Place the beans in a large dish with a little chopped onion, celery and carrot. Cover with $1\frac{1}{2}$ quarts cold water and cook on Full power for 20 minutes. Stir, re-cover and cook on Medium for 1 hour 30 minutes–1 hour 40 minutes, until tender. Top up the water as necessary during cooking, adding boiling water from a kettle.
Garbanzo beans	$1\frac{1}{2}$ cups	
Lima beans	$2\frac{1}{2}$ cups	
Cannellini beans	$1\frac{2}{3}$ cups	
Split peas	1 cup	Place the split peas in a large dish with a little chopped onion, celery and 1 tablespoon lemon juice. Add a little salt and pepper to taste. Cover with $3\frac{3}{4}$ cups water. Cover and cook on Full power for 15 minutes. Stir and cook on Medium for 60–70 minutes, stirring every 30 minutes, until tender. Top up the water as necessary by adding boiling water from a kettle.
Lentils, red	1 cup	Place in a large casserole or bowl and pour in $1\frac{1}{4}$ cups boiling water. Cover and cook on Full power for 15 minutes, or until all the water has been absorbed and the lentils are tender.
Lentils, green	1 cup	Place in a large casserole dish or mixing bowl and pour in $2\frac{1}{2}$ cups boiling water. Cover and cook on Full power for 35–40 minutes, or until the lentils are tender. Top up the water if necessary during cooking by adding extra boiling water from a kettle.

Risotto

Serves 4
¼ cup butter
1 large onion, peeled and finely chopped
¼ green bell pepper, cored, seeded and finely diced
¼ red bell pepper, cored, seeded and finely diced
1 tablespoon tomato paste
1 garlic clove, peeled and crushed
1 teaspoon Italian seasoning
⅔ cup finely chopped mushrooms
2 cups long-grain rice
3 cups hot chicken stock
1 cup finely chopped ham
¼ teaspoon vegetable oil
salt
freshly ground black pepper
1 tablespoon chopped fresh parsley, to garnish

Preparation time: about 15 minutes
Cooking time: about 23 minutes, plus standing
Microwave setting: Full power (High)

1. Place the butter, onion, bell peppers, tomato paste, garlic, herbs and mushrooms in a large bowl. Cover and cook for 8 minutes, stirring halfway through cooking.

2. Stir in the rice, stock, ham, oil, salt, pepper, then cover and cook for 15 minutes, stirring halfway through cooking.

3. Remove from the microwave and leave to stand, covered, for 8 minutes.

4. Stir the risotto with a fork, and sprinkle with chopped parsley. Serve grated Parmesan cheese separately.

Rice and Haddock

Serves 4
1½ pounds smoked cod or haddock fillets
1⅔ cups long-grain rice
3 cups hot chicken stock
salt
¼ teaspoon vegetable oil
¼ cup butter, cubed
1 egg, beaten
2 hard-cooked egg whites, chopped
freshly ground black pepper
1 tablespoon light cream
To garnish:
chopped fresh parsley
1 hard-cooked egg white, chopped
1 hard-cooked egg yolk, sieved

Preparation time: about 15 minutes
Cooking time: about 23 minutes, plus standing
Microwave setting: Full power (High)

1. Place the cod or haddock in a shallow dish. Cover and cook for 3½ minutes. Turn the dish around and cook for a further 3½ minutes.

2. Flake the fish and set aside.

3. Place the rice, hot stock, salt and oil into a large bowl. Cover and cook for 12 minutes.

4. Leave to stand, covered, for 7 minutes.

5. Stir the flaked fish into the rice with the butter, beaten egg, chopped egg whites, pepper and cream. Cover and cook for 4 minutes, stirring halfway through cooking.

6. Garnish with the chopped parsley, chopped egg white and sieved egg yolk, arranged decoratively over the mixture.

Paella

Serves 4
1 onion, peeled and chopped
2 garlic cloves, peeled and crushed
1⅔ cups long-grain rice
3 cups hot stock
few strands of saffron
salt
¼ teaspoon vegetable oil
1 cup frozen peas
6 ounces shelled and deveined cooked shrimp
¾ pound cooked mussels
1 cup diced cooked chicken meat
2 tomatoes, peeled and chopped
cooked shrimp in shells

Preparation time: about 15 minutes
Cooking time: about 30 minutes, plus standing
Microwave setting: Full power (High)

1. Place the onion and garlic in a large bowl, cover and cook for 6½ minutes, stirring halfway through.

2. Stir the rice, stock, saffron, salt and oil into the onion. Cover and cook for 13 minutes, stirring halfway through cooking. Set aside, covered, for 13 minutes.

3. Meanwhile, place the peas in a medium bowl, cover and cook for 3½ minutes. Stir in the shrimp, mussels, chicken and tomatoes. Cover and cook for 7½ minutes, stirring halfway through cooking. Drain and stir into the rice.

4. Serve hot, garnished with shrimp.

Curried Rice

Serves 4
1 large onion, peeled and finely chopped
1 garlic clove, peeled and crushed
½ cup golden raisins
2 tablespoons tomato paste
1 tablespoon mild curry powder
1 teaspoon mild chili powder
1 teaspoon Italian seasoning
salt
¼ teaspoon vegetable oil
1⅔ cups long-grain rice
3 cups boiling beef stock
bay leaves, to garnish

Preparation time: about 10 minutes
Cooking time: 18 minutes, plus standing
Microwave setting: Full power (High)

1. Place the onion in a large bowl, cover and cook for 5 minutes, stirring halfway through cooking.

2. Stir in the garlic, golden raisins, tomato paste, curry powder, chili powder, herbs, salt, oil, rice and stock. Cover and cook for 13 minutes. Leave to stand, covered, for 10 minutes.

3. Fluff the rice with a fork. Serve garnished with bay leaves.

Clockwise: Risotto; Rice and haddock; Curried Paella

Spaghetti Bolognese

Serves 4
4 slices bacon, chopped
1 onion, peeled and finely
*   chopped*
2 garlic cloves, peeled and
*   crushed*
1 celery stalk, finely chopped
1 small carrot, peeled and
*   grated*
$\frac{1}{4}$ cup all-purpose flour
$\frac{1}{2}$ pound ground beef
3 medium tomatoes, peeled and
*   chopped, or 1 × 16-ounce can*
*   tomatoes*
4 tablespoons tomato paste
1$\frac{1}{4}$ cups hot beef stock
1$\frac{1}{3}$ cups chopped mushrooms
salt
freshly ground black pepper
2 teaspoons Italian seasoning
1 quantity cooked spaghetti
*   (page 151), hot*
1 tablespoon grated Parmesan
*   cheese*

Preparation time: about 20
minutes
Cooking time: about 20$\frac{1}{2}$
minutes
Microwave setting: Full power
(High)

1. Place the bacon, onion, garlic,
celery and carrot in a bowl.
Cover and cook for 7$\frac{1}{2}$ minutes,
stirring halfway through.

2. Stir in the flour, beef,
tomatoes and tomato paste.
Cover and cook for 3 minutes.

3. Stir in the stock, mushrooms,
salt, pepper and herbs. Cover.
Cook for 10 minutes, stirring
halfway through.

4. Place spaghetti in a serving
dish, pour over sauce and
sprinkle cheese on top.

Ham and Chicken Lasagne

Serves 4
$\frac{3}{4}$ pound chicken breast
6 ounces green lasagne
$\frac{1}{2}$ teaspoon vegetable oil
3$\frac{3}{4}$ cups boiling water
salt
1 onion, peeled and finely
*   chopped*
1 small green bell pepper,
*   cored, seeded and finely*
*   chopped*
3 tablespoons butter
$\frac{1}{3}$ cup all-purpose flour
1$\frac{1}{4}$ cups milk
$\frac{2}{3}$ cup very hot chicken
*   stock*
$\frac{1}{2}$ cup finely chopped cooked
*   ham*
freshly ground black pepper
$\frac{1}{3}$ cup finely grated Cheddar
*   cheese*

Preparation time: about 15
minutes
Cooking time: about 29$\frac{1}{4}$
minutes, plus standing and
broiling
Microwave setting: Full power
(High)

1. Place the chicken in a shallow
dish. Cover and cook for 6
minutes. Set aside, covered, for
5 minutes. Discard skin and
bones and chop the flesh. Set
aside.

2. Place the lasagne in a 2-inch
deep oblong casserole dish.
Pour over the oil, boiling water
and salt, completely covering
the lasagne with water. Cover
and cook for 9 minutes.

3. Set aside, covered, for 15
minutes. Drain the lasagne and
place it on a separate plate.

4. Place the onion, green bell
pepper and butter in a medium
bowl. Cover and cook for 7
minutes.

5. Sprinkle in the flour and
gradually stir in the milk. Cook
for 4 minutes. Blend in the hot
stock. Stir in the chicken, ham,
salt and pepper.Cook for 2
minutes.

6. Place half the drained lasagne
in a layer at the bottom of the
casserole dish. Pour over half
the sauce. Place the remaining
lasagne over the sauce and
cover with the remaining sauce.
Sprinkle the cheese on top and
cook for 1$\frac{1}{4}$ minutes or until the
cheese has melted.

7. Brown under a preheated
conventional broiler.

Stuffed Cannelloni

Serves 4
Stuffing:
1 small onion, peeled and finely
*   chopped*
1 garlic clove, peeled and
*   crushed*
1 teaspoon Italian seasoning
$\frac{1}{2}$ pound ground meat
2 tablespoons tomato paste
salt
freshly ground black pepper
Sauce:
1 small onion, peeled and finely
*   chopped*
1 garlic clove, peeled and
*   crushed*
1 teaspoon Italian seasoning
2 tablespoons butter, cut into
*   pieces*
$\frac{1}{4}$ cup all-purpose flour
1 × 16-ounce can tomatoes
2 tablespoons tomato paste
8 cannelloni tubes

Preparation time: about 10
minutes
Cooking time: about 28$\frac{1}{2}$
minutes, plus standing
Microwave setting: Full power
(High)

1. To make the stuffing, place
the onion, garlic and herbs in a
bowl. Cover and cook for 4
minutes.

2. Stir in the meat, tomato paste,
and salt and pepper. Cover and
cook for 5 minutes, stirring
halfway through. Set aside,
covered.

3. For the sauce, place the
onion, garlic and herbs in a
medium bowl. Cover and cook
for 4 minutes.

4. Stir in the butter until melted.

Stir in the flour. Blend in the
tomatoes and their liquid,
tomato paste, and salt and
pepper to taste. Cook,
uncovered, for 3$\frac{1}{2}$ minutes,
stirring halfway through
cooking. Purée.

5. Stuff the canelloni tubes with
the meat stuffing. Place in a 5-
cup casserole dish.

6. Pour over sauce. Cook,
covered, for 12 minutes.

7. Leave to stand for 3–4
minutes before serving.

Clockwise: Spaghetti Bolognese;
Macaroni and cheese; Stuffed
cannelloni; Ham and chicken lasagne

Macaroni and Cheese

Serves 4
5 cups boiling water
¼ teaspoon vegetable oil
⅓ 16-ounce package macaroni
Sauce:
¼ cup butter
⅓ cup all-purpose flour
2½ cups milk
½ teaspoon mustard
salt
freshly ground black pepper
1¼ cups finely grated Cheddar
   cheese

Preparation time: about 10 minutes
Cooking time: about 23–25 minutes, plus broiling
Microwave setting: Full power (High)

1. Place the water, oil and macaroni in a large bowl. Cover and cook for 15 minutes. Set aside, covered.

2. Place the butter in a bowl. Cook, uncovered, for 1 minute or until the butter has melted. Stir in the flour, then blend in the milk, mustard and salt and pepper to taste. Cook, uncovered, for 5–7 minutes, stirring every minute.

3. Stir in ¾ cup of the cheese. Drain the macaroni and fold into the cheese sauce. Pour into a casserole.

4. Sprinkle the remaining cheese over. Cook, uncovered, for 2 minutes, or until the cheese has melted. Or, if desired, brown under a preheated conventional broiler.

Vegetable and Cashew Rice

Serves 4
¼ cup butter
1 onion, peeled and chopped
1 garlic clove, peeled and
    crushed
1⅓ cups long-grain brown rice
2½ cups boiling water
½ teaspoon ground turmeric
1 teaspoon sea salt
1 large carrot, peeled and cut
    into thin strips
2 cups green beans broken into
    2-inch pieces
1 small red bell pepper, cored,
    seeded and chopped
3 tablespoons water
4 tomatoes, peeled and
    quartered
freshly ground black pepper
heaped 1 cup cashew nuts,
    toasted

Preparation time: about 10
minutes
Cooking time: about 29
minutes, plus standing
Microwave setting: Full power
(High)

1. Place the butter in a large
casserole and cook for 1 minute
to melt. Add the onion, garlic,
rice, water, turmeric and salt,
blending well. Cover and cook
for 20 minutes until tender.
Leave to stand for 5 minutes,
then drain thoroughly.

2. Meanwhile, place the carrot,
beans and red bell pepper in a
bowl with the cold water. Cover
and cook for 5 minutes, until
tender.

3. Drain the vegetables, then
fold into the rice mixture with
the tomatoes, pepper to taste
and half the cashew nuts.

4. Cook for 3 minutes. Serve
sprinkled with the remaining
cashew nuts.

Pillau Rice

Serves 4
1 onion, chopped
¼ cup butter
2 cardamom seeds
1 bay leaf
1 cinnamon stick
1 cup basmati rice
salt
2½ cups boiling water
1 tablespoon cumin seeds

Preparation time: about 5
minutes
Cooking time: 19–20 minutes
Microwave setting: Full power
(High)

1. Place the onion and half the
butter in a dish. Cover and cook
for 3 minutes.

2. Add the cardamom, bay leaf,
cinnamon stick and rice.
Sprinkle in a good pinch of salt,
then pour in the water. Cover
the dish and cook the rice for
15–16 minutes. Set the rice aside
for 5 minutes.

3. Place the remaining butter
and cumin seeds in a small bowl
and cook for 1–2 minutes, until
the butter has melted and is
sizzling and very hot.

4. Fork up the grains of rice,
then pour the hot butter and
cumin seeds over them, and
serve at once. If you prefer,
remove the whole spices.

Curried Black-eyed Peas

Serves 4
1⅔ cups dried black-eyed peas
1½ quarts cold chicken stock
2 tablespoons butter
2 carrots, peeled and cut into
    thin strips
1 onion, peeled and finely
    chopped
1 celery stalk, finely chopped
2–3 teaspoons curry powder
2 tablespoons all-purpose flour
4 tablespoons tomato paste
1¼ cups beef stock
2 tablespoons Worcestershire
    sauce
½ cup golden raisins
salt
freshly ground black pepper

Preparation time: about 10
minutes
Cooking time: about 1¼–1½
hours
Microwave setting: Full power
(High)

1. Place the peas and stock in a
large casserole. Cover and cook
for 20 minutes.

2. Stir, re-cover and cook on
Medium for 45–60 minutes until
tender, stirring occasionally.
Drain thoroughly.

3. Place the butter in a bowl and
cook on Full power for 1
minute or until melted. Stir in
the carrots, onion and celery.
Cover and cook for 4 minutes,
stirring once.

4. Stir in the curry powder and
cook for 1 minute. Blend in the
flour. Gradually add the tomato
paste, beef stock,
Worcestershire sauce, golden
raisins, salt and pepper to taste.
Cook for 5–7 minutes, stirring
every 2 minutes until thickened.

5. Stir in the peas. Cook for 2
minutes to heat through.

Cook's Tip

Basmati rice should be washed
in several changes of cold water
before cooking to remove as
much excess starch as possible.
This unprocessed Indian rice
has a delicate flavor and fine
scent which is characteristic of
pillau. Take care not to damage
the grains as you wash the rice.
If you cannot find basmati rice
in the supermarket look for it at
delicatessens or Asian stores.

*Curried black-eyed peas; Vegetable and
cashew rice*

SAUCES

A good sauce makes a simple meal special, and with a microwave there is no excuse for lumpy sauce or gravy. The sauce does not stick to a hot pan and burn, nor does it require the constant attention necessary for traditional cooking. Follow the advice on these pages to adapt your favorite sauces to microwave cooking.

Sauce-making in the microwave is far simpler than by traditional methods and has a greater chance of success. Since the sauce is cooked in a bowl or measuring cup it does not stick and burn on the bottom of a hot saucepan. It is also less likely to form lumps if it is beaten regularly during cooking. Traditional principles can be applied with slight adaptation and one-step sauces can be cooked with great ease. Even the more difficult sauces which are based on a liaison of eggs and butter, or those thickened with egg, can be cooked in the microwave.

Cookware

Instead of saucepans and wooden spoons, when making a sauce in the microwave you will need a large bowl or measuring cup and a whisk. A 1-pint glass measuring cup, which can actually hold up to 2½ cups, is large enough for beating 1¼ cups of sauce, but if you are preparing 2½ cups, use a 1-quart measuring cup or bowl.

Bowls and measuring cups replace saucepans for microwave sauces.

One-step Savory White Sauce

This is a basic recipe for a one-step sauce, thickened with flour and enriched with a knob of butter. It can be flavored with chopped herbs, cheese, onion, eggs or anchovies in the same way as a White Sauce (see page 162), which is prepared by the roux method.

Makes 2½ cups
⅓ *cup all-purpose flour*
2½ *cups milk*
salt
freshly ground white or black
 pepper
2 *tablespoons butter*

Preparation time: 5 minutes
Cooking time: 7–10 minutes
Microwave setting: Full power (High)

1. Place the flour in a large measuring cup or bowl. Gradually pour in the milk, beating to make a smooth paste. As the mixture becomes smooth you can add the milk more quickly.

2. Add a little seasoning and the butter. Give the sauce a quick beating, then cook for 3–4 minutes, or until the edges of the sauce have started to thicken slightly around the bowl.

3. Beat the sauce thoroughly, scraping any set bits of flour from the bottom and sides of the measuring cup. Remember, do not put a metal whisk in the microwave.

4. Cook for a further 4–6 minutes, until the sauce is boiling and thickened. Beat at least once during the cooking time.

5. Beat the cooked sauce thoroughly to make sure that it is perfectly smooth. Adjust the seasoning.

Flavorings for One-step Savory White Sauce

Onion sauce Finely chop 1 onion and place it in a small bowl with a knob of butter. Cover and cook on Full power for 3–4 minutes, until softened. Add to the cooked sauce and stir well.

Cheese sauce Stir ¾ cup grated sharp Cheddar cheese into the cooked sauce. Heat for 30 seconds if necessary.

Chive sauce Snip a large bunch of chives into the sauce and add a knob of butter to enrich it. Serve with fish.

Mustard sauce Select a mild mustard – whole-grain is ideal as it gives plenty of flavor; alternatively, use a Dijon mustard. Add 3–4 tablespoons of the mustard to the sauce, or to taste. This is excellent with boiled ham, broiled sausages or mackerel.

Mushroom sauce Add 1⅓ cups finely sliced button mushrooms to the butter and cover. Cook for 2 minutes before stirring in the flour and milk. Continue as in the main recipe. Serve with fish, chicken or vegetables.

Seasoning

The sauce can be seasoned before cooking but, just as when cooking sauces by traditional methods, this first addition of seasoning should be very light and the cooked sauce should be tasted and the seasoning adjusted to taste just before it is served.

Reheating sauces

A sauce can be prepared well in advance and left until required, then reheated in the microwave just before it is to be served.

It is important to prevent a skin from forming on the surface of the sauce while it is standing. Cover the surface with a piece of microwave-safe plastic wrap or waxed paper, pressing it gently over the sauce, right up to the edges of the container. Just before reheating the sauce, peel off the paper and lightly scrape away the sauce with a knife, taking care not to break the paper into the sauce.

Alternatively, sweet dessert sauces can be sprinkled with superfine sugar, in a light, even layer to prevent a skin from forming.

Before reheating, the sauce should be thoroughly beaten to mix it together well and it should be beaten again just before serving.

Freezing sauces

Sauces which are thickened with eggs or which contain cream should not be frozen. However, sauces made by the roux method (Béchamel-type sauces) or one-stage white sauces which are thickened with flour can be successfully frozen. Pack them in small rigid containers or bags supported in containers until the sauce is frozen.

Defrosting sauces

The sauce should be turned into a suitable bowl, then defrosted on a low setting, preferably Defrost. When it has softened it should be thoroughly beaten so that it is as smooth as possible before it is reheated on Full power. Beat the sauce once during heating, then again before serving. When it has just defrosted the sauce may look slightly separated but it becomes smooth again on heating.

Hollandaise Sauce

This rich sauce is one of the mother sauces – it forms the basis for many other well-known sauces which are made by the same method, among them the Sauce Béarnaise (see page 165). The sauce consists of egg yolks which are emulsified with butter in a creamy liaison. It can be served with plain cooked vegetables or fish.

Makes about 1 cup
2 tablespoons water
1 teaspoon lemon juice
2 large egg yolks
salt
white pepper (preferably freshly ground)
½ cup butter

Preparation time: 5 minutes
Cooking time: 4½–5 minutes
Microwave setting: Full power (High)

1. Place the water and lemon juice in a bowl and cook for 2 minutes, until boiling. Some of the water should have evaporated. Take care to watch the water all the time in case your microwave is particularly speedy in which case the water may evaporate too rapidly.

2. Add the yolks to the bowl as soon as it is removed from the microwave and beat vigorously.

3. Place the butter in a measuring cup and heat for 2–2½ minutes, until melted and very hot.

4. Beating all the time, pour the hot butter onto the yolks in a very slow trickle. Do not pour the butter in too quickly or the sauce will curdle. The eggs should absorb the butter to yield a smooth creamy sauce.

5. Place the sauce in the microwave to heat for about 30 seconds, until thickened. Lightly stir the sauce, then serve at once.

6. The prepared sauce can be set aside to be reheated later. Cover its surface with waxed paper or plastic wrap to prevent a skin from forming. Before reheating, remove the paper and cook the sauce for 30 seconds at a time until it is hot. Stir gently and serve.

Speedy Hollandaise

Make the Hollandaise in a blender or food processor. Place the yolks and seasoning in the machine, then add the hot water and lemon juice and process until smooth. Heat the butter for an extra 30–60 seconds, so that it is really hot, then pour it very slowly onto the yolks while the machine is running. The emulsified sauce should be hot and ready to serve.

Variations on Hollandaise Sauce

Lemon Hollandaise Stir 1 teaspoonful finely grated lemon rind into the sauce just before it is heated for the final 30 seconds. Excellent with fish and shellfish, or with chicken.

Mustard Hollandaise Stir 1 teaspoon Dijon mustard into the Hollandaise sauce just before it is served. Serve with beef steaks.

Tomato Hollandaise Add 1 teaspoon concentrated tomato paste to the sauce just before it is heated for the final 30 seconds. Serve with vegetables or seafood.

Hollandaise with capers Stir 1 tablespoon chopped capers into the sauce just before it is served. A good tangy accompaniment for seafood or for broiled veal steaks.

White Sauce

Makes 1¼ cups
1¼ cups milk
*1 small onion, peeled and stuck
    with 6 cloves*
½ carrot, peeled and sliced
½ celery stalk, chopped
2 tablespoons butter
¼ cup all-purpose flour
salt
freshly ground black pepper

Preparation time: about 10
minutes, plus infusing
Cooking time: about 6 minutes
Microwave setting: Full power
(High)

1. Place the milk, onion, carrot
and celery in a medium bowl
and cook for 3 minutes.

2. Leave to infuse for 10 minutes
before straining.

3. Place the butter in a 2½-cup
bowl and cook for 30 seconds
or until melted.

*From left to right: White sauce; Caper
sauce; Egg sauce; Fish sauce; Parsley
sauce; Cheese sauce*

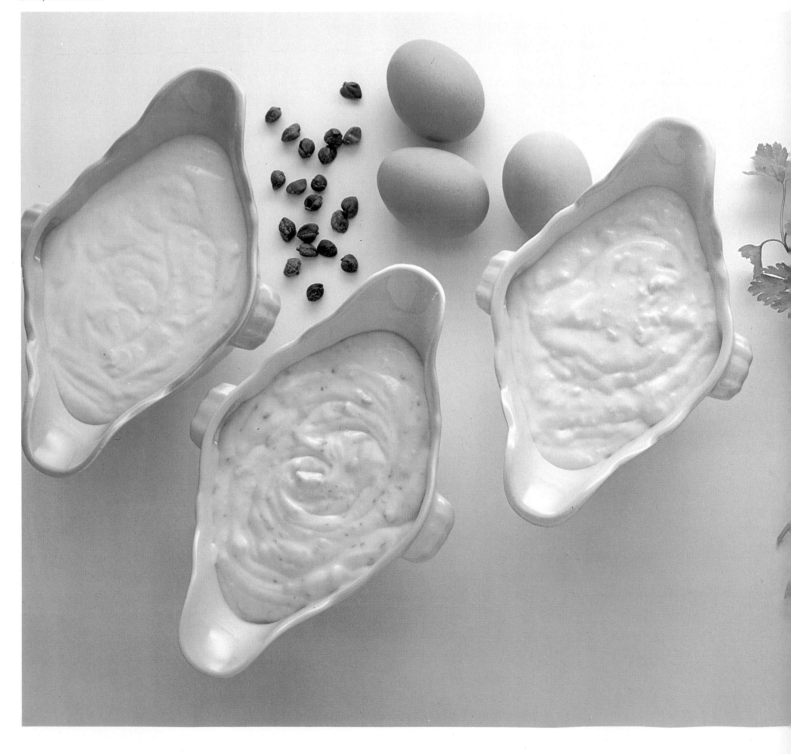

Variations

4. Stir in the flour and gradually blend in the strained milk. Cook for 2½ minutes, stirring every minute, until thick and smooth.

5. Stir in the salt and pepper to taste.

Caper Sauce: Add 1 tablespoon chopped capers and 1 tablespoon caper juice. Serve with boiled chicken, boiled ham or plain fish.

Egg sauce: Add 1 finely chopped hard-cooked egg. Add a pinch of paprika, if liked. Serve with vegetables and fish.

Fish Sauce: Add 2 tablespoons shelled cooked shrimp, ½ teaspoon lemon juice or ½ teaspoon anchovy extract and a pinch of paprika. Serve with vegetables or fish.

Parsley Sauce: Add 1 tablespoon chopped fresh parsley. Serve with fish.

Cheese Sauce: Stir ½ – ¾ cup grated Cheddar cheese into the sauce until it melts. Season with 1 teaspoon mustard. Serve with vegetables, pasta, and fish. This is also an excellent sauce for making a speedy fish or chicken pie, topped with mashed potato.

Cranberry Sauce

Makes about 1 cup
1½ cups fresh cranberries
heaped ½ cup superfine sugar
grated rind of 1 orange
3 tablespoons orange juice

Preparation time: about 3
minutes, plus chilling
Cooking time: about 14
minutes
Microwave setting: Full power
(High) and Defrost

1. Place the cranberries, sugar,
and orange rind and juice in a
small bowl. Cover and cook on
Full power for 4 minutes.

2. Stir the mixture, re-cover and
cook on Defrost for 10 minutes,
stirring halfway through.

3. Purée in a blender or food
processor. Chill. Serve with
roast turkey.

*Clockwise from top: Sauce Béarnaise;
Bread sauce; Tomato sauce; Onion
sauce; Curry sauce. Center: Cranberry
sauce*

Tomato Sauce

Makes 2½ cups
2 tablespoons butter
1 onion, peeled and finely
    chopped
1 garlic clove, peeled and
    crushed
salt
1 teaspoon sugar
1 teaspoon dried oregano
2 tablespoons tomato paste
¼ cup all-purpose flour
4 tomatoes, peeled and roughly
    chopped
freshly ground black pepper
⅔ cup hot chicken stock

Preparation time: about 15
minutes, plus cooling
Cooking time: about 13
minutes
Microwave setting: Full power
(High)

1. Place the butter, onion, garlic,
salt, sugar, oregano and tomato
paste in a large bowl. Cover and
cook for 5 minutes.

2. Stir in the flour, tomatoes and
pepper, then cover and cook for
a further 5 minutes.

3. Stir in the hot stock. Cool the
sauce slightly.

4. Pour into a blender or food
processor and purée until
smooth.

5. Sieve the sauce. Return to the
bowl and reheat for 3 minutes
before serving. Serve with
hamburgers, chops, sausages
and fish.

Curry Sauce

Makes about 2 cups
1 onion, peeled and chopped
1 garlic clove, peeled and
    crushed
1 medium apple, peeled, cored
    and chopped
1 tablespoon ground coriander
1 teaspoon turmeric
½ teaspoon ground cumin
½ teaspoon chili powder
¼ teaspoon ground cinnamon
¼ teaspoon ground ginger
¼ teaspoon grated nutmeg
1½ tablespoons all-purpose flour
1 tablespoon tomato paste
1 teaspoon lemon juice
¼ teaspoon meat extract
2 teaspoons curry paste
2 cups hot stock
salt
freshly ground black pepper

Preparation time: about 10
minutes
Cooking time: 12½–17½ minutes
Microwave setting: Full power
(High)

1. Place the onion, garlic, apple,
coriander, turmeric, cumin, chili
powder, cinnamon, ginger and
nutmeg in a medium bowl.
Cover and cook for 4½ minutes,
stirring halfway through
cooking.

2. Stir in the flour, tomato paste,
lemon juice, meat extract, curry
paste, stock, and salt and
pepper to taste. Cover and cook
for 8–13 minutes, stirring
halfway through cooking.

Sauce Béarnaise

Makes ⅔ cup
6 tablespoons butter
2 tablespoons tarragon vinegar
1 shallot, peeled and chopped
salt
freshly ground black pepper
2 large egg yolks

Preparation time: about 5
minutes
Cooking time: about 1½
minutes
Microwave setting: Full power
(High)

1. Place the butter in a bowl
and cook for 1 minute or until
melted.

2. Beat the tarragon vinegar,
shallot, salt, pepper and egg
yolks into the butter. Cook for
30 seconds, beating the sauce
every 15 seconds.

3. As soon as the sauce is ready,
place the bowl in cold water to
prevent further cooking.

Cook's Tip

To prevent curdling, check the
sauce frequently during
cooking. Serve with broiled
steak.

Bread Sauce

Makes 1¼ cups
1 onion, peeled and stuck with
    8 cloves
about 1¼ cups milk
1½ cups fresh white bread
    crumbs
¼ cup butter, cut into pieces
salt
freshly ground white pepper

Preparation time: about 10
minutes
Cooking time: about 7 minutes,
plus standing
Microwave setting: Full power
(High)

1. Place the onion, 1¼ cups milk,
the bread crumbs, butter, and
salt and pepper to taste in a
medium bowl. Cover and cook
for 5 minutes. Leave to stand,
covered, for 15 minutes.

2. Remove the onion and add 2
more tablespoons of milk to
thin, if necessary. Cook,
uncovered, for 2 minutes
longer, stirring halfway through.

Onion Sauce

Makes 1¼ cups
2 cups peeled and finely
    chopped onions
1 tablespoon butter
2 teaspoons cornstarch
⅔ cup milk
salt
freshly ground black pepper

Preparation time: about 10
minutes
Cooking time: about 6½
minutes
Microwave setting: Full power
(High)

1. Place the onions and butter in
a medium bowl, cover and cook
for 5 minutes, stirring after 2.

2. Blend the cornstarch with a

little of the milk. Stir into the
remaining milk, and add to
the onions. Add the salt and
pepper.

3. Cover and cook for 1½
minutes, stirring once.

Orange Sauce

Makes 1¾ cups
6 tablespoons butter
1½ cups confectioners' sugar, sifted
¾ cup concentrated orange juice
1 tablespoon cornstarch
grated rind of 1 orange
1 egg, separated

Preparation time: about 10 minutes
Cooking time: about 3½ minutes
Microwave setting: Full power (High)

1. Place the butter in a medium bowl, and cook for 1 minute or until melted. Beat the confectioners' sugar into the melted butter with a wooden spoon.

2. Blend the orange juice and cornstarch together and stir into the sugar mixture. Beat in the orange rind and egg yolk, incorporating them thoroughly.

3. Cook for 2½ minutes or until thickened, stirring every 30 seconds. Beat the egg white into the orange sauce.

Gooseberry Sauce

Makes about 2 cups
2¾ cups gooseberries, topped and tailed
⅔ cup water
¼ cup cornstarch
¼ cup superfine sugar

Preparation time: about 10 minutes
Cooking time: about 9 minutes
Microwave setting: Full power (High)

1. Place the gooseberries and ½ cup of the water in a large bowl. Cover and cook for 6 minutes, stirring halfway through cooking.

2. Rub through a strainer or blend in a blender or food processor until smooth.

3. Blend together the cornstarch and remaining water. Stir into the gooseberries. Stir in the sugar and cook, uncovered, for 3 minutes, stirring halfway through.

4. Serve with broiled mackerel or any oily fish.

Applesauce

Makes scant 1 cup
2 tablespoons water
grated rind of ½ small lemon
1 tablespoon superfine sugar
1 tablespoon butter
4 cups peeled, cored and finely sliced cooking apples

Preparation time: about 10 minutes
Cooking time: about 5 minutes
Microwave setting: Full power (High)

1. Place all the ingredients in a large bowl. Cover and cook for 5 minutes, stirring halfway through cooking. Cool the sauce slightly.

2. Pour into a blender and purée until smooth.

3. Return to the bowl and reheat for 3 minutes.

Melba Sauce

Makes 1 cup
3 cups raspberries, sieved
3 tablespoons superfine sugar
2 teaspoons cornstarch
1 tablespoon water
½ teaspoon lemon juice

Preparation time: about 10 minutes, plus cooling
Cooking time: about 2½ minutes
Microwave setting: Full power (High)

1. Place the raspberries and sugar in a 2½-cup bowl.

2. Blend the cornstarch with the water and stir into the raspberries. Cook for 2½ minutes, stirring every minute.

3. Stir in the lemon juice, and allow to cool. Serve with ice cream or cold fruit salad.

Chocolate Custard Sauce

Makes 1¼ cups
1 tablespoon cornstarch
1 tablespoon cocoa powder
2 tablespoons superfine sugar
1¼ cups milk
1 tablespoon butter

Preparation time: about 5 minutes
Cooking time: about 2½ minutes
Microwave setting: Full power (High)

1. Place the cornstarch, cocoa powder and sugar in a 2½-cup bowl. Gradually blend in the milk.

2. Cook for 2½ minutes, stirring every minute, until thick and smooth. Beat in the butter and serve with cold or hot desserts.

Jam Sauce

Makes ¾ cup
4 tablespoons jam
1 tablespoon lemon juice
4 tablespoons water

Preparation time: about 5 minutes
Cooking time: about 3 minutes
Microwave setting: Full power (High)

1. Place the jam, juice and water in a 2½-cup bowl. Cook for 3 minutes, stirring halfway through.

2. Sieve the sauce if necessary. Serve with rice pudding.

Custard Sauce

Makes 1¾ cups
1¼ cups milk
2 drops vanilla extract
1 egg
1 egg yolk
¼ cup superfine sugar
¼ cup all-purpose flour

Preparation time: about 10 minutes
Cooking time: about 2 minutes
Microwave setting: Full power (High)

1. Place the milk and vanilla extract in a 2½-cup bowl and cook for 2 minutes.

2. Place the egg, egg yolk and sugar in a medium bowl and beat together. Add the flour and beat until smooth.

3. Gradually stir the milk into the egg mixture.

4. Cook the custard sauce for 2 minutes, beating every 30 seconds, until thick and smooth.

Clockwise from top: Orange sauce; Gooseberry sauce; Applesauce; Melba sauce; Chocolate custard sauce; Jam sauce. Center: Custard sauce

DESSERTS AND CAKES

Many old-fashioned desserts that traditionally require hours of cooking can be ready in minutes in the microwave with excellent results. Fruit can also be cooked with ease and success, either to be served simply or as the basis for mousses, molds or ice creams.

The speed of microwave cooking means a traditional Christmas Plum pudding can be cooked in minutes rather than hours. The result is delicious – just as expected of old-fashioned methods. If the rise of the pudding is not quite as even as it could be, then it is a small price to pay for the speed and ease of the cooking method.

Fruit

Quartered, sliced or left whole, fruit cooks well in the microwave. The fruit can be poached in syrup to be served hot or cold, and various fruits can be combined in a compote.

Sliced fruits can be cooked until fallen, then sieved or puréed in a blender. The cooled purée can be combined with custard sauce and whipped cream, then chilled to make a delicious fruit fool. Fruit purées also make excellent fillings for crêpes or pastry shells.

When cooking whole fruit, there are a few points to remember. If the fruit is not peeled, then the peel should be scored to prevent it from bursting. The whole fruits should be positioned as far apart as possible in the cooking dish and they should be rearranged at least once during the cooking time.

Crumbles

Traditionally, the characteristics of a good crumble are the crisp, broken texture and a nice brown top. Crumble toppings can be cooked in the microwave but for a good result the traditional basic recipe requires a little adaptation. Since the microwave does not brown the top of the crumble, then add ingredients to improve the appearance as well as the texture. Try some of the following suggested additions, stirring them into a combination of half fat to flour, sweetened with brown sugar. Remember that you can always brown the top under a broiler.

Walnuts and orange Add plenty of chopped walnuts and the grated rind of 1 orange.

Filbert and gingersnap Add plenty of chopped toasted filberts and some crushed gingersnap cookies.

Almond and citrus peel Add toasted, chopped blanched almonds and candied peel.

Piecrusts

Most pastry does not cook well in the microwave (unless the model combines both microwave energy and traditional heat). It is possible to speed up the cooking time of a pastry shell by par-cooking it in the microwave before finishing off in the conventional oven. For puff pastry or piecrusts, it has to be said that traditional or combination cooking methods are by far the best; the traditional methods give a browner finish but puff pastry still rises.

However, suet-crust pastry cooks very well in the microwave in either savory or sweet dishes. It can be rolled with a filling and cooked in a roasting bag or covered dish.

Cooking whole apples

1. The cored apples have their skin scored all the way around so that they will not burst during cooking. They are arranged as far apart as possible in the cooking dish so that they will cook evenly.

2. Here a simple filling of mincemeat is spooned into the middle of each apple. Do not overfill the apples.

3. Halfway through the cooking time the apples are rotated so that both sides of each piece of fruit cook evenly.

Fillings for apples

Nutty apricot filling Mix a little apricot jam with some chopped toasted nuts (filberts, walnuts or cashews) and stir in some cake or cookie crumbs.

Orange and raisin Mix some orange marmalade with raisins and a dash of sherry or rum.

Banana and coconut Mix chopped banana with a little lemon juice, shredded coconut and some orange juice.

GUIDE TO DEFROSTING FRUIT

Quantity of fruit and freezing method	Time in minutes on Full power (High)	Time in minutes on Defrost
1 pound fruit, dry packed with sugar	4–8	—
1 pound fruit, packed with sugar syrup	8–12	—
1 pound tray-frozen fruit	—	4–8

GUIDE TO COOKING FRUIT

Fruit	Preparation	Cooking time in minutes on Full Power (High)
1 pound apricots	Wash and pit, then sprinkle with ½ cup sugar.	6–8
1 pound cooking apples (4 cups)	Peel, core and slice, then sprinkle with ½ cup sugar.	6–8
1 pound gooseberries (3 cups)	Top and tail, then sprinkle with ½ cup sugar.	4
4 medium-sized peaches	Wash and pit, then sprinkle with ½ cup sugar.	4–5
6 medium-sized pears	Peel, halve and core. Dissolve 6 tablespoons sugar in a little water and pour over the pears.	8–10
1 pound cherries or plums (damsons or greengages)	Wash and pit. Sprinkle with ½ cup sugar and the grated rind of ½ lemon.	4–5
1 pound soft berry fruits (4 cups)	Top and tail or hull. Add ½ cup sugar.	3 5
1 pound rhubarb (4 cups)	Trim and cut into short pieces. Add ½ cup sugar and the grated rind of 1 lemon.	8–10

Sweet rich puddings

Rich puddings that are laden with fruit and sugar can be cooked with success in the microwave but they must be watched carefully to make sure that they do not overcook and dry out or burn. Plum Pudding is a typical example – it cooks, or can be reheated, with success but it is vital to check early on in the suggested cooking time to make sure that the mixture is not overcooking. You should stay near throughout the process of cooking such puddings.

Baking

It has to be said that most traditional baking is best left to the realms of conventional cooking methods for fine results. However, the microwave can be used to make a quick cake or some moist gingerbread. There are, however, a few rules to remember.

The shape of the cooking container plays an important role in determining the success of the result. Oblong or square dishes tend to expose the mixture in the corners to overcooking. Round dishes are better and ring dishes are ideal for making cakes. The bottom of the dish can be lined with a circle of waxed paper to facilitate easy removal of the cooked cake.

The cooking container should be greased with butter or margarine but it should not be greased and floured as you would a baking pan for a conventional oven, because this results in an unpleasant floury film on the outside of the cooked cake.

The microwave will not brown the cake, so those that are flavored with chocolate look best. Alternatively, the finished cake can be coated in a frosting and decorated, or topped with toasted nuts, or a little jam and coconut to improve its appearance.

Bakeware

Metal pans should not be used in the microwave. Instead, round dishes, bread dishes and ring dishes should be employed. Look out for specialist microwave cookware or use dishes like those shown here which are suitable for use in the conventional oven as well as in the microwave.

Note: Defrost fruits in their covered freezer containers, if suitable, for the times given above, or transfer the fruit to a suitable covered dish first. The times given will partially defrost the fruit. The fruit should then be allowed to stand at room temperature to finish defrosting. The times given are approximate and will depend upon the freezing method used, the type and shape of the container and the variety of the fruit. Gently shake or stir the fruit during defrosting.

Apple and Golden Raisin Pie

Serves 4–6

⅔ *cup shredded suet*
⅓ *teaspoon baking powder*
2¼ *cups self-rising flour*
⅔ *cup water*
½ *cup fresh whole-wheat bread*
  crumbs
½ *cup soft dark brown sugar*
2 *tablespoons ground*
  cinnamon
¾ *cup golden raisins*
4 *cooking apples peeled, cored*
  and thinly sliced

Preparation time: about 20 minutes
Cooking time: about 11 minutes, plus standing
Microwave setting: Full power (High)

1. Place the shredded suet, baking powder and flour in a bowl. Mix together. Gradually add water to make a soft, but not sticky dough.

2. Roll out two thirds of the dough to ⅛ inch thick and line a greased 1½-quart bowl.

3. Mix together the bread crumbs, sugar, cinnamon and golden raisins.

4. Starting and ending with the apples, make alternate layers with the bread crumb mixture.

5. Roll out the remaining dough and cover the filling, making sure the lid is well sealed. Make 2 cuts in the lid.

6. Cover with plastic wrap, allowing sufficient room for rising. Cook for 5 minutes. Turn the bowl around and cook for a further 6 minutes.

7. Leave to stand, covered, for 5 minutes before unmolding and serving.

Apple and Blackberry Crumble

Serves 4–6

4 *cooking apples, peeled, cored*
  and thinly sliced
3 *cups blackberries or*
  blueberries
6 *tablespoons sugar*
1½ *cups all-purpose flour*
6 *tablespoons soft dark brown*
  sugar
6 *tablespoons butter*

Preparation time: about 20 minutes
Cooking time: about 9 minutes, plus standing and broiling
Microwave setting: Full power (High)

1. Make alternate layers with the apples, blackberries or blueberries and sugar in a casserole.

2. Mix the flour and dark brown sugar together, then cut in the butter until the mixture resembles fine bread crumbs. Sprinkle the mixture over the fruit.

3. Cook for 9 minutes. Leave the crumble to stand for 3 minutes before serving. Brown under a preheated conventional broiler.

Apple and golden raisin pie; Apple and blackberry crumble

Maple Steamed Pudding

Serves 3–4
3 tablespoons maple syrup
1 cup self-rising flour
¼ cup shredded suet
¼ cup superfine sugar
1 eggg
2 tablespoons water
4 tablespoons milk
2 drops vanilla extract

Preparation time: about 10 minutes
Cooking time: about 4 minutes, plus standing
Microwave setting: Full power (High)

1. Place the maple syrup in the bottom of a lightly greased 3¾-cup bowl.

2. Mix the flour, suet and sugar together. Beat in the egg, water, milk and vanilla extract. Spoon the mixture onto the syrup in the bowl.

3. Cover the bowl with plastic wrap and cook for 2 minutes. Remove the plastic wrap and turn the bowl around. Cook for a further 2 minutes.

4. Leave the pudding to stand for 2 minutes before unmolding and serving.

Cold Strawberry Soufflés

Serves 6
2 tablespoons white wine
4 tablespoons water
2 tablespoons unflavored gelatine
1¼ cups strawberry purée
1½ tablespoons lemon juice
½ cup superfine sugar
1¼ cups heavy cream, stiffly whipped
6 egg whites, stiffly beaten
To decorate:
1¼ cups heavy or whipping cream, stiffly whipped
6 strawberries

Preparation time: about 15 minutes, plus setting
Cooking time: about 15 seconds
Microwave setting: Full power (High)

1. Place the wine, water and gelatine in a small bowl. Stir together well and cook for 30 seconds. Stir to ensure the gelatine has dissolved.

2. Add the strawberry purée, lemon juice and sugar to the gelatine mixture and stir well. Allow to cool, stirring once or twice.

3. Carefully fold the cream into the strawberry mixture, then gently fold in the egg whites.

4. Tie waxed paper around the outside of 6 individual ramekin dishes so that it extends ½ inch above the rims. Spoon the soufflé mixture into the ramekin dishes.

5. Chill until set, then remove the paper and decorate each soufflé with piped whipped cream and a strawberry.

Maple steamed pudding; Cold strawberry soufflés

Plum Pudding

Serves 6–8
3/4 cup all-purpose flour
1/4 teaspoon salt
6 tablespoons shredded suet
1/2 teaspoon apple pie spice
1/4 teaspoon ground cinnamon
3/4 cup fresh white bread crumbs
1/4 cup superfine sugar
1/3 cup mixed peel
1/4 cup molasses sugar
1/3 cup candied cherries, chopped
2/3 cup currants
2/3 cup golden raisins
3/4 cup raisins
3 tablespoons chopped blanched almonds
1/4 cup chopped apple
juice of 1/2 lemon
grated rind of 1/2 lemon
4 tablespoons brandy
2 eggs
1/4 cup milk
2 teaspoons corn syrup
2 teaspoons gravy browning

Preparation time: about 15 minutes
Cooking time: about 10 minutes, plus standing
Microwave setting: Full power (High)

1. Mix all the dry ingredients together, then stir in the liquids.

2. Place the mixture in a 1-quart greased bowl. Cover the bowl and cook for 5 minutes.

3. Leave to stand for 5 minutes, then cook for a further 5 minutes.

4. Allow the pudding to stand for 5 minutes.

To reheat
Sprinkle 1½ tablespoons water or brandy over the pudding. Cover and cook for 4 minutes. Leave for 4 minutes. Cover and cook for 3 minutes.

Queen of Puddings

Serves 4
3 egg yolks
1/4 cup superfine sugar
2 1/2 cups milk
2 drops vanilla extract
3 cups fresh white bread crumbs
grated rind of 1 lemon
2 tablespoons jam
Topping:
3/4 cup superfine sugar
3 egg whites, stiffly whisked

Preparation time: about 15 minutes
Cooking time: about 10½ minutes, plus broiling
Microwave setting: Full power (High)

1. Place the egg yolks, superfine sugar, milk and vanilla extract in a 1-quart bowl and beat together. Cook for 4 minutes.

2. Place the bread crumbs and grated lemon rind in a 5-cup casserole and stir in the milk mixture. Cook for 5½ minutes, stirring halfway through cooking. Set aside.

3. Place the jam in a small dish. Cook for 1 minute.

4. Gently spread the jam over the cooked bread crumb and milk mixture.

5. For the topping, fold the sugar into the beaten egg whites. Spread the meringue over the jam and swirl into decorative peaks.

6. Brown the pudding under a preheated conventional broiler.

Plum pudding; Queen of puddings

Fruit-stuffed Crêpes

Serves 4
1 egg
1 egg yolk
1¼ cups milk
1 cup all-purpose flour
pinch of salt
vegetable oil for frying
Filling:
1½ cups dried apricots
hot water
2 drops almond extract
juice of 1 lemon
½ cup blanched almonds,
*   ground*
2 tablespoons superfine sugar
2 tablespoons confectioners'
*   sugar, sifted*

Preparation time: about 35 minutes
Cooking time: about 10 minutes, plus standing
Microwave setting: Full power (High)

1. Beat together the egg, egg yolk and milk.

2. Sift the flour and salt into a large bowl. Make a well in the center and gradually incorporate the egg and milk mixture into the flour to make a batter.

3. Using a conventional stove,

heat a little of the oil in a 6-inch skillet. Pour a small amount of batter into the pan, swirling the batter around. Cook until golden, then turn and cook the second side.

4. Make 8 crêpes in this way. Set the crêpes aside while you make the filling.

5. Place the apricots in a bowl and cover with hot water. Cover and cook for 5 minutes. Leave the apricots to stand, covered, for 20 minutes.

6. Drain the apricots, pour into a blender and purée until smooth.

7. Mix together the apricot purée, almond extract, lemon juice, almonds and superfine sugar. Spread a little of the purée in the center of each crêpe and roll up.

8. Arrange 4 crêpes on a plate and cook for 2½ minutes. Repeat with the remaining crêpes.

9. Sprinkle with confectioners' sugar before serving.

Baked Stuffed Apples

Serves 4
3 tablespoons mincemeat
3 tablespoons strawberry jam
1 teaspoon ground cinnamon
4 large cooking apples, total
*   weight 2¾ pounds, cored, skin*
*   scored around middle*

Preparation time: about 15 minutes
Cooking time: 14 minutes, plus standing
Microwave setting: Full power (High)

1. Mix the mincemeat, jam and cinnamon together.

2. Stand the apples in a shallow dish. Spoon the filling into the cavities in the apples.

3. Cook for 7 minutes. Turn the dish around and cook for a further 7 minutes or until tender.

4. Leave the apples to stand for 4 minutes before serving.

Fruit-stuffed crêpes; Baked stuffed apples

Mixed Fruit Dessert

Serves 4
$\frac{1}{2}$ cup butter
$\frac{1}{2}$ cup superfine sugar
2 eggs
1$\frac{1}{2}$ cups self-rising flour
2 tablespoons water
scant $\frac{1}{2}$ cup mixed dried fruit

Preparation time: about 10 minutes
Cooking time: about 10 minutes, plus standing
Microwave setting: Full power (High)

1. Cream the butter and sugar together until light and fluffy.

2. Beat in the eggs one at a time, then carefully fold in the flour. Stir in the water and mixed dried fruit.

3. Place the mixture in a greased 5-cup bowl. Cover and cook for 5 minutes. Turn the bowl and cook for a further 5 minutes.

4. Remove the cover and leave the pudding to stand for 2 minutes before unmolding. Serve hot.

Honey Cheesecake

Serves 6
1 tablespoon light corn syrup
$\frac{1}{2}$ cup butter
2$\frac{2}{3}$ cups graham-cracker crumbs
12 ounces cream cheese
$\frac{1}{3}$ teaspoon ground cinnamon
1 tablespoon lemon juice
2 tablespoons water
1 tablespoon unflavored gelatine
4 tablespoons clear honey
$\frac{2}{3}$ cup heavy cream, whipped
To decorate:
$\frac{2}{3}$ cup heavy or whipping cream, whipped
walnut halves

Preparation time: about 15 minutes, plus chilling
Cooking time: about 2 minutes
Microwave setting: Full power (High)

1. Place the syrup and butter in a medium bowl. Cook for 1$\frac{1}{4}$ minutes.

2. Stir in the crushed crackers and mix well. Use this mixture to line an 8-inch quiche dish or microwave-safe springform pan.

3. Beat the cheese and cinnamon together until smooth.

4. Place lemon juice and water in a 2$\frac{1}{2}$-cup bowl or measuring cup and stir in the gelatine. Cook for 15 seconds. Stir well to make sure the gelatine has dissolved.

5. Place the honey in another 2$\frac{1}{2}$-cup bowl or measuring cup. Cook for 30 seconds. Pour the honey into the first bowl containing the gelatine and mix well together. Allow to cool slightly.

6. Beat the honey mixture into the cheese mixture, then fold in the whipped cream. Spoon into the quiche dish and chill until set.

7. Decorate the cheesecake with the whipped cream and walnut halves.

Mixed fruit dessert; Honey cheesecake

Pineapple Upside-down Cake

Serves 4
2/3 cup butter
2 tablespoons soft dark brown sugar
3 slices canned pineapple
4 candied cherries
1/2 cup superfine sugar
2 eggs
1 cup self-rising flour, sifted

Preparation time: about 15 minutes
Cooking time: about 7 1/2 minutes, plus standing
Microwave setting: Full power (High)

1. Use 1 tablespoon of the butter to grease a 5-cup soufflé dish.

2. Place 2 tablespoons of the butter and the brown sugar in the dish and cook for 1 minute.

3. Arrange the pineapple slices and cherries in the bottom of the dish in a decorative pattern.

4. Beat the remaining butter and superfine sugar together until light and fluffy.

5. Beat in the eggs and fold in the flour. Gently spread this over the pineapple and cherries.

6. Cook for 3 minutes, turn the dish around and cook for a further 3 1/2 minutes.

7. Leave the pudding to stand for 3 minutes before unmolding.

Chocolate Mousses

Serves 6
6 slices jam jelly roll
4 tablespoons Grand Marnier
8 ounces semisweet chocolate, broken into pieces
2 tablespoons butter
1 tablespoon cold strong black coffee
1 tablespoon brandy
4 egg yolks
4 egg whites, stiffly beaten
To decorate:
2/3 cup heavy or whipping cream, stiffly whipped
1 tablespoon grated chocolate

Preparation time: about 10 minutes, plus setting
Cooking time: about 2 minutes
Microwave setting: Full power (High)

1. Place 1 slice of jelly roll into the bottom of each of 6 small dishes. Sprinkle with the Grand Marnier.

2. Place the chocolate in a medium bowl. Cook for 2 minutes or until it has melted.

3. Beat in the butter, coffee, brandy and egg yolks. Gently fold in the egg whites.

4. Spoon the mousse over the jelly rolls and smooth over the tops. Chill until set.

5. Decorate each dish with swirls of cream and grated chocolate.

Trifle

Serves 6
6 pound cake slices, cut into pieces
12 almond cookies, crumbled
2/3 cup sweet sherry
1/4 cup orange juice
4 tablespoons strawberry jam
2 tablespoons superfine sugar
1 3/4 cups milk
3 eggs
1 egg yolk
2/3 cup heavy or whipping cream, whipped
1 egg white, stiffly beaten
To decorate:
chopped nuts
angelica

Preparation time: about 15 minutes, plus cooling
Cooking time: about 5 1/2 minutes
Microwave setting: Full power (High)

1. Divide the cake slices between 6 glass dishes or 1 large dish. Sprinkle the cookies over the cake.

2. Mix the sherry and orange juice together and pour over the cake and crumbs. Spread a little strawberry jam over the soaked cake and crumbs.

3. Place the sugar and milk in a small bowl. Cook for 2 minutes.

4. Beat the eggs and egg yolk together, then pour the heated milk onto the eggs, beating all the time. Cook for 3 1/2 minutes. Check and beat the custard every 30 seconds.

5. Beat and strain the custard before spooning it over the soaked cake bases. Leave to cool.

6. Fold the cream and egg white together. Gently spread the cream over the custard and decorate with chopped nuts and angelica.

Pineapple Tart

Serves 4–6
1/2 cup butter
1 tablespoon corn syrup
2 2/3 cups gingersnap cookie crumbs
4 tablespoons pineapple juice
2 envelopes unflavored gelatine
1 × 14-ounce can crushed pineapple, drained
2 ounces white marshmallows
1 1/4 cups heavy cream, whipped
To decorate;
candied cherries
pieces of crystallized angelica

Preparation time: about 20 minutes, plus setting
Cooking time: about 2 1/2 minutes
Microwave setting: Full power (High)

1. Place the butter and syrup in a medium bowl. Cook for 1 1/4 minutes.

2. Stir in the cookie crumbs and mix well. Use this mixture to line an 8-inch microwave-safe springform pan with removable bottom.

3. Place the pineapple juice into a 2 1/2-cup bowl and stir in the gelatine. Cook for 10 seconds, then stir until the gelatine has dissolved.

4. Place the crushed pineapple and marshmallows in a medium bowl. Cook for 1 minute or until the marshmallows have melted.

5. Beat the pineapple juice and gelatine mixture into the pineapple and marshmallow mixture. Leave until almost set.

6. Fold the cream into the pineapple mixture and then spoon into the pan, smoothing the top.

7. Decorate the tart with the cherries and angelica. Chill until set. Serve chilled.

Clockwise: Trifle; Chocolate mousses; Pineapple upside-down cake; Pineapple tart

Fresh Fruit Salad

Serves 4–6

$\frac{1}{3}$ cup sugar
$\frac{2}{3}$ cup water
1 tablespoon lemon juice
1 tablespoon Grand Marnier
$\frac{1}{3}$ cup peeled, halved and
  deseeded green grapes
$\frac{1}{3}$ cup peeled, halved and
  deseeded blue grapes
1 dessert apple, peeled, cored,
  quartered and thinly sliced
1 pear, peeled, cored and sliced
1 large orange, peeled and
  segmented
1 papaya, peeled, deseeded and
  diced
$\frac{1}{4}$ honeydew melon, skin
  removed, seeded and diced
1 kiwifruit, peeled and sliced
1 banana, peeled and sliced

Preparation time: about 30
minutes, plus cooling and
standing
Cooking time: about 5 minutes
Microwave setting: Full power
(High)

1. Place the sugar and water in a
bowl and cover. Heat for 5
minutes, then stir and leave to
cool.

2. When the syrup is cool, stir in
the lemon juice and Grand
Marnier.

3. Place all the prepared fruit
into a large glass bowl. Pour the
syrup over the fruit.

4. Leave for 1 hour to let the
flavors mingle.

Baked Bananas

Serves 4

4 bananas, peeled and sliced
4 tablespoons rum
4 tablespoons orange juice
$\frac{2}{3}$ cup gingersnap cookie crumbs
3 tablespoons soft brown sugar
$\frac{2}{3}$ cup heavy cream

Preparation time: about 10
minutes
Cooking time: about 4 minutes
Microwave setting: Full power
(High)

1. Place the sliced bananas in a
glass dish.

2. Mix the rum and orange juice
together and pour over the
bananas.

3. Mix the cookie crumbs and
sugar together and sprinkle over
the bananas.

4. Cover the dish and cook for 2
minutes. Turn the dish around
and cook for a further 2
minutes.

5. Uncover and pour the cream
over the baked bananas. Serve
at once.

Lemon Meringue Pie

Serves 4
unbaked 7-inch pastry shell
finely grated rind of 2 lemons
$\frac{1}{2}$ cup lemon juice
$\frac{1}{4}$ cup cornstarch
1 cup superfine sugar
2 egg yolks, beaten
2 egg whites, stiffly beaten

Preparation time: about 20 minutes
Cooking time: about 10 minutes, plus browning
Microwave setting: Full power (High)

1. Prick the pastry shell all over with a fork and cook for 5 minutes, or until crisp.

2. Make up the lemon rind and juice with cold water to $1\frac{1}{4}$ cups.

3. Mix the cornstarch in a $2\frac{1}{2}$-cup bowl with a little of the lemon water, then gradually stir in the

4. Beat 6 tablespoons of the sugar with the egg yolks. Beat into the lemon mixture. Pour into the pastry shell and leave to cool.

5. Place the beaten egg whites in a bowl and fold in the remaining sugar. Pile over the lemon filling. Cook for $1\frac{1}{2}$ minutes.

6. Place under a preheated conventional broiler to lightly brown the meringue.

Hot Ginger Cake

Serves 4
$\frac{1}{2}$ cup butter
$\frac{1}{2}$ cup superfine sugar
2 eggs
1 cup self-rising flour, sifted
2 teaspoons ground ginger
5 pieces preserved ginger,
   drained and sliced

Preparation time: about 10 minutes
Cooking time: about 6 minutes, plus standing
Microwave setting: Full power (High)
remaining liquid. Cook for $3\frac{1}{2}$ minutes or until the mixture thickens, stirring every minute.

1. Cream the butter and sugar together until light and fluffy.

2. Beat in the eggs, one at a time, then fold in the sifted flour and ground ginger.

3. Arrange the sliced ginger over the bottom of a greased $3\frac{3}{4}$-cup bowl. Spoon the cake batter over the ginger in the bowl, smoothing the top.

4. Cover and cook for 3 minutes. Turn the bowl around and cook for a further 3 minutes.

5. Remove the cover and leave the cake to stand for 2 minutes before turning it out. Serve hot with Custard Sauce (page 166) or Orange Sauce (page 166).

From left to right: Fresh fruit salad; Baked bananas; Lemon meringue pie; Hot ginger cake

Lemon Cake

Makes one 7-inch cake
2 cups self-rising flour
$\frac{1}{4}$ teaspoon baking powder
$\frac{1}{2}$ cup butter
$\frac{1}{2}$ cup soft dark brown sugar
2 eggs
2 teaspoons grated lemon rind
1 tablespoon milk
2 teaspoons lemon juice
3 tablespoons Lemon Curd
    (page 184)
2 cups confectioners' sugar,
    sifted
2 tablespoons water
few drops yellow food
    coloring
8 candied lemon slices, to
    decorate

Preparation time: about 10
minutes, plus cooling
Cooking time: about 5 minutes,
plus standing
Microwave setting: Full power
(High)

1. Sift the flour and baking
powder into a large bowl. Cut in
the butter until the mixture
resembles bread crumbs, then
stir in the sugar.

2. Beat in the eggs, one at a
time, then stir in the lemon rind,
milk and lemon juice.

3. Spoon the batter into a
greased and lined 7-inch round,
$3\frac{1}{2}$-inch deep container. Stand
on an up-turned plate and cook
for 2 minutes.

4. Turn the container around
and cook for a further 2
minutes. Turn around again and
cook for 1 minute.

5. Leave the cake to stand for 5
minutes before unmolding it
upside down onto a serving
plate. Leave to cool completely.

6. Split the cake into 2 layers.
Spread one layer with the lemon
curd and replace the other layer
on top.

7. Mix the confectioners' sugar
with the water and yellow food
coloring. Pour over the cake
and decorate with lemon slices.

Gingerbread

Makes one cake
$2\frac{1}{2}$ tablespoons molasses
1 tablespoon superfine sugar
$\frac{1}{4}$ cup butter
1 cup all-purpose flour, sifted
$\frac{1}{2}$ teaspoon baking soda
$\frac{1}{2}$ teaspoon apple pie spice
$\frac{1}{2}$ teaspoon ground ginger
1 large egg

Preparation time: about 10
minutes, plus cooling
Cooking time: about 5 minutes,
plus standing
Microwave setting: Full power
(High)

1. Place the molasses, sugar and
butter in a medium bowl. Cook
for $1\frac{1}{2}$ minutes.

2. Allow the mixture to cool
slightly, then stir in the sifted
flour, baking soda, spice and
ginger. Beat in the egg.

3. Pour into a greased $1\frac{1}{2}$-quart
deep oblong plastic container.
Stand on an up-turned plate and
cook for 1 minute.

4. Turn the container around
and cook for 1 minute. Turn it
around again and cook for $1\frac{1}{2}$
minutes.

5. Allow the gingerbread to
stand for 5 minutes before
unmolding. Leave to cool
completely. Serve cut in slices
and buttered or with Orange
Sauce (page 166).

Chocolate Banana Ring

Makes one cake
2 eggs
4 tablespoons milk
$\frac{3}{4}$ cup soft brown sugar
$\frac{1}{2}$ cup soft margarine
3 cups peeled and chopped
    bananas
2 cups self-rising flour
$\frac{1}{2}$ teaspoon baking powder
3 tablespoons instant chocolate
    drink powder

Icing:
$\frac{1}{2}$ cup confectioners' sugar
3 tablespoons instant chocolate
    drink powder
1 tablespoon water

Preparation time: about 10
minutes, plus cooling
Cooking time: about 15
minutes, plus standing
Microwave setting: Full power
(High)

1. Place the eggs, milk, sugar,
margarine and bananas into a

blender and purée until smooth.

2. Sift the flour, baking powder
and chocolate powder into a
large bowl. Stir in the banana
purée and mix thoroughly until
well combined.

3. Spoon the batter into a $2\frac{3}{4}$-
quart greased microwave baking
ring. Cook for 5 minutes. Turn
the ring around and cook for a
further 5 minutes.

4. Gently spread any uncooked
cake batter over the surface.
Turn and cook for 5 minutes.

5. Leave the ring to stand for 5
minutes before unmolding.
Leave to cool completely.

6. Mix the sifted confectioners'
sugar and chocolate powder
together. Quickly stir in the
water. Spread over the top and
let some drizzle down the sides
of the cake.

One-step Chocolate Cake

Makes one 7-inch cake
$\frac{3}{4}$ cup soft margarine
heaped $\frac{3}{4}$ cup superfine sugar
$\frac{1}{3}$ cup cocoa
$1\frac{1}{4}$ cups self-rising flour
1 teaspoon baking powder
2 drops vanilla extract
3 tablespoons milk
3 eggs
2 tablespoons confectioners'
    sugar, to decorate

Preparation time: about 10
minutes, plus cooling
Cooking time: about $8\frac{1}{2}$
minutes, plus standing
Microwave setting: Full power
(High)

1. Place all the ingredients,
except the confectioners' sugar,
in a large bowl. Beat well until
the batter is smooth, but be
careful not to overbeat.

2. Spoon the batter into a
greased and lined 7-inch round,
$3\frac{1}{2}$-inch deep container. Stand
the container on an up-turned
plate and cook for 3 minutes.

3. Turn the container around
and cook for a further 3
minutes. Turn around again and
cook for $2\frac{1}{2}$ minutes.

4. Leave the cake to stand for 5
minutes before unmolding.
Leave to cool completely.

5. Unmold the cake upside
down onto a serving plate and
sift confectioners' sugar over
the top to decorate.

*Clockwise: Lemon cake; Gingerbread;
One-step chocolate cake; Chocolate
banana ring*

P RESERVES

The microwave is not a suitable appliance in which to cook vast quantities of preserves but it can be useful for preparing a small quantity of jam or a jar of tasty relish. Try the recipes in this chapter, and follow the guidelines below if you want to prepare small quantities of your favorite traditional recipes.

When making jams and other preserves in the microwave follow the usual principles of preserving but it is also important to use a large cooking container to make sure the ingredients do not boil over in the oven cavity during cooking.

Jams and preserves cooked in the microwave have a fine, full flavor and they are usually better in color than their conventionally cooked counterparts. Do not attempt to cook large quantities of preserves in the microwave – it is difficult to control the boiling and unlikely that you will be able to find a bowl large enough to accommodate all the ingredients with plenty of room for stirring the preserve.

Cookware

Large microwave-safe glass mixing bowls are best for cooking preserves in the microwave. Glazed earthenware mixing bowls absorb some energy and become hot. If you have a very large casserole dish,

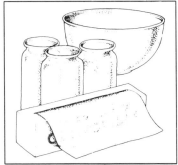

A large mixing bowl or a big casserole dish is essential for allowing preserves to boil in the microwave.

that may also be suitable. If the preserve needs to be covered during cooking use a dinner plate; make sure that it is plain and microwave-safe, and that it does not have any metal decoration.

Evaporation

When cooking in the microwave there can be less evaporation of liquid than when cooking conventionally. This can affect the result when making some chutneys and pickles that require lengthy boiling by traditional methods in order to reduce the liquid content. The balance of sugar and vinegar is important to preserve the chutney or pickle but it can be wavered. Reduce the quantity of liquid slightly and check the progress of the preserve as it cooks – if it is very moist, then remove the lid ahead of the time suggested in the recipe.

Sterilizing jars

The microwave is useful for sterilizing a small number of jars. Do not put jars with metal clips or attachments in the microwave. Make sure that the jars are free of all metal and that they are thoroughly washed. Using boiling water from the kettle, half fill each jar with water and stand the jars in the microwave. Cook on Full power until you can see the water boiling, then continue to cook for 5 minutes. If the jars are to be used immediately, then they should be emptied and dried, then filled with preserve at once. Alternatively, if they are to be left

standing for some time, then cover them with microwave-safe plastic wrap and cook for a further 1–2 minutes, then leave to stand and remove the plastic wrap just before they are to be emptied and used.

Stages in making jams and other sweet preserves

Extracting the pectin The first stage in making any jam, marmalade or preserve is to soften the fruit and extract the pectin. Pectin is the substance which is naturally present in fruit and which makes a preserve gel when it has been cooked.

The pectin combines with the sugar and acid to create the gel, or set. Without pectin the preserve will not gel. Commercial pectin can be obtained and the manufacturer's directions should always be followed.

Selecting the fruit Fruit contains the most pectin when it is slightly underripe. Fruit which is ripe contains a certain amount of pectin but fruit which is overripe has a very low pectin content. So, for best results select slightly underripe fruit and combine it with some which is ripe for flavor.

Softening the fruit The initial step in jam making is softening the fruit. The fruit is prepared according to its type, then cooked with the minimum of liquid – or a measured quantity in the case of marmalades – until very tender. The microwave can be particularly useful for this stage of preparation even if the rest of the preserve is cooked by traditional methods. For example, lemons or oranges can be softened in water in the microwave before they are cut up for marmalade.

Preparing the jars

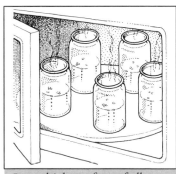

Jars which are free of all metal can be sterilized in the microwave. They should be half filled with boiling water from the

kettle and covered with microwave-safe plastic wrap if they are to be left for any length of time before they are used.

Adding the sugar The sugar is added when the fruit is tender. If the fruit is still slightly tough before the sugar is added, then it will not continue to tenderize after this stage. The sugar should dissolve as quickly as possible and it should lower the temperature of the jam as little as possible. So, for best results, warm the sugar in the microwave for a few minutes before adding it to the fruit. Stir it thoroughly into the fruit, then cook, stirring occasionally, until it has dissolved completely.

Boiling This is the process which excludes most types of preserves from being suitable for microwave cooking. You must allow room for the preserve to come to a rolling boil in the bowl. So the quantities that can be cooked successfully are small.

Testing for doneness

When the preserve has boiled until the water and sugar concentration is just right it must be tested to determine whether gelling point has been reached.

Flake test Take the bowl of preserve from the microwave and use a wooden spoon to give it a stir, then lift the spoon out of the preserve and hold it in the air above the bowl. The preserve should form small flakes as it drips.

Refrigerator test Have a very cold saucer ready in the refrigerator. Spoon some preserve onto the saucer and leave it for a few minutes. Push the preserve with your finger and there should be a clear skin formed on its surface when the preserve is ready.

If the preserve does not pass the test, then return it to the microwave and continue to cook it for a few minutes before testing it again. Do not allow the preserve to cook for more than 3–4 minutes before re-testing,

and less if it is a second or third re-test. Once the preserve is overcooked it will not gel.

Filling jars

Drain and thoroughly dry the sterilized jars and fill them with the preserve. Cover immediately with waxed discs, placing the waxed sides down. The discs should come all the way to the sides of the jar and cover the whole surface of the preserve in order to exclude air and molds or other microorganisms which will spoil the preserve. The preserve should be covered with an airtight lid either immediately, while it is still very hot, or when it has cooled completely.

Labeling and storing

When cooked, label the jars clearly with the name of the preserve and the date when it was made. Store them in a dark, cool, dry place.

Making strawberry jam

1. The fruit is softened. Here strawberries have lemon juice added to them. The lemon juice provides the acid that is necessary for the jam to gel.

2. The sugar is added when the fruit has been softened. The mixture is thoroughly stirred at this stage and until the sugar has dissolved.

3. Testing for doneness – here the saucer test is used to determine whether the jam is ready for putting in jars. The wrinkles which are obvious when the jam is pushed with a finger mean that it is ready for pouring into jars.

Fruit and pectin

All fruits contain some natural pectin but it is present in varying degrees. The fruits which contain the highest amounts include sour apples, crabapples, currants, gooseberries, some grapes and lemons. In most cases, these fruits will gel without any additional pectin. One of the exceptions is when the fruit become overripe and its pectin content lowers.

Fruits with a very low natural pectin content include apricots, figs, pears, raspberries and strawberries. For these fruits to gel they will almost certainly require added pectin or acid.

Commercial pectin to help fruits gel is widely available in liquid and powder forms Recipes will specify if extra pectin is required.

Always follow the directions on the pectin's label but remember, the two forms of pectin are treated differently.

Add powdered pectin to the strained fruit juice before it is heated. Then bring to a full boil and add the sugar and return to a boil.

Liquid pectin, however, is added to the fruit juice and sugar after the mixture has reached a full boil.

Strawberry Jam

Makes about 1 pound
1 pound strawberries, hulled
1 tablespoon lemon juice
1¾ cups sugar

Preparation time: about 5 minutes, plus cooling
Cooking time: about 26 minutes
Microwave setting: Full power (High)

1. Place the strawberries and lemon juice in a large bowl. Cover and cook for 6 minutes or until the strawberries are soft.

2. Stir in the sugar. Cook uncovered for a further 20 minutes or until setting point is reached, stirring halfway through cooking.

3. Allow the jam to cool before spooning into clean, dry jars. Seal and label.

Lemon Curd

Makes about 1 pound
½ cup butter
heaped 1 cup sugar
¾ cup lemon juice
grated rind of 3 large lemons
3 eggs

Preparation time: about 10 minutes, plus cooling
Cooking time: about 8 minutes
Microwave setting: Full power (High)

1. Place the butter, sugar, lemon juice and rind in a large bowl. Cook, uncovered, for 3 minutes, stirring halfway through cooking.

2. Beat the eggs into the mixture. Cook for 5 minutes or until the lemon curd thickens, checking and stirring every minute.

3. Allow the lemon curd to cool before spooning into clean, dry jars. Seal and label.

From left to right; Strawberry jam; Lemon curd; Gooseberry jam; Tomato chutney

Gooseberry Jam

Makes about 1½ pounds
7 fluid ounces water
1 pound gooseberries, topped and tailed
2¼ cups sugar

Preparation time: about 10 minutes, plus cooling
Cooking time: about 30 minutes
Microwave setting: Full power (High)

1. Place the water and gooseberries in a large bowl. Cover and cook for 5 minutes.

2. Stir, and remove the cover. Cook for a further 5 minutes or until the gooseberries are soft.

3. Stir in the sugar. Cook uncovered for 20 minutes or until gelling point is reached, stirring halfway through cooking.

4. Allow the jam to cool before spooning into clean, dry jars. Seal and label.

Tomato Chutney

Makes about 3 pounds
2 large tomatoes, peeled and chopped
3 cups peeled, cored and sliced cooking apples
1 onion, peeled and chopped
2 cups raisins
2 teaspoons salt
2 teaspoons apple pie spice
1 garlic clove, peeled and crushed
heaped 1 cup dark brown sugar
2 cups malt vinegar

Preparation time: about 10 minutes, plus cooling
Cooking time: about 34 minutes
Microwave setting: Full power (High)

1. Place the tomatoes, apples and onion in a large bowl. Cover and cook for 10 minutes, stirring halfway through cooking.

2. Stir in the raisins, salt, apple pie spice, garlic, sugar and vinegar. Cook for 24 minutes, stirring the chutney several times during cooking.

3. Allow the chutney to cool before spooning into clean, dry jars. Seal and label.

Corn Relish

Makes about 3 pounds

*1 large onion, peeled and
    chopped*
*4 cloves garlic, peeled and
    crushed*
*1½ cups peeled and diced
    carrots*
*1 green bell pepper, cored,
    seeded, and chopped*
4 tablespoons vegetable oil
salt
freshly ground black pepper
2 tablespoons cornstarch
2 tablespoons water
3 tablespoons mustard
¼ teaspoon turmeric
1¼ cups white-wine vinegar
½ cup sugar
*3 cups fresh corn kernels or 1½
    10-ounce package frozen
    whole kernel corn*

Preparation time: about 30
minutes, plus cooling
Cooking time: 25 minutes
Microwave setting: Full power
(High)

1. Place the onion, garlic,
carrots and green bell pepper in
a large mixing bowl. Stir in the
oil and salt and pepper. Cook
for 5 minutes.

2. Meanwhile, blend the
cornstarch with the water,
mustard, turmeric and vinegar.
Add the sugar to the onion
mixture, then pour in the liquid
and stir well. Cook for a further
5 minutes.

3. Stir in the corn and mix
thoroughly, then cook for 15
minutes, stirring three times
during cooking.

4. Cool slightly before spooning

into clean, dry jars. Cover
immediately and label. Allow the
relish to mature for at least a
week before eating it. It will
keep for up to 3 months.

Cook's Tip

This tasty relish is a natural
partner for serving with
hamburgers and hot dogs. It is
also an ideal pantry ingredient
to have on hand for serving as
an accompaniment to cold meat
as part of a buffet or quick meal.

Corn is a grain native to North
America and has always been a
staple of the American diet. Use
this recipe to capture the
flavors of summer when fresh
corn is widely available.

The most important factor
affecting the flavor of corn is
how quickly it gets from the
field to your table. When the
ears are picked from the stalk

they instantly start to dehydrate.

Only buy ears of corn with
green husks and plump, firm
kernels. The kernels may be
white or yellow but the color
isn't an indication of taste. If the
kernels are very small, that is a
sign that the corn is still
immature. If the kernels are very
large and firm, that is a sign they
are old and will probably be
tough.

Corn relish

Cranberry Relish

Makes about 2 pounds

4 cups cranberries
2 onions, peeled and finely chopped
3 cloves garlic, peeled and crushed
heaped 1 cup sugar
1 tablespoon whole-grain mustard
$\frac{1}{2}$ cup red-wine vinegar

Preparation time: 10 minutes
Cooking time: 15 minutes
Microwave setting: Full power (High)

1. Place the cranberries, onions, garlic, sugar, mustard and vinegar in a large bowl and stir well. Cover with plastic wrap, allowing a small gap for the steam to escape, and cook for 10 minutes.

2. Uncover and give the relish a good stir, then cook for a further 5 minutes.

3. Have ready two 16-ounce jars, clean and thoroughly scalded. Cool slightly. Stir the relish, then spoon into the jars and seal and label. Store in a cool place for up to 3 months. This is a good relish to serve with hamburgers, baked ham and cold roast meats or poultry (particularly turkey!) or it also goes well with full-flavored sharp Cheddar cheese.

Mango Chutney

Makes about 1$\frac{1}{2}$ pounds

1$\frac{1}{2}$ pounds small green mangos
1 large onion, peeled and chopped
1–2 hot green chilies, seeded and chopped
1 tablespoon salt
2 tablespoons ground coriander
4 cloves garlic, peeled and crushed
$\frac{1}{2}$ cup sugar
$\frac{2}{3}$ cup cider vinegar

Preparation time: 30 minutes
Cooking time: 15 minutes
Microwave setting: Full power (High)

1. Peel the mangos and cut the fruit off the seeds in chunks. Place the mango pieces and the onion in a large bowl. Add the chili(es), salt, coriander, garlic, sugar and vinegar and stir well.

2. Cover the bowl, allowing a small gap for the steam to escape, then cook for 7 minutes.

3. Uncover, and give the chutney a good stir to mix all the ingredients. Continue to cook, without a cover, for a further 8 minutes.

4. Ladle the chutney into clean, dry jars and cover tightly. Allow the chutney to mature for at least a week before serving.

Cranberry relish; Mango chutney

*D*RINKS

Once you own a microwave, there is no need to boil a whole kettle full of water if you just want to make a cup of coffee – simply follow the directions on the chart and heat the water and coffee together in a mug. As well as coffee, try the variety of hearty drinks in this chapter.

The microwave is useful for heating up pots of coffee, for making or reheating individual cups of coffee, or for making tea in various quantities.

At the end of a dinner party, the task of making coffee can be tedious. Having battled through the appetizer, entrée and sumptuous dessert, to find yourself out in the kitchen waiting for the kettle to boil, filling the percolator or battling with the latest technology in the way of coffee machines can be very boring.

A little forethought and the microwave can be combined to ease the situation tremendously. Make fresh coffee just before the meal and leave it ready to reheat when it is to be served. Remember to avoid pots with metal trims or decoration. A big plain pot is best – those which have thin curving spouts can be a problem. As the coffee heats, there can be a build up of heat in the depths of the pot which causes the liquid to boil up and out of the spout in a furious – and noisy – escape.

If you know that you will be needing several pots of coffee, then simply prepare some in advance, then put some on just when you finish the meal – it will brew quite nicely while you work your way through the first batch of microwave-reheated coffee.

Remember, too, that you can always reheat leftover cold coffee in a mug. So next time you have a small amount of fresh coffee left in a pot at the end of a meal, transfer it to a mug, cover and store in the refrigerator until you are ready

to reheat it. It may not be quite as good as fresh coffee, but it will make a morning break special.

Heating milk

Milk can be heated very successfully in the microwave, but do remember that it will boil over just as it does in a saucepan if you do not time it accurately or if you leave it totally unattended.

Pour the milk into a pitcher, or heat a small amount in a mug. (This is also useful for preparing breakfast cereals.)

Milk drinks

These can be made in a pitcher or straight in the mugs. The drinks will boil over if they are cooked for too long, so keep an eye on them while they cook until you are absolutely sure of the timing for a certain quantity of a particular drink in your microwave oven.

Try malted drinks, drinking chocolate or cocoa, prepared in a pitcher or in a mug, simply by combining all the ingredients and heating.

Tea

Tea can be made very simply in the microwave using tea bags. Simply boil the water in a suitable cup or mug, then add the tea bag. This is particularly useful if you want to make just one cup, or if you are preparing a herb or fruit tea from a single bag. It is also useful if you want a specific quantity of tea for use in a recipe, such as a punch.

GUIDE TO HEATING COFFEE AND MILK

	Time in minutes on Full power (High)
Black coffee	
$2\frac{1}{2}$ cups, cold	$4\frac{1}{2}$–5
5 cups, cold	7–$7\frac{1}{2}$
Milk	
$\frac{2}{3}$ cup, cold	1–$1\frac{1}{2}$
$1\frac{1}{4}$ cups, cold	2–$2\frac{1}{2}$
Coffee and milk together	
$2\frac{1}{2}$ cups coffee and $\frac{2}{3}$ cup milk, both cold	5–$5\frac{1}{2}$
5 cups coffee and $1\frac{1}{4}$ cups milk, both cold	8–$8\frac{1}{2}$

Cocoa

Serves 4
$\frac{1}{4}$ cup sugar
3 tablespoons cocoa powder
$3\frac{3}{4}$ cups milk

Preparation time: 5 minutes
Cooking time: 4–$4\frac{1}{2}$ minutes
Microwave setting: Full power (High)

1. Place the sugar and cocoa powder in a large suitable pitcher.

2. Add $\frac{2}{3}$ cup of the milk and mix well. Cook for 1–$1\frac{1}{2}$ minutes, or until very hot.

3. Beat in the remaining milk, then cook for a further 3 minutes, or until the cocoa is hot and steaming but not quite boiling. Serve at once.

Lemon Tea

Serves 4
3 cups weak tea
1 lemon, thinly sliced
sugar to taste

Preparation time: 5 minutes
Cooking time: $4\frac{1}{2}$–5 minutes
Microwave setting: Full power (High)

1. Strain the tea into a large tea pot which is suitable for microwave cooking. Cook for $4\frac{1}{2}$–5 minutes, or until very hot.

2. Add the lemon slices, stir lightly and stand for 5 minutes. Pour into heated glasses, sweeten to taste and serve.

Punches

As well as everyday drinks, the microwave is ideal for making warming punches or mulled wine.

Again, the good old mixing bowl will be a useful utensil. A large casserole dish will do just as well, or a pitcher can be used for smaller quantities. Plain, inexpensive glasses can also be used in the microwave to heat individual glasses of mulled wine. Be certain that the glasses are microwave-safe and do not overheat the liquid causing the glass to break. Do not use cut glass because this reflects the microwaves in the same way as metal.

Fruit drinks

As well as hot drinks and alcoholic drinks, the microwave can be used to prepare fruit drinks which are served chilled.

The best known of these is lemonade, but you can also try using oranges, grapefruit or limes, or a mixture of citrus fruits.

By heating eating apples in a small amount of water, with lemon, cloves and sugar you can make a delicious apple drink.

Make fruit syrups by heating raspberries or strawberries with sugar, then pressing the juices through a strainer. A very sweet syrup of this type can be used to flavor milk shakes or yogurt drinks.

Making punch

1. The flavoring ingredients and water are heated together.

2. The sugar is dissolved in wine and rum, for Hot Rum Punch (see page 192).

3. The flavored liquid is strained into the warmed wine and rum mixture.

Lemonade

Serves 6–8
3 tablespoons water
grated rind of 2 lemons
juice of 4 lemons
heaped 1 cup sugar
iced water or sparkling mineral water to serve

Preparation time: 10 minutes
Cooking time: 4 minutes
Microwave setting: Full power (High)

1. Place all the ingredients except the iced water in a large pitcher suitable for use in the microwave. Alternatively, use a bowl.

2. Cook for 4 minutes, stirring twice during cooking, until the sugar has dissolved completely.

3. Cool, then chill thoroughly before serving the concentrated lemonade topped up with iced water or sparkling mineral water.

Cook's Tip

This concentrated lemonade is ideal for summer. Make a batch to keep in the refrigerator for up to a week, ready for diluting to taste as required.

Exotic Fruit Cordial

Makes about 2½ cups
grated rind and juice of 6 limes
⅔ cup water
heaped 1 cup sugar
⅔ cup passionfruit juice
iced water or sparkling mineral water to serve

Preparation time: 15 minutes
Cooking time: 4–5 minutes
Microwave setting: Full power (High)

1. Mix the lime rind and juice and sugar in a large bowl suitable for use in the microwave. Stir well to dissolve the sugar as much as possible before heating.

2. Cook for 4–5 minutes, stirring twice during cooking, until the sugar has dissolved completely.

3. Stir for a few minutes to cool the lime syrup slightly, then add the passionfruit juice and stir well. Leave to cool.

4. The cordial can be served simply, diluted to taste with water, or it can be used to make exotic cocktails with liquors such as gin, rum or vodka.

Plain mugs and glasses can be used to heat individual portions of drinks in the microwave. Larger quantities can be heated in pitchers, bowls or in tea and coffee pots if they are suitable. Pots with long, thin spouts should be avoided.

Hot Chocolate

Makes 3 cups
*2 ounces semisweet chocolate,
 broken into pieces*
2½ cups milk
5 marshmallows, chopped

Preparation time: about 5
minutes
Cooking time: about 8½
minutes
Microwave setting: Full power
(High)

1. Place the chocolate in a large
pitcher. Heat for 3½ minutes or
until the chocolate has melted.

2. Stir in the milk and heat for 4
minutes.

3. Beat in the marshmallows
until they have melted. Heat for
1 minute, then pour into 4
warmed mugs or glasses.

Hot Whiskey Eggnog

Makes about 3¾ cups
3 cups milk
⅓ cup whiskey
¼ cup superfine sugar
2 eggs, lightly beaten
*1 teaspoon grated nutmeg, to
 decorate*

Preparation time: about 5
minutes
Cooking time: about 6 minutes
Microwave setting: Full power
(High)

1. Place the milk, whiskey and
sugar in a large pitcher. Cook
for 6 minutes, stirring halfway
through.

2. Beat the eggs into the hot
milk mixture. Strain into 4
heatproof or warmed tumblers.
Sprinkle grated nutmeg over
each and serve immediately.

Calypso Coffee

Makes 2½ cups
2½ cups cold, strong black coffee
2 tablespoons superfine sugar
4 tablespoons rum
⅔ cup heavy cream

Preparation time: about 5 minutes
Cooking time: about 4½ minutes
Microwave setting: Full power (High)

1. Place the coffee, sugar and rum in a large pitcher. Heat for 4½ minutes, stirring halfway through.

2. Pour the coffee into 4 warmed glasses or cups.

3. Pour a little cream on the top of each coffee.

Orange Tea

Makes 3½ cups
1 cup orange juice
2½ cups water
1 tablespoon superfine sugar
2 tea bags
To decorate:
4 slices orange
4 mint sprigs

Preparation time: about 10 minutes
Cooking time: about 8 minutes
Microwave setting: Full power (High)

1. Place the orange juice, water and sugar in a large pitcher. Cook for 8 minutes, stirring halfway through cooking.

2. Stir in the tea bags, cover and leave to stand for 4 minutes.

3. Stir the orange tea, remove the tea bags, then pour into the 4 glasses and float a slice of orange on the top. Decorate each glass with a sprig of mint.

From left to right: Hot chocolate; Hot whiskey eggnog; Calypso coffee; Orange tea

Mulled Red Wine

Makes about 3½ cups
2 cups red wine
⅔ cup water
⅔ cup orange juice
2 tablespoons superfine sugar
4 tablespoons brandy
½ teaspoon ground cinnamon
8 orange slices, to decorate

Preparation time: about 5 minutes
Cooking time: about 4 minutes
Microwave setting: Full power (High)

1. Place the wine, water, orange juice, sugar, brandy and cinnamon in a pitcher. Stir well and pour into 4 microwave-safe tumblers.

2. Heat for 4 minutes, stirring halfway through.

3. Decorate with the orange slices.

Mulled Cider

Makes just over 3 cups
2 cups apple cider
⅔ cup apple juice
⅔ cup orange juice
2 tablespoons superfine sugar
½ teaspoon apple pie spice
8 apple slices

Preparation time: about 5 minutes
Cooking time: about 4 minutes
Microwave setting: Full power (High)

1. Place the cider, apple juice, orange juice, sugar and spice into a large pitcher. Stir well and pour into 4 microwave-safe tumblers.

2. Place an apple slice in each tumbler. Heat for 4 minutes, stirring halfway through heating.

3. Decorate with the remaining apple slices.

Hot Rum Punch

Makes 3¾ cups
2 cups water
1 orange
6 cloves
2 Ceylon tea bags
rind of ½ lemon
1 cinnamon stick
⅔ cup dark rum
⅔ cup white wine
⅔ cup orange juice
¼ cup soft dark brown sugar
To decorate:
4 small slices orange
4 small slices lemon

Preparation time: about 5 minutes
Cooking time: about 10 minutes
Microwave setting: Full power (High)

1. Place the water in a large pitcher and cook for 5 minutes.

2. Stud the orange with the cloves and add to the water with the tea bags, lemon rind and cinnamon stick. Stir and cover, then set aside for 5 minutes, removing the tea bags after 3 minutes.

3. Meanwhile, place the rum, wine, orange juice and sugar in measuring cup. Cook for 5 minutes, stirring halfway through.

4. Remove the orange and cloves, rind and cinnamon stick. Strain. Mix the tea and rum mixtures together, then pour into 4 heatproof or warmed glasses. Place a small slice of lemon and orange in each glass.

Mulled cider; Hot rum punch; Mulled red wine

FREEZER TO MICROWAVE

The microwave is an oven in its own right but it is also the perfect partner for your freezer. One of the greatest innovations since the introduction of the freezer for storing food, is the microwave for reducing the defrosting times from hours to minutes.

The microwave cuts defrosting times to a fraction of what they would be if the food were left to stand at room temperature. All microwaves come with a Defrost setting, or low settings that are recommended for defrosting. It is important to read the manufacturer's directions carefully and to follow the owner's manual when using your microwave to defrost food. Also, there are certain rules of thumb for defrosting and reheating foods.

Packing food for freezer-to-microwave use

If a little forethought is put into the packing of food before freezing it can save a lot of effort when the food is to be defrosted and reheated.

When freezing foods like vegetables or individual items, it is best to open freeze the items until they are quite hard, then pack them into bags and seal them. Small quantities or single items can be removed with ease if the food is not frozen into a block.

Try to consider the shape of the package that you are freezing. For example, when freezing stews, sauces or other fluid dishes, pack them into containers which can be fitted into a vessel for microwave reheating. Plastic bags can be used to line casserole dishes or bowls which can be used to reheat the dish at a later date. The food is ladled into the bag which is then sealed and frozen in the outer container. Once the package is firm the casserole or dish can be removed.

Boil-in-bags and roasting bags

These are particularly useful as they can be transferred directly from the freezer to the microwave not only to defrost the food but also to reheat it. Remember to use ties which are suitable for use in the microwave or to replace metal ties before transferring the frozen package to the microwave.

Freezer-to-microwave dishes

These are ideal for cooking food in the microwave, for freezing, then for defrosting and reheating in the microwave at a later date. However, unless you are very well equipped in the kitchen you will probably miss the dishes if they are stored away in the freezer for months. The answer is to line the dish with microwave-safe plastic wrap before putting the food into the dish for freezing. If you cook the food in the dish in the first place, then transfer it to a bowl, wash the dish, then line it with the plastic wrap.

Put the food to be frozen into the lined dish, leave plenty of plastic wrap overhanging the side of the dish. Make sure it covers the whole of the bottom,

Using pouches or bags

1. Commercially frozen vegetables or other foods in a pouch can be reheated successfully in the microwave. The pouch should be placed on a plate or suitable shallow dish. Pierce the pouch to allow steam to escape during cooking.

2. Home-made dishes or home-frozen foods can be packed in boil-in bags or roasting bags ready to be reheated in the microwave. Remember to remove all metal clips and replace them with elastic bands or microwave ties. Loosen the tie to allow the steam to escape and place the package on a plate or shallow dish to catch any juices which may escape.

overlapping it well where necessary. If in any doubt use two layers of plastic wrap.

Freeze the food until solid. Gently loosen the frozen food from the dish with a knife, then pull it out in a block, using the overhanging plastic wrap. Wrap it around the food and pack the whole block in a bag, then label and freeze.

To reheat the food, remove the bag and the plastic wrap. If it is stuck to the food, then place the block on a plate and cook on Full power for 1 minute, or until the plastic wrap can be pulled away from the outside of the food. Place the food in the dish in which it was originally molded and it is ready to be defrosted and reheated.

Removing frozen food from ordinary freezer containers

Whether you are packing food in a dish suitable for heating the food or in a simple storage container, then it is sensible to make sure that it will fit into the microwave oven cavity. For example, packing soups in very tall containers may mean that the block of frozen soup is too tall to fit into the microwave for reheating.

If the food does not come out of the container easily, then remove the lid and place the container in the microwave for a minute or so. Release the block of food and transfer it to a suitable container for reheating it completely.

Remember, do not heat food in containers which are not designed to withstand high temperatures.

Lining dishes before freezing blocks of food

1. Here a lasagne is being prepared for freezing. The dish selected is one that will fit in the microwave. It is lined with microwave-safe plastic wrap. The plastic wrap is smoothed evenly over the bottom and sides of the dish. There is plenty of overhanging plastic wrap for easy removal.

2. The ingredients for the lasagne are layered in the plastic wrap-lined dish.

3. When the lasagne is layered, it is frozen until solid, with the ends of plastic wrap still hanging over the edge of the dish. Here it is removed from the dish, with the help of the plastic wrap and a knife to help ease out the block. The lasagne is packed, labeled and frozen.

Selecting the setting

When defrosting raw foods or foods which do not require further cooking before they are served cold, then select a defrost setting.

Defrost or the low power setting recommended by the manufacturer are ideal for defrosting all foods, whether they are to be reheated before serving, cooked with other dishes or served cold. However, if you are in a hurry, the defrosting time of certain foods (mainly cooked dishes) can be reduced by using a higher setting. This is usually acceptable if the food is reheated following defrosting; the aim is to combine the process of defrosting with reheating. Raw foods begin to cook when defrosted on higher settings.

The higher the setting used, then the more attention needed when preparing the food. A medium setting can be used and only moderate attention has to be paid to the food. Full power can also be used but you must stay near and turn, stir and

Defrosting and reheating a block of frozen food

1. The lid is removed from the container and it is heated in the microwave very briefly until the block of food can be released.

2. The food is transferred to a suitable dish as soon as it can be released.

3. As it defrosts, the block of food is carefully broken up, and lumps of food are eased apart.

rearrange the food regularly; otherwise some parts will overcook before others are defrosted. The advantage of using the higher setting is, of course, in the speed. It is useful if you are in a hurry to defrost and reheat a casserole or spaghetti sauce for a quick supper, or similar foods. To offer some guidance when using a high setting, the charts provide an outline of the timings and brief instructions.

GUIDE TO ONE-STAGE DEFROSTING AND REHEATING

Food	Quantity	Time in minutes on Full power (High)	Method
Purchased frozen foods: defrosting time only			
Bread, rolls	2	1	Place on paper towels.
Bread, sliced	2 slices	1	Turn over once.
Cheesecake	2 pieces, 6 ounces total	30 seconds	—
Orange juice, frozen	$\frac{3}{4}$ cup	1	Transfer to suitable pitcher and stir once
Purchased frozen foods: defrosting and reheating			
Cod in butter sauce (in pouch)	6 ounces	5	Pierce pouch before cooking to allow steam to escape. Place on plate or dish.
Fish cakes	4, 8 ounces total	4	Turn fish cakes over and around once.
French fries, oven baked	4 ounces	2	Rearrange once.
Frozen home-made cooked dishes			
Bread, garlic	$\frac{1}{2}$ French loaf, 6 ounces	$1\frac{1}{2}$	Place on a double thickness of paper towel.
Casserole, beef	4 servings	10–12	Break up the block of casserole as it defrosts, then stir as it reheats.
Cottage pie	4 servings	15	Remove dish from oven after 10 minutes. Cover with foil and stand for 5 minutes. Remove foil and cook for a further 5 minutes.
Complete meal: meat patties new potatoes peas gravy	2, 4 ounces total 4, 5 ounces total 4 ounces 4 tablespoons	8	Cover plate with cover or microwave-safe plastic wrap.
Hamburgers (raw)	4, 8 ounces total	6	Turn burgers over and around 3 times.
Rice, long-grain, cooked	3 cups	8	If in boil-in bag, pierce bag to allow steam to escape. Cover dish if rice is not in a bag. Stir once.
Frozen home-made sauces and soups			
Spaghetti sauce	4 servings	12–14	Break up the block as it defrosts, then stir once as it reheats.

GUIDE TO ONE-STAGE DEFROSTING AND REHEATING

Food	Quantity	Time in minutes on Full power (High)	Method
Onion sauce	$1\frac{1}{4}$ cups	6–7	Break up the block as it defrosts, then beat well halfway through reheating and before serving.
Applesauce	$\frac{2}{3}$ cup	3	Stir once.
Cauliflower soup	5 cups	18	Break up the block of soup as it defrosts, then stir halfway through reheating and again before serving.

Guide to defrosting

Always err on the side of safety and follow the minimum times given in recipes, adding extra if the food is not sufficiently defrosted. Special care should be taken with poultry. When completely defrosted, the wings and legs will be flexible and there won't be any ice in the cavity. The following hints will also ensure good results:

● Pierce any skins, membranes or pouches before defrosting.
● Turn foods over during defrosting.
● If turning is not possible, rotate the dish during defrosting.
● Flex any pouches that cannot be broken up or stirred during the defrosting time and rotate frequently.
● Place any foods like cakes, rolls, turnovers and pastry items on a double sheet of paper towel during defrosting to absorb any excess moisture.
● Any blocks of frozen food should be broken up with a fork during defrosting so that the microwave energy can concentrate on the unfrozen block.
● Separate any blocks of frozen meats like hamburgers, sausages and steaks as they defrost.
● Remove any giblets from the cavity of chickens and other poultry or game birds as they defrost.
● Open all cartons and remove any lids and wrappings before defrosting.
● With items like meat roasts, whole poultry and whole fish, defrost the items until icy, then leave to defrost completely during the standing time.
● If any parts of the food start to defrost at too fast a rate or become warm, then shield or protect these areas with small, smooth strips of aluminum foil, attached with wooden toothpicks if necessary.
● Always observe a standing time – foods will continue to defrost with the heat produced via conduction. Allow foods to defrost until just icy for bet results.
● Home-frozen food tends to take longer to defrost than commercially frozen food because of the ice crystals.
● When freezing a meal, do not overlap foods and place the thicker, denser items toward the edges of the plate.

Guide to reheating

Most foods will reheat in the microwave oven without loss of quality, flavor, color and some nutrients. Follow the guidelines below.
● Arrange foods on a plate for reheating so that the thicker, denser and meatier portions are to the outer edge.
● Cover foods when reheating to retain moisture, unless otherwise stated.
● When reheating observe the standing time to avoid overcooking.
● When reheating potatoes in their skins, breads, pastry items and other moist foods, place them on a sheet of paper towel so that it will absorb any moisture.
● Stir foods regularly while reheating. If stirring is not possible, then rotate the food or dish or rearrange it.

Smoked Haddock with Noodles

Serves 3–4
1 small onion, peeled
6 cloves
1 bay leaf
6 peppercorns
1 small carrrot, peeled
$1\frac{1}{4}$ cups milk
14 ounces frozen smoked
    haddock fillets
3 tablespoons butter
$\frac{1}{3}$ cup all-purpose flour
2 teaspoons chopped fresh
    parsley
$\frac{3}{4}$ cup grated cheese
$\frac{1}{2}$ 16-ounce package noodles
$2\frac{1}{2}$ cups boiling water
1 tablespoon vegetable oil
To garnish:
lemon slices
tomato slices
parsley sprigs

Preparation time: 10 minutes
Cooking time: $28\frac{1}{2}$–30 minutes,
plus standing
Microwave setting: Defrost and
Full power (High)

1. Stud the onion with cloves
and place in a bowl with the bay
leaf, peppercorns, carrot and
milk. Cook on Defrost for 10–11
minutes until hot. Leave to stand
so that the milk is flavored while
cooking the haddock.

2. Pierce the smoked haddock
bags and place on a plate. Cook
on Full power for 10 minutes,
shaking the bags gently after 6
minutes.

3. Place the butter in a bowl and
cook on Full power for 30
seconds to melt. Add the flour,
mixing well. Gradually add the
strained milk and cook on Full
power for 2–$2\frac{1}{2}$ minutes, stirring
every 1 minute until the sauce is
smooth and thickened. Stir in
the parsley and the cheese until
melted.

4. Place the noodles, water and
oil in a deep container. Cover
and cook on Full power for 6
minutes. Leave to stand for 3
minutes, then drain.

5. Flake the haddock into bite-
sized pieces, removing and
discarding any skin. Stir into the
sauce, tossing gently to mix.

6. To serve immediately, arrange
the noodles around the edge of
a shallow serving dish. Spoon
the haddock mixture into the
center. Garnish with lemon
slices, tomato slices and parsley
sprigs.

FREEZING DETAILS
1. Prepare the recipe to the end
of step 5.

2. Cool quickly, pack the
noodles and haddock mixture
separately into rigid containers.
Cover, seal, label and freeze for
up to 2 months.

REHEATING DETAILS
Microwave setting: Defrost and
Full power (High)
Defrosting and cooking time:
30–31 minutes

1. Remove all wrappings. Cook
the haddock mixture on Defrost
for 8 minutes. Leave to stand for
5 minutes.

2. Cook the noodles on Defrost
for 6 minutes. Leave to stand for
2 minutes.

3. Cook the haddock mixture
on Full power for 5–6 minutes,
stirring once.

4. Cook the noodles on Full
power for 4 minutes. Serve as in
step 6 above.

Sweet-and-Sour Soup

Serves 4
2 tablespoons vegetable oil
1 pound lean pork, finely
    chopped
$\frac{1}{4}$ cup all-purpose flour
salt
freshly ground black pepper
1 onion, peeled and chopped
1 green bell pepper, cored,
    seeded and chopped
1 large carrot, peeled and
    grated
1 × 16-ounce can tomatoes
$1\frac{1}{4}$ cups chicken stock
1 tablespoon red-wine vinegar
1 garlic clove, peeled and
    crushed
grated rind of 1 orange
1 tablespoon tomato paste
$\frac{1}{2}$ teaspoon ground ginger

Preparation time: 20 minutes,
including heating browning dish
Cooking time: 24 minutes
Microwave setting: Full power
(High)

1. Preheat a browning dish for 8
minutes (or according to the
manufacturer's directions).
Brush with the oil and cook for
a further 1 minute.

2. Toss the pork in the flour
with salt and pepper to taste.
Add the pork to the browning
dish and turn quickly on all
sides to brown evenly. Add the
onion, green bell pepper and
carrot, cover and cook for 8
minutes, stirring once.

3. Transfer to a large bowl and
stir in the tomatoes with their

Pork Rolls with Cabbage

Serves 4
1 pound pork sausage meat
1 onion, peeled and chopped
1⅓ cups chopped button
    mushrooms
1 tablespoon lemon juice
grated rind of ½ lemon
1 teaspoon dry mustard
2 tablespoons chopped fresh
    parsley
1 egg, beaten
salt
freshly ground black pepper
1 medium cabbage, washed
    and shredded
4 tablespoons water
1 tablespoon soy sauce
1 tablespoon vegetable oil
To garnish:
tomato wedges
parsley sprig

Preparation time: 20 minutes,
including heating browning dish
Cooking time: 16–17 minutes
Microwave setting: Full power
(High)

1. Mix the sausage meat with the
onion, mushrooms, lemon
juice, lemon rind, mustard,
parsley, egg and salt and pepper
to taste, blending well. Divide
into 8 portions and shape into
rolls.

2. Place the shredded cabbage
in a bowl with the water and salt
to taste. Cover and cook for 8
minutes, stirring once. Drain
thoroughly and toss with the soy
sauce to coat lightly.

3. If serving immediately, preheat a large browning dish for 8
minutes (or according to the
manufacturer's directions).
Brush with the oil and cook for
a further 1 minute.

4. Add the pork rolls and turn
quickly on all sides to brown
evenly. Cook for 7–8 minutes,
turning and re-arranging the
rolls once. Serve on a bed of
seasoned cabbage and garnish
with tomato wedges and
parsley.

FREEZING DETAILS
1. Prepare the cabbage mixture
and the uncooked pork rolls to
the end of step 2.

2. Cool quickly, pack the
cooked cabbage mixture in a
rigid container. Cover, seal and
label.

3. Freeze the uncooked pork
rolls interleaved between
freezer plastic wrap and
overwrapped with aluminum
foil. Seal, label and freeze both
for up to 3 months.

REHEATING DETAILS
Microwave setting: Defrost and
Full power (High)
Defrosting and cooking time:
28–32 minutes

1. Remove all wrappings. Place
the pork rolls on a plate and
cook on Defrost for 6–7
minutes, turning and
rearranging once. Leave to stand
while cooking the cabbage.

2. Place the frozen cabbage in a
bowl. Cover and cook on Full
power for 4–6 minutes, stirring
frequently.

3. Cook the pork rolls as in
steps 3 and 4 above. Reheat the
cabbage on Full power for 2
minutes if necessary.

4. Serve the pork rolls on the
bed of cooked cabbage and
garnish with tomato wedges and
parsley sprig.

Cook's Tip

If you are freezing this dish, you
must not use frozen sausage
meat to make the rolls. Only
fresh ingredients should be
used if the dish is frozen
uncooked.

juice, stock, vinegar, garlic,
orange rind, tomato paste and
ginger. Add salt and pepper to
taste. Cover and cook for 15
minutes, stirring twice.

4. Serve hot with crusty bread.

FREEZING DETAILS
1. Prepare the recipe to the
end of step 3.

2. Cool quickly, transfer to a
rigid container, allowing 1 inch
headspace. Cover, seal, label
and freeze for up to 2 months.

REHEATING DETAILS
Microwave setting: Defrost and
Full power (High)
Defrosting and cooking time:
32 minutes

1. Remove all wrappings and
place the frozen soup in a
suitable serving dish. Cook on
Defrost for 12 minutes.
Breaking up and stirring twice.
Leave to stand for 10 minutes.

2. Cover and cook on Full
power for 10 minutes, stirring
twice.

3. Serve hot with crusty bread.

*Sweet-and-sour soup; Pork rolls with
cabbage*

Pasta Scallops

Serves 3–4
6 ounces pasta shells
3 cups boiling water
1 tablespoon vegetable oil
salt
6 bacon slices
1⅓ tablespoons butter
1⅓ tablespoons all-purpose flour
1¼ cups milk
freshly ground black pepper
¾ cup grated cheese
2 hard-cooked eggs, shelled and
*   chopped*
To garnish:
parsley sprigs

Preparation time: 10 minutes
Cooking time: 21–24½ minutes
Microwave setting: Full power
(High)

1. Place the pasta in a deep dish with the water, oil and salt to taste. Cover and cook for 12–14 minutes, stirring once. Leave to stand while cooking the bacon and sauce.

2. Place the bacon on a plate or microwave bacon rack, cover with a paper towel and cook for 3 minutes until crisp.

3. Place the butter in a bowl and cook for 30 seconds to melt. Add the flour, blending well. Gradually add the milk and cook for 3½–4 minutes, stirring every 1 minute until smooth and thickened. Add salt and pepper to taste.

4. Stir in two-thirds of the cheese until melted.

5. Mix the eggs with the hot drained pasta and salt and pepper to taste.

6. Arrange the pasta mixture in 4 deep scallop shells. Spoon the sauce over. Crumble the bacon coarsely and sprinkle over the sauce.

7. To serve immediately, cook for 2–3 minutes, re-arranging the shells twice.

8. Brown under a preheated conventional broiler if wished. Garnish with parsley sprigs.

FREEZING DETAILS
1. Prepare the recipe to the end of step 6.

2. Cool quickly, cover, seal, label and freeze for up to 3 months.

REHEATING DETAILS
Microwave setting: Defrost and Full power (High)
Defrosting and cooking time: 23–24 minutes

1. Remove all wrappings and cook the pasta in the scallop shells on Defrost for 10 minutes. Leave them to stand for 10 minutes.

2. Cook on Full power for 3–4 minutes, re-arranging and turning the uncovered scallop shells twice.

3. Brown under a preheated conventional broiler if wished. Garnish with parsley sprigs.

Salami-stuffed Pasta

Serves 4
6 sheets lasagne
2 teaspoons vegetable oil
3¾ cups boiling water
salt
Filling:
1 large onion, peeled and
*   chopped*
1⅓ cups sliced mushrooms
8 ounces salami, diced
1 × 16-ounce can tomatoes
1½ tablespoons cornstarch
Topping:
¼ cup butter
½ cup all-purpose flour
2½ cups milk
1½ cups grated cheese
bay leaves, to garnish

Preparation time: 20 minutes
Cooking time: 27½–29 minutes
Microwave setting: Full power
(High)

1. Place the lasagne in a deep rectangular dish. Add 1 teaspoon oil, the water and salt to taste. Cover and cook for 9 minutes. Leave to stand for 10 minutes, drain and rinse in cold water.

2. Meanwhile, place the remaining oil and onion in a bowl. Cover and cook for 3 minutes. Add the mushrooms, cover and cook for 2 minutes.

3. Stir in three-quarters of the salami and the tomatoes, blending well. Cover and cook for 3 minutes, stirring twice.

4. Mix the cornstarch with a little water and stir into the salami mixture. Cook for 2 minutes, stirring once, until thickened.

5. Cut the cooked lasagne sheets in half. Spoon equal quantities of the salami mixture onto the pieces of pasta, roll up to enclose and place, seam side down, in a large gratin dish.

6. Place the butter in a bowl and cook for 1 minute to melt. Add the flour, blending well. Gradually add the milk and cook for 5½–6 minutes, stirring every 1 minute until smooth and thickened. Stir in two-thirds of the cheese until melted.

7. Pour the sauce over the pasta, sprinkle with the remaining cheese and salami.

8. To serve immediately, cook for 2–3 minutes, turning once, until heated through. Brown under a preheated conventional broiler if wished. Garnish with bay leaves.

FREEZING DETAILS
1. Prepare the recipe to the end of step 7.

2. Cool quickly, cover, seal, label and freeze for up to 2 months.

REHEATING DETAILS
Microwave setting: Defrost and Full power (High)
Defrosting and cooking time: 29–31 minutes

1. Remove all wrappings and cook the pasta on Defrost for 15 minutes. Leave to stand for 10 minutes.

2. Cook on Full power for 4–6 minutes, turning the dish twice. Brown under a preheated conventional broiler if wished. Garnish with bay leaves.

Leek and Baloney Supper

Serves 4

*8 medium leeks, trimmed and
   washed*
4 tablespoons water
8 slices baloney
2 tablespoons butter
¼ cup all-purpose flour
1¼ cups milk
1 cup grated Cheddar cheese
salt
freshly ground black pepper

Preparation time: 5 minutes
Cooking time: 16–19½ minutes
Microwave setting: Full power
(High)

1. Place the leeks in a dish. Add the water, cover and cook for 10–12 minutes until tender, stirring once. Drain thoroughly.

2. Wrap each leek in a slice of the baloney and place in a flameproof serving dish.

3. Place the butter in a bowl and cook for 30 seconds to melt. Add the flour, blending well. Gradually add the milk and cook for 3½–4 minutes, stirring every 1 minute until smooth and thickened.

4. Stir in three-quarters of the cheese until melted. Add salt and pepper to taste. Spoon over the leeks and sprinkle with the remaining cheese.

5. If serving immediately, cook for 2–3 minutes until the cheese is hot and bubbly.

6. Brown under a preheated conventional broiler if wished.

FREEZING DETAILS

1. Prepare the recipe to the end of step 4.

2. Cool quickly, cover, seal, label and freeze for up to 3 months.

REHEATING DETAILS
Microwave setting: Defrost and Full power (High)
Defrosting and cooking time: 18–21 minutes

1. Remove all wrappings and cook the rolls on Defrost for 8 minutes. Leave to stand for 5 minutes.

2. Cook on Full power for 5–8 minutes.

3. Brown under a preheated conventional broiler if wished.

*Pasta scallops, Salami-stuffed pasta;
Leek and baloney supper*

Danish Pizza

Serves 2
8 bacon slices
¼ cup butter
1 onion, peeled and chopped
1 × 8-ounce can tomatoes,
  drained and chopped
¼ teaspoon Italian seasoning
salt
freshly ground black pepper
1 cup self-rising flour
water to mix
1 tablespoon vegetable oil
4 ounces Samsoe cheese, sliced
3 stuffed olives, sliced
rosemary sprigs, to garnish

Preparation time: 25 minutes, including heating browning dish
Cooking time: 15½ minutes, plus standing
Microwave setting: Full power (High)

1. Place the bacon on a plate or microwave bacon rack, cover with a paper towel and cook for 3 minutes until crisp.

2. Place half the butter in a bowl and cook for 30 seconds to melt. Add the onion, cover and cook for 2½ minutes. Add the tomatoes, herbs and salt and pepper to taste. Cover and cook for 4 minutes, stirring twice.

3. To make the dough, cut the remaining butter into the flour and gradually add about 3–4 tablespoons of water to make a soft dough. Knead lightly until smooth and roll out on a lightly floured surface to a square large enough to fit a small browning dish.

4. Preheat the browning dish for 6 minutes (or according to the manufacturer's directions). Brush with the oil and heat for a further 30 seconds.

5. Place the dough in the browning dish and top with the tomato mixture, spreading it evenly. Arrange the cheese on top and cook for 5½ minutes, turning the dish every 1 minute.

6. Arrange the cooked bacon slices on top of the pizza to form a lattice. Place the sliced olives in the "window" of each lattice.

7. To serve immediately, cook for a further 30 seconds. Leave to stand for 5 minutes, then remove from the dish and garnish with rosemary. Serve with a crisp salad if wished.

FREEZING DETAILS
1. Prepare the recipe to the end of step 6.

2. Cool quickly, place in a rigid container, cover, seal, label and freeze for up to 2 months.

REHEATING DETAILS
Microwave setting: Full power (High)
Defrosting and cooking time: 6 minutes

1. Remove all wrappings. Place the pizza on a double thickness piece of paper towel. Cook for 6 minutes until the pizza is hot and bubbly.

2. Serve, garnished with rosemary, and with a crisp salad if wished.

Cheese and Ham Toasties

Serves 4
8 small slices thin white bread,
  crusts removed
1–2 teaspoons whole-grain
  mustard
4 slices quick-melting processed
  cheese
4 slices cooked ham
3 tablespoons butter

Preparation time: 15 minutes, including heating browning dish
Cooking time: 4–5 minutes
Microwave setting: Full power (High)

1. Spread half the bread slices with mustard to taste. Top each with a slice of cheese and ham. Cover with the remaining bread slices, pressing down well.

2. To serve immediately, place the butter in a bowl and cook for 1 minute to melt.

3. Preheat a large browning dish for 8 minutes (or according to the manufacturer's directions).

4. Brush one side of each sandwich with half the butter. Place buttered side down in the browning dish and allow to brown on the underside, about 1–2 minutes.

5. Quickly brush the second side of each sandwich with the remaining butter, turn over with tongs and cook for 2 minutes, turning the dish once.

6. Cut each sandwich in half

diagonally to form triangles. Serve hot with napkins.

FREEZING DETAILS
1. Prepare the recipe to the end of step 1.

2. Freeze the uncooked sandwiches, wrapped in aluminum foil, sealed and labeled for up to 3 months.

REHEATING DETAILS
Microwave setting: Defrost and Full power (High)
Defrosting and cooking time: 22–23 minutes

1. Remove all wrappings. Place on a plate and cook on Defrost for 5 minutes. Leave to stand for 5 minutes.

2. Cook as in steps 2–6 above. Serve hot with napkins.

Spaghetti Mozzarella

Serves 4
8 ounces spaghetti
5 cups boiling water
1 tablespoon vegetable oil
salt
½ cup butter
1 garlic clove, peeled and
*   crushed*
4 tomatoes, peeled, seeded and
*   quartered*
½ cup ripe olives
1½ cups cubed mozzarella
*   cheese*
3 tablespoons chopped fresh
*   parsley*
freshly ground black pepper

Preparation time: 10 minutes
Cooking time: 13½–14½ minutes,
plus standing
Microwave setting: Full power
(High)

1. Wind the spaghetti into a deep dish with the water, oil and salt to taste until softened. Submerge in the water, cover and cook for about 10 minutes. Leave to stand for 5 minutes.

2. To serve immediately, place the butter in a bowl and cook for about 3–4 minutes, until "nutty" brown. Add the garlic and cook for 30 seconds.

3. Drain the cooked spaghetti and toss in the hot garlic butter with the tomatoes, olives, cheese, parsley and salt and pepper to taste. Serve at once on warmed plates with a simple green salad.

FREEZING DETAILS
1. Prepare the recipe to the end of step 1.

2. Place in a rigid container, cover, seal, label and freeze for up to 1 month.

REHEATING DETAILS
Microwave setting: Defrost and Full power (High)
Defrosting and cooking time: 18–19 minutes

1. Remove all wrappings. Place the pasta in a bowl, cover and cook on Defrost for 6½ minutes. Leave to stand for 2 minutes.

2. Cook on Full power for 4 minutes. Leave to stand for 2 minutes.

3. Continue from step 2 above.

Danish Pizza; Cheese and ham toasties

Ham and Potato Supper

Serves 4–6
$\frac{1}{4}$ cup butter
2 onions, peeled and chopped
2 teaspoons mustard
2 teaspoons chopped fresh
   tarragon or 1 teaspoon dried
   tarragon
3 tablespoons all-purpose flour
1$\frac{1}{4}$ cups milk
1$\frac{1}{4}$ cups white meat stock
5 cups cubed cooked ham
5 cups peeled and cubed
   potatoes
8 tablespoons water
2 tablespoons milk
pinch of grated nutmeg
salt
freshly ground black pepper

Preparation time: 15 minutes
Cooking time: 32–35 minutes
Microwave setting: Full power
(High)

1. Place half the butter in a bowl with the onions. Cover and cook for 4 minutes.

2. Stir in the mustard, tarragon and flour, blending well. Gradually add the milk and stock. Cook for 8–9 minutes, stirring every 2 minutes until smooth and thickened. Fold in the cubed ham.

3. Place the potatoes in a bowl with the water. Cover and cook for 16–18 minutes until tender. Drain and mash with the remaining butter, milk, nutmeg and salt and pepper to taste.

4. Spoon the ham mixture into a large dish. Spoon the potato mixture into a pastry bag fitted with a large star-shaped tip and pipe around the edge to make a border.

5. To serve immediately, cook for 4 minutes, turning the dish a quarter turn every 1 minute.

6. Brown under a preheated conventional broiler if wished.

FREEZING DETAILS
1. Prepare the recipe to the end of step 4.

2. Cool quickly, cover, seal, label and freeze for up to 3 months.

REHEATING DETAILS
Microwave setting: Defrost and Full power (High)
Defrosting and cooking time: 40–42 minutes

1. Remove all wrappings. Cook on Defrost for 20 minutes. Allow to stand for 10 minutes.

2. Cook on Full power for 10–12 minutes, turning the dish every 2 minutes.

3. Brown under a preheated conventional broiler if wished.

From left to right; Herder's pie; Ham and potato supper; Whole-wheat spinach and cheese quiche

Whole-wheat Spinach and Cheese Quiche

Serves 4
1½ cups whole-wheat flour
3 tablespoons shortening
3 tablespoons margarine
2 tablespoons iced water
Filling:
1 pound fresh spinach leaves, washed, or 8 ounces frozen leaf spinach
⅓ cup cottage cheese
2 eggs, beaten
⅓ cup light cream
4 tablespoons grated Parmesan cheese
salt
freshly ground black pepper

Preparation time: 20 minutes
Cooking time: 24–29 minutes, plus standing
Microwave setting: Full power (High) and Defrost

1. Place the flour in a bowl. Cut in the shortening and margarine until the mixture resembles fine bread crumbs. Add the water and bind together to a firm but pliable dough. Place on a lightly floured board and knead until smooth and free from cracks.

2. Roll out the dough on a lightly floured board to a circle large enough to line an 8-inch dish. Press in the dish firmly, taking care not to stretch the dough. Cut the dough away, leaving a ¼-inch overhang to allow for any shrinkage. Prick the bottom and sides well with a fork.

3. Place a double thickness layer of paper towel over the bottom, easing it into position around the edges.

4. Cook on Full power for 3½ minutes, giving the dish a quarter turn every 1 minute. Remove the paper and cook on Full power for a further 1½ minutes.

5. Place the fresh spinach in a bowl, cover and cook on Full power for 5–7 minutes. Drain thoroughly and chop coarsely. Alternatively, cook the frozen spinach on Full power for 6–7 minutes, breaking up the spinach after 3 minutes. Drain thoroughly and chop coarsely.

6. Mix together the cottage cheese, eggs, cream, Parmesan cheese and salt and pepper. Stir in the spinach, blending well. Spoon into the quiche case and cook on Defrost for 14 16 minutes, giving the dish a quarter turn every 3 minutes. Allow to stand for 10–15 minutes. The quiche should set completely during this time.

FREEZING DETAILS
1. Prepare the recipe to the end of step 6.

2. Cool quickly, pack into a rigid container, cover, seal, label and freeze for up to 2 months.

REHEATING DETAILS
Microwave setting: Full power (High)
Defrosting and cooking time: 9–10 minutes

1. Remove all wrappings. Cook on Full power for 4–5 minutes, turning once. Allow to stand for 3 minutes to serve cold.

2. To reheat, cook on Full power for 2 minutes.

Herder's Pie

Serves 4
¼ cup butter
1 large onion, peeled and chopped
1⅓ cups quartered button mushrooms
6 ounces canned pimentos, drained and chopped
1 × 16-ounce can tomatoes, drained
3 cups coarsely ground or finely chopped cooked ham
1 tablespoon all-purpose flour
2 tablespoons tomato ketchup
1 tablespoon Worcestershire sauce
½ teaspoon dried rosemary
freshly ground black pepper
4 cups peeled and cubed potatoes
1 large carrot, peeled and grated
5 tablespoons water
½ cup grated cheese

Preparation time: 5 minutes
Cooking time: 33–35 minutes
Microwave setting: Full power (High)

1. Place half the butter in a large bowl with the onion and mushrooms, cover and cook for 5 minutes, stirring once.

2. Add the pimentos, tomatoes, and ham tossed in the flour, tomato ketchup, Worcestershire sauce, rosemary and pepper to taste, blending well. Cover and cook for 10 minutes, stirring twice. Spoon into a large shallow dish.

3. Place the potatoes and carrot in a bowl with the water. Cover and cook for 12–14 minutes until tender. Drain and mash with the remaining butter and cheese. Pipe or spoon over the

meat mixture to cover. If piping the mixture, spoon into a pastry bag fitted with a large star-shaped tip.

4. To serve immediately, cook for 6 minutes, turning the dish every 1½ minutes.

5. Brown under a preheated conventional broiler if preferred.

FREEZING DETAILS
1. Prepare the recipe to the end of step 3.

2. Cool quickly, cover, seal, label and freeze for up to 3 months.

REHEATING DETAILS
Microwave setting: Defrost and Full power (High)
Defrosting and cooking time: 40 minutes

1. Remove all wrappings. Cook on Defrost for 10 minutes. Allow to stand for 10 minutes. Cook on Defrost for a further 10 minutes.

2. Cook on Full power for 10 minutes to reheat, turning every 2 minutes.

3. Brown under a preheated conventional broiler if wished.

Turkey Hot Pot

Serves 4
1 tablespoon vegetable oil
1½ pounds turkey meat, cubed
¼ cup seasoned all-purpose flour
1 large onion, peeled and sliced
1 garlic clove, peeled and
   crushed
2 carrots, peeled and sliced
1¾ cups beef stock
1 teaspoon vinegar
1 teaspoon sugar
1½ teaspoons tomato paste
½ teaspoon Worcestershire sauce
1 bay leaf
salt
1⅓ cups halved button
   mushrooms

Preparation time: 5 minutes
Cooking time: 51 minutes
Microwave setting: Full power (High) and Medium

1. Place the oil in a large casserole and cook on Full power for 1 minute.

2. Toss the turkey in the flour. Add to the oil with the onion, garlic and carrots, blending well. Cover and cook on Full power for 10 minutes.

3. Add the stock, vinegar, sugar, tomato paste, Worcestershire sauce, bay leaf and salt to taste, blending well. Cover and cook on Full power for 10 minutes.

4. Reduce the setting to Medium and cook for 20 minutes, stirring once. Stir in the mushrooms, cover and cook for a further 10 minutes. Remove and discard the bay leaf.

5. Serve with buttered noodles or boiled rice.

FREEZING DETAILS
1. Prepare the recipe to the end of step 4.

2. Cool quickly, cover, seal, label and freeze for up to 3 months.

REHEATING DETAILS
Microwave setting: Defrost and Full power (High)
Defrosting and cooking time: 37 minutes

1. Remove all wrappings. Cover and cook on Defrost for 25 minutes, stirring twice.

2. Cook on Full power for 12 minutes, stirring twice.

3. Serve hot with noodles or boiled rice.

Braised Liver with Vegetables

Serves 4–6
2 tablespoons vegetable oil
2 tablespoons all-purpose flour
½ teaspoon salt
¼ teaspoon freshly ground black
   pepper
1¼ pounds lambs' liver, thinly
   sliced
4 ounces bacon, chopped
2 onions, peeled and sliced
1 turnip, peeled and chopped
3 celery stalks, chopped
1 carrot, peeled and chopped
1¼ cups boiling beef stock
1 tablespoon tomato paste
To garnish:
4 slices bacon

Preparation time: 15 minutes
Cooking time: 54–56 minutes, plus standing
Microwave setting: Full power (High) and Medium

1. Blend the oil, flour, salt and pepper in a large casserole. Cook on Full power for 2–3 minutes or until the color of the mixture is slightly darkened.

2. Add the liver and bacon, tossing well to coat. Cook on Full power for 5 minutes, stirring once.

3. Add the onions, turnip, celery, carrots, stock and paste. Cover and cook on Full power for 10 minutes, stirring once.

4. Reduce the setting to Medium and cook for a further 35 minutes, stirring twice. Leave to stand for 5 minutes.

5. To serve immediately, pleat the 4 bacon slices and thread onto a wooden skewer or use toothpicks. Cook on Full power

for 2–3 minutes until crisp, then use as a garnish.

FREEZING DETAILS
1. Prepare the recipe to the end of step 4.

2. Cool quickly, cover, seal, label and freeze for up to 2 months.

REHEATING DETAILS
Microwave setting: Defrost and Full Power
Defrosting and cooking time: 42–43 minutes

1. Remove all wrappings. Cook the casserole, covered, on Defrost for 25 minutes.

2. Cook on Full power for 12 minutes, stirring twice. Leave to stand for 3 minutes while completing step 5 above.

Cook's Tip

Liver cooks very successfully in the microwave oven and it can be topped with croutons or served on crisply fried bread to add interest to the texture.

Turkey hot pot; Braised liver with vegetables

Roast Chicken with Walnut and Orange Stuffing

Serves 6
1 × 4-pound chicken
2 tablespoons butter
1 tablespoon all-purpose flour
1¼ cups chicken stock
Stuffing:
¼ cup butter
1 small onion, peeled and finely chopped
2 cups fresh white bread crumbs
½ cup chopped fresh parsley
grated rind of 1 orange
2 tablespoons orange juice
½ cup chopped walnuts
salt
freshly ground black pepper
1 egg, beaten
To garnish:
orange slices
parsley sprigs

Preparation time: 15 minutes
Cooking time: 35½–45½ minutes, plus standing
Microwave setting: Full power (High)

1. To make the stuffing, put the butter in a bowl. Cook for 30 seconds to melt. Add the onion, cover the bowl and cook for 2 minutes.

2. Add the bread crumbs, three-quarters of the parsley, orange rind and juice, walnuts, and salt and pepper. Add sufficient beaten egg to bind. Use to stuff the neck end of the chicken. Secure with wooden toothpicks. Roll remaining stuffing into balls.

3. To serve immediately, shield the tips of the wings with small pieces of smooth aluminum foil. Place on a roasting rack or up-turned saucer in a dish and dot with butter.

4. Cook for 26–34 minutes, giving a half-turn halfway through. Cover with aluminum foil and leave to stand for 15 minutes.

5. Meanwhile, place the stuffing balls in a circle on a plate or roasting rack and cook for 2–3 minutes, turning the plate once. Sprinkle with the remaining parsley.

6. To make the gravy, place 2 tablespoons of the chicken juices in a bowl and stir in the flour. Cook for 3 minutes until the flour turns golden. Gradually add the stock, mixing well. Cook for 2–3 minutes, stirring every 1 minute, until smooth and boiling.

7. Garnish the chicken with orange slices and parsley sprigs.

FREEZING DETAILS
1. Prepare the recipe to the end of step 2.

2. Wrap the chicken and stuffing balls separately in aluminum foil. Seal, label and freeze for up to 3 months.

REHEATING DETAILS
Microwave setting: Defrost and Full power (High)
Defrosting and cooking time: about 1¼ hours

1. Remove all wrappings. Cook the chicken on Defrost for 26 minutes, turning it occasionally. Leave to stand for 5 minutes.

2. Meanwhile, cook the stuffing balls on Defrost for 5 minutes. Leave to stand while following steps 3, 4 and 5.

3. To make the gravy, cook the frozen juices on Full power for 2–3 minutes, stirring once. Continue from step 6 above.

Rabbit Casserole with Bacon and Sage Dumplings

Serves 4
1 tablespoon vegetable oil
1½ pounds boneless rabbit or 4 large rabbit pieces
2 tablespoons seasoned flour
1 onion, peeled and sliced
1 garlic clove, peeled and crushed
3 ounces bacon slices, chopped
4 celery stalks, chopped
2 leeks, sliced and washed
2 carrots, peeled and sliced
1¾ cups hot chicken stock
fresh parsley, thyme and bay leaf tied together
salt
freshly ground black pepper
celery leaves, to garnish
Dumplings:
2 bacon slices, chopped
½ cup self-rising flour
2 tablespoons shredded beef suet
1 tablespoon chopped fresh sage or 2 teaspoons rubbed sage
cold water, to mix

Preparation time: 15 minutes
Cooking time: 66 minutes, plus standing
Microwave setting: Full power (High) and Medium

1. Place the oil in a large casserole and cook on Full power for 1 minute.

2. Toss the rabbit in the flour. Add to the oil with the onion, garlic, bacon, celery, leeks and carrots. Cover and cook on full power for 10 minutes. Add the stock, herbs, salt and pepper. Cover and cook on Full power for 5 minutes.

3. Reduce the setting to Medium and cook for 30 minutes, stirring twice.

4. To serve immediately, place all the dumpling ingredients in a bowl and mix to a soft dough. Place on a floured board and form into 4 dumplings.

5. Stir the casserole and add the dumplings. Cover and cook on Medium for 20 minutes. Allow to stand for 5 minutes. Remove and discard the herbs and garnish with celery leaves.

FREEZING DETAILS
1. Prepare the recipe to the end of step 3.

2. Cool quickly, remove and discard the herbs, cover, seal, label and freeze for up to 3 months.

REHEATING DETAILS
Microwave Setting: Defrost, Full power and Medium
Defrosting and cooking time: about 1 hour

1. Remove all wrappings. Cover and cook on Defrost for 25 minutes, stirring twice.

2. Cook on Full power for 10 minutes, stirring once.

3. Continue from step 4 above.

Roast chicken with walnut and orange stuffing; Rabbit casserole with bacon and sage dumplings

Bacon and Mushroom Pie

Serves 4
Pastry:
2 cups self-rising flour
salt
½ cup shredded beef suet
⅔ cup cold water
Filling:
1½ cups chopped cooked lean
*   ham*
¼ cup all-purpose flour
1 teaspoon rubbed sage
1 onion, peeled and chopped
1 small cooking apple, peeled,
*   cored and grated*
1⅓ cups sliced button
*   mushrooms*
freshly ground black pepper
⅔ cup chicken stock

Preparation time: 20 minutes
Cooking time: 12 minutes, plus
standing
Microwave setting: Full power
(High)

1. Sift the flour and a pinch of
salt into a bowl. Stir in the suet
and water and mix quickly,
using a round-bladed knife, to
form a light elastic dough.
Knead lightly until smooth and
free from cracks.

2. Roll out the dough on a lightly
floured board to a circle about 2
inches larger than the diameter
of a 3¾-cup bowl. Cut a quarter
section from the dough circle
and reserve for a lid.

3. Lift the remaining piece of
dough and ease it into the bowl,
pinching the 2 cut edges
together to seal. Gently mold
the dough onto the bottom and
around the sides of the bowl
with the fingertips.

4. Toss the ham in the flour.
Add the sage, onion, apple and
mushrooms and pepper to
taste. Spoon into the bowl and
pour the stock over.

5. Roll out the remaining dough
to a circle large enough to make
a lid. Dampen the dough edges
with water and cover with the
lid. Pinch the edges together
firmly to seal.

6. Cover with plastic wrap,
snipping 2 holes in the top to
allow the steam to escape. Cook
for 12 minutes, giving the dish a
quarter-turn every 3 minutes.
Allow to stand for 10 minutes.

7. Serve hot with fresh seasonal
vegetables.

FREEZING DETAILS
1. Prepare the recipe to the end
of step 6.

2. Cool quickly, wrap in
aluminum foil, seal, label and
freeze for up to 1 month.

REHEATING DETAILS
Microwave setting: Defrost and
Full power (High)
Defrosting and cooking time:
21–23 minutes

1. Remove all wrappings. Cook
on Defrost for 6 minutes. Leave
to stand for 10 minutes.

2. Cover and cook on Full
power for 5–7 minutes. Serve
hot with fresh vegetables in
season.

Bean Lasagne

Serves 4
6 ounces lasagne
1 teaspoon vegetable oil
3¾ cups boiling water
salt
Beef and bean sauce:
1 tablespoon vegetable oil
1 large onion, peeled and
*   chopped*
½ pound ground beef
2 × 8-ounce cans baked beans
*   in tomato sauce*
2 tablespoons tomato paste
½ teaspoon grated nutmeg
freshly ground black pepper
1 cup grated Cheddar cheese

Preparation time: 10 minutes
Cooking time: 27–29 minutes
Microwave setting: Full power
(High)

1. Place the lasagne in a deep
rectangular casserole. Add the
oil, water and a pinch of salt.
Cover and cook for 9 minutes.
Leave to stand while preparing
the sauce, then drain
thoroughly.

2. Place the oil in a bowl with
the onion, cover and cook for 3
minutes. Add the beef and cook
for 3 minutes, breaking up the
beef and stirring twice.

3. Add the beans, tomato paste,
nutmeg and salt and pepper to
taste, blending well. Cook for 10
minutes, stirring once.

4. Layer the lasagne and beef
and bean sauce in the casserole,
finishing with a layer of sauce.

Trout with Orange

5. To serve immediately, sprinkle with the cheese and cook for 2–4 minutes until heated through. Alternatively, place under a preheated conventional broiler until golden if wished.

FREEZING DETAILS

1. Prepare the recipe to the end of step 4.

2. Cool quickly, cover, seal, label and freeze for up to 3 months.

REHEATING DETAILS
Microwave setting: Defrost and Full power (High)
Defrosting and cooking time: 40–41 minutes

1. Remove all wrappings. Cook on Defrost for 25 minutes. Leave to stand for 10 minutes.

2. Cook on Full power for 3–4 minutes to reheat.

3. Sprinkle with the cheese and cook on Full power for 2 minutes or place under a preheated conventional broiler until golden.

Serves 4
4 × 6-ounce trout, gutted
Stuffing:
2 tablespoons butter
1 small onion, peeled and chopped
⅔ cup chopped mushrooms
6 tablespoons fresh white bread crumbs
2 tablespoons chopped fresh parsley
salt
freshly ground black pepper
1 egg, beaten
Orange sauce:
2 tablespoons butter
pinch of superfine sugar
1 orange, thinly sliced
8 tablespoons orange juice
1½ tablespoons lemon juice
To garnish:
fresh dill or parsley sprigs

Preparation time: 15 minutes, including heating browning dish
Cooking time: 15½ minutes
Microwave setting: Full power (High)

1. Remove the heads from the trout and bone if preferred.

2. Place the butter in a bowl and cook for 30 seconds to melt. Add the onion, cover and cook for 2 minutes. Stir in the mushrooms, cover and cook for 1 minute.

3. Stir in the bread crumbs, parsley and salt and pepper to taste. Bind together with the beaten egg. Use to stuff the trout and place in a shallow oblong dish, top next to tail and stuffing pockets uppermost.

4. Cover and cook for 5 minutes. Turn the dish and cook for 5 minutes. Leave to stand, covered, while preparing the orange sauce.

5. Preheat a small browning dish for 6 minutes (or according to the manufacturer's directions). Add the butter and sugar and swirl to coat. Add the orange slices and turn quickly on all sides to brown lightly. Add the orange juice and lemon juice and cook for 2 minutes.

6. To serve immediately, garnish with the orange slices and dill or parsley sprigs and spoon over the orange sauce.

FREEZING DETAILS

1. Prepare the recipe to the end of step 4.

2. Cool quickly, place in a rigid container, cover, seal, label and freeze for up to 2 months.

3. The orange slices are prepared when the dish is reheated.

REHEATING DETAILS
Microwave setting: Defrost and Full power (High)
Defrosting and cooking time: 23–25 minutes

1. Remove all wrappings and place on a shallow oblong dish. Cover and cook on Defrost for 20 minutes.

2. Cook on Full power for 3–5 minutes to reheat.

3. Prepare the sauce. Garnish with the orange slices and dill or parsley sprigs. Spoon over the orange sauce.

Bean lasagne; Bacon and mushroom pie; Trout with orange

Pork Spareribs Provençal

Serves 6
6 country-style pork spareribs
Marinade:
6 tablespoons vegetable oil
3 tablespoons white-wine
vinegar
1 tablespoon chopped fresh
parsley
2 garlic cloves, peeled and
crushed
Provençal sauce:
1 tablespoon vegetable oil
1 onion, peeled and finely
chopped
1 green bell pepper, cored,
seeded and chopped
1 tablespoon tomato paste
1 × 16-ounce can tomatoes,
chopped
1 teaspoon sugar
1 teaspoon Worcestershire
sauce
2 teaspoons cornstarch
salt
freshly ground black pepper
parsley sprigs, to garnish

Preparation time: about 20 minutes including heating browning dish, plus marinating
Cooking time: 37 minutes
Microwave setting: Full power (High) and Medium

1. Place the spareribs in a shallow dish.

2. Mix the oil with the vinegar, parsley and garlic, blending well. Pour over the chops and leave to marinate for 4 hours.

3. To cook, preheat a large browning dish on Full power for 8 minutes (or according to the manufacturer's directions).

4. Add the spareribs and turn quickly on all sides to brown evenly. Cook on Medium for 26 minutes. Remove, cover with aluminum foil and leave to stand while preparing the sauce.

5. Place the oil in a bowl and cook on Full power for 1 minute. Add the onion and pepper, cover and cook on Full power for 4 minutes. Stir in the tomato paste, tomatoes with their juice, sugar, Worcestershire sauce and cornstarch dissolved in a little cold water. Add salt and pepper to taste and cook the sauce on Full power for 6 minutes, stirring twice.

6. Serve the spareribs with the sauce and garnish with parsley sprigs.

FREEZING DETAILS
1. Prepare the recipe to the end of step 5.

2. Cool quickly, place the chops and sauce in a rigid freezer container. Cover, seal, label and freeze for up to 3 months.

REHEATING DETAILS
Microwave setting: Defrost and Full power (High)
Defrosting and cooking time: 38–40 minutes

1. Remove all wrappings. Place the frozen spareribs and sauce mixture in a serving dish and cook on Defrost for 25 minutes. Allow to stand for 5 minutes.

2. Cook on Full power for 8–10 minutes.

3. Garnish with parsley.

Sweet-and-Sour Meatballs

Serves 4
2 tablespoons vegetable oil
1 onion, peeled and finely
chopped
1 pound lean ground beef
1 cup fresh white or whole-
wheat bread crumbs
1 teaspoon Worcestershire
sauce
salt
freshly ground black pepper
1 egg, beaten
Sauce:
1 tablespoon vegetable oil
1 red bell pepper, cored, seeded
and chopped
1 green bell pepper, cored,
seeded and chopped
2 tablespoons soft brown sugar
2 teaspoons soy sauce
2 tablespoons vinegar
$\frac{1}{2}$ cup orange juice
$\frac{1}{2}$ cup beef stock
2 teaspoons cornstarch
parsley sprig, to garnish

Preparation time: 15 minutes
Cooking time: $18\frac{1}{2}$ minutes
Microwave setting: Full power (High)

1. Heat the oil in a large dish for 30 seconds. Add the onion and cook for 3 minutes, stirring once.

2. Meanwhile, mix the beef, bread crumbs, Worcestershire sauce, salt and pepper to taste and enough egg to bind the mixture.

3. Divide into 8 portions and roll into balls. Place these in a single layer on top of the onion. Cook for 5 minutes, turning once. Leave to stand while preparing the sauce.

4. Place the oil and peppers in a bowl. Cover and cook for 4 minutes, stirring once. Stir in the sugar, soy sauce, vinegar, orange juice, beef stock and cornstarch, blending well. Cook for 3 minutes, stirring every 1 minute.

5. Pour over the meatballs and cook for 5 minutes.

6. Garnish with parsley sprig and serve with boiled rice or baked potatoes.

FREEZING DETAILS
1. Prepare the recipe to the end of step 5.

2. Cool quickly, cover, seal, label and freeze for up to 3 months.

REHEATING DETAILS
Microwave setting: Defrost and Full power (High)
Defrosting and cooking time: 31–35 minutes

1. Remove all wrappings. Cook on Defrost for 8–10 minutes. Leave to stand for 15 minutes.

2. Cook on Full power for 8–10 minutes, turning once. Garnish with parsley and serve with boiled rice or baked potatoes.

Pork spareribs Provençal; Sweet-and-sour meatballs

Celery with Lemon and Almonds

Serves 4
2 tablespoons butter
1 bunch celery, washed and cut
into 3-inch pieces
scant 1 cup chicken stock or
water
7 tablespoons lemon juice
1 tablespoon sugar
salt
freshly ground black pepper
$\frac{1}{2}$ cup slivered almonds
grated rind of 1 small lemon
celery leaves, to garnish

Preparation time: 5 minutes
Cooking time: $23\frac{1}{2}$–$26\frac{1}{2}$ minutes
Microwave setting: Full power
(High)

1. Place the butter in a shallow dish and cook for 30 seconds to melt. Add the celery, tossing well to coat. Cook, uncovered, for 3 minutes.

2. Add the stock or water, lemon juice, sugar and salt and pepper to taste. Cover and cook for 16–18 minutes, turning the dish twice.

3. To serve immediately, leave the celery to stand while preparing the almonds. Place the almonds on a plate and cook for 4–5 minutes, stirring every 1 minute until golden.

4. Serve the celery sprinkled with the lemon rind and toasted almonds. Garnish with celery leaves.

FREEZING DETAILS
1. Prepare the recipe to the end of step 2.

2. Cool quickly, cover, seal, label and freeze for up to 3 months.

REHEATING DETAILS
Microwave setting: Full power (High)
Defrosting and cooking time: 12–14 minutes

1. Remove all wrappings, cover and cook on Full power for 3–4 minutes, turning the dish twice. Leave to stand for 5 minutes.

2. Meanwhile, toast the almonds as in step 3 above.

3. Serve the celery sprinkled with the lemon rind and almonds. Garnish with celery leaves.

Celery with lemon and almonds;
Spinach terrine (with Provençal sauce)

Spinach Terrine

Serves 6–8
20 large fresh spinach leaves
1 pound cream cheese
3 egg yolks
¾ cup finely chopped cooked ham
2 teaspoons lemon juice
salt
freshly ground black pepper

Preparation time: 15 minutes, plus chilling
Cooking time: 9½–10½ minutes
Microwave setting: Full power (High) and Medium

1. Wash the spinach leaves well, shake thoroughly and place in a bowl. Cover and cook on Full power for 1½ minutes. Drain and rinse under cold running water.

2. Use about 8 of the spinach leaves to line an 8-inch microwave bread dish.

3. Mix the cheese with the egg yolks, ham, lemon juice and salt and pepper to taste.

4. Spoon one third of the ham mixture into the bottom of the dish and cover with 4 of the spinach leaves. Repeat twice, finishing with a layer of spinach leaves.

5. Cover with plastic wrap, cutting 2 holes in the top to allow the steam to escape. Cook on Medium for 5 minutes.

6. Give the dish a half turn and cook on Full power for 3–4 minutes or until just set. Allow to cool in the dish.

7. To serve immediately, chill slightly and serve in thin slices with a tomato sauce such as provençal sauce (see Pork spareribs Provençal, page 212). Serve with crusty bread.

FREEZING DETAILS
1. Prepare the recipe to the end of step 6.

2. Cool quickly in the dish. Cover with aluminum foil, seal, label and freeze for up to 3 months.

DEFROSTING DETAILS
Microwave setting: Defrost
Defrosting time: 40–50 minutes

1. Remove all wrappings. Cook on Defrost for 20 minutes.

2. Leave to stand for 20–30 minutes before serving, cut into thin slices, with a sauce (see left).

Vegetable Rissoles

Serves 4
½ cup red lentils
2½ cups boiling chicken stock
1 large onion, peeled and finely chopped
1 celery stalk, finely chopped
2 small carrots, peeled and grated
½ cup finely chopped cooked green beans
1 cup fresh white bread crumbs
3 eggs, beaten
1 teaspoon Italian seasoning
salt
freshly ground black pepper
¾ cup dry white bread crumbs
2–3 tablespoons vegetable oil

Preparation time: about 20 minutes including heating browning dish, plus standing
Cooking time: 27–29 minutes
Microwave setting: Full power (High)

1. Place the lentils and stock in a bowl. Cover and cook for 20 minutes, stirring once. Drain if necessary.

2. Mix the lentils with the onion, celery, carrots, beans, fresh bread crumbs, 2 of the eggs, herbs and salt and pepper to taste. Leave to stand for 30 minutes.

3. Shape the mixture into 8 meatball-shaped rissoles. Dip each of these in the remaining beaten egg and then in the dry bread crumbs to coat.

4. To serve immediately, preheat a large browning dish for 8 minutes (or according to the manufacturer's directions). Brush with the oil and cook for a further 1 minute.

5. Add the rissoles and allow to brown on the underside, about 2–3 minutes. Turn over and cook for 4–5 minutes, re-arranging them twice. Drain on paper towels and serve hot.

FREEZING DETAILS
1. Prepare the recipe to the end of step 3.

2. Freeze, interleaved with freezer wrap and wrapped in foil. Cover, seal, label and freeze for up to 3 months.

REHEATING DETAILS
Microwave setting: Full power (High)
Defrosting and cooking time: 25–29 minutes

1. Remove all wrappings and place the rissoles on a large plate. Cook on Full power for 4–6 minutes, re-arranging them frequently. Leave to stand for 5 minutes.

2. Cook as in steps 4 and 5 above.

Lima Beans in Horseradish Cream

Serves 4

3 cups shelled lima beans
4 tablespoons water
salt
2 tablespoons butter
2 tablespoons all-purpose flour
1¼ cups milk
4 tablespoons heavy cream
4 teaspoons horseradish sauce
¼ teaspoon sugar
freshly ground black pepper
chopped fresh parsley, to
*   garnish*

Preparation time: 5 minutes
Cooking time: 11½–15 minutes
Microwave setting: Full power (High)

1. Place the lima beans in a bowl with the water and a little salt. Cover and cook for 6–8 minutes, shaking the dish once. Leave to stand while preparing the sauce.

2. Place the butter in a bowl and cook for 30 seconds to melt. Stir in the flour, blending well. Gradually add the milk and cook for 4–4½ minutes, stirring every 1 minute until smooth and thickened.

3. Add the cream, horseradish sauce, sugar and pepper to taste, blending thoroughly.

4. Fold in the drained cooked beans, tossing well to coat.

5. To serve immediately, cook for 1–2 minutes to reheat. Sprinkle with chopped parsley and serve.

FREEZING DETAILS
1. Prepare the recipe to the end of step 4.

2. Cool quickly, spoon into a rigid container. Cover, seal, label and freeze for up to 3 months.

REHEATING DETAILS
Microwave setting: Full power (High)
Defrosting and cooking time: 15 minutes

1. Remove all wrappings. Place the frozen bean mixture in a bowl, cover and cook on Full power for 7 minutes, breaking up the beans and stirring twice. Leave to stand for 5 minutes.

2. Cook on Full power for 3 minutes, stirring once. Serve sprinkled with chopped parsley.

Leeks à la Grecque

Serves 4

1 large onion, peeled and
*   chopped*
12 ounces leeks sliced
*   lengthwise and well rinsed*
1⅓ cups halved button
*   mushrooms*
1 garlic clove, peeled and
*   crushed*
2 tablespoons olive oil
½ cup dry white wine
1 × 8-ounce can peeled
*   tomatoes*
1 tablespoon tomato paste
¾ teaspoon Italian seasoning
salt
freshly ground black pepper
chopped fresh basil or parsley, to
*   garnish*

Preparation time: 10 minutes
Cooking time: 14–16 minutes
Microwave setting: Full power (High)

1. Mix the onion, leeks and mushrooms with the garlic and place in a shallow dish.

2. Mix together the oil, wine, tomatoes and their juices, tomato paste, herbs, and salt and pepper to taste, blending well. Spoon over the leek mixture, cover and cook for

14–16 minutes, stirring twice, until tender.

3. To serve, allow to cool, then chill. Garnish with chopped fresh basil or parsley. Serve with lamb or as a starter with crusty bread.

FREEZING DETAILS
1. Prepare the recipe to the end of step 2.

2. Cool quickly, spoon into a rigid container. Cover, seal, label and freeze for up to 3 months.

DEFROSTING DETAILS
Microwave setting: Full power (High)
Defrosting time: 15 minutes

1. Remove all wrappings and place the frozen leek mixture in a bowl. Cover and cook for 5 minutes. Break up and stir well.

2. Leave to stand for 10 minutes until thoroughly defrosted but still chilled. Serve garnished as above.

Caponata

Serves 4

4 tablespoons vegetable oil
4 celery stalks, finely chopped
2 large onions, peeled and
*   sliced*
4 small eggplant, diced
4 tablespoons tomato paste
1 tablespoon capers, drained
½ cup Spanish olives, pitted and
*   chopped*
2 tablespoons water
2 tablespoons red-wine vinegar
1 teaspoon sugar
salt
freshly ground black pepper

Preparation time: 5 minutes
Cooking time: 14 minutes, plus standing
Microwave setting: Full power (High)

1. Place the oil, celery and onions in a large bowl. Cover and cook for 4 minutes, stirring once.

2. Add the eggplant, blending well. Cover and cook for 4 minutes, stirring once.

3. Stir in the tomato paste, capers, olives, water, vinegar, sugar, and salt and pepper to taste. Cover and cook for 6

minutes, stirring once. Leave to stand for 5 minutes.

4. Serve hot or cold with pork or chicken.

FREEZING DETAILS
1. Prepare the recipe to the end of step 3.

2. Cool quickly, spoon into a rigid container, cover, seal, label and freeze for up to 2 months.

REHEATING DETAILS
Microwave setting: Defrost and Full power (High)
Defrosting and cooking time: 24–31 minutes

1. Remove all wrappings and cook on Defrost for 15 minutes. If serving cold, leave to stand for 5–10 minutes.

2. To reheat, cover and cook on Full power for 4–6 minutes, stirring twice.

Western Baked Potatoes

Serves 4

4 large potatoes, scrubbed
½ cup cubed corned beef
2 × 8-ounce cans baked beans
    in barbecue sauce
salt
freshly ground black pepper
½ cup grated cheese

Preparation time: 10 minutes
Cooking time: 19–21 minutes,
plus standing
Microwave setting: Full power
(High)

Lima beans in horseradish cream;
Caponata; Western baked potatoes

1. Prick the potatoes with a fork
and arrange on a double
thickness of paper towels,
spaced well apart. Cook for 10
minutes, turn over and
rearrange, then cook for a
further 6–7 minutes. Allow to
stand for 5 minutes.

2. Split each potato in half and
scoop out the flesh. Mix the
flesh with the corned beef,
beans and salt and pepper to
taste, blending well. Return the
mixture to the potato skins.

3. If serving immediately,
sprinkle with the cheese and
cook for 3–4 minutes to reheat.

Serve with barbecued meats,
sausages or as a snack.

FREEZING DETAILS
1. Prepare the recipe to the end
of step 2.

2. Cool quickly, place in a rigid
box, cover, seal, label and
freeze for up to 3 months.

REHEATING DETAILS
Microwave setting: Full power
(High)
Defrosting and cooking time:
33–34 minutes

1. Remove all wrappings. Place
the potatoes on a double
thickness of paper towels,
spaced well apart. Cook on
Defrost for 30 minutes,
rearranging them twice.

2. Sprinkle with the cheese and
cook on Full power for 3–4
minutes.

Gooseberry and Mint Upside-down Cake

Serves 4
Cake:
½ cup butter
½ cup superfine sugar
2 eggs, beaten
1 cup self-rising flour
pinch of salt
1–2 tablespoons hot water
4–5 tablespoons gooseberry jam
½ teaspoon chopped fresh mint
Custard sauce:
1¼ cups milk
2 eggs
1 tablespoon superfine sugar
1 teaspoon cornstarch
2–3 drops vanilla extract

Preparation time: 20 minutes
Cooking time: 13–14 minutes, plus standing
Microwave setting: Full power (High)

1. Line a 3¾-cup microwave-safe bowl with plastic wrap or grease the bowl well.

2. Cream the butter with the sugar until light and fluffy. Add the eggs, blending well. Sift the flour with the salt and fold into the mixture with a metal spoon. Add enough water to make a soft dropping consistency.

3. Mix the jam with the mint and place in the bottom of the prepared bowl. Spoon the batter on top. Cover with plastic wrap, cutting 2 holes in the top to allow the steam to escape. Cook for 6–7 minutes, turning the bowl once. Leave to stand for 5–10 minutes.

4. To serve immediately, place the milk in a bowl and cook for about 3 minutes or until almost boiling. Lightly beat the eggs, sugar, cornstarch and vanilla extract together. Pour the milk onto this mixture, stir well to blend and strain back into the bowl.

5. Return to the oven in a deep dish containing hand-hot water to come halfway up the sides and cook for 4 minutes, stirring every 1 minute to keep the sauce smooth. The custard sauce should lightly coat the back of the spoon. Serve with the unmolded cake.

FREEZING DETAILS
1. Prepare the recipe to the end of step 3.

2. Cover, seal, label and freeze for up to 3 months.

REHEATING DETAILS
Microwave setting: Defrost and Full power (High)
Defrosting and cooking time: 13–14 minutes

1. Remove all wrappings. Cook on Defrost for 1½–2 minutes. Allow to stand for 10 minutes.

2. Cover and cook on Full power for 1½–2 minutes. Leave to stand while preparing the custard sauce from step 4 above.

Gooseberry and mint upside-down cake; Mocha-honey cake

Mocha-Honey Cake

Makes one 8-inch cake
Cake:
¾ cup butter
6 tablespoons soft light brown sugar
2 tablespoons honey
3 eggs, beaten
heaped 1 cup self-rising flour
3 tablespoons cocoa powder
1 teaspoon instant coffee
4 tablespoons hot water
few drops of vanilla extract
Filling and frosting:
⅓ cup cornstarch
2 cups milk
2 tablespoons instant coffee
1 cup soft light brown sugar
1½ cups butter

2 cups finely chopped walnuts
To decorate:
chocolate curls or crumbled chocolate flakes

Preparation time: about 40 minutes
Cooking time: 12–14 minutes, plus standing
Microwave setting: Full power (High)

1. Line an 8-inch cake dish or soufflé dish with plastic wrap or, alternatively, lightly grease the dish and line the base with waxed paper or parchment paper cut to fit.

2. Cream the butter with the sugar and honey until light and

fluffy. Add the eggs, one at a time, beating well.

3. Sift the flour with the cocoa powder and fold into the butter mixture with a metal spoon.

4. Dissolve the coffee in the water and stir in the vanilla extract. Fold into the cake batter with a metal spoon. Spoon into the prepared dish and cook for 5½–6½ minutes, giving the dish a quarter turn every 1½ minutes. Leave to stand for 5–10 minutes before turning out onto a cake rack to cool.

5. To serve immediately, when cold carefully cut the cake horizontally into 3 equal layers.

6. Make the filling and frosting by blending the cornstarch with a little of the milk in a bowl to form a smooth paste. Place the remaining milk in a bowl with the coffee and sugar, cook for 1½ minutes. Add the blended cornstarch, stirring well to mix. Cook for 5–6 minutes, stirring twice, until smooth and thick. Cover the surface with plastic wrap and leave to cool completely.

7. Beat the butter until creamy. Gradually add the cold coffee sauce, beating well to form a smooth mixture.

8. Mix one-third of the coffee filling with ¼ cup of the walnuts.

Sandwich the cake layers together with this filling. Frost the top and sides of the cake with about half of the remaining coffee mixture. Press the remaining walnuts onto the sides of the cake.

9. Place the remaining coffee mixture in a pastry bag fitted with a large star tip and pipe swirls on top of the cake.

10. Decorate with chocolate curls or crumbled chocolate flakes. Cut into wedges to serve.

FREEZING DETAILS
1. Prepare the recipe to the end of step 4.

2. Place the undecorated cake in a rigid box. Cover, seal, label and freeze for up to 6 months.

DEFROSTING DETAILS
Microwave setting: Defrost
Defrosting time: 8 minutes

1. Remove all wrappings, and place on plate. Cook on Defrost for 3 minutes. Leave to stand for 5 minutes.

2. To fill and decorate the cake continue from step 5 above.

Honey Crunch Crumble

Serves 4
6 cups peeled, cored and sliced
cooking apples
6 tablespoons honey
6 tablespoons butter
2 cups granola-style breakfast
cereal

Preparation time: 10 minutes
Cooking time: 12½–15 minutes
Microwave setting: Full power
(High)

1. Put the apples in a serving dish and drizzle over half the honey.

2. Place the butter in a bowl and cook for 1½–2 minutes to melt.

3. Stir in the remaining honey and the cereal, mixing well to coat. Spoon on top of the apples. Cook for 11–13 minutes, giving the dish a quarter turn every 3 minutes.

4. Serve hot with cream or custard sauce (see Gooseberry and mint pudding, page 218).

FREEZING DETAILS
1. Prepare the recipe to the end of step 3.

2. Cool quickly, cover, seal, label and freeze for up to 3 months.

REHEATING DETAILS
Microwave setting: Full power
(High)
Defrosting and cooking time:
12–13 minutes

1. Remove all wrappings. Cook for 5 minutes, turning the dish once. Allow to stand for 5 minutes.

2. Cook for a further 2–3 minutes. Serve hot with cream or custard sauce (for custard sauce recipe, see Gooseberry and mint pudding, page 218).

Cherry Cream Pie

Makes one 9-inch pie
Crust:
½ cup butter
2⅓ cups bran flakes
1½ tablespoons soft brown sugar
Filling:
1 × 16-ounce can dark cherries
in syrup
1⅓ × 3-ounce package cherry
flavored gelatin dessert
powder
1⅔ cartons cherry yogurt
1¼ cups heavy cream, whipped

Preparation time: 10 minutes,
plus chilling
Cooking time: 4–5½ minutes
Microwave setting: Full power
(High)

1. Place the butter in a large bowl and cook for 1½–2 minutes to melt. Stir in the bran flakes and sugar, tossing well to coat. Press on to the base and sides of a deep 9-inch springform pan with a removable base. Chill to set, for about 30 minutes.

2. Drain the juice from the cherries into a bowl. Add the gelatin and cook for 2½–3½ minutes, stirring once to dissolve completely. Chill until just beginning to set.

3. Beat the mixture with the yogurt until foamy. Fold in half the cream with a metal spoon. Pour into the pie shell. Chill until set.

4. Pipe or swirl the remaining cream on top of the pie and decorate with the cherries. Serve chilled.

FREEZING DETAILS
1. Prepare the recipe to the end of step 3.

2. Place in a rigid container, cover, seal, label and freeze for up to 3 months.

DEFROSTING DETAILS
Microwave setting: Defrost
Defrosting time: 1–2 hours

1. Remove all wrappings. This dessert is best defrosted at room temperature for 6 hours. To speed up this time, however, cook on Defrost for 1 minute. Leave to stand for 1 hour.

Clockwise: Honey crunch crumble;
Cherry cream pie; Winter steamed
pudding

Winter Steamed Pudding

Serves 4
¾ cup self-rising flour
pinch of salt
½ teaspoon apple pie spice
1½ cups fresh whole-wheat bread
crumbs
6 tablespoons shredded beef suet
¼ cup soft light brown sugar
⅓ cup golden raisins
⅓ cup raisins
⅓ cup currants
grated rind of ½ lemon
about 6 tablespoons milk

Preparation time: 10 minutes
Cooking time: 5 minutes, plus
standing
Microwave setting: Full power
(High)

1. Sift the flour together with the salt and apple pie spice. Stir in the bread crumbs, suet, sugar, golden raisins, raisins, currants and lemon rind, blending well. Add sufficient milk to make a soft dropping consistency.

2. Spoon into a greased 3¾-cup microwave-safe bowl or steamed pudding basin and cover with plastic wrap. Cut 2 holes in the top for steam to escape.

3. Cook for 5 minutes, giving the bowl a half-turn twice.

4. Leave to stand for 5 minutes before turning out onto a warmed serving plate. Serve with custard sauce (see Gooseberry and mint upside-down cake, page 218).

FREEZING DETAILS
1. Prepare the recipe to the end of step 3.

2. Cool quickly, cover the bowl with aluminum foil, seal, label.

REHEATING DETAILS
Microwave setting: Full power
(High)
Defrosting and cooking time:
13½–14 minutes

1. Remove all wrappings. Cook on Defrost for 2 minutes. Leave to stand for 10 minutes.

2. Cook on Full power for 1½–2 minutes to reheat. Serve with custard sauce (see Gooseberry and mint upside-down cake, page 218).

Sausage and Horseradish Roll

Serves 6
Pastry:
2 cups self-rising flour
pinch of salt
$\frac{1}{2}$ cup shredded suet
$\frac{2}{3}$ cup cold water
Filling:
1 pound frozen beef link
  sausages
1 tablespoon butter
1$\frac{1}{4}$ cups sliced mushrooms
2 teaspoons prepared
  horseradish
salt
freshly ground black pepper
Provençal sauce (see Pork
  spareribs Provençal, page
  212)
parsley sprig, to garnish

Preparation time: about 10 minutes
Cooking time: 19–19$\frac{1}{2}$ minutes
Microwave setting: Defrost and Full power (High)

1. Place the sausages on a plate and cook on Defrost for 5 minutes, turning and re-arranging once. Leave to stand while preparing the mushrooms.

2. Place the butter and mushrooms in a bowl, cook on Full power for 2 minutes, stirring once. Stir in the horseradish and salt and pepper to taste.

3. Prick the sausages well with a fork. Cook on Full power for 4–4$\frac{1}{2}$ minutes, turning and re-arranging once. Cut into thin slices.

4. Mix the sausages with the mushroom mixture, blending well.

5. Sift the flour and salt into a bowl. Stir in the suet. Add the cold water and mix to a soft but manageable dough. Roll out on a lightly floured board to a 9-inch square.

6. Spread the sausage mixture evenly over the dough square, leaving a $\frac{1}{2}$-inch border around the edge, and carefully roll up like a jelly roll.

7. Place, seam side down, on a piece of waxed paper and roll the paper up loosely around the dough roll, allowing plenty of space for the roll to rise. Carefully tie the ends of the paper with string or elastic bands to cover loosely with plastic wrap.

8. Cook for 8 minutes, turning twice, until well risen and cooked through. Test by inserting a skewer into the center of the roll – the skewer should come out clean and free from pastry.

9. Serve very hot, cut into slices, with the Provençal sauce. Garnish with parsley.

Cook's Tip

Suet pastry can be made lighter by adding 1 cup fresh white bread crumbs with the suet. Bind together with a little extra water if necessary. Change the flavor by adding $\frac{1}{2}$ small grated onion or 1–2 teaspoons chopped fresh herbs.

Turkey Roast with Prune and Mustard Sauce

Serves 4
1$\frac{1}{4}$ pounds frozen boneless
  turkey breast roast
2 tablespoons butter
2 teaspoons dry mustard
salt
freshly ground black pepper
$\frac{2}{3}$ cup port
$\frac{3}{4}$ cup pitless prunes
2 teaspoons cornstarch
$\frac{2}{3}$ cup chicken stock

Preparation time: 15 minutes
Cooking time: 27–28 minutes, plus standing
Microwave setting: Defrost and Full power (High)

1. Place the turkey roast in a lidded dish and cook on Defrost for 8 minutes. Allow to stand for 5–10 minutes until completely defrosted.

2. Spread with the butter and rub with the mustard and salt and pepper to taste. Cover and cook on Full power for 6 minutes.

3. Turn the turkey roast over, baste with the juices, cover and cook on Full power for a further 5–6 minutes. Remove from the dish, wrap in aluminum foil and leave to stand while preparing the sauce.

4. Add the port and prunes to the dish juices. Cover and cook on Full power for 4 minutes.

5. Mix the cornstarch with the stock and stir into the prune and port mixture. Cover and cook on Full power for 4 minutes, stirring twice.

6. Carve the turkey roast into slices and place on a platter. Pour over a little of the sauce, garnish with some of the prunes and serve the rest separately.

Potted shrimp; Turkey roast with prune and mustard sauce; Sausage and horseradish roll

Potted Shrimp

Serves 4

*12 ounces frozen shelled and
    deveined small or medium
    shrimp*
¾ cup butter, diced
salt
¼ teaspoon ground mace
¼ teaspoon cayenne pepper
To garnish:
parsley sprigs
lemon wedges

Preparation time: 5 minutes
Cooking time: 7½–8½ minutes
Microwave setting: Defrost and
Full power (High)

1. Place the frozen shrimp in a
bowl and cook on Defrost for
6–7 minutes, stirring once.
Drain thoroughly and discard
any juices.

2. Place the butter in a bowl and
cook on Full power for 1½
minutes, stirring once, to melt.
Add the shrimp, salt, mace and
cayenne pepper to taste. Divide
equally between 4 small
ramekin dishes.

3. Allow to cool, then chill for
30 minutes in the refrigerator.

4. Garnish with parsley sprigs
and lemon wedges. Serve with
triangles of thin whole-wheat
bread.

Oriental Chicken with Sweet-and-Sour Sauce

Serves 4
4 × 9-ounce frozen chicken
*   pieces*
1 tablespoon vegetable oil
1 onion, peeled and thinly
*   sliced*
1 small green bell pepper,
*   cored, seeded and sliced*
1 small red bell pepper, cored,
*   seeded and sliced*
1 garlic clove, peeled and
*   chopped*
pinch of ground ginger
salt
freshly ground black pepper
1½ tablespoons red-wine
*   vinegar*

1 tablespoon brown sugar
⅔ cup apple juice
⅔ cup unsweetened orange
*   juice*
1 tablespoon cornstarch
1 small carrot, peeled and
*   coarsely grated*
2 canned pineapple rings,
*   coarsely chopped*
2 tablespoons pine nuts
scallion tassel, to garnish

Preparation time: 15 minutes
Cooking time: 51 minutes, plus
standing
Microwave setting: Defrost and
Full power (High)

1. Place the frozen chicken pieces on a microwave roasting rack and cook on Defrost for 14 minutes.

2. Cook on Full power for 20 minutes, turning and re-arranging the chicken every 5 minutes.

3. Place the oil, onion, peppers and garlic in a casserole. Cover and cook on Full power for 6 minutes, stirring once. Add the ginger, salt and pepper, vinegar, sugar, apple and orange juice. Cover and cook on Full power for 4 minutes.

4. Blend the cornstarch with a little water and stir into the sauce with the carrot and pineapple pieces, blending well. Cover and cook for 3 minutes, stirring once.

5. Add the chicken pieces and nuts. Cover and cook on Full power for 4 minutes. Allow to stand for 5 minutes. Garnish with a scallion tassel.

Haddock Mornay Shells

Serves 4
14 ounces frozen smoked
*   haddock fillets*
2 tablespoons butter
¼ cup all-purpose flour
1¼ cups milk
1 egg yolk, beaten
1 teaspoon mustard
salt
freshly ground black pepper
¾ cup grated Cheddar cheese
2 teaspoons chopped capers

Preparation time: 10 minutes
Cooking time: 16–17 minutes,
plus broiling
Microwave setting: Full power
(High)

1. Pierce the packages of haddock and place on a plate. Cook on Full power for 10 minutes, shaking the packages gently after 6 minutes. Leave to stand while preparing the sauce.

2. Place the butter in a bowl and cook on Full power for 30 seconds to melt. Add the flour, mixing well. Gradually add the milk and cook on Full power for 3½–4 minutes, stirring every 1 minute until the sauce is smooth and thickened. Beat in the egg yolk, mustard, salt and pepper to taste and half the cheese.

3. Flake the haddock, discarding any skin. Fold into the sauce with the capers. Spoon into 4 scallop shells or flameproof dishes. Sprinkle with the remaining cheese and cook on Full power for 2 minutes, re-arranging the dishes after 1 minute.

4. Brown quickly under a preheated conventional broiler.

5. Serve with triangles of hot toast, if liked.

Light Summer Curry

Serves 4
1½ pounds frozen firm fish fillets,
*   such as cod or salmon*
1 onion, peeled and chopped
2 tablespoons butter
¼ cup all-purpose flour
2 teaspoons hot Madras curry
*   powder*
scant 1 cup water
1½ tablespoons lemon juice
2 firm tomatoes, peeled, seeded
*   and chopped*
⅔ cup heavy cream
salt

Preparation time: 10 minutes
Cooking time: 25½ minutes
Microwave setting: Defrost and
Full power (High)

1. Place the fish fillets in a dish and cook on Defrost for 12 minutes. Leave to stand while preparing the sauce.

2. Place the onion and butter in a bowl. Cover and cook on Full power for 2 minutes, stirring once. Stir in the flour and curry powder, blending well. Gradually add the water and lemon juice. Cover and cook on Full power for 2½ minutes, stirring every 1 minute.

3. Meanwhile, skin the fish fillets and place in a serving dish. Pour over the sauce. Cover and cook on Full power for 5 minutes, stirring or re-arranging the fish fillets twice.

4. Carefully add the tomatoes and cream with salt to taste. Cover and cook on Full power for 4 minutes, stirring twice. Serve with boiled rice.

Oriental chicken with sweet-and-sour
sauce; Haddock mornay shells

One-dish Chicken Supper

Serves 4

8 frozen chicken thigh pieces
1 pound frozen new potatoes
1 tablespoon vegetable oil
1 onion, peeled and chopped
4 ounces frozen button
  mushrooms
1 × 16-ounce package frozen
  stir-fry vegetables with
  cauliflower, mushrooms,
  peas, onions and carrots
⅔ cup apple juice
salt
freshly ground black pepper
parsley sprig, to garnish

Preparation time: 10 minutes, including heating browning dish
Cooking time: 50 minutes
Microwave setting: Defrost and Full power (High)

1. Place the frozen chicken thigh pieces on a plate and cook on Defrost for 12–14 minutes, turning once. Allow to stand while defrosting the potatoes.

2. Place the potatoes in a bowl and cook on Defrost for 10 minutes, stirring once.

3. Remove the bone from each chicken thigh and cut the meat into slices.

4. Preheat a large browning dish on Full power for 8 minutes (or according to the manufacturer's directions). Brush with the oil and cook on Full power for a further 2 minutes.

5. Stir in the chicken slices and onion and turn quickly on all sides to brown evenly. Cover and cook on Full power for 6 minutes, stirring once.

6. Add the mushrooms, stir-fry vegetables, potatoes, apple juice and salt and pepper to taste. Cover and cook on Full power for 12 minutes, stirring twice.

7. Serve hot, garnished with a parsley sprig and accompanied by crusty brown rolls and a mixed salad.

Rice with Smoked Fish and Corn

Serves 4

1 cup plus 2 tablespoons long-grain rice
1¼ cups boiling water
16 ounces frozen smoked trout or haddock fillets
¼ cup butter, diced
1 cup frozen whole-kernel corn
grated rind of 1 lemon
2 tablespoons chopped fresh parsley
salt
freshly ground black pepper
¼ teaspoon grated nutmeg
2 tablespoons heavy cream
To garnish:
1 hard-cooked egg, shelled and quartered
parsley sprigs

Preparation time: 10 minutes
Cooking time: 28–29 minutes, plus standing
Microwave setting: Defrost and Full power (High)

1. Place the rice in a deep container with the water. Cover and cook on Full power for 12 minutes. Leave to stand, covered, while preparing the fish fillets.

2. Place the fish fillets in a single layer in a large shallow dish and cook them on Defrost for 3 minutes. Allow to stand for 5 minutes.

3. Cook on Defrost for a further 2–3 minutes, until completely defrosted.

4. Cover with plastic wrap, cutting 2 holes in the top to allow any steam to escape and cook on Full power for 6 minutes, turning the dish once. Remove, discard any skin and bones and flake the flesh over the rice. Mix the fish in gently, blending well.

5. Place the butter in a medium bowl and cook on Full power for 1 minute. Add the corn and lemon rind. Cover and cook on Full power for 3 minutes, stirring once. Stir into the rice with the parsley, salt and pepper to taste and nutmeg.

6. Stir in the heavy cream, cover and cook on Full power for 1 minute.

7. Serve garnished with hard-cooked egg quarters and parsley sprigs.

Cook's Tip

For even greater speed, use frozen ready-cooked rice in this dish. Place the frozen rice in a deep dish and cook it on Full power until it has defrosted and warmed through – about 5 minutes. Stir it at least once during this time, then continue as above.

One-dish chicken supper; rice with smoked fish and corn

COMBINATION MICROWAVE COOKING

The combination microwave oven is the most versatile appliance, providing three cooking methods. The food can be cooked by using microwaves only, by traditional methods or it can be cooked on a combination mode, using the microwaves and convected heat together.

Combination cooking is the method of cooking using microwave energy and conventional heat either simultaneously or consecutively. The majority of ovens offering this feature combine the microwave energy with recirculating hot air, produced by the high-speed fan built into the microwave oven. In addition, some models have a broiler built into the microwave oven, in which case a combination of broiling and microwave cooking can be used for certain cooking procedures.

From the range of literature that is available you will find that many terms are used to describe the same cooking process. For example, you may find reference to a *combination microwave oven*, a *convection microwave oven* or a *microwave-convection oven.*

Whatever the term used, the exciting part of this cooking method is the results that can be achieved by combining the proven standards of traditional cooking with the speed of cooking with microwaves.

Combination mode

In combination ovens, the temperature settings are given in degrees Fahrenheit (F). The range of cooking temperatures that can be selected varies; however it is usually in the region of 275°–500°.

The microwave settings that can be used in combination with heat also vary from oven to oven. The majority of ovens allow for the use of 100% or Full power (High), Medium or Low microwave settings in combination with conventional heat sources.

Some microwave ovens are pre-programed to provide a selection of different combinations of microwave energy and temperature settings; in this case you are limited in choice of temperature and microwave energy input. However, other models offer the possibility of unlimited combinations.

Advantages of combination cooking

By using microwaves the cooking process is speeded up, and by using conventional heat the food turns brown and develops a crisp texture, or crust. Because it is a moist cooking method, cooking by microwaves alone produces food with a steamed flavor. However, cooking by the combination method results in food which has a baked flavor.

Pastry, roast meat and baked goods are a few examples of foods that are inferior or unacceptable when cooked by microwaves only. Cook these items by a combination of microwaves and conventional heat and the results are excellent – pastry becomes crisp and flakey with a brown crust; meat roasts very well, giving a traditional result in significantly less time than roasting by conventional means.

Any recipes that require the food to be thoroughly heated or cooked through with a crisp coating or browned topping are also particularly successful in the combination oven. While the crisp coating, or pastry pie top, cooks and browns, the food underneath cooks through without drying out.

Convection cooking

The great advantage of the combination convection oven is that you can use it on the convection mode to cook all your own favorite recipes. Convection cooking uses conventional heat that is recirculated in the oven by means of a fan. The movement

A comparison of combination cooking and traditional baking

1. Combination-cooked bread has a brown, crusty top and a good flavor and texture. The sides and bottom of the loaf are not as brown as expected by traditional baking.

2. Combination-cooked puff pastry is light, well risen and delicious. It does tend to shrink slightly more than pastry cooked by traditional baking and it can rise slightly unevenly.

3. Cakes cooked in a combination microwave are browned on top and they have a good flavor. The sides and bottom do not brown as well as by traditional methods. Take care not to overcook cakes to darken the crust because this will result in a dry middle.

of the hot air within the oven cavity speeds up the cooking process. The air moves around the food, rapidly displacing the cold air from the uncooked food. The result is not only speedy cooking, but even heat distribution.

The effect of cooking in a fan-assisted oven is equivalent to about 65°F hotter than the actual setting selected. So, if you put something in to cook at 350°F, because of the recirculated air, the cooking time is closer to that required at 400°F in a normal oven. If you are cooking something that requires slow cooking, either reduce the setting or the cooking time.

Combination ovens – features available

Most ovens offer one or more features which make cooking easier by taking the guess work out of programing the time, temperature or power level.

Automatic cooking programs automatically calculate cooking times, temperature and/or power levels for the microwave, convection, combination and rotisserie cooking or broiling of specific foods or cooking methods such as baking, roasting, re-heating and defrosting. All you have to do is key in the food's code (and in some cases the weight) and the oven does the rest.

Moisture sensors allow you to microwave foods without having to program cooking times or power levels. In order to work properly the food must be covered. The sensor measures moisture escaping from the covered food and when a specific moisture level is detected the oven shuts off automatically. The feature is especially useful for vegetables and re-heating leftovers. Some models have separate Re-heat or Popcorn features which are actually moisture sensors.

Weight sensors are built-in scales which automatically calculate the cooking time and the cooking method or the defrost time according to the weight of the food.

Automatic or delay start lets you pre-program the oven to start cooking at a specific time. Although it seems attractive for today's busy lifestyles, its usefulness is limited by the fact that many foods should not be left out for long periods of time prior to cooking.

Broil features are used for meats, fish and poultry. How broiling is accomplished differs among manufacturers. Some "broil" using forced hot air (convection) temperatures between 450–475°F, others use sources of radiant heat such as Cal-rods or Quartz elements. In some models the element is stationary, while in others it is adjustable.

Another available option is the combination of radiant heat and forced hot air. In the traditional sense, broiling is accomplished by radiant heat; however, a combination of convection and radiant heat browns the food and seals in the juices giving optimum results. Some broiling features require you to program in the preheat time, while others do it automatically and signal when the temperature is reached.

It is important to follow the manufacturer's guides for allowing the oven to cool between different functions and keeping the oven clean to prevent grease build up.

Rotisseries are found in a limited number of units. They are useful for boneless roasts, chicken, Cornish hens, large kabobs and shellfish such as jumbo shrimp and sea scallops.

Power levels affect the speed at which foods cook. Although some ovens claim to have as many as 100 power levels, the five levels used by most manufacturers as well as in most microwave cookbooks and recipes are: Full power (High or 100%), Medium-High (70%), Medium (50%), Medium-Low or Defrost (30%) and Low (10%).

In order to cook at lower power levels the magnatron tube cycles on and off or the wattage is reduced.

Temperature probes are similar to conventional meat thermometers in that they register the internal temperature of food, such as a roast or casserole. They can be manually programed or pre-programed to operate with microwave, convection or combination cooking. The oven automatically shuts off or switches to a keep warm cycle once the set temperature is reached.

Timers which are independent from the cooking cycle can be used in the same way you would use a conventional timer. Most can be programed up to 99 minutes and 99 seconds.

Slow cook lets you cook at a lower power level for longer periods of time. The principle is similar to crock pot cooking. It is used for soups and stews.

Memories allow you to program more than one function, cooking time or power level at one time. It eliminates the need to re-program the oven each time a particular cycle is complete. For example, if you were cooking in the microwave only mode and you wanted your casserole to cook for half the time on Full power (High) and the remainder of the time on Medium you could program all the information at once rather than waiting for the first cycle to end. The number of memories varies with the oven model, although most at least three.

Keep warm maintains the temperature of the food usually up to 60 minutes after cooking is complete without over-cooking it.

Preheat signal makes an audible sound once the set temperature is reached.

Preheating the oven for combination cooking

You will find most manufacturers state that it is not necessary to preheat the oven for combination cooking. Moreover, most of them suggest that results are, in fact, better if the oven is not preheated. In some cases this is perfectly correct; however, in some ovens if the cooking time is short, and in many cases this is so, the food does not have time to become crisp and well browned unless the oven is preheated. Results vary significantly from oven to oven – some ovens heat up very quickly, others can take up to 20 minutes. So, when it comes to preheating it really

is a case of getting to know your own oven.

The recipes in this book were tested in a preheated oven unless otherwise stated. When roasting meat or poultry, if the size of the food is large enough, there is no need to preheat. Try cooking a few dishes in your oven without preheating it first. If the results are not brown enough or not quite "baked" enough, you will know it is necessary to preheat for any other recipe with a similar cooking time.

Because of the speed of cooking, preheating is not an essential safety and hygiene factor.

Accessories and their uses

Turntables rotate the food 360 degrees. They eliminate the need for you to interrupt the cooking process in order to turn the dish. They do not compensate for stirring or turning over the food, but they do promote even cooking. Some models have a feature which locks the turntable in place. They can be easily removed for cleaning. One of the disadvantages of a turntable is it reduces the capacity of the oven and prohibits the use of larger rectangular-shaped cookware.

Broil pans usually include a drain insert that allows the juices to drip into the pan. Many can double as baking pans.

Trim kits are available if you wish to install your countertop microwave as a wall oven.

Splash trivet is a perforated metal tray that fits into the turntable, standing slightly above it. When the turntable is used as a drip tray for roasting, the trivet helps to prevent the fat from spattering. It can be left in position during all cooking operations.

Oven/baking racks are included with most models. The rack should be used for combination cooking and for cooking in the convection mode since they allow the hot air to circulate underneath.

The rack(s) can also be used to cook more than one dish of food at the same time. Follow the manufacturer's directions for positioning racks and food.

Insulating mats are provided with a limited number of ovens. They are usually covered with a non-stick surface. They are placed between the wire rack and metal baking pans and prevent sparking during combination cooking.

Cookware

You will probably find that you already have plenty of suitable cookware in the kitchen, so it is not a good idea to rush out and buy large quantities of specialist cookware.

Metal baking pans are recommended by some manufacturers for use on combination cooking mode. Do not use metal baking pans if cooking with microwaves only.

Throughout the recipes, microwave-compatible dishes are used instead of baking pans when using the combination mode. The reason for this is simple: the microwaves do not pass through metal, therefore the food does not receive any microwave energy through the sides or bottom of a pan, just from the top. Because of this, microwave-safe dishes, glassware and china give a better result.

Ovenproof glassware and ceramic dishes are ideal for use in the combination oven. Avoid any with metal trims. Remember the combination oven gets very hot so the dishes must be able to withstand the heat. Today most china manufacturers design microwave compatible dinnerware.

Specially manufactured microwave cookware is designed for use in microwave ovens and up to temperatures of 425°F. This type of reusable cookware can be expensive and some of it does not stand up to really heavy wear over long periods of time, cookware made of polysulfone holds up very well. For day-to-day cooking, you are probably better off with ovenproof china or sturdy ovenproof glassware.

Roasting bags are useful to prevent spattering and they can also be used for microwave only cooking. Follow the manufacturer's directions.

Pre-programed settings

Most microwave ovens give you the option of setting the cooking combinations of your choice. Some ovens provide numbered settings, each of which combines a certain microwave input with a particular temperature. The user's manual will tell you exactly what the settings are on your oven if it is pre-programed. Alternatively, the manufacturer may provide all the details you need to know for which setting to use for a variety of cooking processes without spelling out the precise combinations of temperature and microwave power settings.

To follow the recipes in this book, select the setting that offers the combination nearest to the microwave setting and oven temperature stated in the recipe. You may find that the setting you use has a lower microwave input and slightly cooler oven, in which case you will have to increase the overall cooking time. Remember, it is best to slightly undercook the food, then put it back for a few minutes, than overcook it.

Combination broiling

If your appliance offers the feature for broiling in combination with microwave cooking, then maximize the use of it by cooking small pieces of meat or poultry in this way. Microwave energy combined with the use of a hot broiler cooks food very fast and is not suitable for baking cakes or bread, or for roasting meat. Combination broiling can be used for whole fish, poultry steaks, chops or sausages, for gratins and casserole dishes.

Because the broiler browns and crisps the food quickly, a 100% power level (High) microwave setting can be used to cook at a similar rate.

Remember that as with all broiling, you do have to keep a close watch on the food.

Cooking a complete meal

You can cook a complete meal in the combination microwave oven with great success but take time to plan before you start cooking. If possible, cook all microwave only components of the meal first to avoid putting them in a hot oven.

1. Prepare vegetables and sauces cooked by microwaves only in advance, leaving them slightly undercooked so that they can be reheated quickly just before serving.

2. Prepare any other recipes that are cooked by microwaves only, for example, an appetizer or dessert, remembering to slightly undercook if you are going to reheat the dish later.

3. Prepare any dessert that is suitable for cooking in advance and that requires the combination cooking mode.

4. Cook the main dish and make the gravy or any sauce based on the meat juices.

5. Quickly reheat the vegetables on microwaves only and serve.

By following the above guidelines you should produce a meal that is ready in the right order. The vegetables should be heated for just one or two minutes before serving so that they do not have time to dry out in the residual heat from combination cooking.

Care of the oven

Wipe the oven out frequently to remove any spattering or bits of food before they have time to bake onto the surface. Remove and wash the turntable and racks frequently. Always follow the manufacturer's directions when choosing the cleaning materials to use.

It is vitally important to keep the door, its surround and all areas near the opening clean.

SPECIALTIES OF COMBINATION COOKING

The recipes which follow in this chapter provide a variety of different ideas for foods and dishes which can be cooked in a combination microwave oven. Use them as guidelines for adapting your favorite recipes to this method of cooking. The following notes highlight some of the foods which benefit from both the speed of microwave cooking and the conventional heat source. For example, baked potatoes can be cooked by microwaves only very successfully, but when they are cooked on combination mode they are crisp outside in the traditional way. Pastry and bread doughs also cook well by this method.

Combination microwave cooking for baked potatoes

Traditional baked potatoes, fluffy inside and crispy brown outside, are delicious but they require lengthy cooking in the conventional oven. The ordinary microwave cooks potatoes well but it does not turn them crisp and brown. Use the combination cooking mode to get traditional-style results.

The following timings are for large potatoes weighing about 10 ounces each and cooked on a combination of Full power and 500°F.

1 potato   – 7 minutes
2 potatoes –10 minutes
3 potatoes   18 minutes
4 potatoes –25 minutes
5 potatoes –28–30 minutes
6 potatoes –35 minutes

Combination microwave cooking for pastry

Pastry bakes very well on combination mode, the only exception being creampuff dough which does not rise properly and cooking is not recommended by this method.

This chapter offers recipes which include pastry, but the following notes may be useful if you are adapting your own recipes to this type of cooking.

Partially cooking an empty pie shell

An empty pie shell can be partially baked before filling, using the combination mode. Line with a paper towel and weigh the pastry down with dried beans or baking beans to prevent it rising. For a 9-inch pastry shell, allow about 5–7 minutes on Medium and using 500°F without preheating the oven first.

Alternatively, if you want to cook the dough very slightly, chill it well – for at least 45 minutes – and prick it all over, then cook it without the paper towel and beans for 4–5 minutes. If it is well chilled it should not collapse, but it does not cook as well as dough which is lightly chilled and filled with paper and beans. Sweet dough should be cooked with a paper towel and beans in place.

Baking an empty pie shell

An empty pie shell can be completely cooked on combination mode, ready to be filled with a savory or sweet filling which is uncooked or which has been cooked separately (for example, fruit-filled tarts).

To cook a 9-inch pastry shell, first line it with a paper towel and beans, then cook it on Medium and 500°F for 5 minutes in the preheated oven. Remove the beans and paper, then continue to cook for a further 3 minutes, or until the pastry is cooked and lightly browned. The pastry can be allowed to cool before filling, or it can be filled with a savory sauce mixture and served hot.

Quiches

Whether you pre-bake the empty pastry shell before filling it with an egg-and-milk-based filling is largely a matter of personal taste. The dish used also affects the end results – ovenproof glass dishes usually allow enough heat to pass through the bottom to give a well-cooked pastry bottom; thicker china dishes can promote a soggy pastry bottom unless the empty pie shell is partially cooked first.

For a 9-inch tart, allow 3 eggs beaten with $1\frac{1}{4}$ cups milk for the filling. Chopped onion, diced bacon and other raw ingredients which require lengthy cooking should be cooked first in a bowl using microwaves only.

The filled tart should be cooked using Medium and 400°F for 15–20 minutes, by which time the filling should be set and lightly browned.

Yeast doughs cooked by combination mode

Bread recipes are included in this chapter but do remember the other applications for this type of dough, in particular pizza. The combination microwave oven can be used to make excellent pizza. Make one large one, or try making small, snack-size pizzas.

A round of pizza dough which is folded in half to seal in a savory filling is known as Calzone, and this can also be cooked in the combination microwave oven.

Basic pizza dough

Make a basic yeast dough using 1 cup all-purpose or bread flour mixed with a good pinch of salt. Blend $1\frac{1}{2}$ teaspoons active dried yeast with about $\frac{1}{4}$ cup lukewarm water and a pinch of sugar until frothy. Add to the flour and knead thoroughly.

The dough should be allowed to rise in a warm place until doubled in size, then it can be rolled out into a 9–10 inch pizza.

Use a large shallow dish to hold the pizza, greasing it with a little oil before putting the dough in.

The topping can be made up of ingredients of your choice. Onions and garlic should be cooked first with a little oil or butter for about 3 minutes using microwaves only.

Once the pizza is topped, leave it to stand for 10 minutes in a warm place, then cook it using Medium and 500°F for 10–12 minutes. The edges should be crisp and browned and the topping should be cooked.

Calzone

Calzone is made by putting the savory filling on half the circle of pizza dough, then folding over the other half to enclose the filling completely. Pinch the edges together well to thoroughly seal in the filling. A calzone made from pizza dough based on 1 cup flour as above will take about 10–12 minutes to cook on Medium using 500°F. Remember that the exact timing will depend on the ingredients used in the filling – any which need lengthy cooking should be cooked briefly first using microwaves only.

Leek Soup Surprise

Serves 4
12 ounces leeks, sliced
2 cups peeled and cubed
* potatoes*
2 tablespoons butter
2 tablespoons all-purpose flour
2 cups chicken stock
salt
freshly ground black pepper
⅔ cup milk or light cream
8 ounces frozen puff pastry
* dough, defrosted*
beaten egg, to glaze

Preparation time: 20 minutes
Cooking time: 27–31 minutes
Microwave setting: Full power
(High) and Medium
Temperature setting: 500°F

1. Put the leeks in a colander and wash them thoroughly, separating the rings and rinsing out any grit. Shake off the excess water.

2. Put the leeks in a large casserole dish or mixing bowl. Add the potatoes and butter. Cover and cook using microwaves only on Full power for 5 minutes.

3. Stir in the flour, then gradually pour in the stock. Add salt and pepper to taste. Cook on Full power for 15–18 minutes, or until the vegetables are tender. Stir in the milk or cream. Leave to cool.

4. Heat the oven. Ladle the soup into four individual casserole dishes or bowls that are not too wide across the top. Cut the dough into quarters. Roll out each portion into a circle large enough to cover one of the bowls. Cut shapes from the trimmings of dough to decorate the pastry lids and brush with a beaten egg.

5. Brush the edges of the dishes or bowls with a little beaten egg. Lift a pastry circle over each one and press the edge onto the rims of the dishes, taking care not to press the middle down onto the soup. Brush the tops *very* lightly with beaten egg.

6. Bake at 500°F using Medium for 7–8 minutes, or until the pastry is well puffed and browned. Serve at once.

Cook's Tip

These satisfying soup pots make a delicious, warming lunch or supper dish. Use the same idea for other soups if you like.

Ham Soufflé in Artichokes

Serves 4
4 globe artichokes
1½ cups finely chopped or
* ground cooked ham*
3 tablespoons all-purpose flour
2 tablespoons snipped chives
salt
freshly ground black pepper
1 tablespoon milk
2 eggs, separated

Preparation time: 15 minutes,
plus cooling
Cooking time: 28–30 minutes
Microwave setting: Full power
(High) and Medium
Temperature setting: 425°F

1. Cut off and discard the artichoke stems, wash the artichokes thoroughly and place in a large roasting bag. Cook using microwaves only on Full power for about 20 minutes, or until one of the bottom leaves comes off easily. Leave until cool enough to handle.

2. Trim off the leaf tips, pull out the center leaves, then use a small teaspoon to remove the hairy choke.

3. Heat the oven to 425°F. Mix together the ham, flour, chives and salt and pepper to taste, then stir in the milk and egg yolks.

4. Beat the whites until they are stiff, then use a metal spoon to fold them into the ham mixture.

5. Stand the artichokes in a quiche dish and fill with the ham mixture. Bake at 425°F using Medium for 8–10 minutes, or until well risen and browned. Serve immediately with thin bread and butter, hot rolls or Melba toast.

Souffléd Avocados

Serves 4
⅓ cup grated Cheddar cheese
1 tablespoon grated Parmesan
* cheese*
1 teaspoon mustard
1 tablespoon snipped chives
1 tablespoon all-purpose flour
salt
freshly ground black pepper
1 tablespoon milk
1 large egg, separated
2 ripe avocados
lemon juice

Preparation time: 15 minutes
Cooking time: 5 minutes
Microwave setting: Medium
Temperature setting: 500°F

1. Heat the oven. Mix the cheeses, mustard, chives, flour and salt and pepper to taste in a bowl. Beat in the milk and egg yolk.

2. Cut the avocados in half and remove the seeds. Sprinkle with a little lemon juice to prevent discoloration. Place the avocado halves on a quiche dish, using pieces of crumpled paper towels to support them so they are level.

3. Beat the egg white until stiff, then use a metal spoon to fold it into the cheese mixture.

4. Spoon the cheese mixture into the avocados and bake immediately at 500°F using Medium for 5 minutes, or until the soufflé filling has risen and browned. Serve at once.

Leek soup surprise; Ham soufflé in artichokes

Captain's Cobbler

Serves 4
1 large leek, sliced
2 large carrots, peeled and
*   sliced*
1 tablespoon butter
2 tablespoons all-purpose flour
2 cups fish stock
bay leaf
salt
freshly ground black pepper
1 pound white fish fillet,
*   skinned and cut into chunks*
*   (cod or haddock)*
2 tablespoons chopped fresh
*   parsley*
Cobbler topping:
2 cups self-rising flour
3 teaspoons baking powder
$\frac{1}{4}$ cup butter or margarine
1 teaspoon Italian seasoning
$\frac{1}{2}$ cup grated cheese
1 egg, beaten
about 5 tablespoons milk, plus
*   extra to glaze*

Preparation time: 15 minutes
Cooking time: 20–22 minutes
Microwave setting: Full power
(High) and Medium
Temperature setting: 500°F

1. Thoroughly wash the leek, separating the slices into rings to make sure that all grit is removed. Mix the leek with the carrots and butter in a deep casserole dish. Cook using microwaves only on Full power for 5 minutes.

2. Stir in the flour, then gradually pour in the stock. Add the bay leaf and salt and pepper to taste. Cook for a further 5–7 minutes, or until the stock is almost boiling.

3. Add the fish and parsley and mix well, taking care not to break up the fish. Heat the oven.

4. For the topping, sift the flour and baking powder into a bowl and cut in the butter and margarine. Stir in the herbs, cheese, beaten egg and enough milk to make a soft biscuit dough.

5. Place the dough on a lightly floured board and knead it until

just smooth. Cut the dough into eight equal portions and roll each into a ball, then flatten slightly. Without overlapping them, arrange the scones on top of the fish around the edge of the dish. Brush with a little milk.

6. Bake at 500°F using Medium for about 10 minutes, or until the cobblers are risen and browned. Serve freshly cooked.

Cook's Tip

You may like to offer an additional green vegetable (peas or green beans, for example) with the cobbler, but the topping is quite filling and will replace potatoes, pasta or rice.

Bacon-wrapped Trout

Serves 4
4 trout, gutted with heads on
4 bay leaves
4 parsley sprigs
4 strips of lemon rind
4 smoked bacon slices
Garnish:
lemon wedges
fresh bay leaves or parsley
*   sprigs*

Preparation time: 5 minutes
Cooking time: 10 minutes
Microwave setting: Medium
Temperature setting: 500°F

1. Heat the oven. Trim the fins off the trout. Place a bay leaf, parsley sprig and strip of lemon rind in each fish. Wrap a slice of bacon around each trout, then place in two quiche dishes.

2. Put one dish on the turntable and the second on the rack above. Cook at 500°F using Medium for 6 minutes. Swap the positions of the dishes, then cook for a further 4 minutes. Serve immediately, garnished with lemon wedges and bay leaves or parsley sprigs.

Cook's Tip

For more squeamish guests, you may prefer to remove the fish heads before cooking. Cut them off neatly behind the gills using a sharp knife. Use additional parsley sprigs to garnish.

Bacon-wrapped trout; Captain's cobbler

GUIDE TO COMBINATION COOKING POULTRY AND GAME

	Microwave setting	Temperature °F	Time in minutes per 1 pound	Method
Chicken, whole	Medium	425	7–9	Preheat oven. Put chicken in dish and dot with a little fat or brush with vegetable oil. Turn over twice, ending with breast side uppermost.
Chicken quarters – 2	Medium	475–500	Total cooking time 10–12 minutes	Preheat oven. Turn pieces once, starting skin side down and ending with skin uppermost.
Chicken quarters – 4	Medium	475 500	Total cooking time: 15–16 minutes	As above
Turkey	Medium	400	6–7	Do not preheat oven. Place turkey in dish, turn twice, baste several times. Leave to stand 15 minutes before serving.
Duck	Medium	475–500	7–8	Preheat Oven. Place duck in dish. Prick skin all over and rub with a little salt. Turn twice, draining off excess fat. Stand 5 minutes before serving.
Duck pieces – 2	Full power	475–500	5	As above.
	Medium	475–500	Total cooking time: 10–12 minutes	Prick skin, rub with salt. Turn twice, ending with skin side uppermost.
Duck pieces – 4	Medium	475–500	Total cooking time: 25–30 minutes	As above.
Pheasant – 2	Medium	425–475	Total cooking time: 18–20 minutes	Preheat oven. Place in dish, breast side up. Place halved bacon slice on top. Turn over twice, ending breast side up and remove bacon to brown.
Pheasant – 4	Medium	425–475	Total cooking time: 25 minutes	As above.

Marinating poultry or game

Marinating is intended to moisten poultry or game and to infuse it with the flavor of herbs, spices or other ingredients. Although chicken is usually only marinated when the full flavor of spices or wine is required, game birds benefit greatly from being marinated before cooking as their meat tends to be rather dry. Similarly, duck can be marinated in a mixture that will contrast well with its rich tastes and slightly fatty meat.

For marinating, put the poultry or game in a suitable dish – it should be deep enough to hold the marinade but not too wide. Pour in the marinade, cover the dish and chill the poultry for several hours or overnight. Ideally, the poultry should be turned at least once or twice during marinating.

The following marinades can be used for all poultry or game.

Walnut oil marinade Walnut oil gives a distinct flavor to foods which are cooked or marinated in it. Mix 8 tablespoons walnut oil with $\frac{2}{3}$ cup red or white wine. Add a bay leaf, 4 lightly crushed juniper berries and a blade of mace.

Apple marinade Mix $\frac{2}{3}$ cup unsweetened apple juice with 1 teaspoon finely chopped rosemary, 2 tablespoons sunflower oil and plenty of black pepper. Rub the inside of the dish with a cut clove of garlic before putting the poultry or game and marinade in it.

White wine marinade Mix $1\frac{1}{4}$ cups dry white wine with a slice of onion, a large sprig of parsley and a finely chopped stalk of celery.

Roast Chicken with Spicy Rice Stuffing

Serves 4
1 onion, peeled and chopped
¼ teaspoon turmeric
1 teaspoon ground coriander
1 teaspoon ground cinnamon
heaped ½ cup long-grain rice
¾ cup water
2 tablespoons golden raisins
1½ cups peeled, cored and chopped eating apples
salt
freshly ground black pepper
1 × 3½-pound chicken
2 tablespoons butter
1 clove garlic, peeled and crushed
grated rind of ½ lemon

Preparation time: 10 minutes
Cooking time: 25–40 minutes
Microwave setting: Full power (High) and Medium
Temperature setting: 425°F

1. Put the onion in a bowl with the spices, rice and water. Cover and cook using microwaves only on Full power for 10 minutes.

2. Heat the oven. Add the golden raisins, apples and salt and pepper to taste to the rice, then use a spoon to press the stuffing into the body cavity of the chicken.

3. Cream the butter with the garlic and lemon rind. Spread this mixture all over the top of the chicken.

4. Place the chicken in a large quiche dish and roast at 425°F on Medium for 25–30 minutes, or until the chicken is cooked and browned. To check that the bird is cooked, pierce the meat at the thickest part of the body, near the thigh joints. The juices should be free of blood.

Alternative cooking method
The chicken can be cooked at 425°F using Low for about 35–40 minutes.

Cook's Tip

Take this recipe as a guide to cooking any roast stuffed chicken.

Galantine of Chicken

Serves 4–6
1 small leek, chopped
2 tablespoons butter
1 teaspoon rubbed sage
½ teaspoon dried thyme
salt
freshly ground black pepper
3 cups fresh bread crumbs
1 red bell pepper, cored, seeded and chopped
heaped 1 cup dried cooked ham
1 × 3½-pound chicken, boned (see page 61)
vegetable oil for brushing.

Preparation time: 15 minutes
Cooking time: 23–28 minutes
Microwave setting: Full power (High) and Medium
Temperature setting: 425°F

1. Put the leek in a bowl with the butter and cook using microwaves only on Full power for 3 minutes. Mix in the herbs, salt and pepper to taste and half the bread crumbs.

2. Heat the oven. Mix the remaining bread crumbs with the red bell pepper and ham, adding salt and pepper to taste.

3. Open the chicken out flat on a board. Spread half the ham stuffing on it, then put the leek stuffing on top. Top with the remaining ham mixture.

4. Use a trussing needle or large darning needle and strong thread to sew up the chicken into a neat shape. Place in a large quiche dish and brush with oil.

5. Roast at 425°F using Medium for 20–25 minutes; turn the chicken over halfway through cooking. Serve hot or cold, sliced.

Tandoori Chicken

Serves 4

4 chicken pieces, skinned
1 onion, peeled and grated
5 cloves garlic, peeled and
*   crushed*
2 tablespoons peeled and grated
*   fresh ginger root*
2 teaspoons ground coriander
1 teaspoon ground cumin
1 teaspoon ground cinnamon
1 teaspoon turmeric
$\frac{1}{2}$ teaspoon salt
$\frac{1}{4}$ teaspoon black pepper
$\frac{2}{3}$ cup plain yogurt
juice of 1 lemon
***Garnish**:*
1 lemon, cut into wedges
1 lettuce heart
1 onion, peeled and thinly
*   sliced*

Preparation time: 5 minutes,
plus marinating for 24 hours
Cooking time: 15–17 minutes
Microwave setting: Medium
Temperature setting: 500°F

1. Cut three slits in each piece of chicken, then place in a bowl. Mix all the remaining ingredients and pour over the chicken.

2. Cover and leave in the refrigerator for at least 24 hours. This dish is best left to marinate for a couple of days (make sure the chicken is really fresh before you start).

3. Heat the oven. Put the chicken pieces in a quiche dish and pour over the marinade. Roast at 500°F using Medium for 10 minutes, turn the joints and continue cooking for a further 5–7 minutes.

4. Serve garnished with lemon wedges, small lettuce leaves and plenty of onion rings. Pillau rice is a traditional accompaniment (see recipe on page 158).

Alternative cooking method
This recipe can be cooked at 500°F using Low setting for about 10–12 minutes. If you prefer follow the instructions for combination broiling on page 231.

Tandoori chicken

Baked Chicken Kiev

Serves 4
¼ cup butter
2 cloves garlic, peeled and
 chopped
2 tablespoons chopped parsley
salt
freshly ground black pepper
4 boneless chicken breast
 halves, skinned
1 egg, beaten
2 tablespoons water
2–2⅓ cups fresh white bread
 crumbs
Garnish:
1 red bell pepper, cored, seeded
 and chopped
¼ cucumber, sliced
1 lemon, cut into wedges

Preparation time: 15 minutes,
plus chilling
Cooking time: 17–20 minutes
Microwave setting: Medium
Temperature setting: 500°F

1. Mix together the butter,
garlic, parsley and salt and
pepper to taste. Divide into
quarters and form each portion
into a small pat. Wrap in plastic
wrap and chill thoroughly (this
can be done in the freezer).

2. Make a small slit in the middle
of each chicken breast half and
firmly press in a pat of the
butter mixture. Press the meat
back together to enclose

the flavored butter pats
completely.

3. Beat the egg and water
together. Coat each chicken
breast in the mixture, then press
on a thick coating of bread
crumbs. Repeat coating process
to ensure that the coating is
thick and even. Chill for at least
15 minutes.

4. Heat the oven. Arrange the
chicken on a well-greased
quiche dish. Bake at 500°F using
Medium for 17–20 minutes, or
until the coating is well
browned. The chicken should
be firm and the butter center

will have melted.

5. Serve immediately, garnished
with chopped red bell pepper,
cucumber slices and lemon
wedges.

Cook's Tip

A very successful way of
cooking this well-known recipe
– far better than the
inconvenience of deep frying.

Baked chicken Kiev

Cranberry Pheasant

Serves 4

1 cup cranberries
1 onion, peeled and chopped
4 tablespoons sugar
2 tablespoons port
2 firm pears, peeled, cored and
    chopped
1 cup fresh bread crumbs
salt
freshly ground black pepper
2 pheasants, dressed
2 bay leaves
4 bacon slices
Sauce:
2 tablespoons all-purpose flour
1¼ cups red wine
⅔ cup boiling water

Preparation time: 15 minutes
Cooking time: 35 minutes
Microwave setting: Full power
(High) and Medium
Temperature setting: 400°F

1. Put the cranberries and onion
in a bowl. Cover with
microwave-safe plastic wrap or a
plate and cook using
microwaves only on Full power
for 5 minutes. Heat the oven.

2. Mix the sugar, port, pears,
bread crumbs and salt and
pepper to taste into the
cranberry mixture. Rinse and
dry the pheasants. Spoon the

stuffing into the birds, then
place in a quiche dish. Top with
bay leaves and bacon.

3. Roast at 400°F using Medium
for 20 minutes. Remove the
bacon from the top of the birds,
putting it beside them in the
dish. Remove and reserve the
bay leaves for garnish. Roast the
pheasant for a further 5
minutes, or until cooked.

4. Transfer the pheasant to a
warmed serving dish and keep
hot. Crumble the bacon into the
cooking juices and stir in the
flour, wine and boiling water,

then cook using microwaves
only on Full power for 5
minutes, or until the sauce has
boiled and thickened slightly.
Serve the sauce separately.

Cook's Tip

Use this recipe when
cranberries are in season. For
use throughout the year, keep a
package of the berries in the
freezer; cook from frozen for an
extra minute or so.

*Braised Pheasant; Boned Stuffed
Turkey*

Braised Pheasant

Serves 4
2 pheasants, dressed
1 orange, quartered
12 cloves
1 onion, peeled and finely
*   chopped*
2 bay leaves
1¼ cups red wine
2 slices bacon, halved
2 tablespoons butter
2 tablespoons all-purpose flour
salt
freshly ground black pepper
Garnish:
1 orange, sliced
parsley sprigs

Preparation time: 15 minutes
Cooking time: 38–45 minutes
Microwave setting: Medium
Temperature setting: 400°F

1. Heat the oven. Rinse and thoroughly dry the pheasants. Stud the orange quarters with the cloves, then place 2 pieces in each pheasant.

2. Put the onion in a large casserole dish with the bay leaves. Place the pheasant on top, with the breasts uppermost. Pour the wine over and lay the bacon slices on top of the pheasants.

3. Cook at 400°F using Medium for 20 minutes. Turn the pheasants over and cook for a further 10 minutes. Remove the bacon. Turn the birds once more and cook for a final 5–10 minutes.

4. Meanwhile, beat together the butter and flour, and salt and pepper to taste.

5. Transfer the cooked pheasants to a serving platter and keep hot.

6. Beat the butter and flour mixture into the cooking juices. Cook using microwaves only on Full power for 3–5 minutes, or until boiling.

7. Garnish the pheasant with orange slices and parsley sprigs. Serve the sauce separately.

Boned Stuffed Turkey

Serves 8
1 × 10-pound turkey
1½ cups cranberries
3 tablespoons sugar
2 tablespoons orange juice
1⅓ cups peeled and finely
*   chopped onions*
¼ cup butter
4 cups fresh bread crumbs
1 tablespoon rubbed sage
⅔ cup milk
salt
freshly ground black pepper
1 pound pork sausage meat

Preparation time: 45 minutes
Cooking time: 1hr 23–38 minutes, plus standing
Microwave setting: Full power (High)
Temperature setting: 400°F

1. Trim the leg and wing ends off the turkey. To bone the turkey, place it breast side down and using a sharp, pointed knife, cut straight down the middle of the back, from head to tail. Working on one side, cut off all the meat, as near to the bone as possible. Take great care not to puncture the skin. As you near the ends of the joints, turn the meat and skin inside-out to leave the bones completely cleaned. Carefully work underneath the breast meat, cleaning the ribs as far as the main breastbone. Remove the meat from the second side in the same way.
   When you reach the breastbone, very carefully cut the finest sliver of bone off to separate the carcass completely from the meat without cutting the skin at all. The bones can be used along with the giblets to make an excellent stock.

2. Prepare the stuffings: Put the cranberries in a bowl with the sugar and orange juice. Cover and cook using microwaves only on Full power for 3 minutes. Stir well.

3. Put the onions in a bowl with the butter and cook on Full power for 5 minutes. Stir in the bread crumbs, sage and milk, and salt and pepper.

4. Lay the boned turkey, skin side down, flat on the surface. Spread the sausage meat thinly and evenly over it. Spread the sage and onion stuffing evenly over the sausage meat to cover the turkey completely. Spread the cranberry sauce down the middle, then carefully lift the sides of the turkey over the cranberry mixture to enclose it completely. Heat the oven.

5. Using a trussing needle or large darning needle and thread, sew up the bird, then turn it over so that the breast meat is uppermost. Press it into a neat shape, tucking the wing and leg ends underneath and plumping up the middle. Place in a large dish.

6. Roast at 400°F using Medium for 30 minutes. Turn the turkey over, drain off any excess fat and cook for a further 30 minutes. Turn the turkey again so that the breast side is uppermost and cook for a final 15–20 minutes, or until the meat is cooked through. Test whether the turkey is properly cooked by piercing it at the thickest part – there shouldn't be any sign of pink meat and the juices should run clear.

7. Leave to stand for 15 minutes, then serve hot. Alternatively, the turkey can be served cold.

Cook's Tip

If you have a good butcher, then ask him to bone out the turkey for you. If you are attempting the task yourself just set aside enough time and take it slowly!
   If cranberries are not available, use bottled cranberry sauce in the stuffing, pepping it up with a dash of brandy if you like.

GUIDE TO COMBINATION COOKING MEAT

Meat	Microwave setting	Temperature °F	Time in minutes per 1 pound	Method Note: No need to preheat oven for cooking times over 30 minutes.
Beef				
Sirloin Steak medium/well done	Medium	475–500	5–6	Preheat oven. Brush steak with a little oil and place on rack or in a large shallow dish. Turn halfway.
Sirloin Steak well done	Medium	475–500	7–8	As above.
Boneless rump roast	Medium	350	12–15	Place the roast in a dish or on rack. Turn and baste twice during cooking.
Boneless rib-eye roast	Medium	350	12–15	As above.
Rib roast on the bone	Medium	350	10–12	Turn the meat and baste once or twice during cooking.
Brisket	Medium	425–350	14–15	Place meat on bed of diced vegetables (onion, carrot and potato). Add $\frac{2}{3}$–$1\frac{1}{4}$ cups water and season. Cook at 425 for 15 minutes, then reduce the temperature for remaining time. Turn twice during cooking.
Lamb				
Chops	Medium	475–500	7–9	Preheat oven. Arrange chops in dish, sprinkle with herbs. Turn over halfway through cooking.
Steaks (slices off the leg)	Medium	475–500	10–12	As above.
Leg	Medium	375	9–11	Season the meat and place in a dish. Turn and baste two or three times during cooking.
Shoulder	Medium	400	10–12	As above.
Breast, boned and rolled	Medium	425	13–14	As above.
Pork				
Chops	Medium	475–500	7–9	Preheat oven. Arrange in dish, season, turn halfway through.
Loin, boneless top loin roast	Medium	425–375	14–16	Score the rind, rub with salt and place pork in dish. Reduce temperature after 15 minutes. Baste frequently, turn twice, having rind uppermost for 5 minutes at the end of cooking time. Increase temperature again for last 5 minutes. Leave to stand for 5–10 minutes before serving.
Loin, center rib roast	Medium	425–375	15–16	Score the rind and rub with salt. Place the pork in dish, rind uppermost. Cook as above, reducing temperature after 5 minutes. Increase temperature at the end of cooking.
Ham	Medium	425–350	15–16	Rub the rind with salt and score well. Place in dish. Reduce temperature after 5 minutes. Baste frequently, turn twice during cooking.
Pork Belly	Medium	475–500	10	Score the rind, rub with salt. Place in dish and turn twice during cooking. Have rind uppermost to start, underneath for the majority of cooking, then on top for final 3–5 minutes.

Beef Wellington

Serves 4–6
2 pounds beef tenderloin
1 large onion, peeled and finely chopped
1 clove garlic, peeled and crushed (optional)
2 tablespoons butter
1⅓ cups chopped button mushrooms
1 tablespoon chopped parsley
salt
freshly ground black pepper
13 ounces frozen puff pastry dough, defrosted
1 egg, beaten

Preparation time: 20 minutes, plus cooling
Cooking time: 20–25 minutes
Microwave setting: Full power (High) and Medium
Temperature setting: 500°F

1. Tie the piece of beef firmly in shape so that it does not curve as it cooks.

2. Place the onion and garlic (if used) in a bowl with the butter. Cook using microwaves only on Full power for 3 minutes. Heat the oven.

3. Stir the mushrooms, parsley and salt and pepper to taste, into the onion.

4. Place the meat in a quiche dish and cook at 500°F using Medium for 5–10 minutes. The length of time for this initial cooking period depends on how you like your beef: For just red in the middle and quite juicy 5 minutes is enough; for slightly pink in the middle allow 7–8 minutes and for well-done cook for the full 10 minutes. Remove the meat from the oven and set aside to cool.

5. Roll out the pastry dough on a lightly floured board into an oblong large enough to enclose the meat completely. It should measure about 12 × 16 inches and be fairly thick. Spread the mushroom mixture in the middle of the dough.

6. Remove the string from the meat and place the beef on top of the mushroom mixture. Lift the dough over the meat to ensure that it fits, then trim off square shapes from each corner to avoid thick pastry seams.

7. Brush the edges of the dough with a little of the beaten egg, then fold the dough around the meat, pressing the seams firmly together. Turn the package over and place it on a large flat dish. From the trimmings cut a few leaves to decorate the dough.

8. Glaze the dough with beaten egg. Bake at 500°F using Medium for about 12 minutes, or until the dough is well puffed and browned. Serve freshly cooked, cut into slices.

Cook's Tip

This is an expensive dish to prepare but it is truly delicious. If you like, use a neat piece of boneless rump roast instead of the tenderloin steak. Other suitable substitutions are a piece of lean boneless lamb, cut from the leg, or a piece of pork, trimmed of all fat. If using pork, then remember to cook it well first.

Stuffed Leg of Lamb

Serves 6
3½-pound leg of lamb, boned
1¼ cups roughly chopped prunes
4 tablespoons brandy
1 large onion, chopped
2 tablespoons butter
2 cups fresh bread crumbs
salt
freshly ground black pepper
1⅓ cups chopped button mushrooms
1 teaspoon Italian seasoning
Sauce:
2 tablespoons all-purpose flour
1¼ cups red wine
1¼ cups boiling water
bay leaf

Preparation time: 30 minutes
Cooking time: 43–53 minutes
Microwave settings: Full power (High) and Medium
Temperature setting: 375°F

1. Place the lamb in a large roasting dish. Put the prunes in a bowl and sprinkle the brandy over them. Set aside.

2. Cook the onion and butter on Full power for 3 minutes. Stir in the bread crumbs, seasoning and mushrooms. Add the herbs, then the prunes and brandy. Mix well.

3. Press the stuffing into the lamb and roast it at 375°F using Medium microwave setting for 35–45 minutes.

4. Turn the lamb several times during cooking and baste it frequently with the cooking juices. Pierce it at the thickest part to check that it is cooked.

5. Transfer the lamb to a serving platter and keep hot. Drain off the excess fat from the cooking juices, then stir in the flour. Gradually pour in the wine and water, and add the bay leaf.

6. Cook the sauce using microwaves only on Full power for 6–8 minutes, beating well once during cooking. Taste and adjust the seasoning. Discard the bay leaf.

7. Carve the lamb into thick slices and serve the sauce with it.

Roast Beef with Yorkshire Pudding and Roast Potatoes

Par-cook the potatoes first in a dish using microwaves only on Full power. Add a little fat. Put the meat on the rack above the potatoes and cook for the necessary time. Make a batter using 1 cup all-purpose flour to 2 eggs and 1¼ cups milk. Remove the meat and heat a little of the dripping in a quiche dish. Pour in the batter and cook for 10–15 minutes at 500°F using Medium setting. Make the gravy using microwaves only just before serving.

Ground Beef Pie

Serves 4

*1 large onion, peeled and
    chopped*
¾ cup peeled and diced carrots
1 tablespoon vegetable oil
salt
freshly ground black pepper
1⅓ cups sliced mushrooms
1 pound ground beef
1 tablespoon tomato paste
*½ teaspoon dried or 1 teaspoon
    chopped fresh thyme*
2 tablespoons chopped parsley
bay leaf
1 cup boiling water
*Piecrust dough made with 1½
    cups all-purpose flour, 6
    tablespoons margarine and
    3 tablespoons chilled water*
beaten egg, to glaze

Preparation time: 15 minutes
Cooking time: 20–23 minutes
Microwave setting: Full power
(High) and Medium
Temperature setting: 425°F

1. Place the onion, carrots and oil in a bowl or deep pie dish and cover with a plate or with microwave-safe plastic wrap. Cook using microwaves only on Full power for 5 minutes.

2. Heat the oven. Add a good sprinkling of salt and pepper to the onion mixture, then stir in the mushrooms, beef, tomato paste, herbs and boiling water. Set aside.

3. Roll out the dough on a lightly floured board into a piece large enough to cover the top of the bowl or deep pie dish with about 1 inch all around to spare. Trim a narrow strip from the edge of the dough, then dampen the bowl rim and press the strip of dough onto it. Dampen it, then lift the dough lid over the filling, pressing the edges down well. Trim off excess dough. Re-roll it and cut out decorative leaves.

4. Brush the pie with a little beaten egg and bake at 425°F using Medium for 15–18 minutes or until well browned.

5. Serve immediately with baked potatoes and a crunchy green vegetable to make a satisfying winter's meal.

Cook's Tip
Use this simple recipe for meat pie as a guide for adapting your favorite recipes to combination microwave cooking. Remember that the filling should be at least part cooked before the dough top is added.

One combination of appliances that is not exploited to the full is the pressure cooker and the microwave. You can always make tasty, tender meats pie fillings in the pressure cooker, using cuts like chuck steak, then top them with dough and finish the pie by combination cooking to save time.

Beef Lasagne

Serves 4

*1 large onion, peeled and
    chopped*
*2 cloves garlic, peeled and
    crushed*
1 tablespoon vegetable oil
salt
freshly ground black pepper
1 pound ground beef
*1 × 16-ounce can tomatoes,
    chopped*
1 teaspoon dried marjoram
*1⅓ cups chopped button
    mushrooms*
6 ounces no precook lasagne
2 cups Cheese Sauce (page 163)
½ cup grated cheese
2 tablespoons dry bread crumbs

Preparation time: 15 minutes
Cooking time: 33–38 minutes
Microwave setting: Full power
and Medium
Temperature setting: 400°F

1. Put the onion in a large bowl or casserole dish with the garlic and oil. Cook using microwaves only on Full power for 3 minutes.

2. Stir in salt and pepper to taste, the beef, tomatoes, marjoram and mushrooms. Cook for a further 5 minutes, then stir well. Heat the oven.

3. For the lasagne you will need a deep casserole dish. If you have a large oven cavity that does not have a turntable, then you can use an ordinary, large lasagne dish. Otherwise, a deep round dish will give an excellent result. Layer the pieces of lasagne, breaking them up as necessary, with the meat sauce in the dish.

4. Pour the cheese sauce on top. Mix the cheese with the bread crumbs and sprinkle over the top.

5. Bake at 400°F using Medium for 25–30 minutes or until well browned on top and cooked through. To check that the lasagne is cooked, pierce the middle with the point of a knife – the pasta should feel softened.

6. Serve freshly baked, with a crisp fresh salad.

Cook's Tip
Ground pork, lamb, or finely chopped cooked chicken, are good substitutes for beef in this lasagne.

Ordinary lasagne will require pre-cooking before making layers with the meat sauce in the casserole dish. Bring a large saucepan of lightly salted water to the boil and add a few drops of sunflower or other cooking oil. Cook the lasagne in batches for 7–9 minutes until just tender. Drain thoroughly and pat dry on paper towels before proceeding with step 3.

Ground beef pie; Beef lasagne

Bread

Makes 1 large or 2 small loaves
4 cups hard white or whole-
   wheat flour
1 teaspoon salt
¼ cup margarine
1 envelope active dry yeast
1¼ cups lukewarm water
1 teaspoon sugar

Preparation time: 25 minutes,
plus rising
Cooking time: 10–12 minutes
Microwave setting: Medium
Temperature setting: 500°F

1. Line a large bread dish with waxed paper. The paper should stand above the rim of the dish by 1 inch.

2. Place the flour and salt in a bowl. Cut in the margarine. Sprinkle the yeast over the lukewarm water and sugar and leave in a warm place until the yeast has dissolved and the mixture is frothy. Make a well in the dry ingredients and pour in the yeast liquid. Gradually stir in the flour to make a stiff dough.

3. Place the dough on a lightly floured board and knead it until very smooth and elastic, this will take about 10 minutes.

4. Lightly flour the bowl and put the dough back into it. Cover with a damp cloth or a piece of plastic wrap and leave in a warm place until doubled in size.

5. Place dough on a lightly floured board and knead lightly to punch out the gas. Press the dough into the prepared dish and cover with a dampened cloth or a piece of plastic wrap. Leave in a warm place until risen above the rim.

6. Heat the oven. Brush the dough with a little water and bake at 500°F using Medium for 10–12 minutes or until the loaf is cooked and browned on top. Leave in the dish for a few minutes to stand, then unmold the bread gently onto a cake rack to cool and remove the paper. The bottom of the bread will not be brown, but the top should be brown and crusty.

Alternative cooking method
Using 400°F and Low setting, cook a small loaf for 9–10 minutes or a large loaf for about 15 minutes.

Cook's Tip

This recipe gives the basic technique for making dough for breads and buns. If you do not have a suitable large bread dish, use a 7–9-inch deep round dish instead. Alternatively, make 2 small loaves and bake as in the main recipe but for about 9 minutes. A 6-inch soufflé dish can be substituted for a small bread dish.

Currant Buns

Makes 6
2 cups hard white flour
½ teaspoon salt
2 tablespoons butter
⅔ cup milk
1 tablespoon sugar
1 envelope active dry yeast
⅔ cup currants
Glaze:
2 tablespoons sugar
2 tablespoons milk

Preparation time: 25 minutes
Cooking time: 10–12½ minutes
Microwave setting: Full power (High) and Medium
Temperature setting: 500°F

1. Put the flour in a bowl and add the salt. Cut in the butter.

2. Heat the milk and sugar using microwaves only on Full power for about 30 seconds or until lukewarm. Sprinkle the yeast over the milk and leave in a warm place until the yeast has dissolved and the mixture is frothy.

3. Add the currants to the flour. Make a well in the dry ingredients, then pour in the yeast liquid. Gradually mix to make a firm dough.

4. Only on a lightly floured board, knead the dough, until smooth and elastic, about 10 minutes. Lightly flour the inside of the mixing bowl, put the dough back in and cover

with a damp cloth or a piece of plastic wrap. Leave in a warm place until doubled in size.

5. Meanwhile, line the bottom of a 10-inch quiche dish, or large flat dish, with plstic wrap and grease well.

6. Place the risen dough on a lightly floured board and knead lightly. Cut into six pieces. Shape each piece into a neat bun and place on the prepared dish around the edge. As they rise they will touch each other. Cover with a piece of greased plastic wrap and leave in a warm place until well risen. Heat the oven.

7. Bake the buns at 500°F using Medium for about 8–10 minutes, or until browned.

8. Mix the sugar and milk in a large bowl which can go into the hot oven. Cook using microwaves only on Full power for 1½–2 minutes. Check that the mixture does not boil over. Brush this glaze over the hot buns and transfer them to a cake rack to cool completely.

9. Break rolls apart and serve split and buttered, or toasted and buttered.

Soda Bread

Makes one small loaf
2 cups all-purpose flour
1 teaspoon baking soda
½ teaspoon salt
⅔ cup milk

Preparation time: 10 minutes
Cooking time: 10 minutes
Microwave setting: Medium
Temperature setting: 350°F

1. Heat the oven. Put the flour in a bowl with the baking soda and the salt. Make a well in the middle. Gradually stir the milk into the flour to make a soft dough.

2. Place the dough on a lightly floured board and knead very lightly to make a neat round loaf.

3. Lightly grease a quiche dish or similar flat, round dish. Place the loaf on the dish and cut a cross in the top.

4. Bake at 350°F using Medium for 10 minutes, or until the bread is risen and browned. Transfer to a cake rack to cool. This bread tastes best when served warm.

Milk Loaf

Makes one 7-inch round loaf
4 cups hard white flour
1 teaspoon salt
¼ cup butter or margarine
1 envelope active dry yeast
1¼ cups milk
2 teaspoons sugar
1 tablespoon sesame seeds

Preparation time: 25 minutes
Cooking time: 11 minutes, plus standing
Microwave setting: Full power (High) and Medium
Temperature setting: 425°F

1. Put the flour in a bowl and stir in the salt. Cut in the butter or margarine.

2. Heat the milk and sugar using microwaves only on Full power for 1 minute or until lukewarm. Sprinkle over the milk and sugar and leave in a warm place until dissolved and frothy.

3. Make a well in the dry ingredients. Pour in the yeast liquid, then gradually mix in the flour to make a stiff dough.

4. Place on a lightly floured board and knead until smooth and elastic, about 10 minutes. Lightly flour the inside of the bowl, put the dough in and cover with a damp cloth or a piece of plastic wrap. Leave in a warm place until doubled in size.

5. Meanwhile, line a 7-inch round deep dish with plastic wrap and oil.

6. Place the risen dough onto a lightly floured board and knead lightly to punch out the gas. Press the dough into the prepared dish and cover with plastic wrap or a damp cloth.

Leave in a warm place until doubled in size and risen above the rim of the dish.

7. Heat the oven. Brush the loaf with a little water and sprinkle with the sesame seeds. Bake at 425°F using Medium for 10 minutes, or until crisp and very well browned. Leave in the dish for 5 minutes, then place onto a cake rack to cool and remove the paper.

Clockwise: Soda bread; Currant buns; Bread, white and whole-wheat; Milk loaf

Victoria Cake

Makes one 7-inch cake
¾ cup butter or margarine
¾ cup sugar
½ teaspoon vanilla extract
3 eggs
1½ cups self-rising flour
⅔ cup jam
superfine sugar, to dust

Preparation time: 15 minutes
Cooking time: 11–13 minutes
Microwave setting: Medium
Temperature setting: 400°F

1. Grease two 7-inch round shallow dishes (cake, soufflé or fairly deep quiche dishes). Line the bottom of each with a circle of paper towel, cut to fit. Heat the oven.

2. Beat the butter or margarine with the sugar and vanilla extract until very pale and soft. Gradually beat in the eggs, adding a little of the flour if the mixture begins to curdle. Use a metal spoon to fold in the remaining flour.

3. Pour the mixture into the prepared dishes, dividing it equally between them. Smooth the surfaces. Put one dish on the turntable, and the second on the rack above. If the oven shelf is wide enough put both cakes on the same level. Bake at 400°F using Medium.

4. Cook for 8–9 minutes, then remove the top cake from the oven and move the cake below up onto the rack to finish cooking. Cook for a further 3–4 minutes. The cooked cakes should be lightly browned and firm to the touch.

5. Unmold both cakes onto a cake rack to cool and remove the lining paper.

6. Sandwich the cakes together with jam and sprinkle the top with a little superfine sugar.

Alternative cooking method
Cook using 400°F and Low for 10 minutes. Remove top cake, move bottom cake up and cook for a further 1–2 minutes.

Variations

Chocolate Cake Substitute 2 tablespoons cocoa for an equal quantity of the flour. Sandwich the cakes together with whipped cream or chocolate frosting. To make a chocolate frosting, beat ¼ cup butter with ¾ cup sifted confectioners' sugar until smooth and soft. Dissolve 1 tablespoon cocoa in 2 tablespoons boiling water, cool slightly and beat into the frosting. Top the cake with melted chocolate and sprinkle with a little confectioners' sugar.

Lemon Cake Add the grated rind of 1 lemon to the creamed mixture instead of the vanilla extract. Sandwich the cooled cakes together with lemon curd and top the cake with a lemon glacé icing. To make the icing, soft 1 cup confectioners' sugar into a bowl and beat in 1–2 tablespoons lemon juice.

Cherry and Almond cake

Makes one 7-inch cake
1⅓ cups candied cherries
¾ cup butter or margarine
¾ cup sugar
3 eggs
¼ teaspoon almond extract
1¾ cups self-rising flour
1 cup chopped blanched almonds
2 tablespoons milk

Preparation time: 15 minutes
Cooking time: 13–15 minutes
Microwave setting: Medium
Temperature setting: 425°F

1. Heat the oven. Line a 7-inch deep, round dish with a paper towel, cut to fit. Halve the cherries, put them in a strainer, wash under warm water, drain and dry well on paper towels.

2. Beat the butter or margarine and sugar together until very pale and creamy. Beat in the eggs and almond extract, adding a little of the flour if the mixture begins to curdle. Toss the cherries in a little flour. Fold the remaining flour into the cake batter using a metal spoon. Fold in the cherries, then the almonds and milk.

3. Pour the mixture into the prepared dish and lightly smooth the top.

4. Bake at 425°F using Medium for 13–15 minutes, or until the cake has risen and lightly browned. Leave the cake in the dish for a few minutes, then unmold onto a cake rack to cool. Remove the paper when cold.

Madeira cake

Makes one 7-inch cake
¾ cup butter
¾ cup sugar
grated rind of 1 lemon
3 eggs
1¾ cups self-rising flour
2 tablespoons milk
strip of candied citron peel

Preparation time: 15 minutes
Cooking time: 13–15 minutes
Microwave setting: Medium
Temperature setting: 425°F

1. Heat the oven. Line the bottom and sides of a 7-inch deep round dish with paper towels, cut to fit. The paper should stand about 1 inch above the rim.

2. Beat the butter, sugar and lemon rind together until pale and very creamy. Beat in the eggs, adding a spoonful of the flour if the mixture begins to curdle. Use a metal spoon to fold in the flour. Lastly fold in the milk. Turn the mixture into the prepared dish, smooth the surface. Lay the peel on top.

3. Bake the cake at 425°F using Medium for 13–15 minutes, or until the cake is well risen and lightly browned. Leave the cake in the dish for a few minutes, then unmold it onto a cake rack. Remove the paper when cold.

Variation

Light fruit Cake Add ⅔ cup mixed dried fruit to cake batter and omit the peel.

Mocha Layer Cake

Makes one 7-inch cake
¾ cup butter or margarine
¾ cup sugar
3 eggs
1½ cups self-rising flour
2 tablespoons instant coffee
2 tablespoons boiling water
Filling and Frosting:
6 tablespoons butter
1½ cups confectioners' sugar, sifted
2 tablespoons cocoa
1 tablespoon boiling water
2 tablespoons rum or brandy
Decoration:
1½ cups walnut halves

Preparation time: 25 minutes
Cooking time: 9½–10½ minutes
Microwave setting: Medium
Temperature setting: 400°F

1. Grease two 7-inch round sandwich cake dishes and line the bottoms with paper towels, cut to fit.

2. Beat the butter or margarine with the sugar until very pale and soft. Beat in the eggs, adding a little of the flour if the mixture begins to curdle. Dissolve the coffee in the boiling water and leave to cool slightly. Use a metal spoon to fold the flour into the creamed mixture. Lastly fold in the coffee.

3. Pour the mixture into the prepared dishes, dividing it equally between them. Smooth the tops.

4. Bake the cakes, one on the turntable and the second on the wire rack, at 400°F using Medium for 7–7½ minutes, or until the top cake is golden and springy to the touch. Remove the top cake from the oven and transfer the cake from the turntable to the rack. Cook for a further 2½–3 minutes, or until cooked.

5. Leave the cakes in the dishes for a few minutes, then unmold onto a wire rack to cool. Remove the paper towels.

6. To make the filling and frosting, beat the butter with the confectioners' sugar until pale and very soft. Mix the cocoa with the boiling water, then gradually stir in the rum or brandy. Beat this into the butter icing.

7. Reserve a few of the walnut halves and chop the remainder.

8. Sandwich the cakes together with a little frosting. Spread a little around the sides of the cake. Put the chopped walnuts on a sheet of waxed paper and roll the sides of the cake in them. Spread a thin layer of frosting over the top. Put the remaining frosting in a pastry bag fitted with a star tip and pipe a border around the top edge of the cake. Decorate with the reserved walnut halves.

Cherry and almond cake; Light fruit cake; Mocha layer cake

INDEX

ACKNOWLEDGEMENTS

Photographers: Howard Allman 1; Alan Duns 31; James Jackson 159, 186, 187, 198–9, 201, 203, 204, 206, 208–9, 210–1, 213, 214, 217, 218–9, 220, 223, 225, 227; David Jordan 12, 13, 14, 15, 20, 23, 30, 42, 43, 44, 61, 62, 63, 81, 82, 127, 134, 136, 150, 151, 160, 168, 183, 189, 194, 195, 228; James Murphy 2–3, 4–5, 6–7, 8–9, 233, 234–5, 238, 239, 240, 245, 247, 249; Peter Myers 24, 26, 27, 28, 29, 32–3, 35, 36, 37, 39, 40, 41, 48, 49, 51, 52, 53, 54, 55, 56–7, 58, 59, 66–7, 69, 70–1, 72–3, 74–5, 77, 78, 79, 84–5, 86, 87, 88, 91, 92, 93, 94, 95, 96, 97, 98, 99, 102, 104, 105, 107, 108, 109, 110, 111, 115, 116–7, 118, 119, 120, 121, 123, 124, 125, 128, 129, 130, 132, 141, 142–3, 144, 145, 146, 147, 148, 155, 157, 162–3, 164, 167, 170–1, 172, 173, 174, 175, 176, 178–9, 181, 184–5, 190–1, 192–3; Charlie Stebbings 38, 89, 90, 133.

Illustrator: Patricia Capon; Joan Farmer Artists

First published in 1989 by
The Hamlyn Publishing Group Limited
a division of The Octopus Publishing Group
Michelin House, 81 Fulham Road, London SW3 6RB
This 1990 edition published by
The Hamlyn Publishing Group Limited
distributed by Crown Publishers, Inc.
225 Park Avenue South
New York, New York 10003

Produced by Mandarin Offset
Printed and bound in Hong Kong

ISBN 0-517-028905

hgfedcba